International Journal on Advances in Software

2017 vol. 10 nr. 1&2

Printed from e-media with permission by:

Curran Associates, Inc.
57 Morehouse Lane
Red Hook, NY 12571

Some format issues inherent in the e-media version may also appear in this print version.

Printed by Curran Associates, Inc. (2018)

International Academy, Research, and Industry Association (IARIA)
412 Derby Way
Wilmington, DE 19810

Phone: (408) 893-6407
Fax: (408) 527-6351

petre@iaria.org

Additional copies of this publication are available from:

Curran Associates, Inc.
57 Morehouse Lane
Red Hook, NY 12571 USA
Phone: 845-758-0400
Fax: 845-758-2633
Email: curran@proceedings.com
Web: www.proceedings.com

The *International Journal on Advances in Software* is published by IARIA.
ISSN: 1942-2628
journals site: http://www.iariajournals.org
contact: petre@iaria.org

Sponsored by IARIA
www.iaria.org

International Journal on Advances in Software
Volume 10, Number 1 & 2, 2017

Antonio Bucchiarone, Fondazione Bruno Kessler, Italy
Georg Buchgeher, Software Competence Center Hagenberg GmbH, Austria
Dumitru Burdescu, University of Craiova, Romania
Martine Cadot, University of Nancy / LORIA, France
Isabel Candal-Vicente, Universidad del Este, Puerto Rico
Juan-Vicente Capella-Hernández, Universitat Politècnica de València, Spain
Jose Carlos Metrolho, Polytechnic Institute of Castelo Branco, Portugal
Alain Casali, Aix-Marseille University, France
Yaser Chaaban, Leibniz University of Hanover, Germany
Savvas A. Chatzichristofis, Democritus University of Thrace, Greece
Antonin Chazalet, Orange, France
Jiann-Liang Chen, National Dong Hwa University, China
Shiping Chen, CSIRO ICT Centre, Australia
Wen-Shiung Chen, National Chi Nan University, Taiwan
Zhe Chen, College of Computer Science and Technology, Nanjing University of Aeronautics and Astronautics, China PR
Po-Hsun Cheng, National Kaohsiung Normal University, Taiwan
Yoonsik Cheon, The University of Texas at El Paso, USA
Lau Cheuk Lung, INE/UFSC, Brazil
Robert Chew, Lien Centre for Social Innovation, Singapore
Andrew Connor, Auckland University of Technology, New Zealand
Rebeca Cortázar, University of Deusto, Spain
Noël Crespi, Institut Telecom, Telecom SudParis, France
Carlos E. Cuesta, Rey Juan Carlos University, Spain
Duilio Curcio, University of Calabria, Italy
Mirela Danubianu, "Stefan cel Mare" University of Suceava, Romania
Paulo Asterio de Castro Guerra, Tapijara Programação de Sistemas Ltda. - Lambari, Brazil
Cláudio de Souza Baptista, University of Campina Grande, Brazil
Maria del Pilar Angeles, Universidad Nacional Autonónoma de México, México
Rafael del Vado Vírseda, Universidad Complutense de Madrid, Spain
Giovanni Denaro, University of Milano-Bicocca, Italy
Nirmit Desai, IBM Research, India
Vincenzo Deufemia, Università di Salerno, Italy
Leandro Dias da Silva, Universidade Federal de Alagoas, Brazil
Javier Diaz, Rutgers University, USA
Nicholas John Dingle, University of Manchester, UK
Roland Dodd, CQUniversity, Australia
Aijuan Dong, Hood College, USA
Suzana Dragicevic, Simon Fraser University- Burnaby, Canada
Cédric du Mouza, CNAM, France
Ann Dunkin, Palo Alto Unified School District, USA
Jana Dvorakova, Comenius University, Slovakia
Lars Ebrecht, German Aerospace Center (DLR), Germany
Hans-Dieter Ehrich, Technische Universität Braunschweig, Germany
Jorge Ejarque, Barcelona Supercomputing Center, Spain
Atilla Elçi, Aksaray University, Turkey

Gerasimos Marketos, University of Piraeus, Greece
Abel Marrero, Bombardier Transportation, Germany
Adriana Martin, Universidad Nacional de la Patagonia Austral / Universidad Nacional del Comahue, Argentina
Goran Martinovic, J.J. Strossmayer University of Osijek, Croatia
Paulo Martins, University of Trás-os-Montes e Alto Douro (UTAD), Portugal
Stephan Mäs, Technical University of Dresden, Germany
Constandinos Mavromoustakis, University of Nicosia, Cyprus
Jose Merseguer, Universidad de Zaragoza, Spain
Seyedeh Leili Mirtaheri, Iran University of Science & Technology, Iran
Lars Moench, University of Hagen, Germany
Yasuhiko Morimoto, Hiroshima University, Japan
Antonio Navarro Martín, Universidad Complutense de Madrid, Spain
Filippo Neri, University of Naples, Italy
Muaz A. Niazi, Bahria University, Islamabad, Pakistan
Natalja Nikitina, KTH Royal Institute of Technology, Sweden
Roy Oberhauser, Aalen University, Germany
Pablo Oliveira Antonino, Fraunhofer IESE, Germany
Rocco Oliveto, University of Molise, Italy
Sascha Opletal, Universität Stuttgart, Germany
Flavio Oquendo, European University of Brittany/IRISA-UBS, France
Claus Pahl, Dublin City University, Ireland
Marcos Palacios, University of Oviedo, Spain
Constantin Paleologu, University Politehnica of Bucharest, Romania
Kai Pan, UNC Charlotte, USA
Yiannis Papadopoulos, University of Hull, UK
Andreas Papasalouros, University of the Aegean, Greece
Rodrigo Paredes, Universidad de Talca, Chile
Päivi Parviainen, VTT Technical Research Centre, Finland
João Pascoal Faria, Faculty of Engineering of University of Porto / INESC TEC, Portugal
Fabrizio Pastore, University of Milano - Bicocca, Italy
Kunal Patel, Ingenuity Systems, USA
Óscar Pereira, Instituto de Telecomunicacoes - University of Aveiro, Portugal
Willy Picard, Poznań University of Economics, Poland
Jose R. Pires Manso, University of Beira Interior, Portugal
Sören Pirk, Universität Konstanz, Germany
Meikel Poess, Oracle Corporation, USA
Thomas E. Potok, Oak Ridge National Laboratory, USA
Christian Prehofer, Fraunhofer-Einrichtung für Systeme der Kommunikationstechnik ESK, Germany
Ela Pustułka-Hunt, Bundesamt für Statistik, Neuchâtel, Switzerland
Mengyu Qiao, South Dakota School of Mines and Technology, USA
Kornelije Rabuzin, University of Zagreb, Croatia
J. Javier Rainer Granados, Universidad Politécnica de Madrid, Spain
Muthu Ramachandran, Leeds Metropolitan University, UK
Thurasamy Ramayah, Universiti Sains Malaysia, Malaysia
Prakash Ranganathan, University of North Dakota, USA
José Raúl Romero, University of Córdoba, Spain

Tanja E. J. Vos, Universidad Politécnica de Valencia, Spain
Krzysztof Walczak, Poznan University of Economics, Poland
Yandong Wang, Wuhan University, China
Rainer Weinreich, Johannes Kepler University Linz, Austria
Stefan Wesarg, Fraunhofer IGD, Germany
Wojciech Wiza, Poznan University of Economics, Poland
Martin Wojtczyk, Technische Universität München, Germany
Hao Wu, School of Information Science and Engineering, Yunnan University, China
Mudasser F. Wyne, National University, USA
Zhengchuan Xu, Fudan University, P.R.China
Yiping Yao, National University of Defense Technology, Changsha, Hunan, China
Stoyan Yordanov Garbatov, Instituto de Engenharia de Sistemas e Computadores - Investigação e Desenvolvimento, INESC-ID, Portugal
Weihai Yu, University of Tromsø, Norway
Wenbing Zhao, Cleveland State University, USA
Hong Zhu, Oxford Brookes University, UK
Qiang Zhu, The University of Michigan - Dearborn, USA

International Journal on Advances in Software
Volume 10, Numbers 1 & 2, 2017

CONTENTS

Data Quality Considerations for Big Data and Machine Learning: Going Beyond Data Cleaning and Transformations

Venkat N. Gudivada*, Amy Apon†, and Junhua Ding*
*Department of Computer Science, East Carolina University, USA
†School of Computing, Clemson University, USA
email: gudivadav15@ecu.edu, aapon@clemson.edu, and dingj@ecu.edu

Abstract—**Data quality issues trace back their origin to the early days of computing. A wide range of domain-specific techniques to assess and improve the quality of data exist in the literature. These solutions primarily target data which resides in relational databases and data warehouses. The recent emergence of big data analytics and renaissance in machine learning necessitates evaluating the suitability relational database-centric approaches to data quality. In this paper, we describe the nature of the data quality issues in the context of big data and machine learning. We discuss facets of data quality, present a data governance-driven framework for data quality lifecycle for this new scenario, and describe an approach to its implementation. A sampling of the tools available for data quality management are indicated and future trends are discussed.**

***Keywords*-Data Quality; Data Quality Assessment; Data Cleaning; Big Data; Machine Learning; Data Transformation**

I. Introduction

This paper is a substantial extension of the work presented at the ALLDATA 2016 conference [1]. Data quality plays a critical role in computing applications in general, and data-intensive applications in particular. Data acquisition and validation are among the biggest challenges in data-intensive applications. High-quality data brings business value in the form of more informed and faster decisions, increased revenues and reduced costs, increased ability to meet legal and regulatory compliance, among others. What is data quality? It depends on the task and is often defined as the degree of data fitness for a given purpose. It indicates the degree to which the data is complete, consistent, free from duplication, accurate and timely for a given purpose.

The application of relevant practices and controls to improve data quality is referred to as *data quality management.* Defining and assessing data quality is a difficult task as data is captured in one context and used in totally different contexts. Furthermore, the data quality assessment is domain-specific, less objective, and requires significant human involvement.

A. Ubiquity of Data Quality Concerns

Data quality is a concern in many application domains. Consider the software engineering domain. The effectiveness of prediction models in empirical software engineering critically depends on the quality of the data used in building the models [2]. Data quality assessment plays a critical role in evaluating the usefulness of data collected from the Team Software Process frameworks [3] and empirical software engineering research [4]. Cases Inconsistency Level (CIL) is a metric for analyzing conflicts in software engineering datasets [5].

Data quality is studied in numerous other domains including cyber-physical systems [6], assisted living systems [7], citizen science [8], ERP systems [9], accounting information systems [10], drug databases [11], smart cities [12], sensor data streams [13], linked data [14], data integration [15], [16], multimedia data [17], scientific workflows [18], and customer databases [19]. big data management [20], Internet of Things (IoT) [21], and machine learning [22] domains are generating renewed interest in data quality research. A wide range of domain-specific techniques to assess and improve the quality of data exist in the literature [23], [24], [25].

B. Manifestations of Lack of Data Quality

Lack of data quality in the above domains manifests in several forms including data that is missing, incomplete, inconsistent, inaccurate, duplicate and dated. Though the data quality issues date back to the early days of computing, many organizations struggle with these basic elements of data quality even today. For example, capturing and maintaining current and accurate customer data is largely an expensive and manual process. Achieving an integrated and single view of customer data which is gleaned from several sources remains elusive and expensive.

Organizations often overestimate data quality and underplay the implications of poor quality data. The consequences of bad data may range from significant to catastrophic. Data quality problems can cause projects to fail, result in lost revenues and diminished customer relationships, and customer turnover. Organizations are routinely fined for not having an effective regulatory compliance process. High-quality data is at the heart of regulatory compliance. The Data Warehousing Institute

(TDWI) estimates that poor data quality costs businesses in the United States over $700 billion annually [26].

C. Dual Threads of Data Quality Research

Data quality research is primarily advanced by computer science and information systems researchers. Computer science researchers address data quality issues related to the identification of duplicate data, resolving inconsistencies in data, imputation for missing data, linking and integrating related data obtained from multiple sources [24]. Computer scientists employ algorithmic approaches based on statistical methods to address the above issues [27]. Information systems researchers, on the other hand, study data quality issues from a systems perspective [28]. For example, they investigate the contribution of user interfaces towards data quality problems. Though statisticians also confront data quality issues, the magnitude of their datasets pale in comparison to big data and machine learning environments.

D. Operational Data-centric Data Quality Research

Traditionally, data quality research has been exclusively focused on *operational data* — business transactions [29]. This data is structured and is typically stored in relational databases. Integrity constraints have been used as the primary mechanism to enforce data quality. This approach is effective in preventing undesirable changes to data that is already in the database. It does not address issues that originate at the source such as missing, incomplete, inaccurate, and outlier data.

Operational data alone is inadequate to support the needs of an organization-wide strategic decision making. Data warehouses were introduced to fill this gap. They extract, clean, transform, and integrate data from multiple *operational databases* to create a comprehensive database. A set of tools termed *Extract, Transform, and Load* (ETL) are used to facilitate construction of data warehouses. The data in the warehouses is rarely updated but refreshed periodically, and is intended for a read-only mode of operation. Data warehouse construction calls for an extreme emphasis on ensuring data quality before the data is loaded into the warehouse.

Compared to database environments, data warehouses pose additional challenges to data quality. Since data warehouses integrate data from multiple sources, quality issues related to data acquisition, cleaning, transformations, linking, and integration becomes critical. Several types of rules and statistical algorithms have been devised to deal with missing data, identification of duplicates, inconsistency resolution, record linking, and outlier detection [30].

As a natural progression, subsequent data quality research encompassed web data sources. Evaluating the veracity of web data sources considers quality of hyperlinks, browsing history, and factual information provided by the sources [31]. Other investigations used relationships between web sources and their information for evaluating veracity of web data [32].

E. Big Data and Machine Learning Exacerbate Data Quality Concerns

The recent rise and ubiquity of big data have exacerbated data quality problems [20]. Streaming data, data heterogeneity, and cloud deployments pose new challenges. Furthermore, provenance tracking is essential to associate a degree of confidence to the data [33], [34]. To address the storage and retrieval needs of diverse big data applications, numerous systems for data management have been introduced under the umbrella term NoSQL [35]. Unlike the relational data model for the operational databases and the star schema-based databases for data warehousing, NoSQL systems feature an assortment of data models and query languages [36]. In the current NoSQL systems, *performance at scale* takes precedence over data quality. In other words, near real-time processing overshadows everything else. Furthermore, database schema evolution is celebrated as a desirable feature of certain classes of NoSQL systems.

Recently, many organizations have begun implementing big data-driven, advanced and real-time analytics for both operational and strategic decision making. Machine learning algorithms are the foundation for such initiatives, especially for the predictive and prescriptive analytics [37]. However, poor data quality is the major factor impeding advanced analytics implementations [38]. It is often said that the biggest challenge for big data is the quality of big data itself.

In contrast with big data, Machine Learning (ML) presents a different set of data quality concerns. The three components of ML algorithms are model representation, measures for assessing model accuracy, and methods for searching for a best model in the model space (i.e., optimization). As these three components are tightly intertwined, assessing data quality for ML applications is a complex task. For example, applications for which the linear model is the right model, a small number of representative data/observations will suffice for model building and testing. Even if we use an extremely large number of observations to build a linear model, it may not help the model performance. On the other hand, consider an application such as a self-driving car. By late 2016, Google's self-driving car program logged 2 million miles, which was aggregated from 60 vehicles. Still this data does not sufficiently capture different scenarios that depict the complexities of driving on diverse roads under various weather conditions. Such datasets are said to be computationally large, but statistically sparse.

There seems to a belief that more data compensates for using less sophisticated ML models. The current best practices suggest that more data and better models produce superior results. Moreover, a model developed using a stratified sampling performs as good or even better than a model that is built using all the data. Furthermore, for the same feature set, a more complex model such as a *non-linear model* does not perform any better than a simpler model such as the *linear model.*

However, more complex models when coupled with more complex features yield significantly better performance.

In machine learning, often the raw data is not in a form that is suitable for learning. Variables/features are identified and extracted from the raw data. Though features tend to be domain-specific, there is a need to establish generic patterns that help identify the features.

Lack of data quality manifested in the form of missing data, duplicate data, highly correlated variables, large number of variables, and outliers. Poor quality data can pose significant problems for building ML models as well as big data applications. Statistical techniques such as missing data imputation, outlier detection, data transformations, dimensionality reduction, robust statistics, cross-validation and bootstrapping play a critical role in data quality management.

F. Organization of the Paper

The overarching goal of this paper is to describe the nature of the data quality issues and their characterization in the context of big data and machine learning. We discuss facets of data quality, present a data governance-driven framework for data quality lifecycle for this new scenario, and describe an approach to its implementation. More specifically, data quality issues in the context of big data and machine learning are discussed in Sections II and III. In Section IV, we present data quality case studies to highlight the significance of data quality in three diverse applications. These three case studies are expected to motivate the problem and illustrate the complexity of data quality issues.

Next, we define data quality more concretely in terms of several dimensions (aka facets) in Section V. A data governance-driven data quality lifecycle is described in Section VI. A reference framework based on the lifecycle for data quality and its implementation are described in Section VII. A sampling of the tools available for data quality management are mentioned in Section VIII. Future trends are discussed in Section IX and Section X concludes the paper. To help the readers who are not familiar with machine learning, appendices A, B, C, and D introduce essential machine learning concepts, outliers, robust statistics, and dimensionality reduction, from a data quality perspective.

II. Data Quality Challenges in Big Data

Data quality is a problem that has been studied for several decades now. However, primarily the focus has been on the data in operational databases and data warehouses. Only recently, researchers have begun investigating data quality issues beyond the operational and warehousing data. Unlike the case of relational databases, NoSQL systems for big data employ a wide assortment of data models. The attendant question is: Do we need a separate data quality management approach for each NoSQL system? In big data and machine learning domains, data is acquired from multiple vendors. Data is also generated by crowd-sourcing, which is complemented by user-contributed data through mobile and web applications. How do we assess the veracity and accuracy of crowd-sourced and user-contributed data?

The proliferation of digital channels and mobile computing is generating more data than ever before. What is the impact of cloud deployments on data quality? Should data quality investigations move beyond column analysis in relational databases and address issues related to complex data transformations, integration of data from diverse data sources, and aggregations that provide insights into data?

A. Confounding Factors

Data quality in big data is confounded by multiple factors. Some big data is collected through crowdsourcing and these projects are not open for public comments and scrutiny. Also, for the machine-generated data, sufficient meta data is often not available to evaluate the suitability of data for a given task. Furthermore, vendors use multiple approaches for data collection, aggregation, and curation without associating any context for downstream data usage. However, the context plays a central role in determining data suitability for tasks. For example, the types of sampling methods used in data collection determine the valid types of analyses that can be performed on the data.

B. Dealing with Missing Data

Missing data is a major concern in big data. From a statistical perspective, missing data is classified into one of the three categories: Missing Completely At Random (MCAR), Missing At Random (MAR), Missing Not At Random (MNAR) [39]. In MCAR, as the name implies, there is no pattern to the missing data. Data is missing independently of both observed and unobserved data. The missing and observed values have similar distributions. In other words, MCAR is just a subset of the data.

MAR is a misnomer and another name like *Missing Conditionally at Random* better captures its meaning. Given the observed data, data is missing independently of unobserved data. It is possible that there are systematic differences between the missing and observed values, and these differences can entirely be explained by other observed variables. MCAR implies MAR, but vice versa. In MNAR, missing observations are related to the unobserved data. Therefore, observed data is a biased sample.

High rates of missing data require careful attention, regardless of the analysis method used. If MCAR and MAR cases prevail for a variable, such variables can be dropped across all observations in the dataset. However, dropping MNAR variables may lead to results that are strongly biased.

Several approaches exist for dealing with missing data. The simplest approach is to delete from the dataset all observations that have missing values. If a large proportion of observations have missing values for a critical attribute, its deletion will have an effect on the *statistical power*. A variation of the above approach is called pairwise deletion. Assume that a dataset has three variables, v_1, v_2, v_3, and some observations have missing values for the attribute v_2. The entire dataset can be included for analysis by a statistical method if the method does not use v_2. Pairwise deletion allows more of the data in the dataset be used in the analysis. However, each computed statistic may be based on a different subset of observations in the dataset. A correlation matrix computed using pairwise deletion may have negative eigenvalues, which can cause problems for certain statistical analyses.

Another approach to missing data is *mean substitution*. The mean may be calculated for a group of observations (e.g., customers who are based in a specific geographic region) or the entire dataset. Predicting missing values using multiple regression on a set of highly correlated variables is another approach. However, this method may entail overfitting for big data machine learning. Lastly, *multiple imputation* approach is also used for predicting missing values. Methods such as expectation-maximization (EM)/ maximum likelihood estimation, Markov Chain Monte Carlo (MCMC) simulation, and propensity score estimation are used to estimate the missing values. A version of the dataset corresponding to each method is created. The datasets are then analyzed and the results are combined to produce estimates and confidence intervals for the missing values.

C. Dealing with Duplicate Data

Identifying and eliminating duplicate data is critical to big data applications. Duplicates are ubiquitous especially in user-contributed data in social network applications. For example, a user may unintentionally create a new profile without recognizing that her profile already exists. As a result, she may receive multiple notifications for the same event. Householding is closely related to deduplication, and involves identifying all addresses that belong to the same household. Householding obviates the need for sending the same information to multiple addresses of the same family.

Identifying duplicate data is a difficult task in the big data context. There are two major issues. The first is assigning a unique identifier to various pieces of information that belong to the same entity. The unique identifier is used to aggregate all information about the entity. This process is also referred to as *linking*. The second issue is identifying and eliminating duplicate data based on the unique identifiers. Given the volume of data, duplicate elimination is resource-challenged as data is too big to fit in main memory all at once. One solution is to use the Bloom filter, which requires that the associated hash functions be independent and uniformly distributed. Bloom filter is a space-efficient probabilistic data structure for testing set membership.

D. Dealing with Data Heterogeneity

Big data is often characterized by five Vs: volume, velocity, variety, veracity, and value. It is especially the variety (aka data heterogeneity) that poses greatest challenges to data quality. Data heterogeneity is manifested as unstructured, semi-structured, and structured data of disparate types. Traditionally, data quality research focused on structured data which is stored in relational databases. The emergence and the ubiquity of Web data attracted researchers to tackle data quality issues associated with semi-structured data in the Web pages [31].

Information extraction (IE) refers to synthesizing structured information such as entities, attributes of entities, and relationships among the entities from unstructured sources [40]. IE systems have evolved over the last three decades from manually coded rule-based systems, generative models based on Hidden Markov Models, conditional models based on maximum entropy, methods that perform more holistic analysis of documents' structures using grammars, to hybrid models that leverage both statistical and rule-based methods. Most of the IE research targets textual data such as natural language texts. Another line of IE research focuses on extracting text present in images and videos [41]. The next level of IE is to extract information from images and video (aka feature detection and feature extraction), which is extremely difficult and context dependent. IE data quality challenges primarily stem from the uncertainty associated with the extracted information.

E. Semantic Data Integration

As big data is typically loosely structured and often incomplete, most of it essentially remains inaccessible to users [15]. The next logical step after information extraction is to identify and integrate related data to provide users a comprehensive, unified view of data. Integrating unstructured heterogeneous data remains a significant challenge. Initiatives such as the IEEE's Smart Cities and IBM's Smarter Cities Challenge critically depend on integrating data from multiple sources. The difficulties of information extraction and data integration, and attendant data quality issues are manifested in operational systems such as Google Scholar, Citeseer, ResearchGate, and Zillow.

III. Data Quality Challenges in Machine Learning

Traditionally, data quality is assessed before using the data. In contrast, in the machine learning context, quality is assessed before the model is built as well as after. Data quality is assessed before model building using a set of dimensions (see Section V). The effectiveness of a model is evaluated using another subset of the data which was not used for model building. Performance of machine learning models is used as an indirect measure of data quality. Certain pre-processing operations on the data help these models achieve increased effectiveness.

Readers who are not familiar with machine learning concepts are encouraged to consult Appendix A before reading further.

High-quality datasets are essential for developing machine learning models. For example, outliers in training dataset can cause instability or non-convergence in ensemble learning. Incomplete, inconsistent, and missing data can lead to drastic degradation in prediction. The data available for building machine learning models is usually divided into three non-overlapping datasets: *training*, *validation*, and *test*. The machine learning model is developed using the training dataset. Next, the *validation dataset* is used to adjust the model parameters so that overfitting is avoided. Lastly, the *test dataset* is used to evaluate the model performance.

A. Bias and Variance Tradeoff in Machine Learning

Machine learning models are assessed based on how well the they predict response when provided with unseen input data, which is referred to as *prediction accuracy*, or alternatively, *prediction error*. Three sources contribute to prediction error: bias, variance, and irreducible error. *Bias* stems from using an incorrect model. For example, a linear algorithm is used when a nonlinear one fits the data better for a classification problem. Bias is the difference between the expected value and predicted value. The linear model will have high bias since it is unable to learn the nonlinear boundary between the classes. High bias would produce consistently incorrect results.

The *variance* is an error which arises due to small fluctuations in the training dataset. In other words, the variance is the sensitivity of a model to changes to the training dataset. Decision trees, for example, learned from different datasets for the same classification problem will have high variance. In contrast, decision trees have low bias since they can represent any Boolean function. In other words, the trees can fit to the training data well by learning appropriate Boolean functions associated with the tree internal nodes.

A popular way to visualize bias and variance tradeoff is through a bulls-eye diagram shown in Figure 1. The innermost circle is the bulls-eye and this region represents the expected values. When both the bias and variance are low, the expected values and the predicted values do not differ significantly (top-left concentric circles). When the variance is low but the bias is high, the predicted values are consistently differ from the expected values. For the low bias and high variance case, some predicted values are closer to the expected values. However, the difference between the expected and predicted values vary considerably. Lastly, when both the bias and the variance are high, the predicted values are off from the expected values and the difference between the expected and predicted values vary widely.

The *irreducible error* is due to the noise in the problem itself and cannot be reduced regardless of which algorithm is employed.

Bias and variance compete with each other and simultaneously minimizing these two sources of error is not possible. This is referred to as *bias-variance* tradeoff. This applies to all supervised learning algorithms and prevents them from generalizing beyond their training datasets. Generally, parametric models have higher bias, but low variance. They make more assumptions about the form of the model. They are easy to understand, but deliver low predictive performance. In contrast, nonparametric algorithms make fewer assumptions about the form of the model, and have low bias but high variance.

B. Cross-validation and Bootstrapping

When the data available for model building and testing is limited, a technique called *cross-validation* is used [22]. Though one may think that this situation does not arise in big data contexts, availability of sufficiently high-quality data can be a limiting factor. There are many variations of cross-validation including leave-one-out cross-validation (LOOCV) and $k-$fold cross-validation. LOOCV splits a dataset of size n into two parts of size 1 and $n-1$. The $n-1$ data items are used to build the model and the remaining data item is used for model evaluation. This procedure is repeated $n-1$ times, where a different data item is used for the evaluation role. The $k-$fold cross-validation is a computationally efficient alternative to LOOCV. It involves randomly dividing the set of data items into k groups/folds of approximately equal size. The first fold is used for testing, whereas the remaining $k-1$ folds are used to develop the model. This procedure is repeated $k-1$ times, each time a different fold plays the role of test data.

Another technique to deal with limited data is called *bootstrapping*. Assume that we have a small dataset of size n. A bootstrap sample of size n is produced from the original dataset by randomly selecting n data items from it with replacement. Any number of bootstrap samples of size n can be produced by repeating this process. It should be noted that some data items may be present multiple times in the bootstrap sample.

C. Data Transformations

Note that a feature vector has multiple components and each corresponds to a (predictor) variable. The Linear Discriminant Analysis (LDA) is a preferred classification algorithm when the number of classes is more than two. However, LDA assumes that each variable has the same variance. For such cases, data is first standardized by applying the $z-$transform [42]. The mean of the $z-$transformed data is always zero. Moreover, if the original data is distributed normally, the $z-$transformed data will conform to a standard normal distribution, which has a zero mean and a standard deviation of one.

Other machine learning algorithms assume a normal distribution for variables. For variables that are not normally distributed, transformations are used to bring data to normality conformance. Logarithm and square

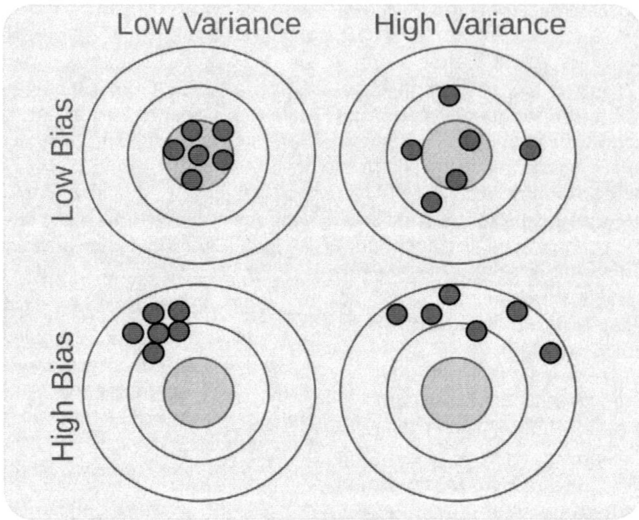

Figure 1: Visualizing bias and variance tradeoff using a bulls-eye diagram

root transformations are appropriate for exponential distributions, whereas the Box-Cox transformation is better suited for skewed distributions.

D. Other Considerations

Outliers are values that are drastically different from rest of the values in a dataset. Outliers may actually be legitimate data, or the result of sampling bias and sampling errors. For example, a malfunctioning or non-calibrated Internet of Things (IoT) device may generate outliers. Furthermore, outliers are also due to inherent variability in the data.

In some cases, the number of predictor variables can be extremely large and the associated problem is known as *dimensionality curse*. The k-nearest neighbor (kNN) algorithm works well when the number of dimensions of the input vector is small. If this number is high, the values computed by the distance metric of the algorithm become indistinguishable from one another. In other words, as dimensionality increases, the distance to the nearest neighbor approaches the distance to the farthest neighbor. The training data, irrespective of its size, covers only a small fraction of the input space. Therefore, no training datasets are big enough to compensate for dimensionality curse.

To overcome the dimensionality curse, variable/feature reduction techniques are used. Machine learning models need is a minimal set of independent variables that are correlated to the prediction, but not to each other. *Variable selection* (aka feature selection) is the process of choosing a minimal subset of relevant variables that are maximally effective for model building. Principal Component Analysis (PCA) and Exploratory Factor Analysis (EFA) are two techniques for variable selection and dimension reduction. Dimensionality reduction also occurs when a group of highly correlated variables is removed and replaced by just anyone variable in the group. Readers who are not familiar with detecting and removing outliers, robust statistics, and dimensionality reduction through PCA and EFA are referred to Appendices B, C, and D, respectively.

IV. Data Quality Case Studies

In this section, we present three data quality case studies. Many organizations still depend on manual data cleansing using methods such as manually reviewing data in spreadsheets or one-off corrections to bad data. The current generation data profiling and data quality assessment tools attest to this statement. The first case study illustrates the dominance of manual processes and labor intensive nature of data quality tasks. Machine learning and big data offer unprecedented opportunities for automating data quality tasks such as outlier detection, identification of inaccurate and inconsistent data, and imputation of missing data. The second and third case studies illustrate the role of machine learning and big data in data quality management.

A. InfoUSA

Producing high-quality data requires significant manual labor. InfoUSA data vendor is a case in point. InfoUSA sells mailing address data of consumers and businesses. The volume of this data is farther from being classified as big data. They collect business data from over 4,000 phone directories and 350 business sources. Consumer data is gleaned from over 1,000 sources including real estate records and voter registration files. Data quality issues such as inconsistency, incompleteness, missing and duplicate data abound in mailing address data. Over 500 InfoUSA full-time employees are engaged in data collection and curation.

B. Zillow

Zillow is a big data-driven real estate and rental marketplace. In contrast with InfoUSA, Zillow uses automated approaches to data acquisition, cleaning, transformation, integration, and aggregation. Zillow is a *living* database of over 110 million homes in the United States. It provides information about homes that are for sale or rent, and also homes that are not currently on the market. It is a living database in the sense that the data is continually kept current. For example, Zillow provides daily updated *Zestimate®* for both home values and fair rental values. *Zestimate®* home valuation is Zillow's estimated market value, which is computed using a proprietary formula. The formula uses both public and user-submitted data and incorporates undisclosed special features, location, and local market conditions. *Zestimate®* home valuation is more accurate for those geographic areas where the number of real estate transactions is large.

Zillow acquires data through publicly available sources such as prior and current real estate transactions, county courthouse real estate deeds and tax assessments. This data is also integrated with local real estate market conditions and historical data. *Zestimate®* values are a measure of Zillow's data quality accuracy. Across the entire real estate market, *Zestimate®* has a median error rate of 4.5% — *Zestimate®* values for half of the homes in an area are within 4.5% of the selling price, and the values for the remaining half are off by more than 4.5%. This is remarkable given that the *Zestimate®* values are computed by an algorithm without a human in the loop.

Zillow uses machine learning algorithms to automate data cleaning tasks such as outlier detection, data matching, and imputation of missing data. It also employs machine learning algorithms for data transformations, integration, and aggregation. These algorithms process 20 TB of data about 110 million homes. Each home is characterized by over 103 attributes. Time series data about homes encompasses a moving window of most recent 220 months. As an example, consider the following information about a home: 2 beds, 20 baths, and 1,000 sq ft of living space. The number of bathrooms can be easily detected as incorrect data using a supervised learning algorithm such as linear regression. Consider another task of integrating data from multiple sources such as MLS-1, MLS-2, county records, and user-provided data. By using weighted text and numeric features, distance metrics, and the k-nearest neighbor (kNN) machine learning algorithm, data from several sources can be matched quite accurately.

C. Determining Duplicate Questions in Quora

Quora is a question-and-answer website where questions and answers are contributed by users. Questions are asked, answered, edited and organized by a community of users. Quora enables users to edit questions collaboratively and suggest edits to answers contributed by other users. Quora uses an internally developed algorithm to rank answers to questions.

A question can be phrased in many different ways. Ability to determine if two differently worded questions are the same is critical to Quora. Such a capability is useful in directing the question asker to existing answers immediately. Furthermore, this obviates the need for Quora to solicit users to answer a question if the answer already exists for the question.

Recently, Quora released a first public dataset which is related to the problem of identifying duplicate questions. This dataset is comprised of over 400,000 lines of potential *question duplicate pairs*. A line is comprised of full text for each question in the pair, unique identifier for the question, and a binary flag indicating whether or not the question pair is a duplicate of each other. Quora ensured that this dataset is balanced - the number of question pairs that are duplicates is almost the same as the number of question pairs that are not duplicates. The goal of this dataset is to encourage natural language processing and machine learning researchers to find solutions to duplicate detection problem. Along the lines of Quora Question Pairs, Kaggle Competitions feature several challenging problems and associated datasets to advance machine learning research. Though it appears that model building is the primary activity in these competitions, data preprocessing and data quality assessment plays an equally important role.

V. Data Quality Dimensions and Assessment

What exactly is data quality? One may define data quality in terms of its fit for a business purpose. This is a generic and qualitative definition. To bring concreteness to the definition, data quality is often measured as a function of a set of *dimensions* such as accuracy, currency, and consistency. A data quality dimension provides a basis to measure and monitor the quality of data. However, we need an objective methodology to assess each dimension. These methodologies may require different sets of tools and techniques to quantify dimensions. Therefore, the resources required for each dimension will also vary. The initial assessment of data quality will form the baseline. Enhanced data quality resulting from new data cleaning, transformation, integration, and aggregation activities is measured against the baseline.

There is no consensus on what comprises the data quality dimensions. The dimensions proposed in the literature vary considerably. Also, they are based on the premise that data is primarily stored relational database management systems (RDBMS) and data warehouses. However, the advent of big data has brought in numerous data models and systems for data management under the umbrella term *NoSQL* [35].

Table I lists a set of data quality dimensions for the big data and machine learning contexts, which are generic and transcend application domains. Some of these dimensions can be evaluated using an ordinal scale. For example, consider the *Data Governance* dimension. Each question in the description column corresponding to this dimension is regarded as a sub-dimension. The latter can be measured using an ordinal scale such as {No data standards exist, Data standards exist but are not enforced, Data standards exist and are enforced}. In contrast, dimensions such as the *Data Duplication* can be quantified numerically. For example, the ratio of the number of duplicate observations to the total number of observations is one such numerical measure. Other dimensions such as *Outliers* require more elaborate methods for its quantification.

VI. Data Governance-Driven Data Quality Life Cycle

Data governance is a set of best practices and controls undertaken by an organization to actively manage and improve data quality. Data governance provides a process-oriented framework to embed and execute data quality activities such as planning, cleaning, profiling, assessing, issue tracking, and monitoring. Data governance identifies clear roles and responsibilities for ensuring data quality through repeatable processes. Data governance, though existed for long, is considered as an emerging discipline given its recent renaissance. Organizations that do not have an effective data governance, tend to take a tactical and quick-fix approach to data quality problems. Data governance, on the other hand, provides an organization-wide, proactive and holistic approach to data quality. It strives to capture data accurately and also enforces controls to prevent deterioration of data quality. Data governance calls for establishing a data governance strategy, policies, procedures, roles and responsibilities.

To identify suitable procedures for assessing various data quality dimensions and to implement the procedures, we need to first understand the data quality lifecycle in a data governance environment. The lifecycle depicts the movement of data through various processes and systems in an organization. Shown in Figure 2 is such a lifecycle suitable for organizations that follow data governance-driven approach to data management. The circled numbers in the figure indicate the ordering of the lifecycle processes.

A. Data Governance Standards

The first component of the data quality lifecycle is the *Data Governance Standards*, which is labeled ① in Figure 2. There are four processes in this component. *Data Dictionary* is a repository of definitions of business and technical terms. It includes information about conventions for naming data, meaning of data, its origin, owner, usage, and format. It may also include relationships of a data item to other data elements, default values, minimum and maximum values. Data dictionaries are also called *data glossaries*. The data dictionary counterpart in a relational database management system is called *system catalog*, which provides detailed information about the logical and physical database structures, table data statistics, authentication and authorization. Advanced data dictionaries may also feature those functions provided by taxonomies and ontologies. The data in the data dictionary is *meta data* since it describes other data.

Reference & Meta Data refers to two types of data. Reference data is any data that can be used to organize, classify, and validate other data. For example, ISO country codes are reference data. They are internationally recognized codes for uniquely identifying countries. Other reference data include codes for airports, zip codes, Classification of Instructional Programs (CIP) codes.

Reference data is critical to data validation. For instance, some data entered by application users can be validated against reference datasets. *Master data* is another category of data, which is often erroneously equated to the reference data. They are clearly different though they are interdependent. Master data represents core business data such as products, services, customers, and suppliers. It represents entities that come into play in business transactions such as a customer placing an order for a product. Meta data refers to additional data about data whose scope is beyond the data dictionary. Such meta data is typically generated by other processes in the data quality framework.

The next process, *Data Models & Business Rules*, documents a range of data models and policies. Data models go beyond the relational data model and may include NoSQL data models such as column-family and graph models. *Business Rules* specify complex relationships between data elements from a validation perspective. They also encompass rules for missing data imputation, spotting data integrity violations, resolving inconsistent data, linking related data, detection of outliers, and purging dated data, among others.

The last process, *Roles & Responsibilities*, involves identifying various roles for data quality management and associating responsibilities with each role. Roles may include an owner, program manager, project leader, chief data officer, business analyst, data analyst, and data steward. For example, a data analyst's role may include addressing issues raised in data quality reports and tracking resolution of these issues. Responsibilities associated with each role vary from one organization to another.

TABLE I: Data quality dimensions

Dimension Name	Description
Data Governance	Do organization-wide data standards exist and are they enforced? Do clearly defined roles and responsibilities exist for data quality related activities? Does data governance strive to acquire and maintain high-quality data through proactive management?
Data Specifications	Are data standards documented in the form of a data dictionary, data models, meta data, and integrity constraints?
Data Integrity	How is data integrity maintained? How are data integrity violations detected and resolved?
Data Consistency	If data redundancy exists, how is data consistency achieved? What methods are used to bring consistency to data that has become inconsistent? If data is geographically replicated, how is the consistency and latency managed?
Data Currency	Is the data current? Do procedures exists to keep the data current and purge stale data?
Data Duplication	Are there effective procedures in place to detect and remove duplicate data?
Data Completeness	Is the data about entities complete? How is missing data managed?
Data Provenance	Is a historical record of data and its origination maintained? If the data is acquired through multiple sources and has undergone cleaning and transformations, does the organization maintain a history of all changes to the data?
Data Heterogeneity	If multi-modality data about an entity is available, is that data captured and used?
Streaming Data	How is streaming data sampled, filtered, stored, and managed for both real-time and batch processing?
Outliers	How are outliers detected and addressed? Are there versions of datasets that are outlier-free? Does each version correspond to a different method for outlier detection and treatment?
Dimensionality Reduction	Do the datasets feature dimensionality reduced versions? How many versions are available?
Feature Selection	Do datasets have versions that exclude features that are either redundant, highly correlated, or irrelevant? How many versions are available?
Feature Extraction	Do the datasets provide a set of derived features that are informative and non-redundant, in addition to the original set of variables/features? How many such derived feature sets are available?
Business Rules	Does a process exist to identify, refine, consolidate, and maintain business rules that pertain to data quality? Do rules exist to govern data cleaning and transformations, and integrating related data of an entity from multiple sources? What business rules govern substitutions for missing data, deleting duplicate data, and archiving historical data? Are there rules for internal data audit and regulatory compliance?
Data Accuracy	Data can be syntactically accurate and yet semantically inaccurate. For example, a customer's mailing address may meet all the syntactic patterns specified by the postal service, yet it can be inaccurate. How does the organization establish the accuracy of data?
Gender Bias	Is the data free from factors that lead to gender bias in machine learning algorithms?
Confidentiality & Privacy	Are procedures and controls implemented for data encryption, data de-identification and re-identification, and differential privacy?
Availability & Access Controls	How is high data availability achieved? What security controls are implemented to protect data from unauthorized access? How are user entitlements to data access and modifications defined and implemented?

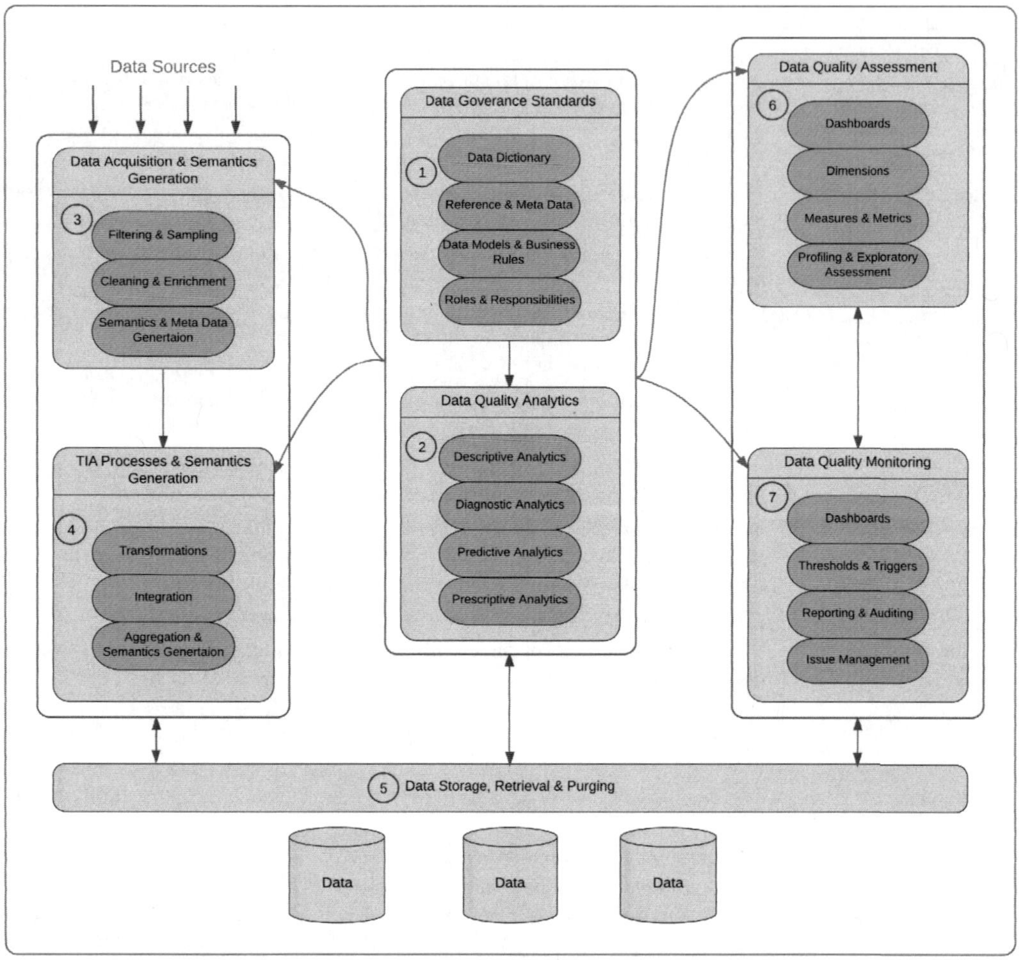

Figure 2: A data governance-driven framework for data quality lifecycle

B. Data Quality Analytics

This component provides four categories of analytic functions: descriptive, diagnostic, predictive, and prescriptive. These functions collectively provide the algorithms and statistical methods required for implementing the components identified by ③, ④, ⑥, and ⑦ in Figure 2. The analytic function categories are interrelated and overlap considerably.

Descriptive Analytics provides a process and a set of tools for measuring and assessing data quality. The goal is to describe data quality both quantitatively and qualitatively using statistical exploratory data analysis techniques. The next step is to determine what factors are contributing to poor data quality — *Diagnostic Analytics.* These analytics help to determine the relative contributions of factors such as missing, incomplete, inconsistent, and duplicate data towards poor data quality.

Predictive Analytics enable answering *what-if* questions related to data quality improvement. For example, what is the magnitude of data quality improvement if 90% of incomplete data is resolved? A natural evolution of predictive analytics leads to *Prescriptive Analytics.* The latter suggests an actionable plan, for example, for resolving 90% of incomplete data.

Both *Data Governance Standards* and *Data Quality Analytics* components provide principles, practices, and tools that drive the other four components. For example, descriptive, diagnostic, predictive, and prescriptive analytics are used for various tasks including data acquisition, transformations, integration, aggregation, data quality assessment and monitoring.

C. Data Acquisition & Semantics Generation

This component is comprised of three processes: Filtering & Sampling, Cleaning & Enrichment, and Semantics & Meta Data Generation. Big data applications typically acquire data from multiple sources. Some of this is streaming data. To manage the complexities of velocity and volume facets, streaming data is often sampled and filtered. Data is sampled randomly for retention and further processing. Also, the data is averaged over a moving window and only the averaged data is retained. Moreover, data may be filtered based on certain predicates. For example, if the values fall within a predefined range, such data is retained. Alternatively, data values that fall outside a predefined range are retained. Such data represents anomalies and outliers and is useful for detecting unusual events.

The next process is Cleaning & Enrichment, which primarily targets data standardization, detection and removal of duplicates, inconsistent data resolution, imputation for missing data, incomplete data strategies, and matching data across multiple sources (aka data/record linking). Cleaning & Enrichment process uses analytic functions to automatically or semi-automatically accomplish the above tasks. A meta data by-product of cleaning and enrichment is *annotation*, which is used to explain the evolution of data.

Several pieces of additional information are captured during the data acquisition phase. In the case of IoT devices, for instance, the types of sensors used, precision and scale for data calibration, and sampling methods employed is recorded. This meta data essentially captures semantics about the IoT data. These semantics and meta data is essential to determining suitable statistical analysis methods in downstream big data and machine learning applications.

Data cleaning procedures employ a range of ad-hoc data transformations. These transformations are relatively simple compared to those described in Section VI-D. An example of a simple cleaning procedure is the one that normalizes data — when some observations are measured in meters while others are measured in kilometers, all measurements are converted either meters or kilometers. Missing values can be automatically determined in some cases, if the missing value in conjunction with other available values and associated constraints entail a unique solution. Some quantitative approaches to data cleaning are based on detecting outliers. As discussed in Section B, detection of outliers is not a trivial task.

Imputation is a statistical technique for estimating missing values. Though several imputation methods are available, there is no imputation method that works in all cases. An imputation model is selected based on the availability of auxiliary information and whether or not the data to be inputed is subject to multivariate edit restrictions. A practical strategy is to impute missing values without considering edit restrictions and then apply minimal adjustments to the imputed values to comply with edit restrictions.

There are three basic numeric imputation models: imputation of the mean, ratio imputation, and generalized linear regression model. In the imputation of the mean model, imputation value is the mean computed over the observed values. The usability of this model is limited since it causes a bias in measures of spread, which are estimated from the sample after imputation.

In the ratio imputation model, the imputation value of variable x_i is computed as the product of $\hat{R}y_i$, where y_i is a covariate of x_i and $\hat{R}$ is an estimate of the average ratio between x and y. $\hat{R}$ is computed as the ratio of the sum of observed x values to the sum of corresponding y values. Lastly, in the *generalized linear regression model*, the missing value $\hat{x_i}$ is imputed as:

$$\hat{x_i} = \hat{\beta_0} + \hat{\beta_1}y_{1,i} + \hat{\beta_2}y_{2,i} + \cdots + \hat{\beta_k}y_{k,i}$$

where $\hat{\beta_0}, \hat{\beta_1}, \ldots, \hat{\beta_k}$ are estimated linear regression coefficients of the auxiliary variables $y_1, y_2, \ldots, y_k$.

In another method called *hot deck imputation*, missing values are imputed by copying values from similar records in the same dataset. This imputation method is applicable to both numerical and categorical data. The main consideration in the *hot deck imputation* method is determining which one of the observed values be chosen for imputation. This leads to the following variations: *random hot-deck imputation*, *sequential hot deck imputation*, and *predictive mean matching*. Others include k nearest neighbor imputation and an array of methods for imputation of missing longitudinal data [43]. Imputation results in datasets with very different distributional characteristics compared to the original dataset [44].

D. TIA Processes & Semantics Generation

Transformation, Integration, Aggregation (TIA) & Semantics Generation are the four processes that underlie this component. Many statistical procedures assume data normality and equality of variance. Data is transformed for improving data normality and equalizing variance. Such data transformations include inversion and reflection, conversion to a logarithmic scale, and square root and trigonometric transforms. It should be noted that these transformations are more complex than the ones discussed in Section VI-C, and use sophisticated rule-based approaches.

Large organizations typically have very complex data environments comprised of several data sources. This entails the need for integrating and aggregating data from these sources. Integration requires accurately identifying the data associated with an entity originating from multiple sources. However, not all data source providers use the same identification schemes consistently. Several tools are available for data integration such as the Talend Open Studio and Pentaho Data Integration. Once the data is integrated, aggregates are precomputed to speed up the analysis tasks. Transformation, integration, and aggregation processes generate substantial meta data as well as semantics, which are also captured and stored.

E. Data Storage, Retrieval & Purging

This component provides persistent storage, query mechanisms, and management functionality to secure and retrieve data. Both relational and NoSQL database systems are used to realize this functionality [36]. Several data models and query languages are provided to efficiently store and query structured, semi-structured, and unstructured data [35]. Rules-driven processing is employed to purge expired and stale data.

F. Data Quality Measurement and Assessment

This component provides four primary functions: dashboard view of current data quality, definition of data quality dimensions and associated measures & metrics to quantify dimensions, tools for measuring data quality through exploratory profiling. *Data quality assessment* is the process of evaluating data quality to identify errors and discern their implications. The assessment is made in the context of an intended use and suitability of data for that use is evaluated.

Dashboards are graphical depictions of data quality along and across the dimensions. Recall that data quality dimensions and their assessment at a conceptual level are discussed in Section V. Measures and metrics are used to quantify data quality dimensions. *Measures* are intended to quantify more concrete and objective attributes such as the number of missing values. In contrast, *metrics* quantify abstract, higher-level, and subjective attributes such as data accuracy.

There are four measurement scales: nominal, ordinal, interval, and ratio. The measurement scale determines which statistical methods are suitable for data analysis. The *nominal scale* is the most basic and provides just a set of labels for measurement. There is no inherent ordering to the labels. For example, gender is measured on a nominal scale comprised of two labels: male and female. The *ordinal scale* is a nominal scale when ordering is imposed on the labels. For instance, the Mohs scale of mineral hardness is a good example of ordinal scale. Mohs hardness varies from 1 to 10, where 1 corresponds to talc and 10 to diamond. However, the scale is not uniform. For instance, the diamond's hardness is 10 and the corundum's is 9, but the diamond is 4 times harder than the corundum.

In contrast with the ordinal scale, the *interval scale* has equal distance between the values. However, the scale does not have an *inherent* zero. For instance, a temperature is measured using an interval scale in weather prediction applications. However, 0 degrees Fahrenheit does not represent the complete absence of temperature. It does not make sense to add values on an interval scale, but the difference between two values is meaningful. It should be noted that 0 on the Kelvin scale is absolute zero — complete absence of temperature. Finally, a *ratio scale* is an interval scale with an inherent zero. The ratio of two values on the ratio scale is meaningful. For instance, 10 degrees Kelvin is twice as hot as 10 degrees Kelvin. As another example, money is measured on a ratio scale.

Data profiling is an exploratory approach to data quality analysis. Statistical approaches are used to reveal data usage patterns as well as patterns in the data [27], [30]. Several tools exist for data quality assessment using data profiling and exploratory data analysis. Such tools include Tableau [45] and Talend Open Studio [46]. Other tools are listed in Section VIII.

G. Data Quality Monitoring

This unit builds on the Data Quality Assessment component's functionality. Its primary function is to continually monitor data quality and report results through dashboards and alerts. Data quality is impacted by processes that acquire data from the outside world through batch and real-time feeds. For example, an organization may procure data feeds from multiple vendors. Issues arise when different values are reported for the same data item. For instance, financial services companies obtain real-time price information from multiple vendors. If the timestamped price for a financial instrument received from vendors differ, how does the system select one of the values as the correct price? *Vendor source hierarchy* is an approach to solving this problem. It requires imposing an ordering on the vendors based on their reputation. If multiple prices are available for an instrument, select the price from that vendor who has the highest reputation. An approach to improving data quality using the conflicting data values about the same object originating from multiple sources is presented in [47].

Corporate mergers and acquisitions also contribute to data quality degradation. These actions entail changes to, for example, the identifiers of financial instruments. The changes will make their way into data vendor feeds. Automated real-time and batch feed ingestion systems will record price information under the new identifiers, effectively causing data quality decay by not recognizing the relationship between the old and new identifiers. Streaming data feeds as well as high volume batch feeds require automated and real-time processing. Whether or not to accept a data record must be determined on the fly. If a data record is accepted whose data quality is suspect, such information is recorded as meta data to help data quality monitoring processes. User interfaces also contribute to data quality decay. Irrespective of data availability, users are forced to enter values for the required fields on a form.

Another source of data quality degradation is when systems are merged or upgraded. The systems being merged may be operating under different sets of business rules and user interfaces. The data may also overlap between the systems. Even worse, the overlapping data may be contradictory. Systems merging typically requires substantial manual effort and decisions made in resolving data issues must be documented in the form of meta data. Lastly, transformations, integration, and aggregation also contribute to data quality decay. These processes may entail loss of data precision and scale, and replacement of old identifiers with new ones.

VII. A Reference Architecture for Implementing the Data Governance-driven Framework for Data Quality Life Cycle

Shown in Figure 3 is a reference architecture for implementing the data governance-driven lifecycle framework of Figure 2. The bottom layer persistently stores all types of data managed by relational and NoSQL systems. In addition to application data, business rules, reference and master data, and meta data are also stored. The next layer above is the hardware layer powered by both conventional CPUs as well as the processors specifically designed for machine learning tasks such as the neuromorphic chips.

The Parallel and Distributed Computing layer provides software abstractions, database engines, and open source libraries to provide *performance at scale* required in big data and machine learning environments. The immediate layer above is dedicated for functionality needed for four types of data analytics – descriptive, diagnostic, predictive, and prescriptive. Various machine learning algorithms comprise the underlying basis for achieving the data analytics functions.

The data access layer is responsible for enforcing the data governance-driven approach to implementing data quality. It has a rules engine to execute and mange business rules. This layer also controls encryption, security, privacy, compression, and provenance aspects of the data. The layer above the data access layer primarily provides authorization and access control features. It also features privileged functions for system administrators. The architecture specifies various types of query APIs for applications, interactive users, and system administrators. The entire architecture can be implemented with *Free and Open Source Software* (FOSS).

VIII. Tools for Data Quality Management

Given the data volumes and the tedious and error-prone nature of the data quality tasks, tools are essential for cleaning, transforming, integrating, and aggregating data and to asses and monitor data quality. The following taxonomy for data quality tools is for exposition purpose only. However, it is difficult to demarcate functions based on this taxonomy in open-source and commercial data quality tools.

The first category of tools provide functions to support descriptive analytics. These tools in the field are referred to as *data profiling* or *data analysis* tools. They primarily target column data in relational database tables, and column data across tables. They help to identify integrity constraint violations. It should be noted that integrity constraints go beyond what can be declaratively specified in relational databases. Complex integrity constraints can be specified in the form of business rules.

Another category of tools provides functions for diagnostic analytics. For instance, if there is an integrity constraint violation, these tools help to discover the root cause of these violations. The third category of tools focuses on how to fix the problems revealed by diagnostic analytics. Data cleaning, integration, and transformation tools come under this category. This functionality is provided by prescriptive analytics tools. The fourth category of tools help to explore *what if* scenarios and perform *change impact analysis* – what is the impact of changing a value on overall data quality or on a specific data quality dimension?

Historically, data cleaning tools performed mostly name and address validation. The expanded functionality in the current generation tools include standardization of fields (e.g., canonical representation for date values), validating values using regular expressions, parsing and information extraction, rule-based data transformations, linking related data, merging and consolidating data from multiple sources, and elimination of duplicates. Some tools go even farther and help to fix missing data through statistical imputation. However, data quality tools do not address the data accuracy dimension. This is typically a manual process which requires significant human involvement. A similar situation exists for data quality monitoring. Data cleaning tool vendors are beginning to address this need through audit logs and automated alerts.

Profiler is a proof-of-concept, visual analysis tool for assessing quality issues in tabular data [48]. Using data mining methods, it automatically flags data that lacks quality. It also suggests coordinated summary visualizations for assessing the quality of data in context. Some of the leading software vendors for data quality tools include Informatica, IBM, Talend, SAS, SAP, Trillium Software, Oracle, and Information Builders.

Informatica offers three data quality products: Informatica Data Quality, Informatica Data as a Service, and Data Preparation (Rev). IBM offers InfoSphere Information Server for Data Quality, which also integrates data governance functionality. Trillium Software markets Trillium Refine^{TM} and Trillium Prepare^{TM}. Trillium Refine^{TM} is used for data standardization, data matching, and data enrichment through annotations and meta data. In contrast, Trillium Prepare^{TM} focuses on data integration from diverse sources through automated workflows and built-in logic, which obviates the need for any programming. Only Trillium Software offers data quality tools under Software as a Service (SaaS) model. Talend provides an array of products for data quality (end-to-end profiling and monitoring), data integration, master data management, and big data processing through NoSQL databases, Apache Hadoop and Spark [46]. In addition to commercially licensed software, Talend offers an open source community edition with limited functionality.

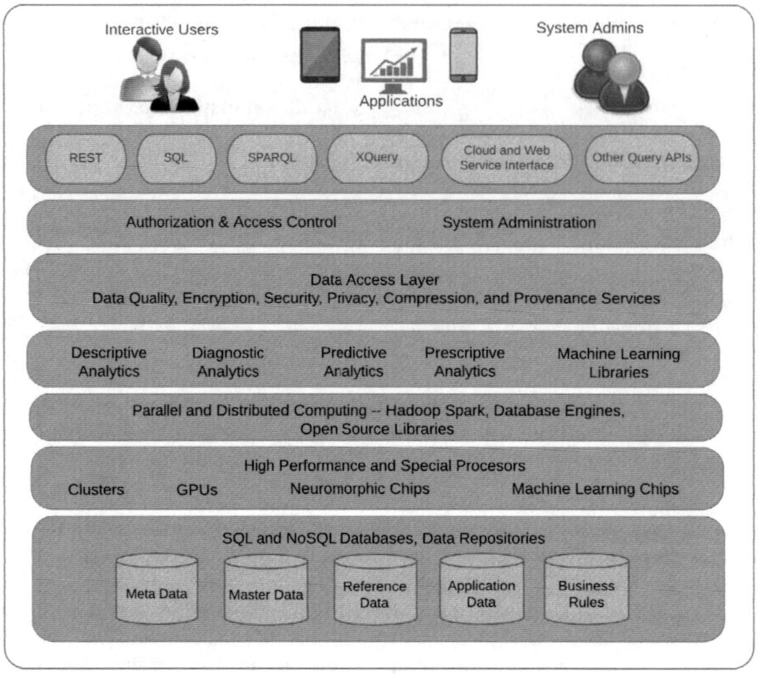

Figure 3: A reference architecture for implementing the data quality lifecycle framework for big data and machine learning

IX. Recommended Practices and Future Trends

Data quality has been an active area of research for over four decades [49]. The progress has been hampered by the domain-specific considerations and attendant narrowly focused solutions. Solutions to simple problems such as recognizing customers as they interact through a wider range of channels and developing a single customer view remains elusive even today. It is common for organizations to have 50 or more customer contact databases. Incomplete and missing data, inaccurate data, dated data, and duplicate data are the most common data quality problems. Exponential growth in data generation coupled with social and mobile channels exacerbate the data quality problem.

Integrity Constraints (ICs) do not prevent bad data. ICs are only one step of a multi-step process for ensuring data quality. Requiring a field to be non-empty in a user interface is not sufficient to ensure that a user provides a meaningful value. Furthermore, constraining a field to a valid range of numerical values does not assure that the values chosen are necessarily accurate. Constraint enforcement through user interfaces often leads to user frustration. In manually generated data contexts, if data entry operators are forced to provide values, they may enter incomplete and inaccurate values. In many cases, they lack the domain knowledge to provide the correct data especially in time-constrained transaction environments. Advances in natural language understanding, language modeling, and named entity recognition will help to alleviate this problem [50].

Current generation user interfaces are designed to accept or reject data values. An accepted value implies complete confidence in its correctness. Instead, the interface should enable specifying a degree of confidence in addition to the value itself. It should be possible to edit the data items with low confidence score at a later time to increase their confidence score. Provenance tracking should be tightly integrated with this method. Furthermore, statistical machine learning methods should be leveraged to suggest appropriate data values. For example, they can suggest values based on an underlying statistical model of data distribution.

Annotation should be an integral part of data quality tools. Annotating unusual or incomplete data is invaluable for data cleaning, integration, and aggregation processes. Annotation makes it easier to identify suspect data that needs correction. Though automated approaches to outlier detection are highly desirable, currently outlier detection and treatment is a manual process. In the short- to medium-term, approaches used in visual analytics [51] should be brought to bear in outlier detection. This approach helps to transition a completely manual process to a semi-automated process. In visual analytics, analysts use their domain knowledge and judgment to validate information provided by algorithms.

Both Big Data Analytics and Data Science as new academic disciplines will accelerate data quality research. Furthermore, big data-driven machine learning [52] is expected yield solutions that will achieve automatic domain adaptation through supervised and unsupervised learning. Privacy-preserving data quality assessment will gain importance to protect the privacy risks of various stakeholders [53]. As the number of data sources increases, the complexity of the transformations required to integrate these data is surging. Data quality errors are often spotted in the transformed data. New algorithms are needed to identify the original data elements and their sources corresponding to these errors [54].

X. Conclusions

The advent of big data and attendant renaissance in machine learning offers both opportunities for and challenges to data quality research. The true cost of fixing a software bug goes up based on how far down the software development lifecycle the bug is found. The IBM Systems Science Institute reports that the cost of fixing a bug that is discovered after the product has been released is four to five times as the one discovered during design, and up to 100 times more than the one discovered during the maintenance phase. A similar scenario is generally true for the costs associated with fixing problems caused by poor data quality.

Historically, data quality tasks were manually carried out with rudimentary support from data quality tools. Manual and even semi-automated approaches are impractical in the big data context. On the positive side, machine learning and other advances in computer science offer unprecedented opportunities to automate data cleaning, assessment and monitoring tasks.

Until recently, data quality research has primarily focused on structured data stored in relational databases and file systems. The recent emergence of NoSQL systems for big data management renders much of the traditional data quality research inadequate and less relevant. In this paper, we described a data governance-driven framework for data quality lifecycle and a reference architecture for implementing the framework. Our next step is to implement the architecture shown in Figure 3 using open source tools and libraries. We expect the application of the resulting system on big data scale datasets to reveal both the strengths and weaknesses of our proposed architecture.

Appendix A
Machine Learning Systems

The facets of a machine learning systems include (1) a representation (aka model) for the system, (2) methods and data used for training the system, (3) convergence and instability issues associated with the datasets and training methods, (4) evaluation of the effectiveness of the system using test data, and (5) model selection - searching for the best model in the model space. We use the terms machine learning *algorithm* and *model* synonymously.

Input to machine learning algorithms is usually represented as $n-$ dimensional (feature) vectors. Each component in the vector corresponds to a *(predictor) variable* value (aka *feature*). All input vectors are of the same dimension. The output of a machine learning algorithm can be a scalar or a vector. The dimensions of this response vector and the input vectors need not be the same. A *labeled input instance* refers to both the feature vector and the expected result.

A. Prediction and Clustering

Broadly speaking, there are two major classes of machine learning algorithms: prediction and clustering. *Prediction problems* involve predicting an outcome for a given input. For example, given an email, predict its class: *spam* or *not spam*. Other examples include predicting whether a credit card transaction is a fraud, whether or not to approve an application for bank credit, and predicting credit scores of consumers.

Regression and *classification* are both prediction problems. Regression predicts a value from a continuous set, for example, predicting the credit score of a consumer, which is a real number. Classification, on the other hand, classifies an input to one of the predefined classes. For instance, classifying hand-written digits into one of the ten classes, where each class corresponds to a decimal digit. Both regression and clustering use *supervised learning*.

Clustering refers to another class of machine learning algorithms. Their primary function is to organize a set of objects into two or more classes in a way that the objects in a class are maximally similar to each other, while maximally different from the objects in other classes. Examples of clustering include categorizing students in a class based on their predominant learning style, classifying customers into groups to enable targeted marketing for new products and services, and identifying clusters of functionally related genes.

B. Supervised, Semi-supervised, and Unsupervised Learning

Supervised, semi-supervised, and unsupervised are the three major approaches to training machine learning algorithms. In *supervised learning*, an algorithm learns from the *training data*, which is provided in the form of *labeled instances*. The result of learning is a model such as a decision tree or an artificial neural network. The model is used to predict a response when it is presented with input data which is not seen before by the model. For supervised learning algorithms, one typically needs to choose values for the model parameters. For instance, the number of trees is one of the model parameters for the random forest models. Model parameters are determined using experimentation and *hyperparameter tuning.*

In *unsupervised learning*, an algorithm learns on its own using the supplied data. Often, unsupervised algorithms are used to automatically generate labeled instances, which are then used in supervised learning. *Semi-supervised learning* is a hybrid of supervised and unsupervised learning. It makes use of mostly unlabeled data for training. In other words, the training data is comprised of a small amount of labeled data and a large amount of unlabeled data.

C. Parametric and Non-parametric Learning

Parametric vs. *non-parametric* is another way to classify machine learning algorithms [55]. Parametric algorithms employ a known functional form such as a linear function to map input (feature) vectors to response vectors. The chosen functional form determines the number of parameters of the model. For example, for the linear regression model, the model parameters are intercept and slope. The model parameters are learned from the training data. Perceptron and linear discriminant analysis are two other examples of parametric learning algorithms. Non-parametric algorithms, on the other hand, do not assume a functional form *a priori*. Using the training data, these algorithms learn functional forms and their parameters. Non-parametric algorithms require large training datasets. Examples of such algorithms are $k-$ nearest neighbors (kNN), support vector machines, artificial neural networks, and *naive* Bayes classifiers.

D. Linear and Nonlinear Learning Algorithms

Linear vs. nonlinear is yet another way to classify machine learning algorithms. As the name implies, linear machine learning algorithms typically employ a linear function to map input vectors to response vectors. Linear algorithms include gradient descent optimization, linear regression, logistic regression, and linear discriminant analysis. Nonlinear machine learning algorithms include classification and regression trees (CART), *naive* Bayes, kNN, learning vector quantization (an extension of kNN), and support vector machines.

E. Ensemble Machine Learning, Bagging, and Random Forests

Variations on the algorithms discussed above include *ensemble learning, bagging,* and *random forest.* An ensemble algorithm combines the predictions from multiple machine learning algorithms to make a more accurate prediction than any individual model. Bootstrap aggregation (aka bagging) is an ensemble learning algorithm. It is a general procedure to reduce variance for high variance algorithms such as the Classification and Regression Tree (CART). First, we create many random subsamples of the training dataset with replacement. Second, using each subsample, we train a CART model. Given a new input instance, it is classified using each of the CART models. The input belongs that class which is arrived at by the majority of the CART models.

Even with bootstrap aggregation/bagging, CART trees may posses significant structural similarities, which results in high correlation in their predictions. This is due to the fact that a *strong predictor* typically gets included in almost all trees. This makes the trees correlated and thus their predictions are also correlated. Ensemble methods work better if the predictions from the underlying individual models are either uncorrelated or weakly correlated.

Boosting (aka boosted tree) overcomes the correlated predictions problem by creating a strong model from a number of weak models. It first creates a model from the training data. A second model is then created, whose goal is to correct the shortcomings in the first model. This process is continued until the ensemble correctly predicts the training dataset or a pre-specified number of models have been added. *AdaBoost* is the first successful boosting algorithm for binary classification problems. It can also be used to boost the performance of any machine learning algorithm. AdaBoost makes a prediction based on the weighted average of the weak classifiers.

Random Forests approach overcomes the *correlation between trees problem* in *bagged trees* by de-correlating the trees. As in bagging, a number of trees on *bootstrapped* training data are developed. However, each time a split in a tree is considered, only a random sample of a subset of predictors is allowed for the split to be based upon.

F. Evaluating Prediction Accuracy

For regression prediction problems (e.g., linear and nonlinear models) evaluation measures include R^2, adjusted R^2, Akaike Information Criteria (AIC), Bayesian Information Criteria (BIC), and Mallow's Cp.

Machine learning algorithms for binary classification prediction problems are evaluated using the *confusion matrix* shown in Table II. Consider the problem of predicting flight delays. This is a binary classification problem — given an input vector, which represents variables (e.g., origin airport, destination airport, flight number, month, day of the month, day of the week, actual departure time, scheduled departure time, actual arrival time, and scheduled arrival time), the classifier will predict whether or not the flight will be delayed (a yes/no response).

Consider the table cell labeled "True Positive (TP)." The value in this cell indicates the number of times the model predicted delays correctly - the model predicted flight delay and the flight was actually delayed. A bigger value is better for this case. The value in the cell labeled "False Positive (FP)" indicates the number times the model predicted delays when actually there were no delays. Smaller values are desired for this case. Next, the value

TABLE II: Structure of a confusion matrix

		Predicted Value		
		POSITIVE	NEGATIVE	Row Total
Actual Value	POSITIVE	True Positive (**TP**)	False Negative (**FN**)	P'
	NEGATIVE	False Positive (**FP**)	True Negative (**TN**)	N'
	Column Total	P	N	

in cell labeled "False Negative (FN)" indicates the number of times the model did not predict delays when there were delays. A smaller value for this case is preferred. Lastly, the value in the cell labeled "True Negative (TN)" indicates the number of times the model did not predict delays when there were no delays. Here again, a bigger value is better.

Let $P = TP + FP$ and $N = FN + TN$. Four metrics are defined — PPV, TPR, ACC, and F1 score — as shown in Table III. Which metric is relevant depends on the problem being addressed. In the case of the airline delay prediction problem, accuracy is a more relevant metric.

For multi-class classification prediction problems (e.g., classification trees), *classification error rate* is used as the evaluation metric. The latter measures the fraction of the training observations in a *region* that do not belong to the most common class. Other measures include the Gini index, which measures the total variance across all the classes. An alternative to the Gini index is *cross-entropy*. Gini index and cross-entropy are quite similar numerically.

APPENDIX B
OUTLIERS

Extreme values in the data are not necessarily outliers. For instance, for a univariate case, a perfect SAT score from a rural high school in the United States is an extreme value, but not an outlier. For a multivariate case, a similar example is a student from a rural background pursuing a Ph.D. degree at a prestigious university. Errors in data acquisition processes and recording contribute to extreme values.

We first define some terminology to facilitate discussion about outlier detection. Univariate context involves only one input variable, whereas the multivariate context refers to the presence of more than one input variable. In statistics, the terms *statistic* and *estimator* are related but are distinct concepts. A statistic relates to a *sample*. For example, *sample mean* is a statistic. An *estimator* also relates to a sample, but in the context of an unknown property of a statistical model. An *estimator* is a rule for estimating the unknown property of the model.

Both *location equivariance* and *scale equivariance* are important properties for all statistical *measures of location*. Location equivariance refers to the fact that if a constant is added to each data point in the dataset, the measure of location will be increased by that constant value. Likewise, scale equivariance corresponds to multiplication by a constant — when each point in the dataset is multiplied by a constant results in a change in the measure of location by the same constant. For multivariate data, properties for measures of location are referred to as *affine equivariance*. The latter extends the notion of equivariance beyond location and scale to measures of multivariate dispersion. For example, covariance matrices are affine equivariant, but are not *robust* in the presence of outliers.

A. Implications of Outliers

Outliers can have a dramatic impact on the performance of machine learning algorithms and statistical procedures including clustering and factor analysis [44]. Clustering is especially sensitive to outliers. Outliers can also distort Pearson's correlation coefficient, pose difficulties in regression analysis, and erroneously imply collinearity among the input (aka predictor) variables. Correlation coefficients based methods such as factor analysis and structural equation modeling are negatively impacted by the outliers.

B. Outlier Detection

A commonly used approach tags a data point as an outlier, if its value is more than two or three standard deviations from the mean. This approach may actually mask an outlier since outliers can inflate the standard deviation. For unimodal and symmetrically distributed data, the box-and-whisker plot method is a popular approach for outlier detection. For skewed distributions, data is first transformed using a logarithmic or square root function. Other methods such as the one proposed by Hiridoglou & Berthelot [56] for positive observations, take the skewness into consideration.

Approaches to multivariate outlier detection must maintain *affine equivariance*. A commonly recommended approach for multivariate outlier detection is the Mahalanobis distance (D^2). Other methods include Minimum Volume Ellipsoid (MVE), Minimum Covariance Determinant (MCD), Fast MCD, and Minimum Generalized Variance (MGV) [44].

TABLE III: Evaluation measures based on confusion matrix

Evaluation Metric Name	Computing the Metric
Precision or positive predictive value (PPV)	$\frac{TP}{TP+FP}$
Recall (sensitivity or true positive rate (TPR))	$\frac{TP}{TP+FN}$
Accuracy (ACC)	$\frac{TP+TN}{P+N}$
F1 score (harmonic mean of precision and sensitivity)	$\frac{2 \cdot TP}{2 \cdot TP+FP+FN}$

Appendix C
Robust Statistics

Robust statistics are statistical methods that are not significantly affected by outliers [57]. They provide good performance for data coming from a wide range of probability distributions, especially for data that is not normally distributed. Modern robust statistical methods offer considerably *higher statistical power* and a greater understanding of data drawn from different probability distributions [58].

A *trimmed mean* is the mean computed by excluding a certain percent of the largest and the same percent of the smallest values from a dataset. For example, the 10% trimmed mean is the mean computed by excluding 10% percent of the largest and 10% percent of the smallest values from the dataset. The trimmed mean calculation requires first sorting the data points from the smallest to the largest. The trimmed mean shields the influence of data points at both ends that may unfairly affect the *traditional mean.*

A related concept is *Winsorizing data.* Instead of removing the 10% of the smallest values, they are set equal to the smallest value that is not trimmed. Likewise, 10% of the largest values are set equal to the largest value that is not trimmed. In other words, 10% of the smallest values are set equal to the value corresponding to the 10th percentile, while the 10% of the largest values are set equal to the value corresponding to the 90th percentile. A simple robust analog of the Pearson's correlation is the *Winsorized correlation.* For example, a 90% Winsorized correlation is calculated using the standard correlation formula after trimming 5% of the smallest and 5% of the largest values.

The notion of *breakdown point* is a key consideration in assessing the impact of outliers. When the proportion of corrupted data points in a dataset exceeds a threshold called the *breakdown point* of an estimator, the estimator can produce arbitrarily erroneous results. There are two types of breakdown points: *finite sample breakdown point,* and *asymptotic breakdown point.* The finite sample breakdown point of an estimator is the proportion of data that can be given arbitrary values without affecting the estimator's validity. Consider the calculation of mean of the sample $\{x_1, x_2, x_3, \ldots, x_n\}$. Making any one of the values in the sample arbitrarily large renders the sample mean invalid — a single bad value causes the sample mean *breakdown.*

The finite sample breakdown point is necessarily associated with the sample size n. In contrast, the *asymptotic breakdown point* is a single number, which is the limit of the finite sample breakdown point as n goes to infinity. For the sample mean, the finite sample breakdown point is $\frac{1}{n}$, and the asymptotic breakdown point is zero. In contrast, for the sample median, the finite sample breakdown point is $\lfloor \frac{n-1}{2n} \rfloor$, and the asymptotic breakdown point is one-half. If a statistic has a breakdown point of 0.2, then 20% of the data points in the dataset could be outliers without markedly impacting the statistic. Median and *trimmed mean* are examples of statistics with higher breakdown points. However, they are less accurate in estimating model parameters.

Appendix D
Dimensionality Reduction

The $k-$ nearest neighbor (kNN) algorithm is a non-parametric method used for both classification and regression. When kNN is used for classification, the output is the name of the class to which the object represented by the input vector belongs. The class assigned to the object is that class which is the most common among its k nearest neighbors. In kNN based regression, the output is the property value for the object represented by the input vector, which is the average of the property values of its k nearest neighbors. For instance, a credit score of a new customer is the average of the credit scores of the k nearest or similar customers. If the variables come from skewed distributions, the effectiveness of the *majority voting based classification* of kNN is diminished. Instances of a more frequent class tend to dominate the class prediction as these instances tend to be common among the k nearest neighbors due to their sheer number.

The kNN algorithm requires a distance metric to determine the k nearest neighbors of a given object. Distance metrics used by the kNN include the Euclidean, Hamming, Manhattan, Mahalanobis, and Minkowski. Euclidean distance is a good measure for cases where the input variables are similar in type. In contrast, Manhattan distance is more appropriate for cases where the input variables are dissimilar in type as in age, height, weight, and gender. Distances between vectors are non-computable if the component values are missing in the input vectors.

A. Dimensionality Reduction through Variable Selection

Other names for the variable selection include *feature selection, attribute selection,* and *variable subset selection. Subspace learning* (aka *feature transformation*) is another approach to dimensionality reduction. It is based on the premise that a combination of the original features may be more useful for machine learning. Subspace learning transforms the original features to a new feature space, which has lower dimensionality.

Fisher criterion plays an important role in dimensionality reduction for classification problems. It seeks a feature representation which minimizes the *within-class distance* while maximizing the *between-class distance. Fisher score* is a feature selection method based on the Fisher criterion. Linear Discriminant Analysis (LDA) is a supervised subspace learning method based on the Fisher criterion.

B. Principal Component Analysis and Exploratory Factor Analysis

Principal Component Analysis (PCA) is another technique for feature selection. It is effective in situations where the variables are highly correlated. The PCA operates under the premise that the *manifested/observed* and *measured variables* are of interest rather than the *unmanifested latent constructs* in the dataset (which are of interest in Exploratory Factor Analysis). PCA performs analysis using all the variance in the (observed) variables, without consideration for the underlying latent structure of the variables. PCA reduces the number of (observed) variables to a smaller number of principal components. Each component is formed as a weighted linear combination of the variables. These components account for most of the variance of the variables. Note that the total amount of variance in PCA is equal to the number of observed variables being analyzed.

The number of principal components extracted is same as the number of observed variables. The first principal component accounts for most of the variance in the dataset, the second component accounts for the second largest amount of variance, and so on. The first few components that account for most of the variance are retained, while the remaining components are discarded. The principal components are uncorrelated with each other. Instead of the original variables, the first few principal components, for example, are used in linear regression.

In contrast with PCA, Exploratory Factor Analysis (EFA) enables exploring the underlying structure of a dataset as well as serving as a general-purpose dimensionality reduction technique. EFA and PCA are functionally equivalent, but are different in how they accomplish their functions. EFA premises that there are latent variables or factors in the dataset that give rise to the observed variables. EFA employs a set of extraction and rotation techniques, which are designed to model the unobserved or latent constructs in the dataset. EFA identifies the underlying factor structure for a set of observed and measured variables. The user interactively determines the number of factors to retain for analysis.

REFERENCES

[1] V. Gudivada, D. Rao, and W. Grosky, "Data quality centric application framework for big data," in *Proceedings of the The Second International Conference on Big Data, Small Data, Linked Data and Open Data (ALLDATA 2016)*. Lisboa, Portugal: IARIA, Feb. 2016, pp. 24 - 32.

[2] M. F. Bosu and S. G. MacDonell, "Data quality in empirical software engineering: A targeted review," in *Proceedings of the 17th International Conference on Evaluation and Assessment in Software Engineering*. New York, NY: ACM, 2013, pp. 171–176.

[3] Y. Shirai, W. Nichols, and M. Kasunic, "Initial evaluation of data quality in a tsp software engineering project data repository," in *Proceedings of the 2014 International Conference on Software and System Process*. New York, NY: ACM, 2014, pp. 25–29.

[4] M. Shepperd, "Data quality: Cinderella at the software metrics ball?" in *Proceedings of the 2nd International Workshop on Emerging Trends in Software Metrics*. New York, NY: ACM, 2011, pp. 1–4.

[5] P. Phannachitta, A. Monden, J. Keung, and K. Matsumoto, "Case consistency: A necessary data quality property for software engineering data sets," in *Proceedings of the 19th International Conference on Evaluation and Assessment in Software Engineering*. New York, NY: ACM, 2015, pp. 19:1–19:10.

[6] K. Sha and S. Zeadally, "Data quality challenges in cyber-physical systems," *J. Data and Information Quality*, vol. 6, no. 2-3, pp. 8:1–8:4, Jun. 2015.

[7] J. McNaull, J. C. Augusto, M. Mulvenna, and P. McCullagh, "Data and information quality issues in ambient assisted living systems," *J. Data and Information Quality*, vol. 4, no. 1, pp. 4:1–4:15, Oct. 2012.

[8] S. A. Sheppard and L. Terveen, "Quality is a verb: The operationalization of data quality in a citizen science community," in *Proceedings of the 7th International Symposium on Wikis and Open Collaboration*. New York, NY: ACM, 2011, pp. 29–38.

[9] L. Cao and H. Zhu, "Normal accidents: Data quality problems in ERP-enabled manufacturing," *J. Data and Information Quality*, vol. 4, no. 3, pp. 11:1–11:26, May 2013.

[10] H. Xu, "What are the most important factors for accounting information quality and their impact on ais data quality outcomes?" *J. Data and Information Quality*, vol. 5, no. 4, pp. 14:1–14:22, Mar. 2015.

[11] O. Curé, "Improving the data quality of drug databases using conditional dependencies and ontologies," *J. Data and Information Quality*, vol. 4, no. 1, pp. 3:1–3:21, Oct. 2012.

[12] P. Barnaghi, M. Bermudez-Edo, and R. Tönjes, "Challenges for quality of data in smart cities," *J. Data and Information Quality*, vol. 6, no. 2-3, pp. 6:1–6:4, Jun. 2015.

[13] A. Klein, "Incorporating quality aspects in sensor data streams," in *Proceedings of the ACM First Ph.D. Workshop in CIKM*. New York, NY, USA: ACM, 2007, pp. 77–84.

[14] D. Kontokostas, P. Westphal, S. Auer, S. Hellmann, J. Lehmann, R. Cornelissen, and A. Zaveri, "Test-driven evaluation of linked data quality," in *Proceedings of the 23rd International Conference on World Wide Web*. New York, NY: ACM, 2014, pp. 747–758.

[15] S. K. Bansal and S. Kagemann, "Integrating big data: A semantic extract-transform-load framework," *Computer*, vol. 48, no. 3, pp. 42–50, 2015.

[16] N. Martin, A. Poulovassilis, and J. Wang, "A methodology and architecture embedding quality assessment in data integration," *J. Data and Information Quality*, vol. 4, no. 4, pp. 17:1–17:40, May 2014.

[17] K.-S. Na, D.-K. Baik, and P.-K. Kim, "A practical approach for modeling the quality of multimedia data," in *Proceedings of the Ninth ACM International Conference on Multimedia*. New York, NY: ACM, 2001, pp. 516–518.

[18] A. Na'im, D. Crawl, M. Indrawan, I. Altintas, and S. Sun, "Monitoring data quality in kepler," in *Proceedings of the 19th ACM International Symposium on High Performance Distributed Computing*. New York, NY: ACM, 2010, pp. 560–564.

[19] H. M. Sneed and R. Majnar, "A process for assessing data quality," in *Proceedings of the 8th International Workshop on Software Quality*. New York, NY: ACM, 2011, pp. 50–57.

[20] V. Gudivada, R. Baeza-Yates, and V. Raghavan, "Big data: Promises and problems," *IEEE Computer*, vol. 48, no. 3, pp. 20–23, Mar. 2015.

[21] Y. Qin, Q. Z. Sheng, N. J. Falkner, S. Dustdar, H. Wang, and A. V. Vasilakos, "When things matter: A survey on data-centric internet of things," *Journal of Network and Computer Applications*, vol. 64, pp. 137 – 153, 2016.

[22] Y. S. Abu-Mostafa, M. Magdon-Ismail, and H.-T. Lin, *Learning From Data*. AMLBook, 2012.

[23] C. Batini, C. Cappiello, C. Francalanci, and A. Maurino, "Methodologies for data quality assessment and improvement," *ACM Comput. Surv.*, vol. 41, no. 3, pp. 16:1–16:52, Jul. 2009.

[24] V. Ganti and A. D. Sarma, *Data Cleaning: A Practical Perspective*, ser. Synthesis Lectures on Data Management. Morgan & Claypool Publishers, 2013.

[25] D. Loshin, *The Practitioner's Guide to Data Quality Improvement*. Burlington, Massachusetts: Morgan Kaufmann, 2010.

[26] TDWI. (2016) The data warehousing institute. Last visited: 14 May 2017. [Online]. Available: https://tdwi.org/Home.aspx

[27] J. W. Osborne, *Best practices in data cleaning: a complete guide to everything you need to do before and after collecting your data*. Thousand Oaks, CA: SAGE, 2013.

[28] D. McGilvray, *Executing Data Quality Projects: Ten Steps to Quality Data and Trusted Information*. San Francisco, CA: Morgan Kaufmann Publishers Inc., 2008.

[29] D. Rao, V. N. Gudivada, and V. V. Raghavan, "Data quality issues in big data," in *IEEE International Conference on Big Data (Big Data)*. Santa Clara, California: IEEE Computer Society, Oct 2015, pp. 2654–2660.

[30] A. Maydanchik, *Data quality assessment*. Bradley Beach, New Jersey: Technics Publications, 2007.

[31] X. L. Dong, E. Gabrilovich, K. Murphy, V. Dang, W. Horn, C. Lugaresi, S. Sun, and W. Zhang, "Knowledge-based trust: Estimating the trustworthiness of web sources," *Proc. VLDB Endow.*, vol. 8, no. 9, pp. 938–949, May 2015.

[32] X. Yin, J. Han, and P. S. Yu, "Truth discovery with multiple conflicting information providers on the web," *IEEE Transactions on Knowledge and Data Engineering*, vol. 20, no. 6, pp. 796–808, jun 2008.

[33] J. Cheney, P. Buneman, and B. Ludäscher, "Report on the principles of provenance workshop," *SIGMOD Rec.*, vol. 37, no. 1, pp. 62–65, Mar. 2008.

[34] Y.-W. Cheah, "Quality, retrieval and analysis of provenance in large-scale data," Ph.D. dissertation, Indianapolis, IN, 2014, indiana University.

[35] V. N. Gudivada, D. Rao, and V. V. Raghavan, "NoSQL systems for big data management," in *2014 IEEE World Congress on Services*. Los Alamitos, CA, USA: IEEE Computer Society, 2014, pp. 190–197.

[36] V. Gudivada, D. Rao, and V. Raghavan, "Renaissance in database management: Navigating the landscape of candidate systems," *IEEE Computer*, vol. 49, no. 4, pp. 31 – 42, 2016.

[37] V. Gudivada, "Data analytics: Fundamentals," in *Data Analytics for Intelligent Transportation Systems*, M. Chowdhury, A. Apon, and K. Dey, Eds. New York, NY: Elsevier, Apr. 2017, pp. 31 – 67, ISBN: 978-0-12-809715-1.

[38] C. Lehmann, K. Roy, and B. Winter. The state of enterprise data quality: 2016. Last visited: 14 May 2017. [Online]. Available: http://pages.blazent.com/rs/184-CZE-628/images/Blazent_State_of_DataQuality_2016.pdf

[39] P. D. Allison, *Missing Data*. SAGE Publications, 2001.

[40] S. Sarawagi, "Information extraction," *Foundations and Trends Databases*, vol. 1, no. 3, pp. 261–377, Mar. 2008.

[41] K. Jung, K. I. Kim, and A. K. Jain, "Text information extraction in images and video: a survey," *Pattern Recognition*, vol. 37, no. 5, pp. 977 – 997, Jan. 2004. [Online]. Available: https://doi.org/10.1016/j.patcog.2003.10.012

[42] M. H. DeGroot and M. J. Schervish, *Probability and Statistics*, 4th ed. Pearson, 2011.

[43] J. M. Engels and P. Diehr, "Imputation of missing longitudinal data: a comparison of methods," *Journal of Clinical Epidemiology*, vol. 56, pp. 968 – 976, 2003.

[44] H. Finch, "Distribution of variables by method of outlier detection," *Frontiers in Psychology*, vol. 3, pp. 1–12, 2012.

[45] Tableau Software. (2016) Tableau cloud analytics. Last visited: 14 May 2017. [Online]. Available: http://www.tableau.com/

[46] Talend Software. (2016) Talend Open Studio. Last visited: 14 May 2017. [Online]. Available: https://www.talend.com/

[47] H. Müller, J.-C. Freytag, and U. Leser, "Improving data quality by source analysis," *J. Data and Information Quality*, vol. 2, no. 4, pp. 15:1–15:38, Mar. 2012.

[48] S. Kandel, R. Parikh, A. Paepcke, J. M. Hellerstein, and J. Heer, "Profiler: Integrated statistical analysis and visualization for data quality assessment," in *Proceedings of the International Working Conference on Advanced Visual Interfaces*. New York, NY, USA: ACM, 2012, pp. 547–554.

[49] S. Sadiq, N. K. Yeganeh, and M. Indulska, "20 years of data quality research: Themes, trends and synergies," in *Proceedings of the Twenty-Second Australasian Database Conference - Volume 115*. Darlinghurst, Australia: Australian Computer Society, Inc., 2011, pp. 153–162.

[50] J. R. Talburt, "Special issue on entity resolution overview: The criticality of entity resolution in data and information quality," *J. Data and Information Quality*, vol. 4, no. 2, pp. 6:1–6:2, Mar. 2013.

[51] S. Venna, R. Gottumukkala1, and V. Raghavan, "Visual analytic decision-making environments for large-scale time-evolving graphs," in *Cognitive Computing: Theory and Applications*, ser. Handbook of Statistics, V. Gudivada, V. Raghavan, V. Govindaraju, and C. R. Rao, Eds. New York, NY: Elsevier, Sep. 2016, vol. 35, pp. 81 – 115.

[52] V. Gudivada, D. Rao, and V. Raghavan, "Big data driven natural language processing research and applications," in *Big Data Analytics*, V. Govindaraju, V. Raghavan, and C. R. Rao, Eds. New York, NY: Elsevier, 2015, pp. 203 – 238.

[53] J. Freudiger, S. Rane, A. E. Brito, and E. Uzun, "Privacy preserving data quality assessment for high-fidelity data sharing," in *Proceedings of the 2014 ACM Workshop on Information Sharing & Collaborative Security*. New York, NY, USA: ACM, 2014, pp. 21–29.

[54] A. Chalamalla, I. F. Ilyas, M. Ouzzani, and P. Papotti, "Descriptive and prescriptive data cleaning," in *Proceedings of the 2014 ACM SIGMOD International Conference on Management of Data*, ser. SIGMOD '14. New York, NY: ACM, 2014, pp. 445–456.

[55] T. Hastie, R. Tibshirani, and J. Friedman, *The Elements of Statistical Learning: Data Mining, Inference, and Prediction*, 2nd ed. New York, NY: Springer, 2009.

[56] M. Hiridoglou and J.-M. Berthelot, "Statistical editing and imputation for periodic business surveys," *Survey Methodology*, vol. 12, no. 1, pp. 73–83, 1986.

[57] R. R. Wilcox, *Introduction to robust estimation and hypothesis testing*, 4th ed. Boston, MA: Academic Press, 2016.

[58] R. R. Wilcox and H. J. Keselman, "Modern regression methods that can substantially increase power and provide a more accurate understanding of associations," *European Journal of Personality*, vol. 26, no. 3, pp. 165–174, 2012.

Cloud Data Denormalization for Platform-As-A-Service

Aspen Olmsted
Department of Computer Science
College of Charleston, Charleston, SC 29401
e-mail: olmsteda@cofc.edu

Abstract— **In this paper, we investigate the problem of representing transaction data in PAAS cloud-based systems. We compare traditional database normalization techniques with our denormalized approach. In this research, we focus on transactional data related to an organization's customers. Some optimization comes from the absence of a known customer object, which allows for the vertical merging of tuples. Instead of storing detail transactional data, data is stored in aggregate form. The journaling features of the data store allow for full audits of transactions while not requiring anonymous data to be materialized in fine-grained levels. The horizontal merging of objects is also deployed to remove detail lookup data instance records and one-to-many leaf node records.**

Keywords-web services; distributed database; modeling; cloud computing

I. INTRODUCTION

In this work, we investigate the problem of representing transactional data in a platform as a service (PAAS) cloud-based system. In traditional client-server architectures, database normalization is used to ensure that redundant data does not exist in the system. Redundant data can lead to update anomalies if the developer is not careful to update every instance of a fact when modifying data. Normalization is also performed to ensure unrelated facts are not stored in the same tuples resulting in deletion anomalies. Our earlier work [1] focused on the minimization of storage requirements for anonymous transaction data in PAAS cloud storage. This work extends that research, by increasing the optimizations to include enterprise integration, mobile integration and the modeling of the workflow and lifecycle of objects in a PAAS system.

Data representation in the cloud has many of the same challenges as data representation in client/server architectures. One challenge data representation in the cloud has that is not shared with client/server is the minimization of data. This challenge exists because the costs of cloud data storage are significantly higher than the costs for local storage. When we say higher costs, we mean the simple, measurable costs for the disk storage, not the true costs of managing and accessing the data over the life of the application. Organizations have traditionally budgeted the costs of disk drives for local storage which are in the tens of dollars per gigabyte. Similar cloud storage can be in the hundreds of dollars per gigabyte per month [1]. Often this storage is expressed as the number of tuples in the data store instead of the number of bytes on the disk drive holding the data. For example, force.com [2] charges for blocks of data measured in megabytes but they calculate usage as a flat 2KB per tuple. Zoho Corporation also tracks data storage by the tuple for serval of their cloud products including Creator [3] and CRM [4]. The tuple count method is used as it is easier to calculate in a multi-tenant system where the physical disk drives are shared by many clients.

In this paper, we present an algorithm that will minimize the number of tuples used to store the facts for a software system. We use a motivating example from a cloud software system developed by students in our lab. The algorithm performs three main operations:

- The horizontal merging of objects – several distinct relations are combined into one.
- The vertical merging of objects – several distinct instances of the same type of facts is combined into one.
- Business rule adoption – instead of storing tuples to represent availability of lookup data, we replace the tables with pattern based business rules

We apply our algorithm to a system in the humanities application domain and show an approximately 500% reduction in tuple storage.

Date [5] invests a good deal of his text on the definition of denormalization. He argues that denormalization is when the number of relational variables is reduced, and functional dependencies are introduced where the left-hand side of the functional dependency no longer is a super key. The practical realization of Date's denormalization is that the primary key does not directly determine attributes in the tuple, leading to update and deletion anomalies in exchange for better performance or storage. In our work, we perform many optimizations. When we horizontally merge relations, then we are performing a true denormalization in Date's definition. Other optimizations such as vertical merging do not fit Date's definition of denormalization. We choose to stay with the term denormalization algorithm as it is a set of steps taken after the normalization process to optimize an aspect of the data model.

The organization of the paper is as follows. Section II describes the related work and the limitations of current methods. In Section III, we give a motivating example where our algorithm is useful and describe our denormalization algorithm. Section IV describes additional enhancements through the design of business rule objects. Section V explores reporting from the denormalized objects utilizing the object version history stored in the journal. Section VI contains our comparison of the proposed method and the traditional database normalization method. We explore the denormalization when applied to an object's workflow and lifecycle in Section VII. In Section VIII, we add an additional optimization to handle one-to-many lookup storage of data. Section X investigates the denormalization algorithm when applied to mobile computing. Section XI considers our data model in the context of web-service database. In Section XII, we analyze the security vulnerabilities that are reduced through our data modeling technique. Section XIII gives a discussion of our experience through this work. We conclude and consider future work in Section XIV.

II. Related Work

Sanders and Shin [6] investigate the process to be followed when denormalization is done on relational data management systems (RDBMS) to gain better query performance. Their research was performed before the cloud database offerings became prevalent. In the cloud, database performance is less of an issue to storage requirements because the systems are designed to distribute queries across many systems.

Conley and Whitehurst [7] patented the idea of denormalizing databases for performance but hiding the denormalization for the end user. Their work focuses on merging two relations into one relationship to eliminate the processing required to join the records back together. Their work uses horizontal denormalization to gain performance. Our work uses both horizontal and vertical denormalization to minimize storage space and increase usability.

Most denormalization research work was done in the late 1990s and was focused on improvement in query performance. The performance was an exchange for a loss of correctness and usability of the data. Recently, folks like Andrey Balmin have looked at denormalization as a technique to improve the performance of querying XML data. Like the previously mentioned research, this work differs from our work in the desired end goal. Our end goal being the minimization of data storage and improvement in end user usability.

In Bisdas' [8] blog, he demonstrates ways that end users can improve data visualization by vertically merging hierarchical data in the Salesforce, data model. He takes advantage of the trigger architecture to create redundant data in the hierarchy. Taber [9] also recommends denormalization to improve data visualization. The problem with both solutions is that data storage requirements are increased while correctness is jeopardized by the redundant data.

In one of our previous publications [10], we study UML models from the perspective of integrating heterogeneous software systems. In this work, we create an algorithm to sort cyclical UML class data diagrams to enable transaction reformation in the integration. In the process, discoveries were made on the freshness of data at different layers in the UML graph. The knowledge is useful in this study when considering anomalies that can happen in response to data updates.

Additional semantics for models can be added by the integration of the matching UML Activity and Class diagrams. UML provides an extensibility mechanism that allows a designer to add new semantics to a model. A stereotype is one of three types of extensibility mechanisms in the UML that allows a designer to extend the vocabulary of UML to represent new model elements [11]. Traditionally the semantics were consumed by the software developer manually and translated into the program code in a hard coded fashion.

Developers have implemented business rules in software systems since the first software package was developed. Most research has been around developing expert systems to process large business rule trees efficiently. Charles Forgy [12] developed the Rete Algorithm, which has become the standard algorithm used in business rule engines. Forgy has published several variations on the Rete Algorithm over the past few decades. In this work, we focus on the representation of the business rules in the data model.

Our previous work [13] on data modeling for the cloud focuses on benefits gained by aggregating anonymous data. These benefits and the research behind that study is covered here along with further work to minimize data storage requirements for one-to-many data along with schema denormalization when using predefined object schemas.

III. Denormalization

We demonstrate our work using a Tour Reservation System (TRS). TRS uses web services to provide a variety of functionalities to the patrons who are visiting a museum or historical organization. We use the UML specification to represent the meta-data. Figure 1 shows a UML class diagram for an implementation of this functionality. The Unified Modeling Language includes a set of graphic notation techniques to create visual models of object-oriented software systems [13]. In this study, we use data collected by the Gettysburg Foundation on visitors to their national battlefield. The system is modeled and implemented on the force.com [2] cloud platform.

Figure 1 shows a normalized UML class model of reservation transactions of visitors to the Gettysburg National Battlefield. In the model, the central object ticket represents a pass for an entry that is valid for a specific date and time and a specific activity. Activities are itinerary items the visitor can be involved in while visiting the battlefield. In the normalized model, each ticket is linked to a specific activity

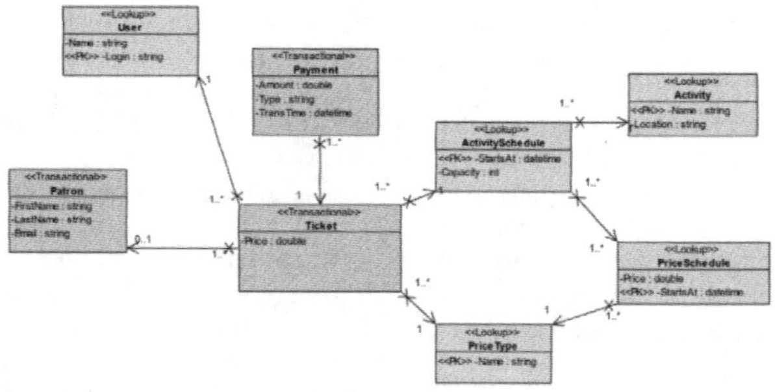

Figure 1. Normalized Transaction Model.

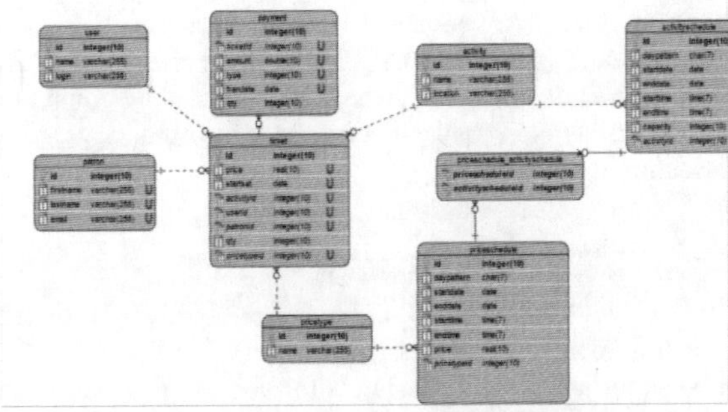

Figure 2. Denormalized Transaction Model.

schedule entry that will designate the date and time the pass is valid for entry. Each activity schedule is linked to an activity object that designates the name and location of the activity.

Each ticket is linked to a user in the Gettysburg organization who was responsible for the transaction. Each ticket can be linked to a patron object. In the case of advanced reservations, there will be a valid patron object linked to the ticket. Advanced reservations are transactions that take place through the organization's website or over the phone to a reservation agent. In the case of walk-up transactions, there will not be a linked patron. A walk-up transaction is a transaction that takes place when a visitor arrives on the site without a prior reservation and pays for the ticket at the front desk.

In Figure 1, the multiplicity of the association between the patron and the ticket is a zero or one to many. A multiplicity that can be zero represents anonymous data. Anonymous data is data that does not need to be specified in order for the transaction to be valid. In the example transaction, the patron can remain anonymous but still visit the battlefield and partake in the activities. In the case of the sample Gettysburg data, 60 percent of ticketing transactions were anonymous.

In the case of the force.com [2] PAAS, data storage is charged by the tuple. With an enterprise license to the platform, the organization is granted access to one gigabyte of data storage. The storage is measured by treating every tuple as two kilobytes. This form of measurement allows the organization 500,000 tuples in the enterprise data storage option. The data collected for the normalized data model would allow the Gettysburg organization to store around nine months' worth of data. With the anonymous transaction, the ticket and the payment data is only important on the original transaction level for auditing. For example, the accounting department may want to see the details behind a specific ticket agent's cash total for the day. Another example would be the marketing department wants to see the ticket price patterns within an hour of the day.

The force.com [2] platform uses an Oracle relational database to deliver the data storage services but adds a journal feature so history can be stored on all changes to an object over time. This journal can be used at no additional data storage cost. The field level changes stored in the journal would allow aggregate data to be stored for anonymous transactions and still have the detail to perform the audits mentioned earlier.

If an object is used between two other objects where the middle object is the "many" side of the one-to-many relationship and the one side of the other relationship, then the same data can be represented by moving the attributes to the object on the composition side of the relationship. The middle object is then able to be removed, reducing the number of tuples representing the same amount of data. In Figure 1, the "Activity Schedule" object fits this profile and can be horizontally merged with the "Ticket" object. In our previous work [10], we study UML data model freshness requirements and document the relationship between data changes and location in the UML graph. In our findings, we see that middle object nodes are less predisposed to changes than leaf nodes. The lower amount of data changes reduces the change of update anomalies.

In Figure 1, we also designate objects that are updated in transactions differently than objects that are navigated for transactional lookup values. Two stereotypes are added to the diagram:

- Transactional – The classes designated with the orange color and the <<Transactional>> tag are updated during transactional activities.
- Lookup – The classes designated with the green color and the <<Lookup>> tag are not updated

Algorithm 1. Denormalization Algorithm.

INPUT: normalizedObjects (XMI representation of UML class diagram)
OUTPUT: denormalizedEntities (XMI representation of denormalized entities)

```
foreach object in normalizedObjects
  add entity to denormalizedEntities
  foreach attribute in object
    add attribute to entity
    if object is transactional
      mark attribute as unique
  add id attribute as primary key
  mark id as autoincrement

foreach entity in denormalizedEntities
  if entity is both a many side and a one side of two
relationships
   and a lookup object
    foreach attribute in object
      if attribute is PK
        add attributes to many side entity
        if attribute is a datetime type expand date pattern
    swap graph location entity of the one sides

foreach association in normalizedObjects
  if association is one-to-may and many side is transactional
    add foreign key to many side entity
    add quantity field to entity on many side
```

during transactional activities. The data in these classes are created by administrative activities. During transactions, the data is searched for the proper values.

The Denormalization Algorithm, Algorithm 1, transforms a normalized model stored in a UML class diagram into a denormalized model represented as an entity-relationship diagram. The algorithm assumes input and output of the models in the XMI [14] format. XMI is a standard exchange format used to represent structural models in a non-proprietary way.

The algorithm first loops through each object in the normalized model and adds the object and attributes as entities in the denormalized entity-relationship diagram. If the object has the transactional stereotype, then the attributes are marked unique. Surrogate Identifier fields are added to each object's definition to be used as an auto-incrementing primary key.

The next pass of the algorithm is to find objects that can be eliminated from the middle relationship of two "one-to-many" relationships. The original model, in Figure 1, had an activity schedule object that consumed a lot of data space by storing a lot of tuples to represent the occurrences an activity can take place. We use a stereotype of "PK" applied to attributes in the original model to designate the primary identifier for instances of an object. This designation allows us to shift the attribute down the association and swap the positioning of the objects. In this iteration over the objects, we also look for date-time data types that are part of the primary key. When we locate an occurrence, we replace the attribute with a date-time specification occurrence. The date-time specification includes a starting date, ending date, starting time, ending time and day of the week pattern.

The final pass of the algorithm adds foreign keys and aggregation counters. The aggregation significantly reduces the count of tuples stored. An example of this is shown in Figure 1. Instead of having an instance of each ticket, we add the quantity field to store the aggregate count for the unique attributes.

Algorithm 2. History Creation Algorithm.

INPUT: object
OUTPUT: collection of object's version history

```
Set thisObject = newest version of object
Set objectVersions = empty list
Set fieldVersions = distinct saveDates values from object journal
Sort fieldVersions by saveDate descending
Set lastDate = maximum(saveDate)
Foreach version in fieldVersions
   If lastDate = version.saveDate
      objectVersions.add(thisObject)
   Set thisObject.[version/attribute] = version.value
   Set lastDate = version.saveDate
Return objectVersions
```

Figure 2 shows an entity-relationship diagram of a transformed model of Figure 1. Unique attributes have been applied where aggregations should be performed. The activity schedule entity has been shifted out in the graph, and the quantity fields have been added to the aggregated transactional objects.

IV. BUSINESS RULES

Business rule engines have sprung up to allow the separation of business rules from the core application code. The systems are designed to allow the end users to change the business rules freely without changing the original application code. In 2007, International Data Corporation implemented a survey where they asked 'How often do you want to customize the business rules in your software?'. Ninety percent of the respondents reported that they changed their business rules annually or more frequently. Thirty-four percent of the respondents reported that they changed their business rules monthly [15].

Figure 2 shows two tables that implement business rules:

- Activity Schedule – This table implements the date-time pattern mentioned earlier to store the business rules for when a particular activity is valid.
- Price Schedule – This table implements the date-time pattern mentioned earlier to store the business rules for when a particular price is available.

In each case objects in Figure 1, which inserted instances to represent availability, are replaced with rule instances to represent the availability. So instead of having a tuple per availability instance, a single tuple can represent the pattern. In the case of activity schedules, the example year had over 26,000 instances of availability that were replaced with 30 instances of the business rule.

V. OBJECT HISTORY ANALYSIS

One of the main reasons an enterprise develops or purchases a software solution is to allow the organization to increase their knowledge of their operations through the analysis of the data collected in the software solution. The denormalization solution presented earlier may limit the data

TABLE I. EMPIRICAL RESULTS.

Table	*Normalized Tuples*	*Denormalized Tuples*
user	*31*	*31*
patron	*17,610*	*17,610*
ticket	*738,981*	*157,780*
activity schedule	*26,697*	*30*
price schedule	*220*	*24*
activity	*17*	*17*
Total	*783,556*	*175,492*

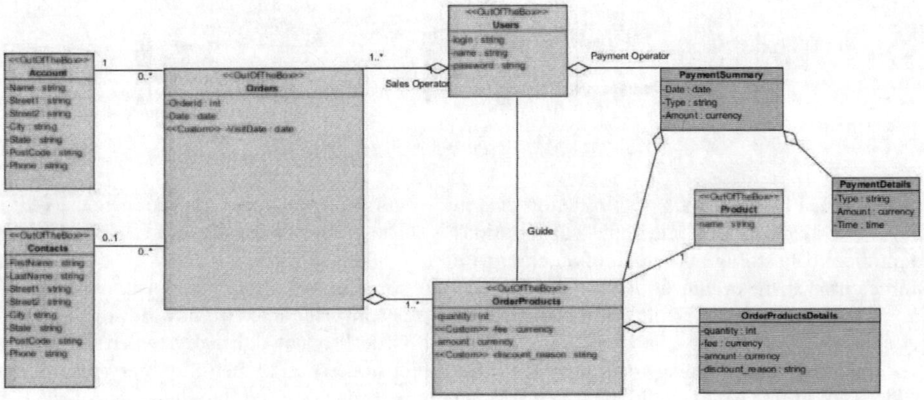

Figure 3. Order Data Model.

available from the denormalization process. The data is presented to the users through dashboards, reports or exports. A dashboard is presented as a graphical chart to measure where the organization stands compared to a goal. Examples of these would be sales to date compared to same period last year. A report has a set of input parameters that control the data displayed. The data displayed in the report tends to include tables with aggregated values. Exports allow for the exporting of data into a two-dimensional table saved as a comma separated value (CSV) format. In this format, attributes represent the columns of the data. Columns are escaped with double quotes and separated by commas. For our purposes, we will refer to all three categories generically as reports.

Current state and historical comparison are the two categories of reports a user may want to pull in their analysis. In current state reports, only the latest version of the object is needed. In historical comparison reports, all versions of an object may be needed depending on the level of aggregation. An example of a historical comparison report would be a report that compares sales for the month compared to sales last year in the same month.

In our work, we developed Algorithm 2 to create an in-memory copy of all historical versions of a specific object. We use code to generate the data and then generate the report output. If the organization wanted to allow end users to report on historical versions, they could modify Algorithm 2 to write records as temporary tuples and then call the reporting tool.

VI. EMPIRICAL RESULTS

The empirical results demonstrate the success of representing the example transaction data with significantly lower cloud storage costs. TABLE I shows the tuple counts for the original data model and the denormalized data model. Both data models represent the complete 2014 calendar year of visitor transactions for the Gettysburg National Battlefield. The denormalized model creates a 78% reduction in the number of tuples. In the specific case of the force.com [2] platform, the reduction in the number of tuples allows the

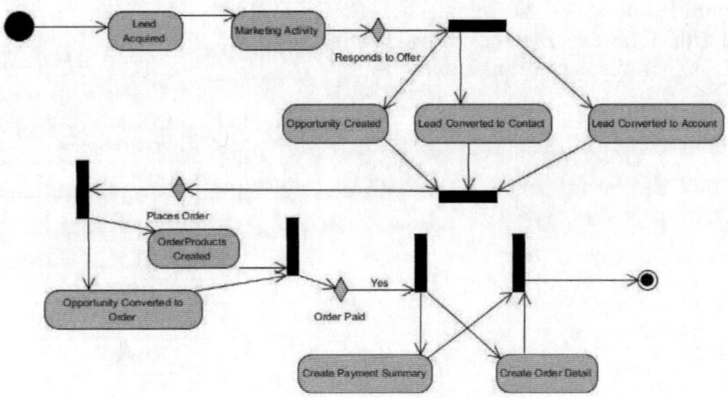

Figure 4. Advanced Reservation Workflow Model.

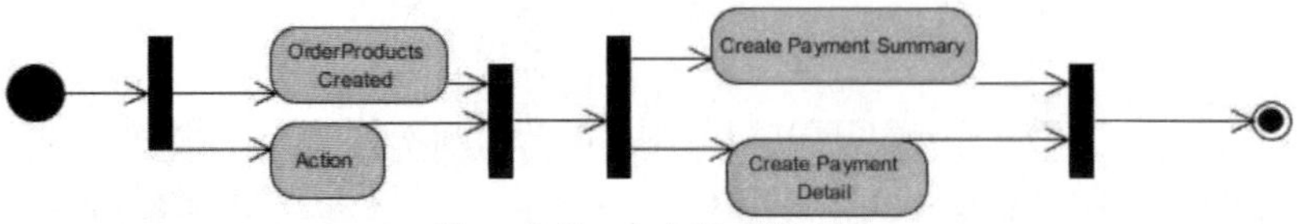

Figure 5. Frontdesk Workflow.

organization to store nearly three years of transaction data in the data storage provided without additional subscriptions costs. In the minimal data storage provided to an enterprise customer of force.com [2], the organization receives 500,000 tuples. Additional data storage is available to the organization for a monthly subscription price of 2,000 tuples per dollar. Using the normalized data model to represent the transactional data a complete year of cannot be stored without purchasing more data storage.

VII. MODELING WORKFLOW

The first phase of research in this paper modeled the reservation transactions using domain specific objects. Using domain-specific objects is the method to use if a designer is implementing greenfield engineering. The cloud PAAS platform we used in the first phase of the research, includes a full Customer Relationship Management (CRM) system to store interactions with customers Out of the box the CRM provides objects to hold sales orders and the workflow with the customer before they place an order. Figure 4 shows the model of the workflow for the advanced sales operations. Leads are acquired through public events such as conference tabeling and information sessions. After a lead is acquired a marketing activity takes place where the lead is related to the new activity. Marketing activities may include email marketing, phone calls, in-person meetings and online meetings using a technology such as Skype or Google Hangouts. When more information is gathered about the potential visit from the customer, the lead is converted into a contact object, account object, and opportunity object. The contact object holds an individual's biographical details such as first name, last name, email, address, and phone numbers. The account object holds details about the organization the customer is associated with. This data includes organization name, address, and phone number. The opportunity object stores the details of the products the visitor is likely to order. These objects are shown in Figure 3.

The workflow continues when the customer makes a commitment about their visit. At this point, the opportunity is converted into two new out-of-the-box objects; Orders and OrderProducts. Finally, when the payment is made by the customer, a PaymentSummary record, and a PaymentDetail record is inserted into the system. The PaymentDetail record is stored for auditing purposes and is purged after the fiscal period is closed out. Individual payment details were only used by the individual operators to settle out their daily cash drawers and by management to audit individual operator cash drawers. Once the fiscal period has closed the details of multiple payments related to individual transactions is no longer needed.

Figure 4 models the workflow used with non-anonymous transactions. To model the collection of the anonymous data, we included Figure 5. The model of the collection of anonymous data is a much shorter workflow where less data is collected. Figure 3 included two detail objects; OrderProductDetails and PaymentDetails. When data is created in the anonymous workflow the summary level object is aggregated on the user and visitation date. The detailed data is required on anonymous transactions for auditing purposes until the fiscal period is reconciled. The payment and order detail objects are purged after the fiscal period is closed. TABLE II shows the tuple count of the normalized data and the denormalized data from this methodology. The table shows an eight-nine percent reduction of the tuple count.

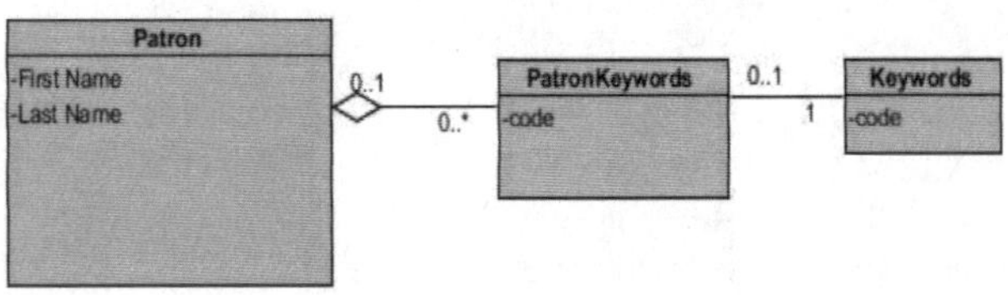

Figure 6. One-to-Many Relationship.

TABLE II. EMPIRICAL RESULTS.

Table	*Normalized Tuples*	*Denormalized Tuples*
Accounts	7,550	7,550
Contacts	15,172	15,172
OrderProducts	519,422	110,675
Orders	176526	16,545
Payments	717,446	7,310
Products	38	38
Users	178	178
Total	1,436,332	157,468

VIII. ONE TO MANY LOOKUP CODES

In traditional database design, one-to-many relationships are represented in separate objects. Figure 6 shows a relationship we observed in another organization. The New York Philharmonic stores keywords as a way to tag patrons with different attributes. This design is the output of the normalization process used to eliminate update and deletion anomalies [16]. Relational databases use b-tree indexes that allow a change in the lookup value to be populated down to the joining table in log N time.

An analysis of the data reveals that on average each patron had six keywords associated with their record. To represent five hundred thousand patrons with this design requires a little over three million five hundred thousand tuples. Bitmap indexes allow a database field to store bits to represent different discrete values in a single field. In the example above, a multi-select field stored in patrons to represent the keywords associated with patrons would reduce the tuples to around five hundred thousand. A single bit of the multi-select field uses a bit to represent the presence or absence of the lookup value. A bitmap index stores separate lists of the tuples where the bitmap is turned on to allow the search time for queries, updates, and deletes to be below N search time. The bitmap allows more data to be stored in fewer tuples but also allows fast retrieval time.

IX. DEPARTMENTAL FUNCTIONAL INTEGRATIONS

Enterprise transaction processing systems support several different use cases to fulfill the entire set of requirements of an organization. An organization will partition an enterprise system at the department level for several different reasons. Two of these reasons are a simplification of the functional model and to enable geographic proximity to the users entering the transactional data.

The result of the departmental partitioning is a duplication of data across departmental systems, and the management of this duplication is a difficult problem. Often an organization will enter this data manually in each local system. The organization is forced to tolerate the data inconsistencies that come from the difference in human interpretation of the source data and transcription differences.

We sampled a few enterprise organizations data in search of duplication of biographical information (customers, addresses, and telephone numbers). Biographical information is easier to correct than other domains as there are standard algorithms to clean the data. These algorithms include address standardization using the postal service CASS database [1] and move update database [2]. We applied the cleaning of the biographical data to the sample. After, we found there was still a 17% duplication of biographical data collected in the individual departmental systems over a 10-year period.

Functional differences across enterprise departments make it difficult for a single system to meet all the needs of the organization. An organization could choose to relax functional requirements in exchange for better data quality, but this option is often not considered. We surveyed the 41 member organizations of CIO Arts [3] to find the threshold between functional requirement priority and system partition preference. The member organizations are performing arts centers that have three specialized departmental system needs (Box Office, Fund Development, and Event Management). In the study, it is clear that even low priority functional requirements take precedence over choosing a single enterprise system.

Disperse Geographic locations also require departments to use separate systems to enable each department to keep its data local. Localization avoids network partition problems and improves system performance. Cloud providers offering infrastructure as a service or platform as a service are an alternative to geographic partitioning. Unfortunately, these platforms are relatively new compared with the live cycle of vertical market enterprise systems. Typically, vertical market systems are built using a client-server architecture that requires low latency response time, making them inappropriate for cloud providers. In our CIO Arts survey, we found all organizations used a Microsoft Windows client-server application.

Often system integrations are built to enable data to be automatically exchanged between departmental systems. The integration is instead of having a single enterprise system. These processes can have high latency in the case of large volumes of transactional data updates. The latency problem can lead to incorrect data and improper decision-making. With cloud-based enterprise systems, the data needs to be pulled or pushed between systems.

TABLE III shows the bandwidth differences for synchronization of one year of our example data between two cloud systems. The denormalized data represents an eighty-eight percent reduction in bandwidth requirements and also represents a similar reduction in synchronization times.

X. OFFLINE MOBILE APPLICATIONS

Mobile computing has become ubiquitous over the past decade due to the proliferation of smartphones, tablet

TABLE III. BANDWIDTH IN KB.

Table	*Normalized Bandwidth*	*Denormalized Bandwidth*
Accounts	1,888	1,888
Contacts	3,793	3,793
OrderProducts	25,971	5,534
Orders	35,305	3,309
Payments	53,808	548
Products	8	8
Users	18	18
Keywords	1,214	0
Total	122,004	15,097

devices, and 4G mobile data coverage. Data storage and computation for the applications running on the mobile devices are accessed from distributed web services running in cloud computing environments. The software industry has responded by developing applications that require continuous connectivity, but this assumes safe computing environments and no user error. In reality, applications operate in a very different environment from the software developer's assumptions. Internet connectivity will come and go as the mobile device moves between cell and hotspot range. Malicious users may want to pollute the data collection process by replaying data packets or manipulating data in the original request. Application users may accidentally submit multiple times, forget to submit or submit incorrect data.

To solve the problem of providing mobile application access to data in the presence of a network partition, we developed a caching algorithm that persisted a local copy of the data on the mobile device as data was retrieved from the cloud. The data fetch operation attempts to call a web-service to retrieve fresh data when a user interacts with the application. If a network partition is discovered, then the locally cached data is used instead of web-service data. The reduced tuples required to store the data (shown in TABLE II) and the reduced bandwidth required to transfer the data (shown in TABLE III) allows more data to be cached locally. These reductions are important with mobile devices that have limited storage capacity and lower bandwidth available.

XI. Fine-grained web-service Calls

Many No-SQL databases handle tuple insertion via web-services. Each tuple create, read, update and delete (CRUD) operation requires a web-service call. When these databases are hosted in the cloud, the latency becomes an important bottleneck to minimize. In our testing, a back office web-service call can be fulfilled in one to three milliseconds on average. The same web-service call to a cloud provider requires between thirty and sixty milliseconds to fulfill on average.

The reduction of tuples of our design methodology assists in reducing the combined latency required in a typical software application. Over the workflow of a typical application the time the reduction is significant. The client reads data from the server to display each form. With our methodology, make fewer calls are made on the form setup, and there are also fewer calls made when the application updates data.

XII. Loss of Cloud Datastore Availability

The loss of availability to a system deployed in the cloud is a security risk that all enterprises must consider when migrating from a self- hosted solution to a vendor-hosted solution. Tuple-based licensing is a treat to availability or budget when overages occur. Tuple and data limit overage policies vary by cloud service provider, but, the threat of system availability loss should cause an organization to consider our modeling strategy to minimize the threat and the damage when an overflow occurs. There are three overage policies in use by cloud service providers:

- Bill for overage – The bill for overage policy allows continued use of the system after the overage occurs, but the organization is charged a fee based on the amount of overage. Often the fees are much higher per tuple then they are on the fixed price policies. The fixed price policy would be the pre-negotiated subscription fee the organization pays for their typical data. Salesforce uses the bill for overage policy for their cloud hosting data storage system. When an organization surpassed the tuple limits, a warning is displayed inside the administrative application for the platform to notify the user of the overage.
- Data insert or web-service call denial – This policy denies access to future writes, or system calls until the overage has been resolved. Salesforce uses this policy for web-service calls per day. In the out-of-the-box web services, a call is made per tuple affected. Once the daily limit is reached, the organization cannot invoke the web-service again until the next day. The possibly of no availability represents a large vulnerability for an organization and modeling must take this vulnerability into effect.
- Throttling – Throttling is a policy that slows access down once tuple limits have been reached. The throttling policy has been used by database systems for years in the back office, to ensure one thread does not overwhelm other concurrent threads on the server. In the cloud several data stores, such as MongoDB, throttle inserts per thread [22].

In all three of the licensing policies, a design methodology that reduced tuples will reduce the potential of downtime and over costs.

XIII. Discussion

At first glance, the problem addressed by our research in this study appears to be a self-inflicted problem created by a licensing model used by several of the PAAS service providers. As we investigated the problem in depth, we quickly realized that traditional client-server database normalization models did not fit distributed cloud-based data store models. The normalization algorithms we teach and learn in database classes are tiered assuming an iterative approach to move down the tiered normalization level. The approach has a single goal of minimizing redundancy to alleviate update or deletion anomalies. The iterative approach includes a final phase in which the designer will denormalize the database structure to gain performance, concurrency or storage enhancements. In exchange for the better performance, concurrency or storage the designer or implementer is willing to accept the greater possibilities of deletion or update anomalies. Our initial problem was focused on the reduction of the storage requirements. The change was not aimed at less disk space usage, but less subscription cost for the data service consumed.

Over the course of the research project, we realized that the client-server model adds many other difficulties that can be eliminated in the denormalization phase. The client-server model has an innate preference for many smaller tables with a few attributes each over larger tables with many attributes stored per tuple. In practice, this has led to three major difficulties. The first challenge is experienced when an end user, of the application that generated the data, tries to gain access to the data stored in the database. The difficulty stems from the complexity of understanding the relationship between the many individual tables and the semantics of each table. Second, there is also complexity added to the development of integration systems that consume and write the data. With increased complexity comes increased development and maintenance costs. Finally, there is complexity in enforcing higher level constraints on data when the data is distributed across many smaller relationships. The need for correct data has increased as more and more data has become available for use in Management Information Systems (MIS) reports, data science prediction models and Executive Information Systems (EIS) visualizations. The best way to ensure correct data is to declare constraints as close to the database store as possible. The constraint declaration is simplified when the model is denormalized as we did in this project.

XIV. CONCLUSION

In this paper, we propose several algorithms for object denormalization when transforming an application domain object model to a data model used in a cloud PAAS data store. Our solution is based on navigating the relationships in a UML class diagram and horizontally compressing classes between multiple one-to-many relationships, aggregating relationships on anonymous relationships, using temporal offering patterns and rolling up one-to-many relationships.

The techniques used in our work met our goals of reduced tuple storage while increasing the usability of the data for the end users. Like the denormalization methods of the late 1990s, aimed at squeezing out a little more performance or a little more storage, our methods can be applied as individual strategies to save tuple space for a particular "use case." For example, if a developer needed to model data passed between a mobile application and a cloud application, the denormalized model could be used to represent the data transferred. Likewise, if a developer had many one-to-many relationships and needed to reduce tuples, then our specific approach could be applied in that instance to reduce the storage requirements of the many sides of the relationship.

In this research, we studied a specific application domain related to humanities organizations. The algorithms can be applied to similar application domains that contain entity objects representing transactions and customers. Future work needs to test our algorithms in other application domains to ensure the work applies across different application domains.

REFERENCES

[1] A. Olmsted and G. Santhanakrishnan, "Cloud Data Denormalization of Anonymous Transactions," in *Cloud Computing 2016, The Seventh International Conference on Cloud Computing, GRIDs, and Virtualization*, Rome, Italy, March 20-24 2016, ISBN: 978-1-61208-460-2, pp 42-46.

[2] Brainsell blog, "Salesforce, SugarCRM and SalesLogix — Data Storage Costs Compared," 2016. [Online]. Available: https://www.zoho.com/creator/pricing-comparison.html. [Accessed 2017.5.5].

[3] Salesforce.com, inc, "Run your business better with Force.," 2006. [Online]. Available: http://www.salesforce.com/platform/products/force/?d=70130000000f27V&internal=true. [Accessed 2016.02.03].

[4] Zoho Corporation, "Creator Pricing Comparison," 2016. [Online]. Available: https://www.zoho.com/creator/pricing-comparison.html. [Accessed 2016.02.03].

[5] Zoho Corporation, "Compare Zoho CRM editions," 2016. [Online]. Available: https://www.zoho.com/crm/comparison.html. [Accessed 2016.02.03].

[6] C. J. Date, "Denormalization," in *Database Design and Relational Theory*, O'Reilly Media, 2012.

[7] G. L. Sanders and S. Shin, "Denormalization Effects on Performance of RDBMS," in *Proceedings of the 34th Hawaii International Conference on Systems Sciences*, 2001.

[8] J. D. Conley and R. P. Whitehurst, "Automatic and transparent denormalization support, wherein denormalization is achieved through appending of fields to base relations of a normalized database." USA Patent US5369761 A, 29 November 1994.

[9] A. Bisda , "Salesforce Denormalization Delivers New Power for Nurtures," DemandGen, 29 07 2014. [Online]. Available: http://www.demandgen.com/salesforce-denormalization-delivers-new-power-nurtures/. [Accessed 2015.5.5].

[10] D. Taber, Salesforce.com Secrets of Success: Best Practices for Growth and Profitability, Prentice Hall, 2013.

[11] A. Olmsted, "Fresh, Atomic, Consistent and Durable (FACD) Data Integration Guarantees," in *Software Engineering and Data Engineering, 2015 International Conference for*, San Diego, CA, 2015.

[12] Object Management Group, "Unified Modeling Language: Supersturcture," 05 02 2007. [Online]. Available: http://www.omg.org/spec/UML/2.1.1/. [Accessed 2015.5.5].

[13] C. L. Forgy, "Rete: A fast algorithm for the many pattern/many object pattern match problem," *Artificial Intelligence*, vol. 19, no. 1, p. 17–37, 1982.

[14] A. Olmsted and G. Santhanakrishnan, "Cloud Data Denormalization of Anonymous Transactions," in *Cloud Computing 2016*, Rome, Italy, 2015.

[15] Object Management Group, "Unified Modeling Language: Supersturcture," 05 02 2007. [Online]. Available: http://www.omg.org/spec/UML/2.1.1/. [2015.5.5].

[16] Object Management Group, "OMG Formal Versions of XMI," 06 2015. [Online]. Available: http://www.omg.org/spec/XMI/. [Accessed 2015.11.11].

[17] Ceiton Technologies, "Introducing Workflow," [Online]. Available: http://ceiton.com/CMS/EN/workflow/introduction.html#Customization. [Accessed 2014.15.09].

[18] J. Ullman and J. Widom , A First Course in Database Systems, Pearson, 2007.

[19] "Certification Programs," United State Postal Service, [Online]. Available: https://www.usps.com/business/certification-programs.htm. [Accessed 2015.5.5].

[20] United States Postal Service, [Online]. Available: https://www.usps.com/business/move-update.htm. [Accessed 2015.5.5].

[21] CIO Arts, Inc, [Online]. Available: http://www.cioarts.org/. [Accessed 2015.5.5].

[22] Normally Pleasant Mixture, "mongo-throttle," [Online]. Available: https://www.npmjs.com/package/mongo-throttle. [Accessed 2017.01.27].

A Framework for Spatial Analytics using Heterogeneous Data Sources

Cláudio de Souza Baptista, Tiago Eduardo da Silva, Brunna de Sousa Pereira Amorim
Federal University of Campina Grande
Campina Grande, Paraíba, Brazil
baptista@computacao.ufcg.edu.br, tiagoes@copin.ufcg.edu.br, brunnasousa@copin.ufcg.edu.br

Hugo Feitosa de Figueirêdo
Federal Institute of Education, Science and Technology of Paraíba
Esperança, Paraíba, Brazil
hugo.figueiredo@ifpb.edu.br

José Mário Pereira Dantas
Court of Accounts of the State of Acre – TCE-AC
Rio Branco, Acre, Brazil
mario.dantas@tce.ac.gov.br

***Abstract*—Several solutions for the integration of Business Intelligence (BI) and Geographic Information Systems (GIS) have been proposed in recent years aiming at improving the decision making process. The term Spatial Analytics has been coined to tools that perform analysis on spatial and conventional data organized according to the multidimensional approach. Nevertheless, no consensus has been reached regarding the best way to accomplish such integration, making it difficult to perform analysis on spatial cubes from heterogeneous multidimensional data sources. In this article, we investigated the state of the art on Spatial Analytics, and propose a framework that enables spatial analytics on cubes from heterogeneous multidimensional data servers. The proposed framework provides a visual query language for the spatial analysis. To validate the proposed framework, a practical example is conducted and applied to accountability processes of the Court of Accounts of the State of Acre, in Brazil. To perform such case study, the framework was extended to access cubes from Microsoft SQL Server Analysis Services (SSAS) and GeoMondrian.**

Keywords- Business Intelligence; GIS; Analytics; GeoBI; SOLAP.

I. Introduction

With the increasing volume of data coming from a large variety of sources, there has been a considerable increase in investments on technologies capable of extracting information from these data and, consequently, help managers in the decision making process. *Business Intelligence* (BI) tools provide a historical, updated and predictive view of business operations of a company, enabling the identification of patterns, the availability of new functionalities and products, and improving the relationship with costumers. *On-line Analytical Processing* (OLAP) is one of the most used BI tools. An OLAP tool enables rapid exploration and analysis of data stored in multiple aggregation levels, according to the multidimensional approach. In this context, most companies are adopting BI tools in order to become more competitive in the marketplace.

In addition to this, most companies heavily deal with the spatial dimension in their datasets. Hence, it is important to investigate how to explore that dimension in order to improve the decision making process. However, traditional BI technologies do not take advantage of spatial data. On the other hand, Geographical Information Systems (GIS) were designed to work on georeferenced data using the Online Transaction Processing (OLTP) approach, and thereby preventing an efficient and deep data analysis.

More recently, corporations have demanded the integration of GIS and OLAP technologies arising a new category of tools known as *Spatial Online Analytical Processing* (SOLAP), or simply Spatial Analytics.

This article proposes a new framework that enables the analysis of spatial cubes coming from multiple and heterogeneous multidimensional data sources. This article is an extended version of the Geoprocessing 2016 Conference paper by Silva et al. [1]. In this extended version, we included a discussion on the design of the spatial cubes, provided more details on the framework extension points and addressed more spatial cube operators.

The integration of GIS and BI technologies may happen through three distinct approaches: prioritizing the resources of GIS (GIS-dominant), overlapping visual and graphical resources of OLAP tools (OLAP-dominant), and the full integration approach (SOLAP) that aggregates the functionalities of GIS with graphs, tables and maps [2].

The need for integrating GIS and OLAP technologies have boosted new SOLAP academic solutions. Recently, several research works have been published on SOLAP addressing several approaches. Aissi et al. address the use of recommendation on SOLAP tool [3]. Li et al. propose a map-reduce architecture for SOLAP [4]. Leonardi et al. discuss SOLAP for trajectory data [5]. Diallo et al. focus on mobile GeoBI [6]. Nonetheless, there is no consensus on how to properly integrate GIS and OLAP technologies. The proposed solutions differ in several aspects, mainly the data model. Without a consensus on the data model, it is very hard to provide spatial cubes on the Web.

Spatial cubes are characterized as data cube that contain spatial data in the fact table or in dimensions, or in both. Vector data is used with at least three data types: points, linestrings and polygons, or collection of those. Spatial operators include topological, metric, set, directional and network. Topological operators include: inside, meets, crosses, cover, overlaps, contains, disjoint and equals. Metric operators include: area, perimeter, length, distance, far, near, and buffer. Set operators are Union, Intersection, and Difference. Direcional operators are: left, right, above, below, north, south, east, west, northeast, northwest, southest, and southwest. Network operators include connected, next, previous, shortest_path. Other spatial operators include: minimum bounding rectangle, centroid, convex_hull [7].

Still regarding GIS and BI systems integration, some works investigated and proposed ways to provide data on the Web to ensure interoperability. Dubé et al. [8] present a XML format to provide and exchange SOLAP cubes via Web Service. In 2011, the Open Geospatial Consortium (OGC) [9] published a white paper that analyzes how the OGC standards (i.e. WMS, WFS, WPS, etc.) could be extended in order to intensify the use of geospatial information and the interoperability of GeoBI applications [10].

Some core features of Spatial Analytics solutions were observed:

- Queries through visual specification language using spatial operators;
- An integrated view of multidimensional and spatial data; using maps, tables and charts; and
- Extensibility to provide access to heterogeneous multidimensional data sources (cube servers).

We enumerate the desirable key requirements of Spatial Analytics solutions:

I. to enable the creation of queries through a visual query language: visual languages improve usability specially concerning Spatial Analytics where queries are quite complex to express;
II. to provide an integrated view of both multi-dimensional and spatial data: enables to analyze data on maps, graphics and tables, simultaneously;
III. to support spatial operators to enable deep analysis: spatial data demands spatial operators such as topological, metric, directional; which enhances user experience in such dimensional data;
IV. to provide access to heterogeneous multidimensional data sources (cube servers): the access to heterogeneous cube servers promote interoperability and data integration without needing to migrate data among these cubes;
V. to enable geocoding data to provide spatial analysis in non-spatial OLAP sources: currently, some cube servers are not spatially aware. Hence, geocoding enables to use such cube servers in a SOLAP solution.
VI. to use open technologies to reduce costs: enabling the use of free source and open technologies may increase ROI (Return of Investment) in SOLAP projects;
VII. to be extensible so that new features can be added: the conception of a white box framework enables code reuse so that programmers may incorporate further features to fulfill new requirements; and
VIII. to enable data visualization through maps, tables and graphs: incorporate into the dashboards maps, tables and graphs to enhance usability in the decision making process.

The lack of consensus for GIS - OLAP integration and standards for the provision of spatial and multidimensional data hinders the use of different data sources at the same time. Hence, the extraction of useful information to improve the decision making process at corporations is impaired.

Our proposed framework can be classified as an Enterprise Application Framework, as it is concerned with the OLAP domain [11]. According to Sommerville, a framework is a software that can be extended to create a more specific application [12]. The main contributions of our research is the proposal of a framework for Spatial Analytics that contains interfaces and abstract classes that can be implemented and extended to support new data sources, making easy the integration of heterogeneous data cubes. Hence, we offer a reusable software to interoperate spatial datawarehouses from heterogeneous data sources.

Furthermore, in order to validate the proposed framework we present a case study on the accountability analysis of the TCE-AC (Court of Accounts of the State of Acre – Brazil). In the case study, we extended our framework for Spatial Analytics to access cubes stored in two different sources: *Microsoft SQL Server Analysis Services* (SSAS) and *GeoMondrian*.

The rest of this article is organized as follows. Section II discusses related work on Spatial Analytics. Section III addresses the architecture of the proposed framework. Section IV presents a case study involving the Court of Accounts of the State of Acre – Brazil. Finally, Section V highlights the conclusions and further work to be undertaken.

II. Related Work

SOLAP has been a very active research area for a long time. Surveys on SOLAP can be found in [13][14][15]. Salehi et al. propose a formal model for spatial datacubes [16]. Aguila et al. address a conceptual model for SOLAP [17]. Baltzer focuses on spatial multidimensional querying [18]. Glorio and Trujillo highlight the optimization of spatial queries [19]. Ziouel et al. propose an approach for cartographic generalization of SOLAP applications [20].

Several SOLAP tools have been developed over the last years in many contexts. Rivest et al. propose a generic SOLAP tool, called JMap Spatial OLAP, that provides an interactive data exploration through charts and maps. The proposed tool is based on Relational OLAP (ROLAP) architecture and supports the three types of spatial dimensions: geometric, non-geometric and mixed. A disadvantage of the proposed tool is that it does not allow the use of spatial operators (metrical or topological).

Bimonte et al. developed the GeWOlap SOLAP tool, highlighting the synchronization of different forms of data visualization [21]. Their architecture comprises three layers: data, SOLAP server and client layers (user interface). Nonetheless, the authors' proposed tool does not enable the use of spatial operators (metric or topologic) and uses proprietary technology. In [22] the authors discuss the use of the GeWOlap tool in the domain of agriculture.

Escribano et al. proposed a tool called Piet, integrating GIS and OLAP technologies and executing the precomputation of the map layers [23]. The Piet architecture also comprises three layers: data, SOLAP server and client layers. The query processor can process four types of queries: geometric, geometric aggregation, OLAP and GIS-OLAP. A language named GISOLAP-QL is proposed. This query language has two parts: the first part retrieves spatial data and the second one retrieves multidimensional data. The Piet tool does not have an interactive interface that hides query language details. Piet consists of two applications: a Web application for OLAP queries and a desktop for spatial queries. Therefore, it does not have an integrated view of multidimensional and spatial data.

Another challenge faced in SOLAP solutions is the issue of aggregation performance when queries involve considerable amounts of spatial data. Li et al. combine SOLAP approach with the Map-Reduce model for processing large amounts of data in parallel [24]. Aissi et al. propose a multidimensional query recommendation system aiming to help users to retrieve relevant information through SOLAP, improving the data exploitation process [25].

Scotch and Parmanto [26] propose the SOVAT tool (Spatial OLAP Visualization and Analysis Tool) to help public health researchers and professionals in the decision making process. SOVAT main features include performing statistical and spatial analysis, providing a detailed data exploration, and viewing data through charts and maps. However, the tool does not provide metric and topologic spatial operators.

The Golapware tool was developed and used to process GeoMDQL, a geographic-multidimensional query language to spatial analysis [27]. The SOLAP server is an extension of the Mondrian OLAP server. The server contains an engine responsible for SOLAP processing called GOLAPE (Geographical Online Analytical Processing Engine) and it supports spatial queries using the GeoMDQL language. The Golapware tool does not offer interface components for visual interaction of queries with the user, resulting in a more complex data analysis.

Stole and Hanrahan [28] present a data analysis interface that extends the Pivot Table interface. Polaris is an interface used in exploratory analysis of large multidimensional relational databases, and has a set of graphic components to specify relational queries visually and to view data (visual specification language). Polaris interface enables visual analysis through a visual specification language called VizQL. However, this language does not provide support for spatial operators and can manipulate only points (latitude and longitude). Although it supports map overlay, where these layers may come from another data source, it does not allow overlapping of layers originated from geometrical fields. On the other hand, our proposed solution extends the VizQL language to visual spatial analysis. This extension aims to overcome spatial analysis drawbacks found in that language. The tool was built to relational databases, so it neither supports hierarchies and levels, concepts related to multidimensional cubes, nor allows the use of spatial operators.

Lamas et al. [29] developed an integration of the MapServer with the Saiku Analytics analysis tool (OLAP), making possible spatial dimension data visualization using maps. With the Web tool, thematic maps that represent spatial distribution of a particular cube measure can be created using different color tones. The color gradation represents different intervals of the selected measure in territorial units. The Saiku tool provides an interface to navigate and select the cube metadata (measure, dimension, etc.) building a thematic map. For this purpose, the tool offers two components (columns and rows) in which users may select the dimensions and measures to analyze, respectively. It is not possible to create spatial filters to build maps because the tool does not provide spatial operators.

Dubé et al. presented an XML file exchange SOLAP cubes through web services [8]. The proposed XML file does not depend on the OLAP/GIS tool and represents all the necessary data (facts and members) and metadata (scheme), besides supporting spatial dimensions. The advantage of exchanging data through Web Services is that the communication is not limited to traditional client-server platforms, but also supports ubiquitous mobile computing environments.

The aforementioned solutions differ in the data model and there is no standard for provision and analysis of spatial data. In this perspective, the Open Geospatial Consortium (OGC) published in 2012 a report (white paper) containing an evaluation of the ways that the OGC standards (e.g., WMS - Web Map Service, WFS, WPS - Web Processing Service, etc.) could be extended, in order to promote the use of geospatial information and the interoperability of GeoBI applications.

Table I presents a comparison among the related work concerning the eight desirable requirements presented in Section 1. Cells that contain an "X" mean that a given solution implements a given feature and those that contain a "–" mean that a given solution does not implement a particular feature.

This article presents a framework for Spatial Analytics, known as SOLAP_Frame that enables the connection to multiple and heterogeneous data sources. The framework was developed using open source technologies. Furthermore, the proposed framework presents an integrated visualization of multidimensional and spatial data, allowing for the creation of queries by means of a visual specification language with support to spatial operators and data visualization through maps, tables and charts. Finally, SOLAP_Frame also enables the geocodification of the data and is extensible, providing support for addition of new functionalities, such as new operators or data visualization methods. To the best of our knowledge, this is the first work to propose a framework for Spatial Analytics that is able to interoperate with new heterogeneous data sources.

TABLE I. RELATED WORK COMPARISON

Solutions	**Requirements**							
	I	*II*	*III*	*IV*	*V*	*VI*	*VII*	*VIII*
JMAP	X	X	-	-	-	X	X	X
GeoWOLAP	X	X	-	-	-	-	-	-
SOVAT	X	X	-	-		-	-	X
Piet	-	-	-	-	-	-	-	-
Golapware	-	X	X			X	-	X
Polaris	X	X	-	-		-	-	X
Saiku	X	X	-	-	-	X	-	X

All works addressed in this article have in common an architecture in which the client is strongly connected to the SOLAP server, which prevents the analysis of data from other SOLAP servers.

Piet and Golapware solutions do not have interactive interfaces in which the user can specify a query. This obliges the user to master a certain query language. The Piet solution has two different interfaces: one for multidimensional analysis and another for spatial analysis. In other words, they do not provide a data integrated view. SOVAT and Piet solutions lack of a Web interface, so the remote access via Internet is not possible. GeoWOLAP, Piet and Mapwarehouse solutions do not present one or more of the following data visualization forms: chats, graphics and maps.

Except Golapware and Mapwarehouse solutions, the other tools do not allow using spatial operators to slice and dice data cubes, minimizing the query's power expression. The analyzed solutions support only one type of data integration: either integrated or federated. All solutions, except Piet and Golapware, have a language to visually specify the query. However, only the Polaris solution defines a specification language for data visualization and query definition. GeoWOLAP, SOVAT, Piet and Polaris solutions do not use open source technologies, and GeoWOLAP, SOVAT, Piet and Golapware are not extensible.

Several attempts have been expended toward building SOLAP tools. However, in the studied solutions, it is not possible to reuse the client layer due to the lack of standards on communication between SOLAP server and client. Hence, based on the key features analyzed in Table I, it is clear that no solution addressed in the state-of-the-art can be considered satisfactory.

III. THE SOLAP_FRAME FRAMEWORK

This section presents the SOLAP_Frame architecture. In the next subsections, we describe the architecture and the extension points of our proposed SOLAP framework.

A. *The Spatial Cube Data Model*

In our framework the data structure is a cube composed of measures and dimensions. The dimensions have hierarchies composed of levels and are responsible for the categorization of the SOLAP cube. Levels, on the other hand, are composed of members. The class diagram that represents the cube can be seen in Figure 1.

In each cube dimension, the members are grouped into levels, that are arranged into hierarchies. A hierarchy defines different levels of detail. In a hierarchy, the levels follow an order that represents the hierarchy level depth. Members relate with themselves, that is, a member of a certain level is son of a superior level member.

Levels and members have properties, which have a type and a value. The property type characterizes the property domain a number, text, date or geometry. The value is an element of the property domain. The level lists properties common to members, so it is possible to know the properties of the members in advance.

Measures are the quantitative values used to measure characteristics of the analyzed phenomenon. In the cube, they are organized as a special dimension called measures dimension, whose members are measure names organized in a special hierarchy called measures hierarchy. This hierarchy has a special level called measures level. In the proposed model, the attributes *isMeasureDimension*, *isMeasureHierarchy* and *isMeasureLevel* of the *Dimension*, *Hierarchy* and *Level* classes, respectively, are responsible for identifying the measures dimension, hierarchy and level.

Each cube component should have, at least, two attributes: unique name and name. The unique name unequivocally identifies the cube's component, and the name is presented to the user. Each member of the measures dimension has a set of measure values associated to it. There is a measure value for each combination of different dimensions. In the proposed framework, the measure values are not associated to the cube itself, but to the result of a multidimensional query.

Cube components are considered spatial if a level member, a hierarchy or a dimension contain a spatial property, a spatial level or a spatial hierarchy, respectively. Lastly, a cube is spatial if it has, at least, one spatial measure or spatial dimension.

B. *Extension of the Vizql Query Language*

Based on Polaris, an interface proposed by Stolte and Hanrahan [30], the goal of the interface proposed in this work is to facilitate the process of data analysis. The framework's interface proposed here has a visual specification language that is an extension of the VizQL [31] formalism. We extended VizQL specifications to retrieve and visualize spatial data in multidimensional cubes.

Through the tabular algebra, VizQL partitions the data according to the visual specification defined for table settings, that is, VizQL tab expressions. The available VizQL tabs are: Columns, Rows, Filters and Tableaus.

Tab Layers was added to VizQL to support spatial analysis (Figure 2). Polaris tab Layers is used only for data segmentation and in Polaris commercial version, it was renamed to Tableau.

A fundamental concept in Geographic Information Systems (GIS) is overlay. A GIS system has data organized in layers that can be overlapped, facilitating the data analysis through visual data correlation. In a cube, data is organized into hierarchy levels, so a spatial level can be used as a map layer. However, there is no tab in the VizQL language for the overlay spatial operation.

A new tabular algebra operator called *SpatialConcatenation* was added to VizQL. For this new operator, the operands must be spatial fields and their names are assigned to the set of names resulted from the application of this operator, where the fields can be either qualitative or quantitative.

In the VizQL language, each table cell has a panel that displays data relative to that cell. To allow data visualization in maps with overlaying, a new type of panel was added: the spatial panel. Thus, panels can display spatial or conventional data.

The spatial panel is a result of panel overlapping of the tabular algebra resulting tables applied to the tab "Layers". This means that, to show a query result in the map, the tables are overlapped and merged into one, unlike the tab "Tabular" that shows one table at a time. Another difference is that the conventional panel aggregates measure values while the

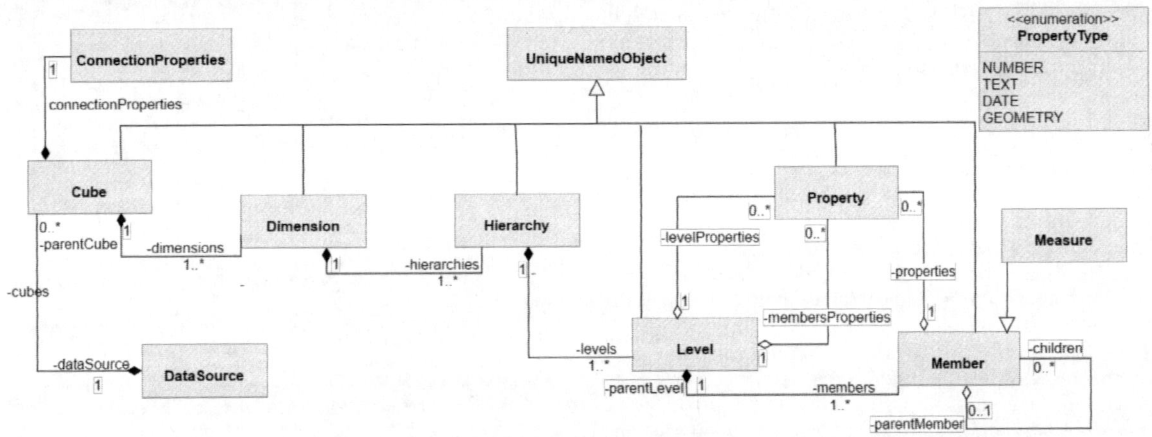

Figure 1. Spatial cube data model

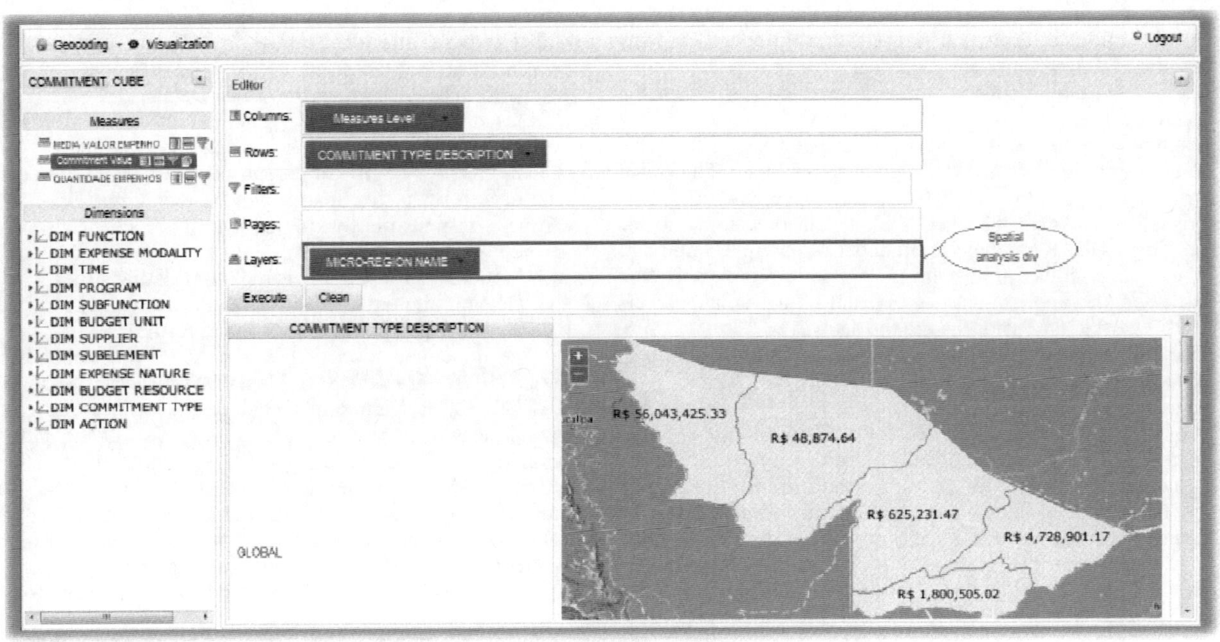

Figure 2. Layers div for spatial analysis

spatial panel aggregates measures by geometry, also known as feature.

The features are grouped by fields. Each set created by this grouping is a layer, making layer overlap possible, for example, in a map. When adding levels to the tab "Layers", the table cell will be composed of layers. In addition to the tab "Layers", spatial constraints are specified in VizQL, according to OGC specification. The OGC (Open Geospatial Consortium) developed standards to model, access, store and share geographic data. The topological operators defined by OGC, based on DE-9IM model (Dimension Extended Nine-Intersection Model) include Touches, Within, Crosses, Overlaps, Disjoint, Contains, Equals, Intersects and Relate. These operators are available for the geographic filter specification. The OGC also specifies Buffer, ConvexHull, Envelop, Boundary, Centroid and PointOnSurface operators. They can be used in geometric filters.

C. Architecture

The framework architecture comprises three layers: client, application and data layers, as shown in Figure 3.

The client layer comprises a set of graphical Web interfaces in which the user can connect to a multidimensional spatial cube, geocode members, pose queries by means of a visual specification and visualize the result set.

The data layer comprises the multidimensional data sources to be analyzed and the spatial data repository. The framework is capable of accessing several multidimensional servers (cube servers), employing different technologies and manufacturers. The framework also supports the geocoding of cube members, enabling the spatial analysis of non spatial OLAP cubes. The application data repository is stored in the *PostgreSQL* DBMS, with the PostGIS spatial extension. The spatial data resulting from the geocoding of members of the cube are stored in this repository, characterizing a Data Warehouse federated approach. Any spatial DBMS can be used for this purpose, simply extending the proposed solution through its extension points.

The application layer is responsible for the implementation of the whole application logic. This layer has six modules: visual query specification, data visualization, map manager, spatial data repository access and the SOLAP engine. We highlight the SOLAP engine as the main module of this layer, providing communication between the application and the multidimensional servers (OLAP or SOLAP) attached to the data layer.

The visual query specification module controls the query execution and result set visualization, turning the interactions between users and the graphical interface into objects that compose the query visual specification. After receiving the result set from a visual query, the visual specification module forwards this result set with its markup to the data visualization module so that the data can be transformed and presented in the specified format. Depending on the markup type, data may have to be transformed, for example, grouped to compose the map layers or graphic axes. After transformed, the data set is forwarded to the most appropriate component of the interface for visualization (e.g., tables, maps, charts, text and caption).

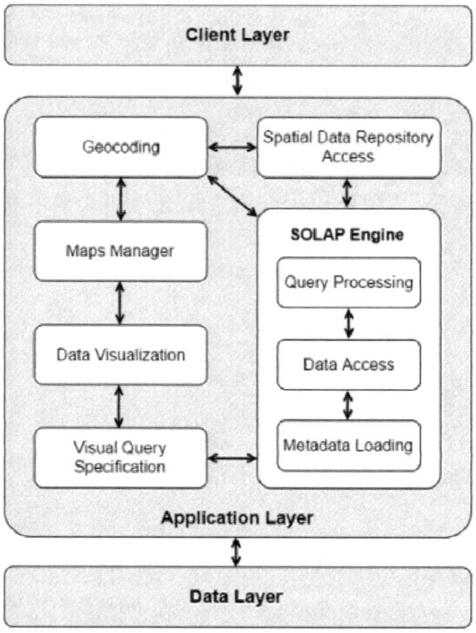

Figure 3. The SOLAP_Frame architecture

The map management module is responsible for displaying data on maps. For such, this module receives, from the data visualization module, a set of spatial and numerical data, query results, and the markup. The repository access module, in turn, was implemented to retrieve the metadata and the data from the spatial tables stored in the spatial data repository. The metadata and the data in the spatial tables are used by the geocoding module, which is accessed using the Java Database Connectivity (JDBC) driver for the PostgreSQL database management system (DBMS) with the PostGIS spatial extension.

The SOLAP engine is composed of three sub-modules: data access, metadata loading and query processing. This engine is responsible for: implementing the connection to a given multidimensional data source; loading of metadata from cubes to be analyzed; translating the visual specification into the destination query language; submitting the translated query; and receiving the result set.

The implementation of the SOLAP engine depends on the manufacturer of the SOLAP server to be accessed.

The data access module enables the connection to the multidimensional data source and the choice of the cube to be analyzed. This module is also in charge of executing queries in the language of the accessed technology and of returning the results of these queries. To accomplish the data access module, it is necessary to inform the connection properties that match both source and cube properties. The source properties state where and how to connect to the multidimensional data source, while the cube properties address which cube belonging to a given source should be accessed. The data access module knows how to handle heterogeneous sources.

The metadata loading and the query processing modules of the SOLAP engine interact with the data access module, which is specialized, that is, its implementation depends on the adopted technology.

The metadata loading module is responsible for retrieving cube metadata. In order to connect to a multidimensional data source, the *ConnectionProperties* and *DataSource* objects must be informed. The metadata coming from this connection will be turned into Cube objects, which will be loaded into memory for posterior use by other modules of the proposed framework.

The query processing module is responsible for translating the visual queries into the target technology native language; executing them using the data access module; and returning the result set. In order to retrieve the data, besides the connection properties, a visual query is passed as parameter to the processing query module.

D. *The SOLAP_Frame Extension Points*

SOLAP_Frame contains extension points that enable to connect it to heterogeneous data sources. In this section we give details of the communication interfaces.

1) *The SOLAP Engine Facade*

The main extension point of the proposed framework is the implementation of the SOLAP engine facade. This facade is responsible for the communication between the proposed solution and the multidimensional data source. The message exchange between our framework and the SOLAP engine consists of requesting metadata and data from a cube. The facade standardizes this message exchange. To request metadata from a cube to the SOLAP engine, the facade contains the *loadCube* method that receives as parameters the connection properties of both the data source and cube and returns an object that represents the cube.

To request data from a cube to the SOLAP engine, the facade contains three methods: *processQuery*, *getLevelMembers* and *filterLevelMembers*. The *processQuery* method receives as parameter an object that models the query, which is part of the visual specification defined by the user. This visual query should be translated into the query language of the source technology; and then executed. The query result must be modeled in a return object called *VisualQueryResult*.

The *getLevelMembers* method receives as parameter an object that represents a hierarchical level. This level is used to retrieve the members of the cube. Finally, the *filterLevelMembers* method receives as parameter, besides the level, a filter that can be either conventional or spatial. This filter will be used to select the members to be retrieved.

Our framework will automatically identify the implementation of the front end by means of the Contexts and *Dependency Injection services* (CDI) present in the Java Enterprise Edition platform, and will register it. A name and a type must be associated to the SOLAP engine in order to be presented to the user. The type is used by the BI engine manager to ensure the mapping between types and implementations available.

2) *The Connection properties interface*

The communication process requires that the user provides the connection properties. This information will be used every time the SOLAP engine needs to communicate with a data source. Thus, another extension point in our framework is the implementation of this user interface.

The connection properties depend on the technology to be used. Hence, the parameters that must be informed vary according to the technology.

The front end for the SOLAP engine contains a method called *getLoaderPopup*, which returns an object called *LoaderPopup*, which, in turn, contains the necessary information for the exhibition of the component. This object is used by the interface, that lists all the available. The *LoaderPopup* object is composed of another object called *LoaderBean*, that needs to be implemented. The *LoaderBean* is the controller responsible for preparing the component for exhibition and for enabling access to the properties of connections created by the user.

3) *The XMLA engine*

In order to provide access to several heterogeneous multidimensional data sources, we also developed a SOLAP engine for servers that provide their data through the XMLA protocol. To enable the XMLA engine to access a specific technology, it is necessary to implement the abstract classes described in the following. In the implementation of the SOLAP engine for XMLA, we used the XMLA driver supplied by the Open Java API for OLAP (olap4j), which is also an open specification for the construction of OLAP applications based on the JDBC protocol. Once connected to the data source, the user chooses the cube that will be analyzed. After that, an alias is assigned to the cube. This alias will be used to identify the cube in the system.

After the selection of the cube, its metadata will be loaded. For such, it is necessary to convert the metadata from the native format into the target one. The metadata loading is carried out by the *Olap4jXMLACubeMetadataDAO* class, and the abstract class *AbstractOlap4jXMLACubeConverter* implements the basic methods necessary for the conversion of the cubes from the native format to the format used in the solution.

The methods of the *AbstractOlap4jXMLACubeConverter* abstract class are spatial related and depends on the technology used by the XMLA server. This is due to the fact that XMLA does not specify a standard format for the transportation of spatial data. Furthermore, the Multidimensional Expressions (MDX) query language, used by the XMLA server, does not specify spatial functions. Figure 4 presents a class diagram for the XMLA engine.

To load the data, the *AbstractOlap4jXMLAQueryDAO* class supplies the basic functionalities necessary for the correct operation of the framework. However, it is necessary to implement the method responsible for translating MDX filters into the language for the chosen technology. The abstract method is necessary due to the fact that our framework deals with spatial filters. Since these spatial filters are not standardized for MDX, they vary according to the technology used.

IV. Case Study Applied To The Court Of Accounts Of The State Of Acre – Brazil

In order to evaluate the SOLAP_Frame, we ran a case study on public accountability of the Court of Accounts of the State of Acre – Brazil (TCE-AC). We used a real dataset from that Court. The aim of this case study was to help in the decision making process related to the definition of more efficient management strategies to achieve an effective control of public spending. More specifically, citizens may inspect public budget and expenditure from a macro-level (e.g. the whole State) to a micro-level (e.g. a specific city).

To run this case study, the framework was extended to connect to two multidimensional data sources: *SQL Server Analysis Services* and *GeoMondrian*, of which the first one provides access to conventional data, and second one provides access to spatial data. Three cubes are available for the analysis: Commitment, Liquidation and Payment. The Commitment cube uses the opensource *GeoMondrian* server, while the other ones utilize the Microsoft SSAS.

The fact tables to be analyzed are represented by the measures: Commitment values, Liquidation values and Payment values. Besides the measures modeled in the *Spatial Data Warehouse* (SDW), the cubes have two additional measures: number and mean of the values.

The Spatial DW used in the cube implementation is modeled by the conceptual schemata presented in Figures 5, 6 and 7. These DW projects are tailored for the TCE-AC domain.

The facts have the following dimensions in common: Action, Supplier, Function, Expense Nature, Program, Expense Subelement, Subfunction, Time, Budget Resource Source Type and Budget Unit. The Commitment and Payment cubes have the Expense Modality dimension in common. The Liquidation and Payment cubes have the Summary Commitment dimension in common and the Commitment Type dimension features only measures of the Commitment cube, while the dimension Bank Account features only measures of the Payment cube.

Some dimensions have members organized by hierarchies, such as: Action, Supplier, Subelement, Bank Account, Time and Budget Unit. The members of these dimensions were organized in the following level of detail.

- Action Dimension: members organized in action type and action;
- Supplier Dimension: members organized in supplier type, cpf, cnpj and supplier name;
- Subelement Dimension: members organized in expense element and subelement;
- Bank Account Dimension: members organized in bank, agency, account type and account;
- Time Dimension: members organized by year, month and day;
- Budget Unit Dimension: members organized in state, meso-region, microregion, city, management unit and budget unit. These regions are defined by a Brazilian Government Agency called IBGE (www.ibge.gov.br).

The Budget Unit dimension is a spatial dimension because of its spatial attributes: State Name, Mesoregion Name, Micro-region Name, City Name; and its spatial hierarchy: State – Meso – Micro – City. The spatial portion of the DW that refers to the Commitment cube was migrated to PostgreSQL so the GeoMeondrian can access these data.

A. *Query Examples*

In order to assess the framework in the case study we analyzed some queries involving Spatial Analytics.

Query 1: "Display a map with the average of Commitment values detailed by state, mesoregion, micro-region and city."

In order to solve this query, the Commitment cube was used. The Average Commitment Value measure was added to the tab "Columns", while the hierarchy State – Mesoregion – Micro-region – City of the Dim Budget Unit dimension was added to the tab "Layers". This hierarchy has four spatial levels: State, Mesoregion, Micro-region and City.

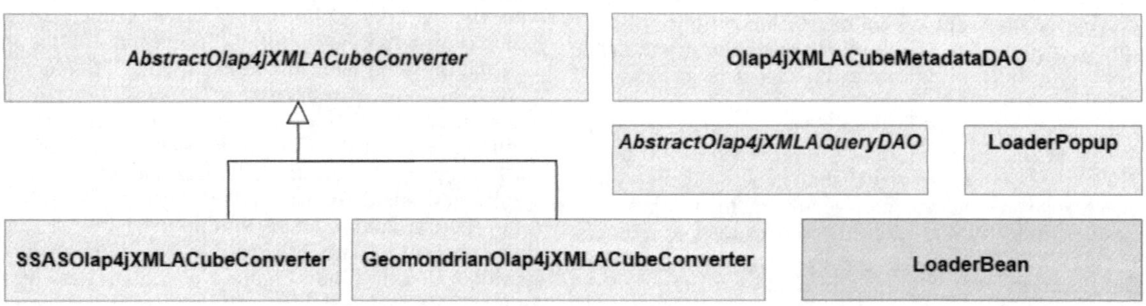

Figure 4. Class Diagram for the XMLA Engine.

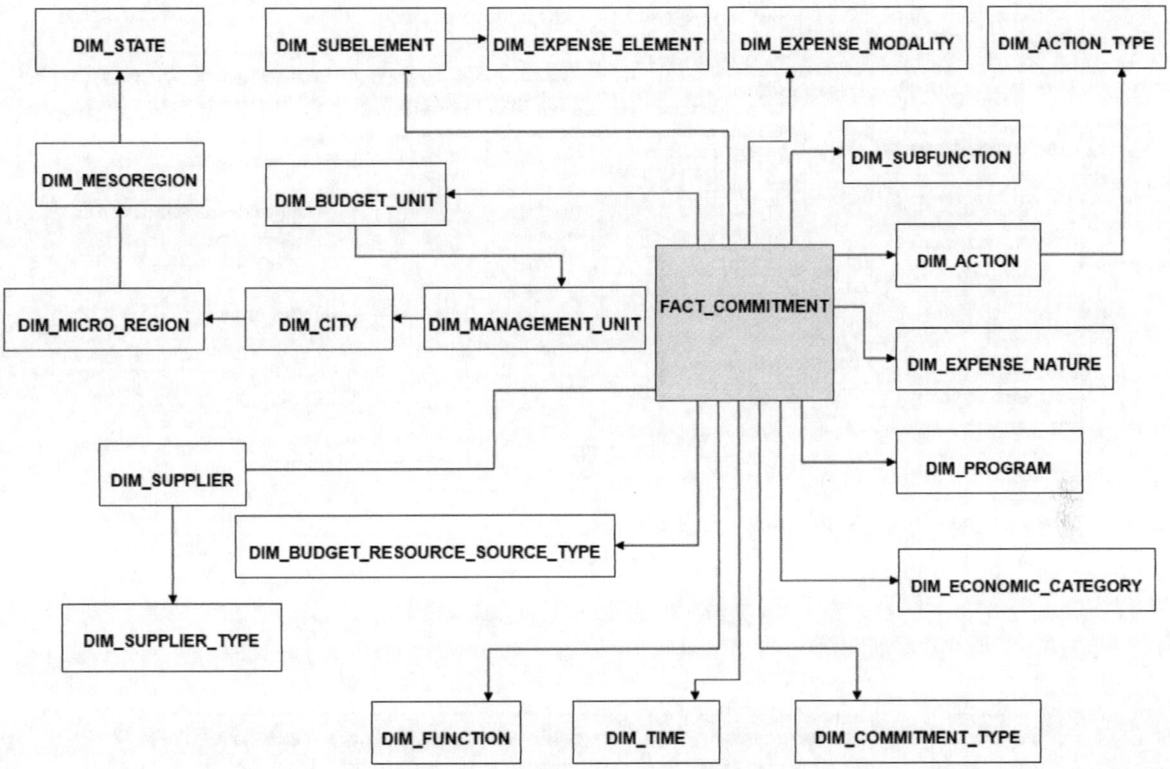

Figure 5. DW schema for the Commitment cube

Adding the hierarchy to the tab, its less level of detail is displayed with the navigation icon +, that is used to increase the level of detail (Figure 8). For data details, the + icon was used to State, Mesoregion (Figure 9) and Micro-region levels. Data visualization was specified by selecting the spatial panel type and the text type marking, where the selected measure was used as a geometry label. If there is no measure value associated with the geometry, the geometry will not be displayed on the map. The goal of this query is to exemplify the hierarchy navigation and the text type visualization in spatial panels (maps).

Query 2: "Display a thematic map with the sum of the Commitment values for each city."

Also, using the Commitment cube for this query, the Commitment Value measure was added to the tab "Columns" while the spatial hierarchy City Name was added to the tab "Layers". The marking type Caption was used for data visualization in the map. (Figure 10).

The caption created for the measure Commitment Value is of type value range, and the amplitude of the measure value is used to group geometries. It is also possible to create captions for the group type, where records are evenly divided in the ranges of values. The level City Name was used as a label to the geometries. This query exemplifies the display of the type Caption in maps.

Query 3: "What is the sum of the liquidated values in the neighbor cities of the city of Rio Branco, concerning the functions Administration, Agriculture and Legislative?"
This query demonstrates the use of the spatial filters available in the framework. In this example, the cube Liquidation was used; the Liquidation Value metric was added to the tab "Columns", the hierarchy Function Description was added to the tab "Rows", and the hierarchy District Name, to the tab "Layers".

The members of the Function Description level were filtered. A geographic filter was added to the cities, and the spatial operator Touches was used to filter neighbor cities of the city of Rio Branco. To visualize the data, we used a caption in spatial panels. Figure 11 presents the query result.

Query 4: "How much was spent with undergraduate education, elementary education and regular education in 2012, detailed by month, in the Rio Branco micro-region and Tarauacá city?"

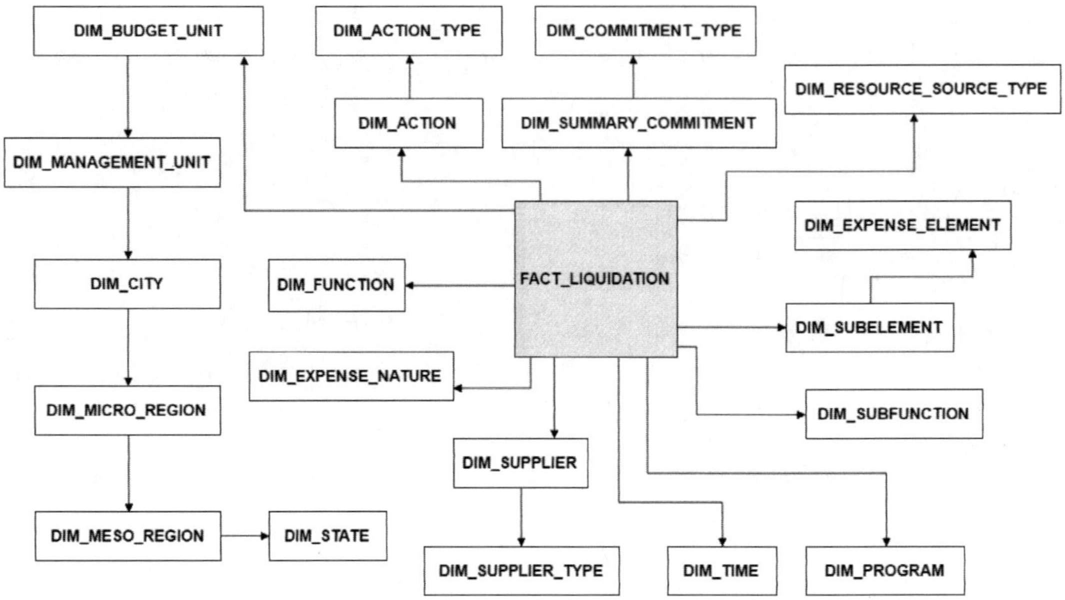

Figure 6. DW schema for the Liquidation cube

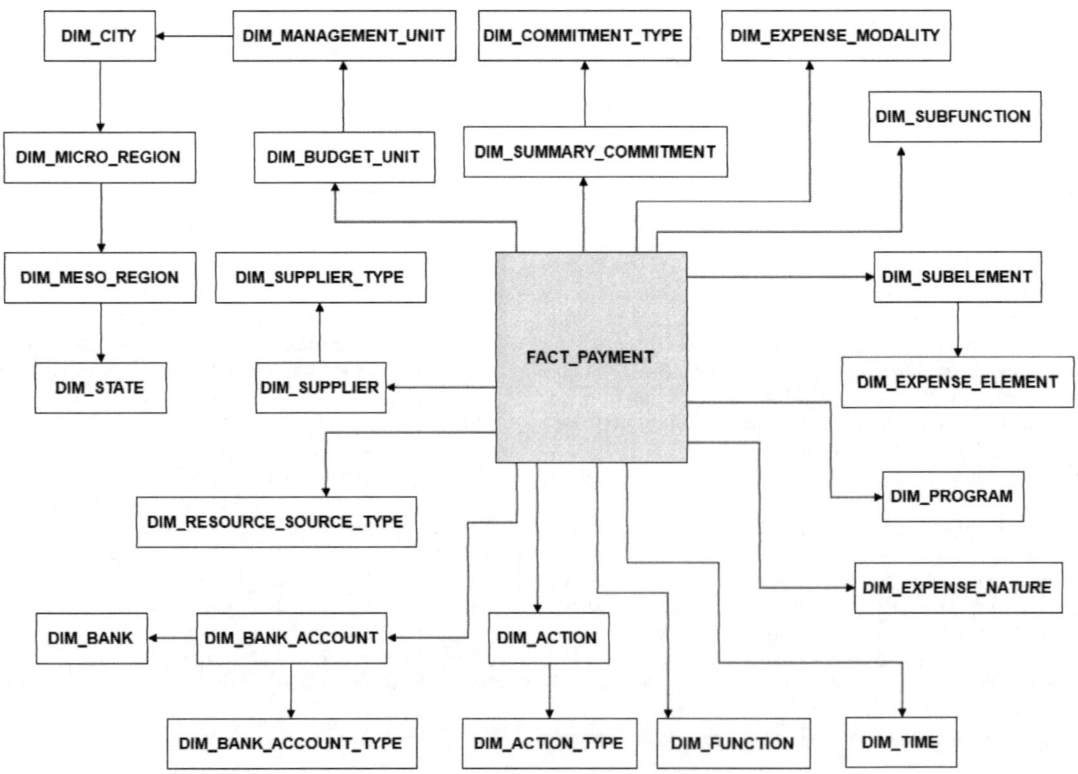

Figure 7. DW schema for the Payment cube

In order to present an example of pagination and overlap of layers, the Payment Value measure was added to the tab "Columns", the Program Description hierarchy was added to the tab "Rows", the Year – Month – Day hierarchy to the tab "Tableau" and the hierarchies City and Micro-region to the tab "Layers". The member 2012 of the Year level was selected and, to detail the pages by months, a drill-down was made. The member Rio Branco of the Micro-region level and the member Tarauacá of the City level were selected. To visualize the data, we used a caption in spatial panels. Figure 12 presents the query result.

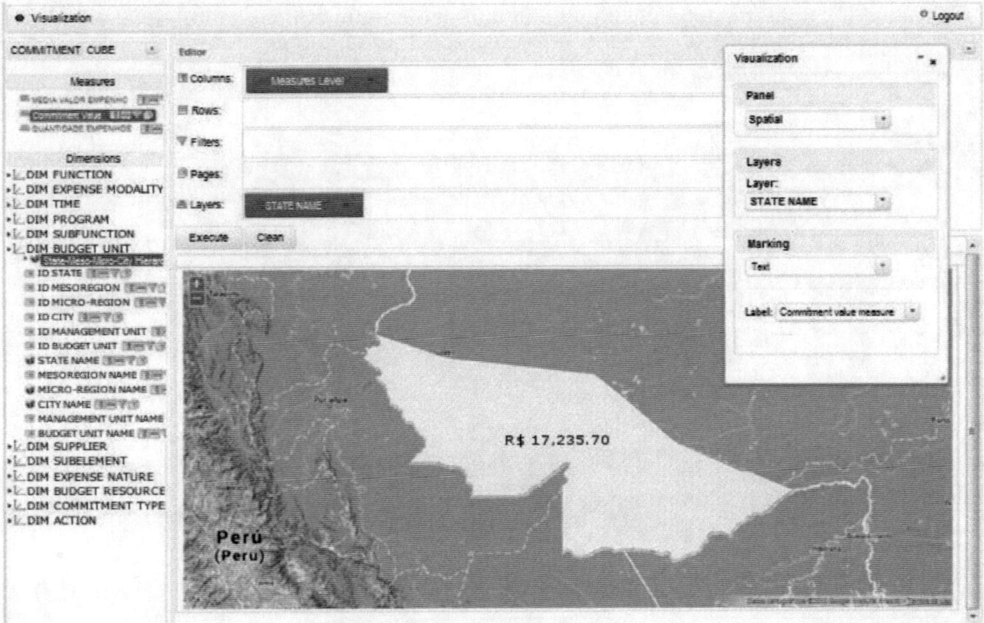

Figure 8. Query 1 result – State level.

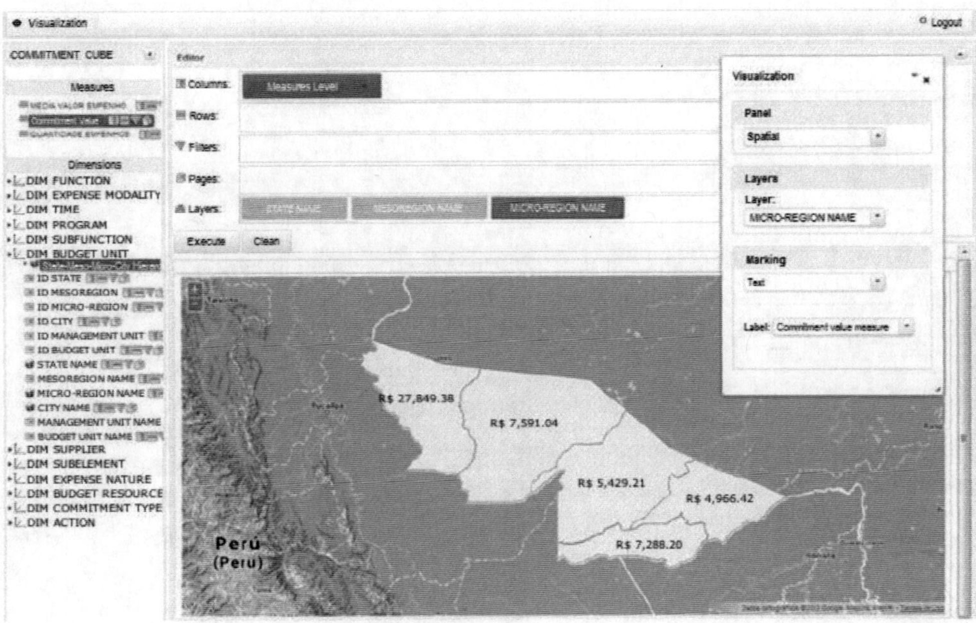

Figure 9. Query 1 Result – Mesoregion Level

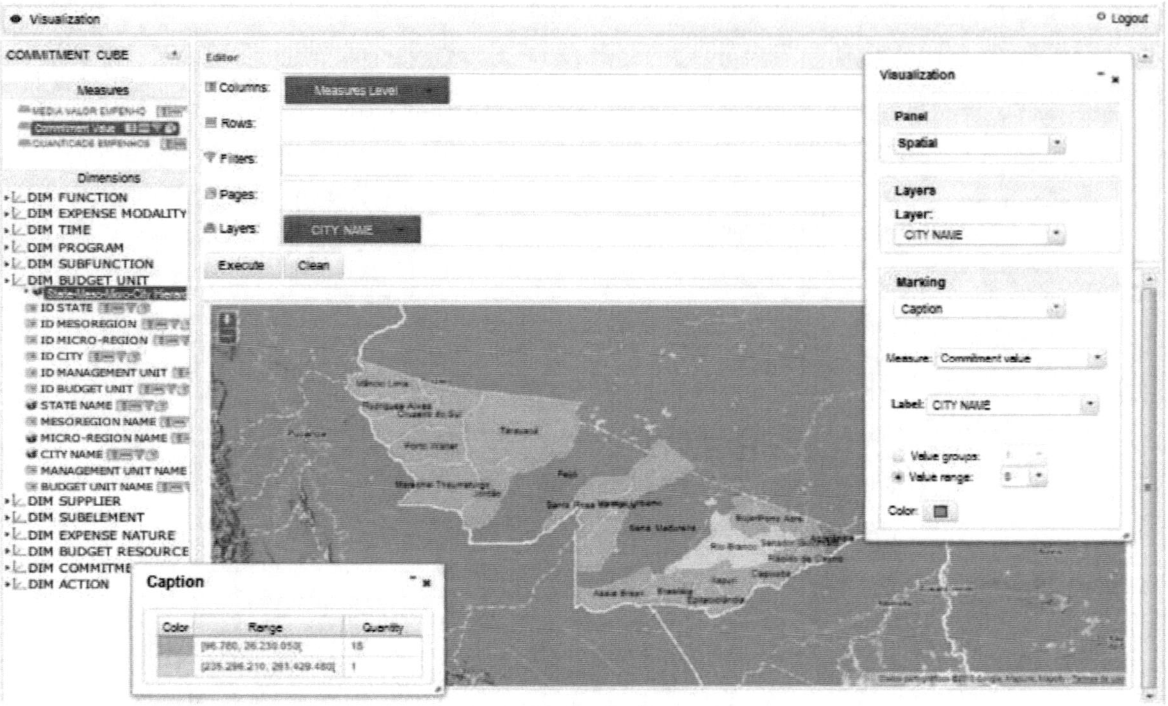

Figure 10. Query 2 result.

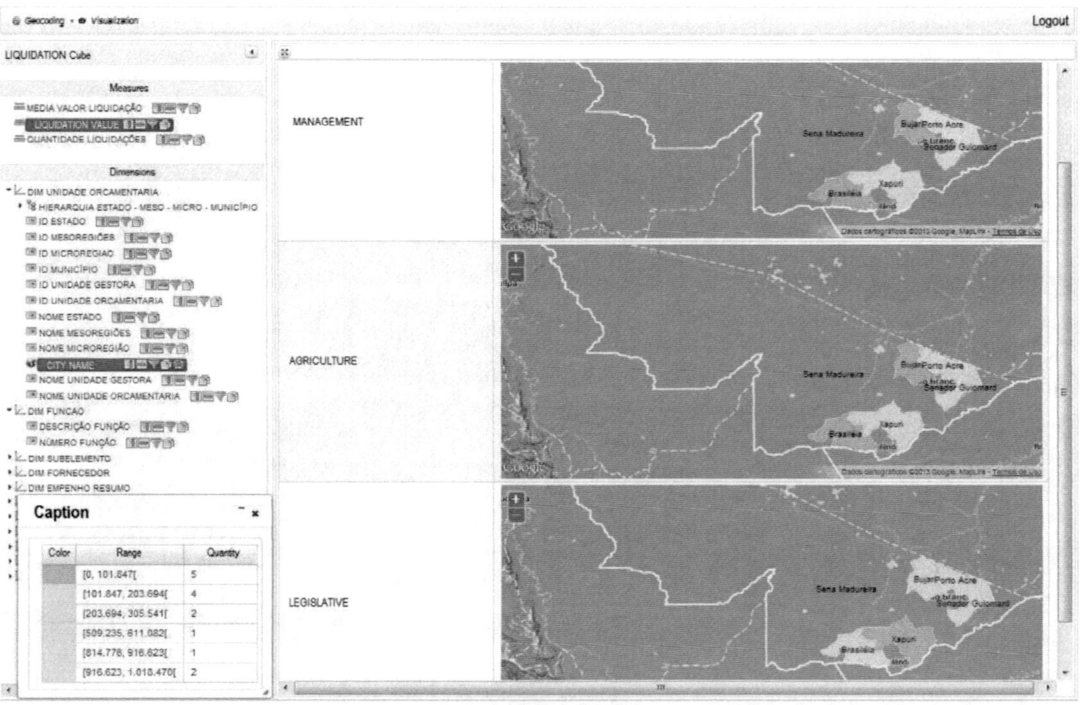

Figure 11. Query 3 result.

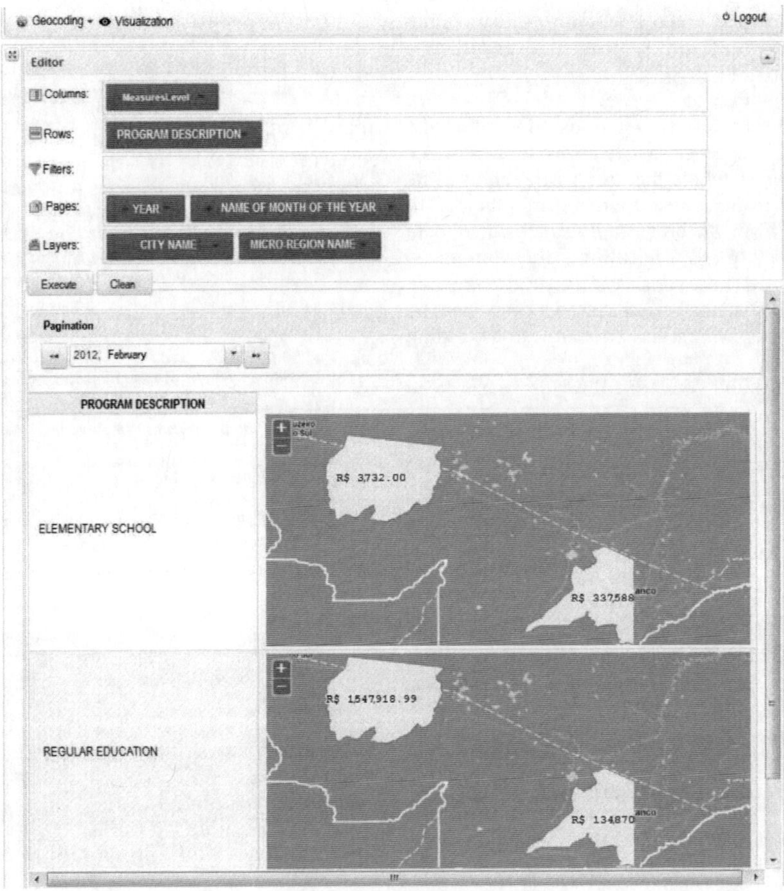

Figure 12.Query 4 result

V. Conclusions and Future Work

As presented in this work, several solutions for integration of spatial and multidimensional data have been proposed over the last few years. The main goal of these solutions was to propose improvements in the analytical process of data, providing a single environment to the multidimensional sources of spatial components analysis.

From the survey of the state-of-the-art presented, it was possible to compare the strengths and weaknesses of the main existing solutions. Because there is no standard to make spatial cubes available on the Web, we may conclude that these solutions do not provide techniques to analyze spatial cubes from heterogeneous multidimensional data sources. Based on the observed issues, a list of requirements needed for a SOLAP analysis tool was created, and the main requirements include the access to various sources of multidimensional data and data geocoding; support for topological spatial operators and a visual language for query specification and data visualization.

To fulfill these requirements, we presented a framework capable of performing spatial analytics on data provided by many sources of multidimensional spatial data. The main effort is to extend the SOLAP engine to access the data sources. Our framework has a set of graphic interfaces that enables the user to create connections to access data cubes; to perform analysis by visual query specification and data visualization; to create conventional or spatial filters to filter data; to geocode dimension members; to compare data by a tabular structure and to use maps to view the query results.

In the framework proposed in this work, our spatial cube model proved to be satisfactory for allowing spatial analysis in cubes from different sources. The extension of the visual language specification VizQL enabled the use of topological spatial operators and the display of data in maps, with overlaying. The framework also provides support for spatial analysis, through a data integration federated approach and made a geocoding service available, providing spatial analysis in pure OLAP servers.

In order to allow the user access to heterogeneous data sources, extension points were created and documented so that the framework can be extended. The Microsoft SSAS and GeoMondrian cube servers were accessed by extensions from the proposed framework, making possible to evaluate features by a practical example based on daily real problems, showing that spatial analysis in cubes from different sources can be performed efficiently. The example obtained relevant data to solve real problems related to a Brazilian Court of Audit (TCE-AC).

A comparative evaluation between the framework proposed in this work and related solutions shows that the framework addressed the necessary features to a SOLAP solution. Therefore, we conclude that this work achieved its goals, having as the main contribution an architecture in which spatial cubes from different multidimensional data sources can be analyzed, fulfilling the proposed requirements.

We also conclude that many expansion points can be explored in future works, which will cooperate for building a more robust framework.

As a future work we point out the following issues to be undertaken:

- Interoperability: although this solution enables analyzing cubes from different data sources, it does not allow the interoperability between cubes. As a future work, a suggestion is the development of a module to provide interoperability between cubes;
- SOLAP Operators: adding new SOLAP operators to the framework;
- Data Availability: adapting the proposed framework architecture to provide services via Web Services;
- Usability: an evaluation study of the interface concerning usability;
- Data visualization: investigate new forms of data visualization;
- Raster representation for data: adding raster data into the framework; and
- Data mining: adding data mining techniques to promote prediction.

ACKNOWLEDGMENT

The authors would like to thank the Court of Accounts of the State of Acre – Brazil (TCE-AC).

REFERENCES

[1] T. E. Silva, D.F.B, Leite, and C.S. Baptista, "SOLAP_Frame: A Framework for SOLAP using Heterogeneous Data Sources," The Eighth International Conference on Advanced Geographic Information Systems, Applications, and Services - GEOProcessing 2016, April 24 - 28, 2016 - Venice, Italy.

[2] S. Rivest, Y. Bédard, M. Proulx, F. Hubert, and J. Pastor, "SOLAP technology: Merging business intelligence with geospatial technology for interactive spatio-temporal exploration and analysos of data," ISPRS P&RS, vol. 60, no. 1, 2005, pp. 17-33.

[3] S. Aissi, M. S. Gouider, T. Sboui, L. B. Said, "Enhancing spatial data warehouse exploitation: A SOLAP recommendation approach," SNPD 2016, pp. 457-464.

[4] J. Li, L. Meng, F. Z. Wang, W. Zhang, Y. Cai, "A Map-Reduce-enabled SOLAP cube for large-scale remotely sensed data aggregation," Computers & Geosciences, vol. 70, pp. 110-119, 2014.

[5] L. Leonardi, S. Orlando, A. Raffaetà, A. Roncato, C. Silvestri, G. L. Andrienko, N. V. Andrienko, "A general framework for trajectory data warehousing and visual OLAP," GeoInformatica, no. 18, vol. 2, pp. 273-312, 2014.

[6] B. A. A. Diallo, T. Badard, F. Hubert, S. Daniel, "Context-based mobile GeoBI: enhancing business analysis with contextual metrics/statistics and context-based reasoning," GeoInformatica no. 18, vol. 2, pp. 405-433, 2014.

[7] P. Rigaux, M. Scholl, A. Voisard, "Spatial Databases with Application to GIS," Morgan Kaufmann, 2001.

[8] E. Dubé, T. Badard, and Y. Bedard, "XML enconding and Web Services for Spatial OLAP data cube exchange: an SOA approach," CIT, vol. 17, no 4, 2009, pp. 347-358.

[9] Open Geospatial Consortium (OGC), "Open Geospatial Consortium OGC(R)," [Online]. Available: http://www.opengeospatial.org/, last access date: 11/10/2016.

[10] Open Geospatial Consortium (OGC), "Geospatial Business Intelligence (GeoBI)," OGC White Paper, 2012.

[11] M. E. Fayad and D. C. Schmidt, "Object-oriented application frameworks," Communications of the ACM, vol. 40, no. 10, 1997, pp. 32-40.

[12] I. Sommerville, Software Engineering, 10th edition, 2015, Pearson.

[13] L. Gómez, B. Kuijipers, B. Moelans, and A. Vaisman, "A Survey of Spatio-Temporal Data Warehousing," JDWM, vol. 5, no. 3, 2009, pp. 28-55.

[14] S. Bimonte, A. Tchounikine, M. Miquel, and F. Pinet, "When Spatial Analysis Meets OLAP Multidimensional Model and Operator," International Journal of Datawarehousing and Mining, vol. 6, no. 4, 2010, pp. 33-60, IGI Publishing.

[15] G. Viswanathan and M. Scheneider, "On the requirements for user-centric spatial data warehousing and SOLAP," in Proceedings of the 16th DASFAA, 2011, pp.144-155.

[16] M. Salehi, Y. Bédard, and S. Rivest, "A formal Conceptual Model and Definition Framework for Spatial Datacubes," Geomatica, vol. 64, no 3, 2010, pp. 313-326.

[17] P. Aguila, R. Fidalgo, and A. Mota, "Towards a more straightforward and more expressive metamodel for SDW modeling," in DOLAP 2011, pp. 31-36.

[18] O. Baltzer, "Computacional Methods for Spatial OLAP," Ph.D. thesis, 2011.

[19] O. Glorio and J. Trujillo, "Designing Data Warehouses for Geographic OLAP Querying by Using MDA," in Proceedings of the International Conference on Computational Science and its Applications, 2009, pp. 305-519.

[20] T. Ziouel, K. A. Derbal, and K. Boukhalfa. "SOLAP On-the-Fly Generalization Approach Based on Spatial Hierarchical Structures," CIIA 2015, pp. 279-290.

[21] S. Bimonte, A. Tchounikine, and M. Miquel, "Spatial OLAP: Open Issues and a Web Based Prototype," in M. Wachowicz & L. Bodum (Eds.), Proceedings of the 10th AGILE International Conference on Geographic Information Science, 2007.

[22] S.Bimonte, A web-based tool for spatio-temporal multidimensional analysis of geographic and complex data. In: Papajorgji, P.(ed). New technologies for constructing complex agricultural and environmental systems. Chapter 3, 2012, IGI Global.

[23] A. Escribano, L. Gomez, B. Kujipers, and A. Vaisman, "Piet: a GIS-OLAP implementation," in Proceedings of the ACM 1oth international workshop on Data Warehousing and OLAP, 2007, pp. 73-80.

[24] J. Li, L. Meng, F. Z. Wang, W. Zhang, and Y. Chai, "A Map-Reduce-enabled SOLAP cube for large-scale remotely sensed data aggregation," Computers & Geosciences, vol. 70, 2014, pp. 110-199.

[25] S. Aissi, M. S. Gouider, T. Sboui, and L. B. Said, "Personalized recommendation of SOLAP queries: theoretical framework and experimental evaluation," SAC 2015, pp. 1008-1014.

[26] M. Scotch and B. Parmanto, "SOVAT: Spatial OLAP Visualization and Analysis Tool," in Proceedings of the Proceedings of the 38th Annual Hawaii International Conference on System Sciences (HICSS'05) - Track 6 - Volume 06, Washington, DC, USA, 2005.

[27] J. Silva, V. Times, and A. Salgado, "An Open Source and Web Based Framework for Geographical and Multidimensional Processing," SAC 2006, pp. 63-67.

[28] C. Stolte and P. Hanrahan, "Polaris: A System for Query, Analysis and Visualization of Multi-Dimensional Relational Databases," in Proceedings of the IEEE Symposium on Information Vizualization 2000, Washington, DC, USA, 2000.

[29] A, Lamas, F. Sotelo, M. Borobio, and J.I. Varela "Creación de un módulo espacial OLAP para SAIKU" VII JORNADAS DE SIG LIBRE, 2013.

[30] C. Stolte and P. Hanrahan, "Polaris: A System for Query, Analysis and Visualization of Multi-Dimensional Relational Databases," in Proceedings of the IEEE Symposium on Information Vizualization 2000, Washington, DC, USA, 2000.

[31] P. Hanrahan, "VizQL: A Language for Query, Analysis and Visualization", SIGMOD 2006, June 27-29, 2006, Chicago, Illinois, USA. ACM, 2006.

ViSiTR: 3D Visualization for Code Visitation Trail Recommendations

Roy Oberhauser
Computer Science Dept.
Aalen University
Aalen, Germany
email: roy.oberhauser@hs-aalen.de

Abstract—**The rapid digitalization occurring in our society depends on massive amounts of data and software running on various devices. This, in turn, entails the creation and maintenance of an ever-increasing volume of computer program code. This situation is exacerbated by a limited pool of trained human resources that must quickly comprehend various sections of program code. Thus, effective and efficient automated tutor systems or recommenders for program comprehension are imperative. Furthermore, advances in game engine and PC performance have hitherto been insufficiently utilized by software engineering tools to leverage the potential that 3D visualization of code structure and navigation can provide. This paper introduces ViSiTR (3D Visualization of code viSitation Trail Recommendations), an approach that utilizes program code as a knowledge base to automatically recommend code visitation trails with visual 3D navigation to support effective and efficient human program code comprehension. A case study with a prototype demonstrated the viability of the approach but found scalability issues for large projects.**

Keywords - program code comprehension; recommendation systems; learning models; intelligent tutoring systems; knowledge-based systems; software engineering; engineering training; computer education; software visualization.

I. INTRODUCTION

This is an extended paper of [1]. The increasing demand for and utilization of software throughout society and industry results in soaring volumes of (legacy) program code and associated maintenance activity. Although the total lines and growth of program code worldwide is untracked and unknown, it's been estimated that well over a trillion lines of code (LOC) exist with 33bn added annually [2], while a study of 5000 active open source software projects shows code size doubling on average every 14 months [3].

This has ramifications on the amount of relatively expensive labor involved in software development and maintenance. Approximately 75% of technical software workers are estimated to be doing maintenance [4]. Moreover, program comprehension may consume up to 70% of the software engineering effort [5]. As an example, the Year 2000 (Y2K) crisis [6] with global costs of $375-750 billion provided an indicator of the scale and importance of program comprehension. Moreover, the available pool of programmers to develop and maintain code remains limited and is not growing correspondingly. This is exacerbated by high employee turnover rates in the software industry, for example 1.1 years at Google [7].

Thus, there is resulting pressure on programmers to rapidly come up to speed on existing code or comprehend and maintain legacy code (a type of knowledge) in a cost-effective manner. It thus becomes imperative that programmers be supported with automated tutors and recommenders that efficiently and effectively support program code comprehension. In this space, recommendation systems for software engineering provide information items considered to be valuable for a software engineering task in a given context [8].

However, such recommenders often lack integrated visualization support, hampering their ability to achieve more comprehensive program comprehension support. This relates to an essential difficulty of software construction asserted by F. P. Brooks Jr., namely the invisibility of software, since the reality of software is not embedded in space [9]. The most common formats used for the comprehension of program code include text or the two-dimensional Unified Modeling Language (UML).

In prior work, we introduced ReSCU [1], a knowledge-centric recommendation service and planner for program code comprehension. This was enhanced with support for cognitive learning models in C-TRAIL [10]. Separately, we developed a 3D flythrough visualization approach called FlyThruCode [11] that offers opportunities for grasping software program structures utilizing information visualization to support exploratory, analytical, and descriptive cognitive processes.

This paper introduces ViSiTR (3D Visualization of code viSitation Trail Recommendations), an approach for the 3D visualization of automatically recommended program comprehension code trails in alignment with various cognitive learning model styles and the "holey quilt" theory [12]. ViSiTR can be viewed as an intelligent tutor system with a 3D visual interface, applying a practical form of granular computing [13] and concepts like knowledge distance [14] to automatically recommend knowledge navigation as a Hamiltonian cycle [15], a special case of the traveling salesman problem (TSP) [16], in an unfamiliar knowledge landscape consisting of program code.

The paper is organized as follows: the next section discusses related work. This is followed by Section III, which provides background information. Section IV then describes the solution concept that is followed by a description of a prototype implementation. Section VI then presents a case study, which is followed by a conclusion.

II. Related Work

An overview of recommendation systems in software engineering is provided by [8]. In the Eclipse Integrated Development Environment (IDE), NavTracks [17] recommends files related to the currently selected files based on their previous navigation patterns. Mylar [18] utilizes a degree-of-interest model in Eclipse to filter our irrelevant files from the File Explorer and other views. The interest value of a selected or edited program element increases, while those of others decrease, whereby the relationship between elements is not considered. In support of developers with maintenance tasks in unfamiliar projects, Hipikat [19] recommends software artifacts relevant to a context based on the source code, email discussions, bug reports, change history, and documentation. The eRose plugin for Eclipse mines past changes in a version control system repository to suggest what is likely also related to this change based on historical similarity [20]. To improve navigation efficiency and enhance comprehension, the FEAT tool uses concern graphs either explicitly created by a programmer [21] or automatically inferred [22] based on navigation pathways utilizing a stochastic model, whereby a programmer confirms or rejects them for the concern graph. With the Eclipse plugin Suade [23], a developer drags-and-drops related fields and methods into a view to specify a context, and Suade utilizes a dependency graph and heuristics to recommend suggestions for further investigation. To support the usage of complex APIs in Eclipse, the Prospector system [24] recommends relevant code snippets by utilizing a search engine in combination with Eclipse Content Assist. Strathcona [25] analyzes structural facts of an incomplete code selection and utilizes heuristic matches to determine the most similar example. The Eclipse plugin FrUiT [26] supports example framework usage via association rule mining of applications that utilize a specific framework. Codetrail [27] connects source code and hyperlinked web resources via Eclipse and Firefox. Yin et al. [28] propose applying coarse-grained call graph slicing, intra-procedural coarse-grained slicing, and a cognitive easiness metric to guide programmers from the easiest to the hardest non-understood methods. Cornelissen et al. [29] survey work on program comprehension via dynamic analysis.

Although we attempted to provide a more detailed practical comparison with many of the above program comprehension tools, we abandoned our effort since the tool software was mostly either inaccessible or after download we were unable to get it to successfully execute. Our comparison is thus based on research paper descriptions. In contrast to the related work above, various facets differentiate the ViSiTR approach. ViSiTR is able to recommend code region visitations and plan a code trail order without necessitating an explicit context or prior history, without requiring the intervention or confirmation of a human expert. Furthermore, the approach is unique in applying a conceptual mapping of geographical points of interest (POI) and the traveling salesman problem/planning (TSP) to source code and the generation of code trail planning, with a Hamiltonian cycle to avoid unnecessary revisitations.

With regard to 3D software visualization tools across the various software engineering areas, an overview and survey is given by Teyseyre and Campo [30]. Software Galaxies [31] provides a web-based visualization of dependencies among popular package managers and supports flying. Every star represents a package that is clustered by dependencies. CodeCity [32] is a 3D software visualization approach based on a city metaphor and implemented in SmallTalk on the Moose reengineering framework. Buildings represent classes, districts represent packages, and visible properties depict selected metrics. Wettel et al. [33] showed a significant increase in terms of task correctness and decrease in task completion time. Rilling and Mudur [34] use a metaball metaphor combined with dynamic analysis of program execution. X3D-UML [35] provides 3D support with UML in planes such that classes are grouped in planes based on the package or hierarchical state machine diagrams. A case study of a 3D UML tool using Google SketchUp showed that a 3D perspective improved model comprehension and was found to be intuitive [36].

In contrast to the above work, ViSiTR supports visual code trails that can be recommended, captured, and replayed via 3D fly-thru visitation using multiple and dynamically switchable metaphors, custom and automatic annotation/tagging, and the display of localized contextually-relevant program code data (code, metrics, UML) in a heads-up display, thereby intermixing 2D data while flying through the 3D space. Because the source code is transformed into an XML description, various programming languages can be easily supported. Its plugin architecture permits the integration of program code data from various separate tools.

III. Background

For our purposes, it may be helpful to view program code comprehension from the holey quilt theory perspective [12], based on [37] and [38]. According to this metaphor "novice programmers' early comprehension models can be characterized by a pattern of 'holey knowledge' (i.e., an incomplete patchwork of fabric, with empty cells and missing stuffing)" [38] quoted in [12].

For the programmer, her or his program comprehension knowledge base can be viewed as a block model as shown in Figure 1 both functionally (the "what" in green) and structurally (the "how" in gold). Structure includes both the text surface of the program (right column), including its syntax, semantics, and style as well as its control structure (middle column). Its function goals (left column) considers its intent or goals at various levels. The finest granularity considered is on the atom (bottom) row, considering language elements and the result of any statement. The third row is labeled block, and consists of grouping within some region of interest (ROI). The second row labeled relations deals with the relations between method calls. The top row deals with the macro-structure of the overall program. The knowledge level (depth dimension) about any element within this structure can vary from fragile to moderate to deep, and is often correlated with the time on task (depth dimension), which can vary from low to medium to high.

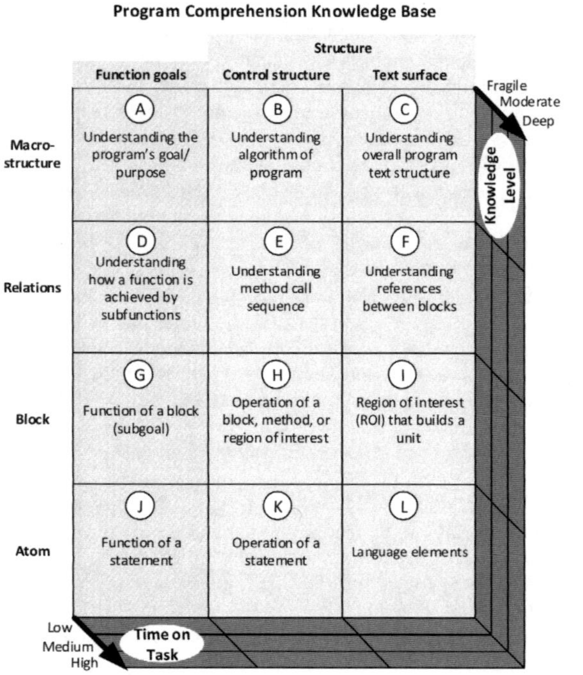

Figure 1. Depiction of the "holey quilt" theory of program comprehension, adapted from [12].

Given this perspective, a hermeneutic view of program comprehension is assumed, consisting of a dynamic process of program code interpretation that involves recurrent transitions between some overall picture down to various myopic code snippets and back to the overall picture again, successively assembling a (hopefully) coherent and consistent picture based on an interpretation of its syntax, semantics, and intention.

In the constructivist theory of human learning, humans actively construct their knowledge [39]. We thus view program comprehension as individualistic for aspects such as capacity, speed, motivation, and how mental models are constructed. Additionally, programmers possess different application-independent general and application-specific domain knowledge. Information processing habits of an individual are known as cognitive learning styles. ViSiTR provides individual and automated support for various learning model (*M:*) styles, primarily ordering or adjusting concept location (code area) visitation scope.

M:Bottom-Up: in this learning model, chunking [40] is used with the program model being correlated with a situation model [41]. Microstructures are mentally chunked into larger macrostructures as comprehension increases, as depicted by the row ordering in Figure 1 from bottom up. ViSiTR assumes a package hierarchy.

M:Top-Down: this model [42] is typically applicable when familiarity with the code, system, domain, or similar system structures already exists. Beacons and rules of discourse are used to hierarchically decompose goals and plans, as depicted by the rows in Figure 1 from top down. To automate support, ViSiTR assumes a cluster hierarchy and starts trails from the highest hierarchy.

M:Topics/Goal: when programmers are given a specific task, they tend to utilize an as-needed strategy to comprehend only those portions relevant for the task [43]. This correlates with ROIs of Figure 1. To support this simply, ViSiTR supports investigating a limited code subset via topic filtering. Topic filters (positive and negative) can be shared and support a goal (e.g., optimize memory) or apply to a specific topic (e.g., security, database access, user interface).

M:DynamicPath: in this model, ordering is oriented on actual invocation execution traces [44], which correlates with block E of Figure 1.

M:Exploratory: this model supports either discovery or analysis to confirm a hypothesis, with the learner actively deciding and controlling the navigation. It is supported by default, since a user can deviate at any time.

IV. SOLUTION APPROACH

The ViSiTR solution approach, incorporating various concepts from [1], [10], and [11], focuses on supporting the learning, understanding, and navigation of unfamiliar program source code by programmers in an automated, systematic way, without requiring additional knowledge, historical information, or human expert assistance. In alignment with the holey quilt theory, we hold the view that a programmer's view of any complex team-based software project given limited time constraints is unlikely to ever be comprehensive, leaving knowledge level "holes" from a knowledge level scale between none to deep knowledge. Thus, a major intent is to provide efficient code trails that focus on the important methods to comprehend given some limited timeframe.

A. Principles

The ViSiTR solution approach is based on these principles (P:):

P:POI: program source code locations are identified and viewed as Points-of-Interest (POI) (or knowledge entities), analogous to geographical locations in navigational systems and ROI in the holey quilt theory. Each POI is identified by some unique name, for instance in Java its fully qualified name (FQN) consisting of the concatenation of a package name, class name, colon, and method name. A POI can be viewed as a granule or information entity of interest in a knowledge "landscape", but this could be a function in non-object-oriented languages, an object method, a class, or a package.

P:POIRanking: to determine the importance of a POI (or knowledge granule) for human comprehension, they are ranked relative to each other. The algorithm MethodRank described below exemplifies such a ranking that fulfills this principle.

P:POILocality: POI locality, which can be conceptually viewed as knowledge closeness from the perspective of knowledge distance [14], is taken into consideration. This is intended to address the cognitive burden of context switches to a human when viewing program source code, by ordering POIs such that the number of unnecessary switches in a POI visitation order is reduced. The POI Distance calculation described later is an example for applying this principle.

P:Timeboxing: the amount of time available for concentrated comprehension and learning is assumed to be limited, and we assume learning is chunked into one or more sessions. Thus, the visitation time for POIs is estimated, and only the subset of priority ordered POIs that can be feasibly visited in the given timebox (deadline is midnight if no other time is provided) is first selected, and this prioritized subset is then reordered according to locality for that session. We assume that a session will not be interrupted, but that following sessions may not occur, therefore we use priority sorting first, and then resort the session subset by locality to limit jumping or thrashing.

P:CodeTrails: the recommendation service provides code trails as output with a navigation and visitation order recommendation for the POIs, whereby POI locality is taken into account. A mapping of the TSP and related planning algorithms are applied to these granules (the POIs) and the associated knowledge distance between them. While the path suggested may not necessarily be the most optimal path, it provides an efficient path nonetheless through the knowledge landscape (source code). In ViSiTR, POI visitation planning via the generated code trails focuses on invocation relationships rather than class relationships. Not following class relationships can be viewed as supported by an empirical eye-tracking study finding that "software engineers do not seem to follow binary class relationships, such as inheritance and composition" [45]. Two modes are supported: initial trail mode that generates a trail from scratch, and refactor trail mode that dynamically incorporates user actions and re-optimizes the trail based on the visited POI and the session time left. Visited POIs (including deviations) are detected via events and automatically removed from the next suggested trail.

P:User profile: user's knowledge level (e.g., familiar vs. unfamiliar) and competency level (junior vs. senior) are taken into consideration.

B. *Visualization Principles*

ViSiTR includes these visualization principles (P:V:):

P:V:Multiple 3D metaphors: The input for a model instantiation is an import of project source code. One of the first issues faced in visualization is how to best model and visualize the program code structures. Because of the lack of any standardization or norms in this area, and to support the spectrum of individual preferences, support is provided for modeling and switching between *multiple visualization metaphors*, analogous to the concept of skins. Our initial model focuses primarily on modeling and visualizing object-oriented packages, classes, and their relationships such as associations and dependencies. Initially, we support two metaphors "out-of-the-box" to provide examples of skins, and custom mappings to other objects types are possible. In the *universe* metaphor, each planet represents a class with planet size based on the number of methods, and solar systems represent a package. Multiple packages are shown by layer solar systems over one another. In the *terrestrial* metaphor, buildings can represent classes, building height can represent the number of methods, and glass bubbles can group classes into packages. Relationships are modeled visually as light beams or pipes by default.

P:V:Cockpit: analogous to an airplane cockpit, this provides information to the user on the border of the screen, and has input fields for searching for a class or method or navigating directly to a class. Buttons can be depressed to indicate preferences. A minimap on the upper right of the screen provides a high-level overview of the entire landscape and one's relative location in a small area.

P:V:Heads-Up Display (HUD): This provides a transparent glass on the screen with additional context-specific information. The type of information displayed can be changed via left/right arrows on the screen edges. The transparency level can be adjusted in the cockpit to provide a less opaque background if desired (e.g., to view code better). Various HUD screens are provided: *Tags* for automatic and manual persistent annotations/tags; *Source Code* where the program text is shown in scrollable form; *UML* where UML diagrams are dynamically generated in 2D; *Metrics* which shows text-based metrics due to the large number of possible metrics (any of which may be of interest to the user); *Project Management* to manage the metaphor, load a project record, or import a new project; and *Filtering* that provides selectors for adjusting the visibility of packages by interest.

P:V:Flythrough navigation: both mouse and keyboard support for 3D navigation (motion) in all directions is provided, as is autopilot or lockon to navigate to a specific class.

P:V:Intermixing 3D/2D: support for dynamically generated 2D UML is integrated in the 3D environment, enabling the usage of this standard notation to support the understanding of a particular area of interest.

P:V:CodeTrails: We provide the ability to capture and record a visitation trail as well as provide a playback ability, displaying the previous, current, and the next visitation node. Furthermore, the trail can be recommended and adjusted adhoc by the ViSiTR service. The HUD features can be used to view the code for any visited class.

C. *ViSiTR Solution Architecture*

ViSiTR consists of a visual client that utilizes a recommender service. The architecture for the recommender service is shown in Figure 2 and consists of four primary modules: *Cognitive Learning, Knowledge Processing, a Database Repository, and Integration.*

The *Cognitive Learning* module supports various program code learning Models, Goals, Topics, execution Traces, and visitation History. The *Knowledge Processing* module includes the components POI Prioritizer for ranking POIs, a POI Filter that filters based on visitations or topics, a Trail Estimator for visitation times, and a Trail Planner for planning the POI visitation time and order. The *Database*

Repository utilizes appropriate database types to retain metadata, knowledge, or data in forms such as a graph database for modeling the source code as a graph of nodes with properties, and a relational/NoSQL database for dealing with non-graph-related knowledge related to source code. The *Integration* module includes a Web Service API (application programming interface) for development tool integration, an Input Processor to process inputs, transformations, and events (such as a POI visit) including analysis and tracing inputs, and a Trail Generator for generating a planned trail into a desired format.

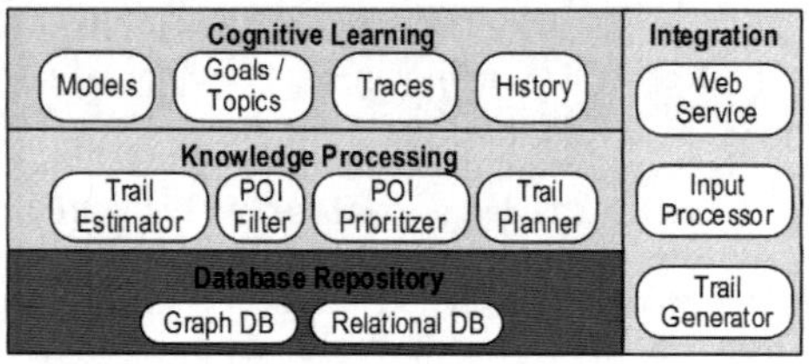

Figure 2. ViSiTR recommender service architecture.

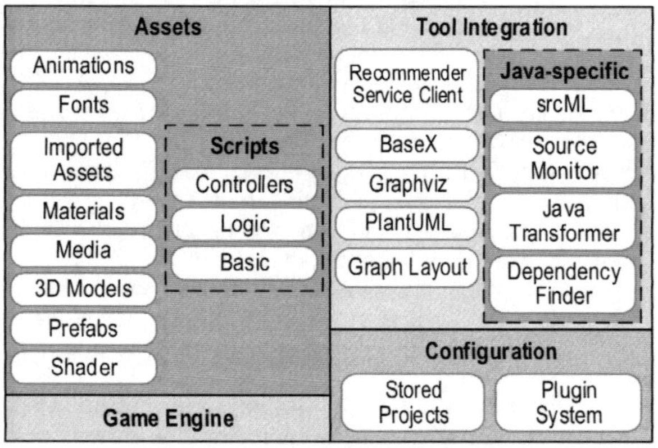

Figure 3. ViSiTR visual client architecture.

Figure 3 shows the visual client architecture which is based on a game engine and supports extensibility via plugin-ins. Assets are used by the game engine and consist of Animations, Fonts, Imported Assets (like a ComboBox), Materials (like colors and reflective textures), Media (like textures), 3D Models, Prefabs, Shaders (for shading of text in 3D), and Scripts. Scripts consist of Basic Scripts like user interface (UI) helpers, Logic Scripts that import, parse, and load project data structures, and Controllers that react to user interaction. Logic Scripts read Configuration data about Stored Projects and the Plugin System (input in XML about how to parse source code and invocation commands). Logic Scripts can then call Applications consisting of General and Java Applications. General Applications currently consist of BaseX, Graph Layout consists of our own version of the KK layout algorithm for positioning objects, Graphviz, PlantUML, and integration with for instance the recommender service as a web service client. Java Applications consist of Dependency Finder, Java Transformer that invokes Groovy scripts, Campwood SourceMonitor, and srcML. Via the designed Plugin system, additional tools and applications can be easily integrated. This was used to integrate the Recommender Service Client which invokes the Recommender Service.

D. ViSiTR Service MethodRank Calculation

With regard to *P:POIRanking*, it is assumed that in general, given no other knowledge source besides the source code and assuming limited learning time, it is more essential for the user to become familiar with the methods of a project that are used frequently throughout the code, rather than ones that are only sparsely utilized. Thus, a variation of the PageRank [20] algorithm call *MethodRank* is used to prioritize the POIs, whereby instead of webpages methods are mapped, and instead of hyperlinks, we map invocations. Thus, those methods that have the most references (invocations) in the code set are ranked the highest. While this does not consider runtime invocations (such as loops), it can be an indicator for a method with broader relative utilization and thus likely of greater interest for comprehension. One might argue that certain utility methods such as print or log would perhaps then be ranked highest, but we provide pattern matching mechanisms to include or exclude methods of no interest so the focus can be on domain-relevant methods. Or one might argue against PageRank for webpages, in that the highest ranked webpages are not necessarily the most important, since importance can be viewed differently by various individuals and their distinct perspective and intentions. However, *MethodRank* does provide an indicator of the methods that are heavily used throughout the static code and should thus be understood.

E. ViSiTR Service POI Distance Calculation

To address *P:POILocality*, an underlying assumption is that (sub)packages map vertically to (sub)layers and classes serve as a type of horizontal grouping of methods. Thus, the distance between any two POIs (given in (3)) A and B (analogous to geographical distance) is determined by their *vertical* (1) and *horizontal* (2) distance where *ld()* is a layer depth function.

$$VerticalDistance = ld(A) + ld(B) - 2(ld(common)) \quad (1)$$

For instance, given layer A = foo.a.b and layer B = foo.x.y.z (closest common package is foo) so $VerticalDistance = 3 + 4 - 2(1) = 5$.

$$HorizontalDistance = \begin{cases} 0 & if\ class(A) = class(B) \\ 1 & otherwise \end{cases} \quad (2)$$

For instance, the POIDistance between methods in the same class is 0, between classes in the same package 1.

$$POIDistance = VerticalDistance + HorizontalDistance \quad (3)$$

Depending on the implementation, a higher layer may only represent a greater abstraction (e.g., only interfaces) and not necessarily be that far in cognitive "distance".

Nevertheless, any sublayers between them should still be cognitively "closer".

F. ViSiTR Service Hamiltonian POI Visitation Trail

Assuming the principles of proper modularity and hierarchy are applied in a given project, a greater distance between POIs is equivalent to a larger mental jump. Thus, to reduce mental effort, once the distance for all pairs has been calculated, we desire the overall shortest trail that provides the visitation order for all POIs such that each POI is visited exactly once except that the starting point is also the end point, i.e., a Hamiltonian cycle. The calculation problem is equivalent to the well-known TSP.

G. ViSiTR Service Knowledge Processing

ViSiTR knowledge processing stages are shown in Figure 4 and described below.

Figure 4. ViSiTR knowledge processing stages.

1) Input Processing: the source code as text files is imported and analyzed. A list of all the POIs in the project as FQNs is determined. The layer of each POI is determined by counting the subpackage depth of its FQN. Whether the project actually utilizes a layer structure or not is irrelevant. This is then used to apply the aforementioned POI distance calculation.

2) POI Filtering: POIs already visited by this user (either in the expected order or out of order) are filtered from the set for the initial planning or replanning.

3) POI Prioritization: the aforementioned MethodRank calculation is used to create an ordered list of POIs.

4) POI Time Planning: the actual POI visitation time is stored per user. Given no prior actual POI visitation time, a default visitation time can be estimated based on a user's profile utilizing a basis time per line of code in seconds, and factors correlated with the size and complexity of the current POI method, the knowledge level (stranger or familiar), and the competency level (junior or senior). Based on the limited session time available and the set of POIs, the POI Time Planner component limits the set to an ordered list by priority that is cut off at the point that the cumlative time exceeds the timeboxed session. This reduces the size of the FQN set for locality planning and traversal.

5) POI Locality Planning: from the resulting set, the POIs are then ordered using a planner for a Hamiltonian cycle and a TSP path that takes locality into account, such that those nearby are visited first before jumping to POIs at a further distance.

6) Trail Generation: the trail with the recommended POI visit order is generated.

H. ViSiTR Client Visualization Process

Enabling visualization in the ViSiTR client consists of: 1) *modeling* program code project constructs, structures, and artifacts as well as visual objects, 2) *mapping* these to a metaphor of visual objects, 3) *extraction* via tools of a concrete project's structure (via source code import and parsing) and metrics, 4) *visualization* of the model with alternative metaphors, and 5) supporting *navigation* through the model in 3 dimensional space (simulating movement by moving the camera based on user interaction).

V. IMPLEMENTATION

To support validation of the solution concept and architecture, a prototype was realized in Java that analyzes and generates code trails given Java program code as input. For simplification, only normal class methods are considered and method overloading is ignored (a single FQN is used for methods of the same name in trails), but this could be extended via more complex method signatures to handle any method type and overloading where only parameters differentiate methods.

A. ViSiTR Service Implementation

To permit the code trail processing and generation to be location-independent (run anywhere, be it local, organization, or cloud and not necessarily burden client PCs) and easily integrate with with various integrated development environments (IDEs), the ViSiTR service was realized as a Web service. It is REST-based (Representational State Transfer), processing client events (e.g., visitations) and outputting updated trails. Thus, if larger projects require more processing, the service could be placed on a more powerful cloud-based server. The *Database Repository* used H2 as a relational and Neo4j as a graph database. To support flexible integration, the output trail format is XML.

The actual POI visitation time is tracked via navigation events received via the web service, with the table METHODRATING_TIMEONMETHOD storing MethodID, UserID, and visitation time (in seconds). POIs that were already visited (expected or not) are then filtered and removed from the replanned trail.

MethodRank requires a data structure with methods (as FQNs) and their target invocation relationships and counts. For this, static code analysis of a project's methods and invoke relationships is performed using jQAssistant 1.0.0 and the GraphAware Neo4j NodeRank plugin [47]. A Cypher query selects all Method FQNs and their invoked Method FQNs and the result is exported to a CSV file. Self-references (such as recursion) are ignored. A separate simplified graph is then created by importing the CSV file into the Static Analysis Program with FQN(Method)->INVOKES->FQN(TargetMethod) relationships in the Neo4j server. GraphAware NodeRank then provides NodeRanks (i.e., MethodRanks) for every node (Method) for the number of invocations with the NodeRank stored in each node's property (Figure 5 shows a partial graph in Neo4j). The result is retrieved via the Neo4j REST API in JSON

```xml
<?xml version="1.0" encoding="UTF-8" standalone="no"?>
<session>
  <sessionguid>f479bf2e-d8a3-484b-80eb-79d3091441f4</sessionguid>
  <user>Default</user>
  <timeboxfinishuntil>2017-02-09T23:00Z</timeboxfinishuntil>
  <filterregexinclude/>
  <executablepath>/home/debian/git/ba/sampledata/ProgramSource/Builds/Saxon.jar</executablepath>
  <sourcerootpath>/home/debian/git/ba/sampledata/ProgramSource/Saxon</sourcerootpath>
  <topicsfilepath>/home/debian/git/ba/sampledata/SERE-Topicmap.xml</topicsfilepath>
  <trailsoutputpath>/home/debian/git/ba/sampledata/trail-output/generated/trail.xml</trailsoutputpath>
  <topic/>
  <prioritizationmode>WEIGHTING</prioritizationmode>
  <userprofile>JUNIOR_ENGINEER</userprofile>
  <knowledgelevel>STRANGER</knowledgelevel>
  <history>
    <trailstep actualvisittimestamp="2017-02-09T17:30:57.718Z" suggestedvisitlocation="" suggestedvisittimestamp=""><![CDATA[net.sf.saxon.tree.tiny.TinyBuilder:characters]]></trailstep>
    <trailstep actualvisittimestamp="2017-02-09T17:32:49.590Z" suggestedvisitlocation="" suggestedvisittimestamp=""><![CDATA[net.sf.saxon.event.ProxyReceiver:characters]]></trailstep>
  </history>
  <trail>
    <trailstep suggestedvisittimestamp="2017-02-09T17:34:00.785Z"><![CDATA[net.sf.saxon.tree.tiny.CompressedWhitespace:getCompressedValue]]></trailstep>
    <trailstep suggestedvisittimestamp="2017-02-09T17:34:00.785Z"><![CDATA[net.sf.saxon.tree.tiny.CompressedWhitespace:compress]]></trailstep>
    <trailstep suggestedvisittimestamp="2017-02-09T17:34:00.785Z"><![CDATA[net.sf.saxon.tree.util.FastStringBuffer:ensureCapacity]]></trailstep>
```


Figure 7. Example ViSiTR code trail XML format.

(example shown in Figure 6). The JSON was parsed, converted to FQNs, and placed in the H2 MethodRank table.

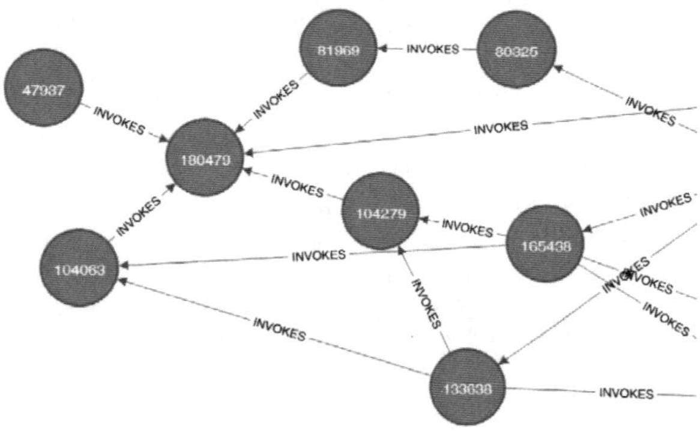

Figure 5. Example partial MethodRank graph in Neo4j.


```json
[
  {
    "id": 41,
    "labels": ["STATICANALYSIS",
      "STATIC_de.ba.Class:getString(java.lang.String)"],
    "MethodRank": 504220
  },
  {
    "id": 90,
    "labels": ["STATICANALYSIS",
      "STATIC_de.ba.GlobalSettings:getInstance()"],
    "MethodRank": 335443
  },
  {
    "id": 1801,
    "labels": ["STATICANALYSIS",
      "STATIC_de.ba.package1.Helpers:someHelp()"],
    "MethodRank": 156736
  }
]
```


Figure 6. Example NodeRank request result in JSON.

Users are differentiated by a user ID. The visitation time is adjusted by a factor (default = 0.5) to halve the estimated time if it is a senior engineer, and a factor (0.5) also if the user is already familiar with the code. All user sessions are time-boxed (default setting is termination at midnight, but any end time can be set). Once the prioritized POI list is calculated, POIs are selected in priority order to be included in the trail until the accumulated expected visitation times exceed remaining session time. The Hamiltonian path calculation is then applied on this subset.

To order the POI trail according to POI locality, the Trail Planner component integrated OptaPlanner, specifically optimizing the trail with regard to the TSP. For sufficient IDE interaction responsiveness during trail generation, the OptaPlanner solving time was explicitly limited to a maximum of 5 seconds to likely provide sufficient time for at least a solution to be found (depending on the project size, session time, and computation hardware) but not necessarily an optimum (absolute shortest path).

Figure 7 shows a sample of the XML-based code trail that is sent to the ViSiTR client, with the tags explained as follows: `sessionguid` is a unique id for the session. `user` can be a unique username for tracking. `timeboxfinishuntil` is an absolute time for the expected end time for the session. `filterregexinclude` is a regular expression for the packages to be included, if nothing is provided then all are assumed. `executablepath` is the path to the project executable. `sourcerootpath` is the path to the root of the program source files. `topicsfilepath` is a path to the file that contains topics of interest, if it is empty then all topics are assumed. `trailsoutputpath` is the location of the trails file. `topic` provides a list of the topics if given, if empty then all topics are assumed. `prioritizationmode` provides the type of trail prioritization desired. `userprofile` indicates if the user is a junior or senior engineer (relates to how fast they may comprehend code). `knowledgelevel` relates to whether the programmer is a stranger or familiar with this code project. `history` tracks the `trailsteps` visited with the actual methods visited including the `actualvisittimestamp`. `trail` provides a list of the suggested `trailsteps` in the suggested order and with the `suggestedvisittimestamp` as an absolute time.

To demonstrate the REST-based integration capability of ViSiTR recommender service within common IDE tools, an Eclipse IDE client was developed, shown in Figure 8. The upper part shows the current project, the middle part is used for starting and navigating a session, and the bottom displays the upcoming trail locations (methods). Double-clicking causes the method to be shown in the Eclipse source view.

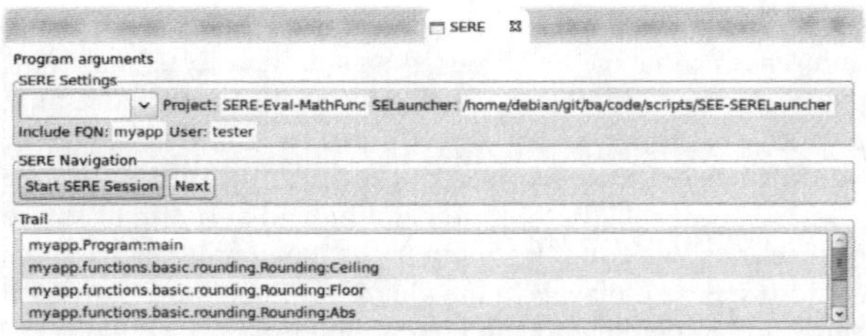

Figure 8. An Eclipse IDE ViSiTR client plugin showing a code trail retrieved from the ViSiTR service.

Code trail integration was accomplished using REST and JSON via a Unirest client invoked in a Groovy Script. The returned XML-based code trail was then parsed in the client.

B. *Visualization Client Implementation*

Existing software structures are imported and converted into a common XML-centric model. XML was selected as the primary data format to support the greatest amount of interoperability with various existing software development tools. BaseX [17] is used as an XML repository and XQuery used for queries. srcML [18] v.0.9.5 was selected to convert source code (such as Java) into XML documents and provides various code metrics. Campwood SourceMonitor v.3.5 is used because it creates code metrics across multiple programming languages. To determine dependencies such as coupling and inheritance, DependencyFinder was selected, which also provides data on code structure, dependencies, and metrics from binary Java. Furthermore, Groovy scripts were used for the integration of the various tools.

The project structure consists of the following files:

- *metrics_{date}.xml*: contains metrics obtained from tools such as SourceMonitor and DependencyFinder, which are grouped by project, packages, and classes.
- *source_{date}.xml*: holds all source code in the srcML XML format
- *structure_{date}.xml*: contains the project structure and dependencies, obtained from tools such as DependencyFinder.
- *swexplorer-annotations.xml*: contains user-based annotations with color, flag, and text including manual tags placed by a user and automatic tag patterns placed automatically where matches occur.
- *swexplorer-metrics-config.xml*: contains thresholds for metrics that support visual differentiation.
- *swexplorer-records.xml*: contains a record of each import of the same project done at different times with a reference to the various XML files such as source and structure for that import. This permits changing the model to different timepoints as a project evolves.

Additional HUD screens include: search, filtering (e.g., inclusion/exclusion of packages and classes), tagging, and a minimap (right corner) for orientation.

Minimum PC specifications are a CPU supporting Streaming SIMD Extensions 2 and DX9 GPU with Shader Model 2.0. Recommended is a DX11 GPU and 1GB video RAM. Java 7 and .NET Framework 3.5 or higher are required.

VI. Case Study

In prior work [10], validation of the various learning models was performed: *M:Top-Down* and *M:Bottom-Up* utilizing the package hierarchy, *M:Topics/Goal* which utilizes filtering of packages and classes by names, *M:DynamicPath* which prioritizes methods that appear in various runtime traces by both how often (frequency) within a trace and that they occur within different trace files, and *weighted mode* that uses configurable parameter weighting inputs. Furthermore, the empirical study utilized program code obfuscation to limit any intuitive mental model creation or semantic ordering, assessing its effectiveness and efficiency for program comprehension knowledge navigation within unfamiliar program code (i.e., unfamiliar presented knowledge), while retaining the equivalent program structure.

This case study thus focuses on validating the viability of the 3D visualization solution and its scalability. For this study, two Java projects were used: the Saxon XSLT 2.0 and XQuery processor consisting of 331K lines of code (LOC), 17K methods, and 1655 classes in 38 packages with 53K inter-class dependencies. The ViSiTR client ran on a Fujitsu Lifebook AH531with Windows 10 Pro (x64) 2.4GHz i5-2430M 8GB RAM and SSD disk.

A. *ViSiTR client visualization*

In the universe metaphor, Figure 9 shows the loaded Saxon project consisting of 53 solar systems (without applying any filters to hide any packages or classes), and showing all dependencies. This can be navigated via 3D fly-thru and visual responsiveness for 3D fly-thru navigation showed no issues. In Figure 10, dependencies were deselected and solar systems become recognizable and distinguishable based on package names. In Figure 11, a single package, the net.sf.saxon package is shown as a solar system including internal package dependencies. Figure 12 shows the source code view in the HUD for the net.sf.saxon.Platform class (class name is labeled on a square in the middle of the planet, these are also used for tagging by stacking the squares in customizable colors) with the selected object in white. Planet orbits are in turquoise and dependencies as purple light beams. Planet size can vary based on some metric like number of methods.

Within the terrestrial metaphor, Figure 13 shows the loaded Saxon project with 53 packages represented by glass bubble cities viewed here from above (dependencies are hidden). Figure 14 shows the source code view in the HUD for the net.sf.saxon.Platform class (class name is labeled on a stackable square of tags on the top of any building), with classes in a package grouped within a glass city bubble and dependencies shown as purple pipes. If desired, building size can be set to vary based on some metric such as number of methods. Both metaphors were found to be easily navigable via 3D fly-thru, and scalability, performance, and responsiveness for the client showed no issues once the project was loaded.

Code trail navigation is shown in Figure 15 for the universe metaphor, with the current location shown on the trail strip above the cockpit menu. On the right of this strip, the current and upcoming two POIs are shown, and on the left, a play/pause button and a rewind and forward button are available for trail navigation. The slider on the left side center adjusts the speed with which one is transported between POIs by the automated trail guidance. Figure 16 shows the HUD in source code view with the terrestrial metaphor. Figure 17 shows the HUD in the UML view with a dynamically generated class diagram showing the dependencies between classes in 2D and those in 3D can be seen in the background.

B. 3D Code Trail Evaluation

The performance and scalability of the ViSiTR prototype was measured. The ViSiTR service was run with VirtualBox version 5.1.14 in a virtual machine image of Debian 8 x86, single CPU, and 1.7GB RAM hosted on a Fujitsu Lifebook AH531with Windows 10 Pro (x64) 2.4GHz i5-2430M 8GB RAM and SSD disk. The host was also used to run the ViSiTR client.

To provide a contrast to the relatively large Saxon project, which includes two dynamic traces - one with 100K lines and the other with 17,497 lines, we also measured a custom small project called MathFunc consisting of 5 packages, 6 classes, 22 methods, and 37 dependencies without any trace input.

Table I compares the measured performance (wall clock time in seconds (s) or hours (h)) for various activities with the MathFunc and the Saxon project. Client-side project preparation, involving external tools and including code parsing, dependencies, and metrics was 15 secs for MathFunc and 300 secs for Saxon. Server-side project preparation was 400 secs for MathFunc and 6 hrs for Saxon. This project preparation time, which among other things involves source code parsing, dynamic trace analysis, and static graph call invocation analysis, is usually incurred once for stable projects. Client project loading delays on the Unity game engine were 5 secs for MathFunc and 220 secs for Saxon. All objects are created on initial loading before providing navigational capability. Trail creation, which involves TSP-based POI prioritization, was 15 secs for MathFunc and 110 secs for Saxon. Trail optimization, which sends a user event and requests a code trail optimization (adaptation) based on the data, was 12 secs for MathFunc and 65 secs for Saxon.

TABLE I. ACTIVITY PERFORMANCE

Activity	*MathFunc*	*Saxon*
Client-side project preparation	15s	300s
Server-side project preparation	400s	6h
Client project loading latency	5s	220s
Trail creation	15s	110s
Trail optimization	12s	65s

In our previous empirical study in C-TRAIL [10] using obfuscated code, we had focused on small projects to support reconstruction of the code structure to avoid straining cognitive abilities. For larger projects using code trails, ViSiTR performance showed the code trail service to be the primary bottleneck both in preparation and at runtime. While this service was run locally on the notebook, the service could instead be placed in the cloud to utilize more powerful hardware and reduce the 6h preparation time.

While we were able to successfully prototype the code trail recommendation with 3D visualization, larger projects created noticeable performance issues, although not in the visualization but rather in the recommendation service. In future work, we plan to address the initial prototype's performance issues via profiling, platform tuning, algorithm optimizations, dedicated server hardware for the service, and enabling background loading of visual objects on the client for very large projects. These are needed to enable a comprehensive empirical study to determine acceptance and improved comprehension by programmers.

Understanding the project requires a programmer to visualize the overall structure in abstractions in their mind; UML also requires some cognitive processing within its metaphor of boxes and lines. Even if visual metaphors provide an additional cognitive burden requiring further processing, in our opinion based on results from our previous study they also provide an additional motivation incentive that can offset this burden for various user groups (such as students) and keep them interested in the project code longer while still viewing real source code.

VII. CONCLUSION AND FUTURE WORK

This paper described the ViSiTR approach to code trail visualization, describing its theoretical background in the holey quilt theory and cognitive learning models. The solution concept was described and implementation details of a prototype provided. A case study evaluated its viability for code trail visualization and its scalability for larger projects.

As an automated tutor and recommender system in the program code comprehension space, ViSiTR applies a conceptual mapping of geographical POIs to code locations, considers the locality or knowledge closeness of such granules, and applies TSP to an unfamiliar knowledge landscape consisting of program code. It incorporates MethodRanking as a variant of PageRanking and granular distance in the form of POI locality. Furthermore, it recommends a knowledge navigation order by generating a code trail as a Hamiltonian cycle. While the ViSiTR prototype showed the feasibility and viability of 3D visual code trails, the evaluation also showed that optimizations of the prototype implementation are needed to improve its scalability and permit empirical studies with larger projects.

Our approach does not consider extraneous artifacts related to program comprehension, such as configuration files and documentation, since these typically must be analyzed and provided by humans. In future work we will consider providing a way to include this information.

Future work includes prototype performance and scalability optimization and testing with workstations, a comprehensive empirical study with different projects and user groups, support for additional programming languages, support for displaying different and directed relationship categories and cardinalities, and additional visualization paradigms. Application of the elaborated ViSiTR solution principles to other domains beyond software engineering could provide beneficial knowledge navigation guidance and recommendations in form of a trail for other unfamiliar knowledge landscapes.

ACKNOWLEDGMENT

The author thanks Claudius Eisele for his assistance with the implementation of the service and Dominik Bergen for the client implementation and evaluation.

REFERENCES

[1] R. Oberhauser, "ReSCU: A Trail Recommender Approach to Support Program Code Understanding," Proceedings of the Eighth International Conference on Information, Process, and Knowledge Management (eKNOW 2016). IARIA XPS Press, 2016, pp. 112-118.

[2] G. Booch, "The complexity of programming models," keynote talk at AOSD 2005, Chicago, IL, March 14-18, 2005.

[3] A. Deshpande and D. Riehle. "The total growth of open source," In: IFIP International Federation for Information Processing. Vol. 275. 2008, pp. 197–209.

[4] C. Jones, "The economics of software maintenance in the twenty first century," Version 3, 2006. [Online]. Available from: http://www.compaid.com/caiinternet/ezine/capersjones-maintenance.pdf 2017.02.23

[5] R. Minelli, A. Mocci, and M. Lanza, "I know what you did last summer: an investigation of how developers spend their time," Proc. IEEE 23rd International Conference on Program Comprehension, IEEE Press, 2015, pp. 25-35.

[6] L. Kappelman, "Some strategic Y2K blessings," Software, IEEE, 17(2), 2000, pp. 42-46.

[7] PayScale, "Full List of Most and Least Loyal Employees." [Online]. Available from: http://www.payscale.com/data-packages/employee-loyalty/full-list 2017.02.23

[8] M. Robillard, W. Maalej, R. Walker, and T. Zimmermann, Recommendation Systems in Software Engineering. Springer, 2014.

[9] F. P. Brooks, Jr., The Mythical Man-Month. Boston, MA: Addison-Wesley Longman Publ. Co., Inc., 1995.

[10] R. Oberhauser, "C-TRAIL: A Program Comprehension Approach for Leveraging Learning Models in Automated Code Trail Generation," Proceedings of the 11th International Conference on Software Engineering and Applications (ICSOFT-EA 2016), SciTePress, 2016, pp. 177-185.

[11] R. Oberhauser, C. Silfang, and C. Lecon, "Code structure visualization using 3D-flythrough," Proc. of the 11th International Conference on Computer Science & Education (ICCSE), IEEE, 2016, pp. 365-370.

[12] T. Clear, "The hermeneutics of program comprehension: a 'holey quilt' theory," ACM Inroads, 3(2), June 2012, pp.6-7.

[13] A. Bargiela and W. Pedrycz, Granular computing: an introduction. Springer Science & Business Media, vol. 717, 2012.

[14] Y. Qian, J. Liang, C. Dang, F. Wang, and W. Xu, "Knowledge distance in information systems," J. of Systems Science and Systems Engineering, 16(4), 2007, pp. 434-449.

[15] M. Rahman and M. Kaykobad, "On Hamiltonian cycles and Hamiltonian paths," Information Processing Letters, 94(1), 2005, pp. 37-41.

[16] E. Lawler, J. Lenstra, A. Kan, and D. Shmoys. The traveling salesman problem: a guided tour of combinatorial optimization. Wiley, New York, 1985.

[17] J. Singer, R. Elves, and M.-A. Storey, "NavTracks: Supporting Navigation in Software Maintenance," Proc. Int'l Conf. on Software Maintenance, 2005, pp. 325–334.

[18] M. Kersten and G. Murphy, "Mylar: A degree-of-interest model for IDEs," Proc. 4th international conf. on aspect-oriented software development, ACM, 2005, pp. 159-168.

[19] D. Cubranic, G. Murphy, J. Singer, and K. Booth, "Hipikat: A project memory for software development," Software Eng., IEEE Trans. on, 31(6), 2005, pp. 446-465.

[20] T. Zimmermann, A. Zeller, P. Weissgerber, and S. Diehl, "Mining version histories to guide software changes," Software Eng., IEEE Trans. on, 31(6), 2005, pp. 429-445.

[21] M. Robillard and G. Murphy, "FEAT: A tool for locating, describing, and analyzing concerns in source code," Proc. 25th Int'l Conf. on Software Eng., IEEE, 2003, pp. 822–823.

[22] M. Robillard and G. Murphy, "Automatically Inferring Concern Code from Program Investigation Activities," Proc. 18th Int'l Conf. Autom. SW Eng., IEEE, 2003, pp. 225-234.

[23] M. Robillard, "Topology Analysis of Software Dependencies," ACM Trans. Software Eng. and Methodology, vol. 17, no. 4, article no. 18, 2008.

[24] D. Mandelin, L. Xu, R. Bodik, and D. Kimelman, "Mining Jungloids: Helping to Navigate the API Jungle," Proceedings of PLDI, Chicago, IL, 2005, pp. 48–61.

[25] R. Holmes, R. J. Walker, and G. C. Murphy, "Approximate structural context matching: An approach to recommend relevant examples," IEEE Transactions on Software Engineering 32(12), 2006, pp. 952–970.

[26] M. Bruch, T. Schaefer, and M. Mezini, "Fruit: IDE support for framework understanding," Proc. 2006 OOPSLA workshop on eclipse technology eXchange, eclipse '06, ACM, 2006, pp. 55–59.

[27] M. Goldman and R. C. Miller, "Codetrail: Connecting source code and web resources," Journal of Visual Languages & Computing, 20(4), 2009, pp.223-235.

[28] M. Yin, B. Li, and C. Tao, "Using cognitive easiness metric for program comprehension," Proc. 2nd Int. Conf. on Softw. Eng. and Data Mining, IEEE, 2010, pp. 134-139.

[29] B. Cornelissen, A. Zaidman, A. Van Deursen, L. Moonen, and R. Koschke, "A systematic survey of program comprehension through dynamic analysis," Softw. Eng., IEEE Trans. on, 35(5), 2009, pp.684-702.

[30] A. Teyseyre and M. Campo, "An overview of 3D software visualization," Visualization and Computer Graphics, IEEE Transactions on, vol. 15, no. 1, (2009, pp. 87-105.

[31] A. Kashcha, "Software Galaxies." [Online]. Available: http://github.com/anvaka/pm/ 2017.02.23

[32] R. Wettel and M. Lanza, "Program comprehension through software habitability," in Proc. 15th IEEE Int'l Conf. on Program Comprehension, IEEE CS, 2007, pp. 231–240.

[33] R. Wettel et al., "Software systems as cities: A controlled experiment," in Proc. of the 33rd Int'l Conf. on Software Engineering, ACM, 2011, pp. 551-560.

[34] J. Rilling and S. P. Mudur, "On the use of metaballs to visually map source code structures and analysis results onto 3d space," in Proc.. 9th Work. Conf. on Reverse Engineering, IEEE, 2002, pp. 299-308.

[35] P. McIntosh, "X3D-UML: user-centred design, implementation and evaluation of 3D UML using X3D," Ph.D. dissertation, RMIT University, 2009.

[36] A. Krolovitsch and L. Nilsson, "3D Visualization for Model Comprehension: A Case Study Conducted at Ericsson AB," University of Gothenburg, Sweden, 2009.

[37] C. Schulte, "Block Model: an educational model of program comprehension as a tool for a scholarly approach to teaching," Proc. Fourth International Workshop on Computing Education Research, ACM, 2008, pp. 149-160.

[38] C. Schulte, T. Busjahn, T. Clear, J. Paterson, and A. Taherkhani, "An introduction to program comprehension for computer science educators," Proc. 2010 ITiCSE Working group reports (ITiCSE-WGR '10), ACM, 2010, pp. 65-86.

[39] J. Novak. Learning, creating, and using knowledge. Lawrence Erlbaum Assoc., Mahwah, NJ, 1998.

[40] S. Letovsky, "Cognitive processes in program comprehension," Journal of Systems and Software, 7(4), 1987, pp. 325-339.

[41] N. Pennington, "Stimulus structures and mental representations in expert comprehension of computer programs," Cognitive psychology, 19(3), 1987, pp.295-341

[42] E. Soloway, B. Adelson, and K. Ehrlich, "Knowledge and processes in the comprehension of computer programs," In: The Nature of Expertise, A. Lawrence Erlbaum Associates, 1988, pp. 129-152

[43] J. Koenemann and S. Robertson, "Expert problem solving strategies for program comprehension," Proc. of the SIGCHI Conference on Human Factors in Computing Systems, ACM, 1991, pp. 125-130.

[44] B. Cornelissen, A. Zaidman, A. Van Deursen, L. Moonen, and R. Koschke, "A systematic survey of program comprehension through dynamic analysis," Softw. Eng., IEEE Trans. on, 35(5), 2009, pp.684-702

[45] Y. Guéhéneuc, "TAUPE: towards understanding program comprehension," Proc. 2006 conf. Center for Adv. Studies on Collaborative research (CASCON '06) IBM Corp., 2006.

[46] L. Page, S. Brin, R. Motwani, and T. Winograd, "The PageRank citation ranking: bringing order to the Web," In:World Wide Web Internet And Web Information Systems 54.1999-66, 1998, pp. 1–17.

[47] GraphAware. Neo4j NodeRank. [Online]. Available from: https://github.com/graphaware/neo4j-noderank 2017.02.23

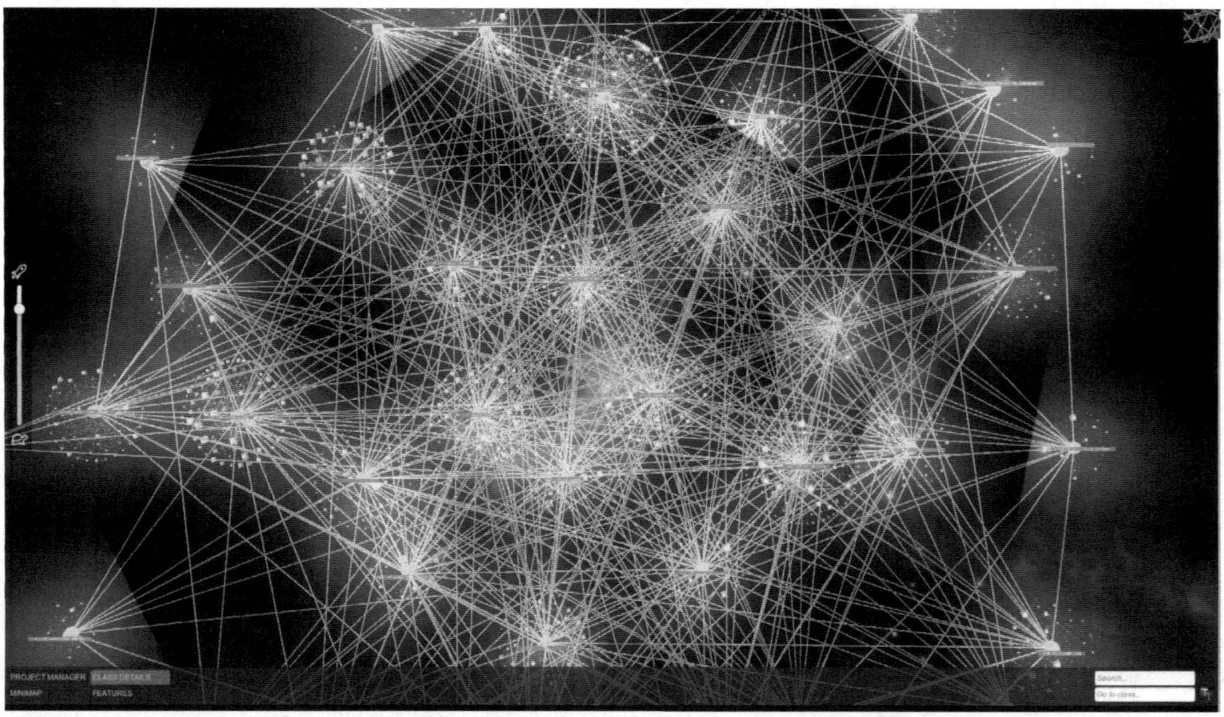

Figure 9. Saxon project with dependencies shown in the ViSiTR universe metaphor.

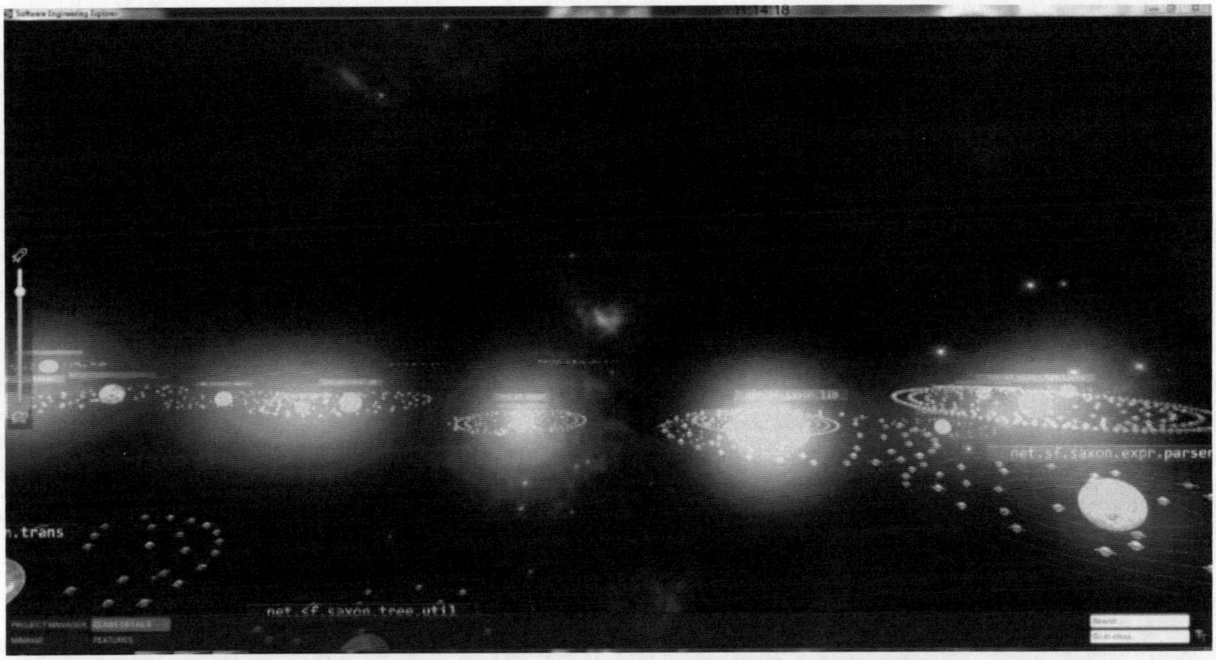

Figure 10. Saxon project without dependencies shown in the ViSiTR universe metaphor.

Figure 11. The net.sf.saxon package shown as an isolated solar system with internal dependencies in the ViSiTR universe metaphor.

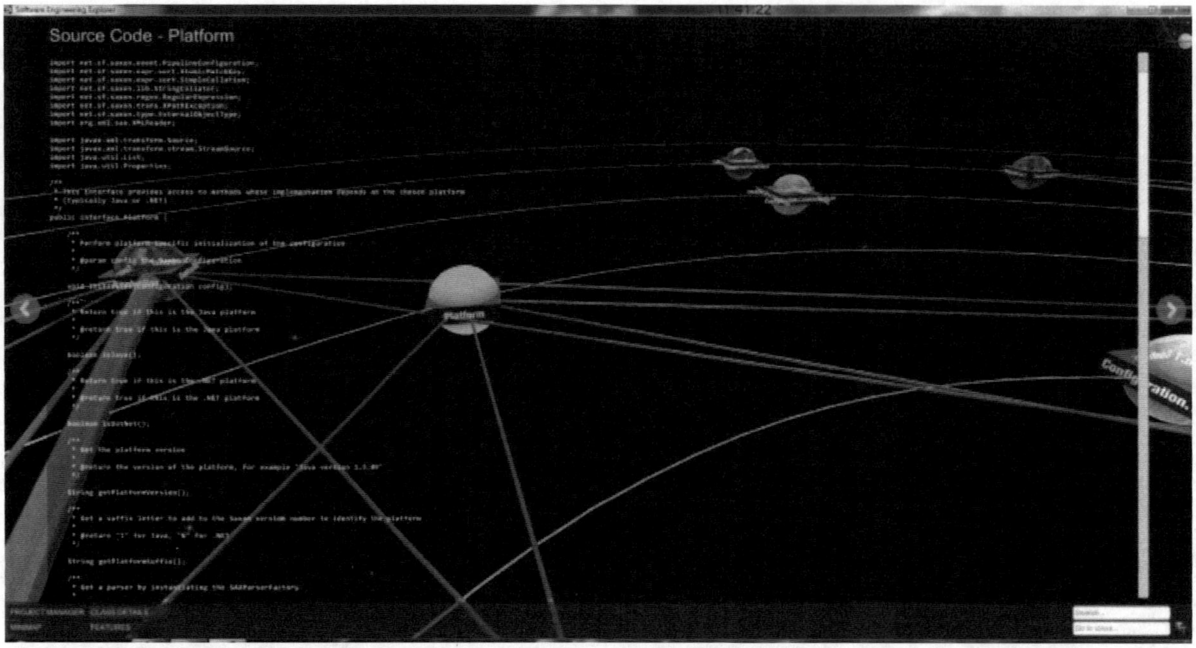

Figure 12. HUD source code view of the saxon Platform class as a planet with dependencies in the ViSiTR universe metaphor.

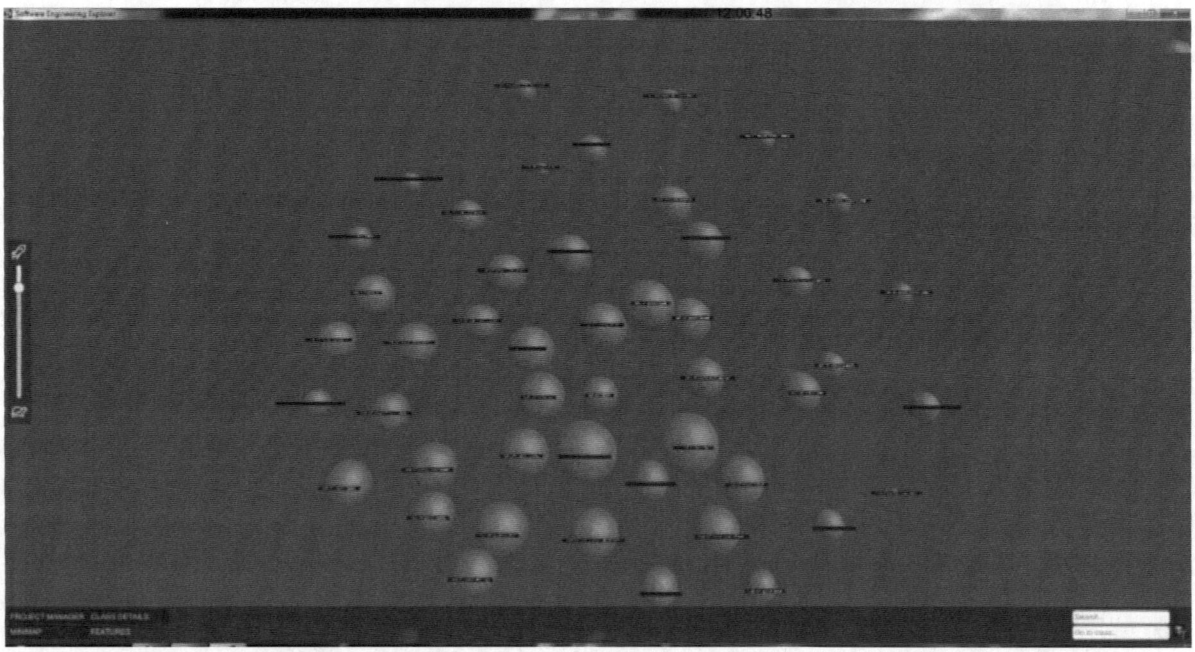

Figure 13. The Saxon project with dependencies shown in the ViSiTR terrestrial metaphor.

Figure 14. HUD source code of saxon Platform class as building in glass city bubble with dependencies in ViSiTR terrestrial metaphor.

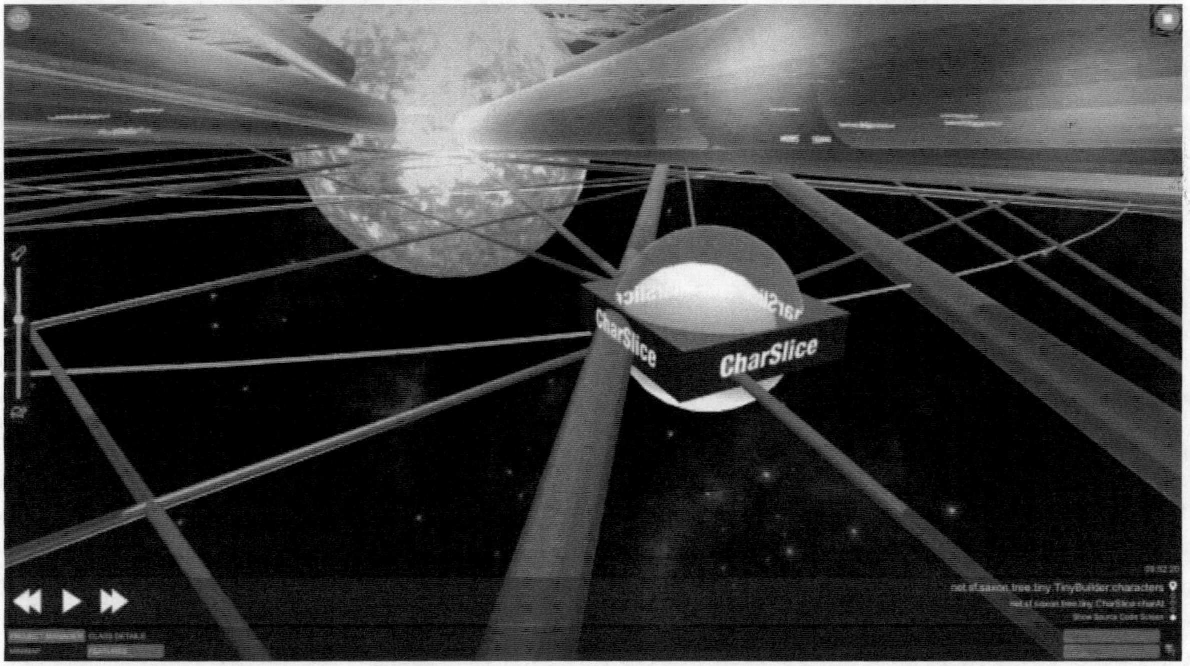

Figure 15. Visitation of CharSlice during automated code trail navigation in the ViSiTR universe metaphor.

Figure 16. Visitation of ProxyReceiver showing HUD source code view during automated code trail navigation in the ViSiTR terrestrial metaphor.

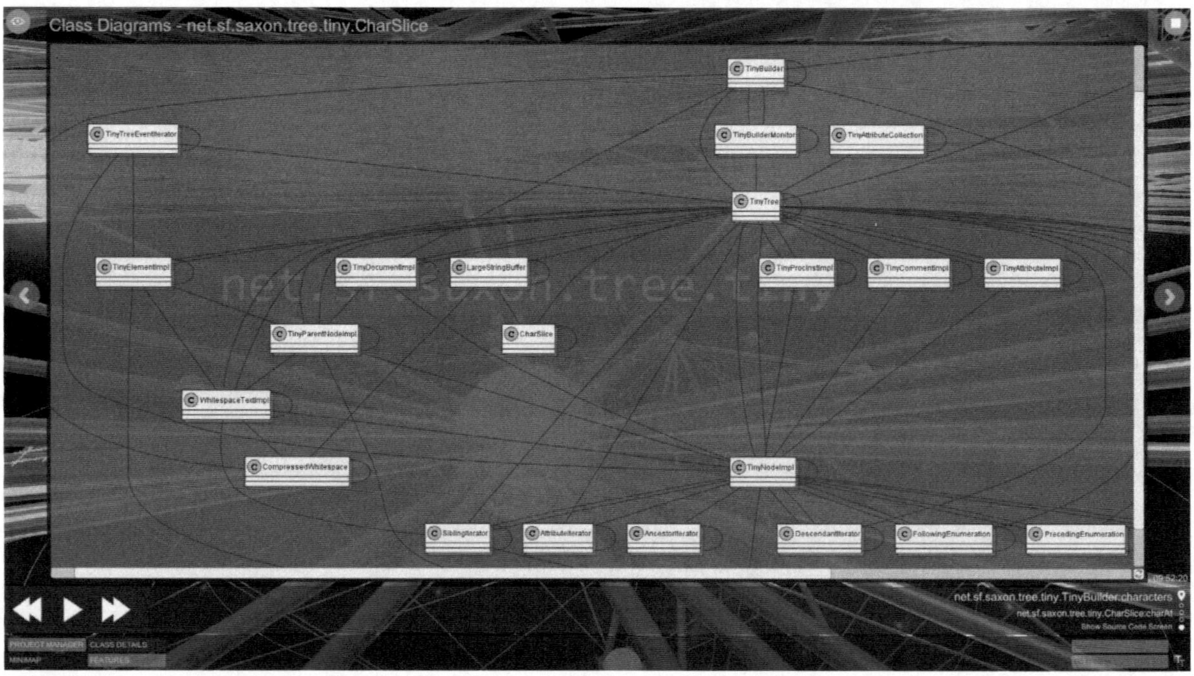

Figure 17. Dynamically generated UML class diagram showing dependencies for CharSlice during code trail visit in the ViSiTR universe metaphor.

Interface Construction, Deployment and Operation – a Mystery Solved

Alexander Hagemann
Hamburger Hafen und Logistik AG
Bei St. Annen 1
20457 Hamburg, Germany
Email: hagemann@hhla.de

Gerrit Krepinsky
Hamburger Hafen und Logistik AG
Bei St. Annen 1
20457 Hamburg, Germany
Email: krepinsky@hhla.de

Christian Wolf
Hamburger Hafen und Logistik AG
Bei St. Annen 1
20457 Hamburg, Germany
Email: wolf@hhla.de

Abstract—**The increasing digitalization pressure within the industry resulted in a continuously growing demand on IT supported business processes over the past decades. This pressure changed singular mainframe applications into large, distributed application landscapes usually operated in a 24/7 hours mode. Simultaneously, this enforced increased support demands to the application management as well as further application integration requirements during development. Therefore, decoupled, robust and supervise able applications are required. Since the behavior of these applications is determined solely by their communication behavior on interfaces, it becomes apparent that interfaces are of overall significance within such distributed application landscapes. But in our experience, interfaces usually do not get the required attention during design, construction, deployment and operation, which is in contrast to their importance. Instead, only technical reports like, e.g., syntactical descriptions, are usually given and important functional as well as operational aspects have been omitted. This leads to unstable and unnecessary complex interface implementations threatening the 24/7 hours mode of operation. To address the aforementioned issues, this paper contributes a new comprehensive approach on interface design, construction, deployment and operation for distributed application landscapes. This includes guidelines for a functional interface design and interface migration patterns for deploying application interfaces into a 24/7 hours running environment.**

Keywords*–*interface; interface aspects; communication requirements; communication services; messaging; communication error handling; business process; interface design; interface versioning; interface migration; interface operation.

I. Introduction

In recent years, growing business demands enforced an increasing information technology (IT) support of many business processes. To rule the resulting functional complexity within the IT, several applications are usually necessary. A direct consequence of this fragmentation is the distribution of business processes over applications, which have to communicate with each other in order to fulfill the requirements of the business processes. This communication requires well defined interfaces between applications due to functional [1] as well as technical reasons.

Generally, the design of application interfaces is a difficult and critical task [1], [2], [3], since the behavior of applications belonging to the class of reactive systems, i.e., applications responding continuously to the environment, is determined by their interfaces only [4]. Consequently, badly designed interfaces may lead to functional misbehavior and may propagate internal application problems directly to communication partners [5], [6].

Wrong assumptions during the interface design phase about functional domain behavior and communication technologies can have devastating effects with respect to interface operations and the integration of further applications into the application landscape [7], [8]. Furthermore, interfaces have relatively long life cycles and their implementations are usually costly to modify. A change of an interface specification always requires either its backward compatibility to previous interface versions, or a change of all applications implementing the interface.

Operating a large application landscape in a 24/7 hours mode imposes additional challenges concerning interface deployment and operation because all applications implementing a new interface must be launched into an already running environment [8]. Once this has been done, interface supervision and communication error detection by the application management are also necessary to enable the agreed operational availability of the application landscape [9].

To overcome the above mentioned restrictions, this paper gives an overall overview on all aspects concerning interfaces. It extends the approach for functional interface design and interface transition into operation presented in [1] by adding further important aspects like communication technology selection and transmission protocol definition, including error handling and runtime supervision. Further examples are given presenting an implementation of the proposed transmission protocol and illustrating the functional interface design approach in more detail.

Beginning with a review on related work in Section II, Section III presents some interface theory and resulting aspects necessary to be considered for a successful interface design. By introducing typical requirements enabling a founded selection of an appropriate communication technology in Section IV, Section V deals with a transmission protocol offering further communication services thus enabling a reliable and robust communication. Further details on error handling and communication supervision are described in Section VI, followed by a conrete implementation example of the transmission protocol in Section VII.

Thereafter, Section VIII gives an introduction and comparison of different design approaches for the construction of a functional interface specification, followed by an industrial example of a concrete interface design in Section IX. Finally, Section X deals with the interface launch into an already running application landscape.

II. Related work

The increased distribution and complexity of business functionalities enforces IT personal responsible for complex application landscapes to use well-designed integration solutions. Due to the ever increasing dependencies between applications on functional, semantic, technical and operational levels, a holistic integration approach is necessary to successfully manage changes within application landscapes [8]. Thus, the design of interfaces becomes the key for successful application integration.

Within the literature, a lot of information exists regarding different aspects of interfaces like performance, reliability, routing etc. Typically, these documents either deal with technical protocols only and omit functional interface properties, like, e.g., the Internet Protocol (IP) [10], the Hypertext Transfer Protocol (HTTP) [11], File Transfer Protocol (FTP) [12], Java Messaging Service (JMS) [13], Remote Method Invocation (RMI) [14], Advanced Message Queueing Protocol (AMQP) [15] and the Blink Protocol [16], or are bound to specific functional domains like the Financial Information eXchange [17], the FIX Adapted for Streaming [18] or the various United Nations Electronic Data Interchange for Administration, Commerce and Transport (UN/EDIFACT) protocols [19]. But none of them gives explicit guidelines for an interface design. Other common approaches like service oriented architectures (SOA) [20] or the representational state transfer (REST) [21] protocol represent rather general architectural styles. Both are more suitable giving architectural guidelines for application design, than for the construction of concrete interfaces.

More specific work on interface design has been done by Henning [2] and Bloch [3] defining principals and high level processes for good interface designs. Both authors argue that it is hard to design good interfaces due to the required understanding of the underlying functional context. Additional aspects on interface design have been introduced by Iridon [22] to decouple application implementations from domain models [7], using a canonical model, as well as Bonati et al. [8] for supporting different interface versions in parallel during operations.

However, none of these works gives a holistic view on interface design, construction, deployment and operation as presented in this paper. This includes specific guidelines for a functional interface design as well as interface migration patterns for deploying application interfaces into an environment operating 24/7.

III. Interface basics

In order to design an appropriate interface, the general structure of an interface must be considered. Once this has been done, it will become obvious which information must be provided to define an interface. Drilling down into an interface, which is located in the application layer in the Open Systems Interconnection model (OSI model) [23], [24], typically, a three layered structure, as shown in Figure 1, becomes visible. Each of these layers has a dedicated important purpose that can be summarized as follows:

- *functional layer*: this topmost layer is responsible for the functional semantics of the information exchanged. Using the analog of natural speech, the functional layer defines the meaning of words spoken.

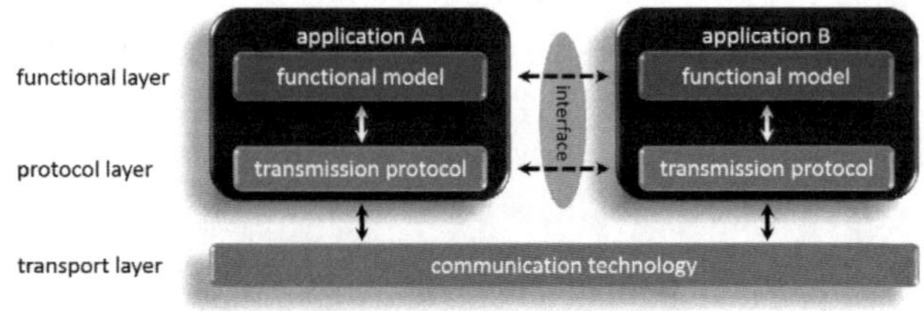

Figure 1. The different layers of an interface. Dotted arrows denote virtual connections within each layer. The communication takes part using the connections denoted by solid arrows. Note that the functional and the protocol layers are located within the application layer of the OSI model, while the transport layer typically encapsulates all layers below the application layer [23], [24].

- *protocol layer*: Within this layer the transmission protocol used to exchange the information is defined. Similar to natural speech, the protocol layer represents the language spoken, e.g., English.
- *transport layer*: Here, the necessary physical transportation of the information is carried out. This layer correlates to the signal transfer using sound waves in a manner similar to natural speech.

Each of these layers communicates virtually with its counterpart located at the other application. Therefore, a layer physically passes the information to its underlying layers until the information is physically transported to the other application. At this point, the information is passed upwards up to the corresponding layer. Only if both sides within one layer use identical functional models or transmission protocols, respectively, communication will take place. Otherwise, the communication is broken.

Given the layered structure of an interface, different aspects arise, which must be considered during the design, implementation, integration and operational phases of an interface life cycle. These aspects focus on different issues and enable the development of robust interfaces. All aspects are independent with respect to each other, focusing on a specific property an interface must satisfy.

A. Functional aspect

While two or more applications are communicating with each other over an interface, the applications assume different functional roles, called *server* and *client*, respectively. An application is called *server* with respect to an interface if it is responsible for the business objects, business events and related business functions that are exposed to other applications through this interface. If business objects and business functions of different business processes are affected, the necessary messages may be combined into a single interface.

Providing an interface is equivalent to defining an interface contract [8] that must be signed by an application in order to communicate with the *server*. The interface may support synchronous and asynchronous communication as well as message flows in both directions, i.e., sending and receiving messages.

Note that this definition deviates slightly from the commonly used client-server definition where the *server* offers a service

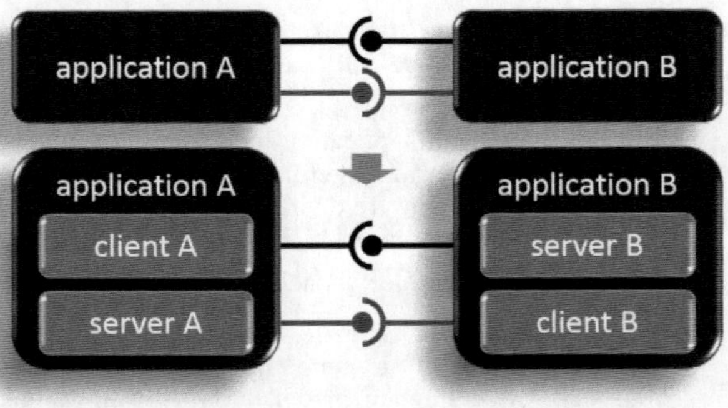

Figure 2. Applications assuming multiple roles simultaneously, i.e., one part of the application serves as a *server* while another part serves as a *client*, as indicated in the top part of the figure. Note that both supported interfaces are not identical.

which can be accessed by *clients* via a synchronous request-reply communication protocol only [25]. Because synchronous communications couples *server* and *client* tightly at runtime, asynchronously based communication should generally be preferred, avoiding these disadvantages [9].

A *client* is an application consuming an interface provided by a *server*. Despite the fact that the interface contract is initially defined by the *server*, a common agreement on the contract is made when the *client* connects to the *server*. Thereafter, none of the participating applications may change the interface contract without agreement of the other party.

Often an application assumes multiple roles with respect to different interfaces concurrently, i.e., the application can be *server* and *client* simultaneously, see Figure 2. It is important to emphasize that this behavior is valid with respect to different interfaces only while for a single interface, the roles of the participating applications are always unambiguous.

B. Semantical aspect

The semantical aspect focuses on the kind of information that may be exposed by the *server* via an interface. Generally, any internal implementation detail of the *server*, i.e., the server model, must never be exposed on an interface. Instead, the information exposed must always be tied to the underlying business processes, thus binding the interface implementation to the domain model [7], [8].

Integration within an IT application landscape requires the decoupling of business and software design due to different responsibilities. In other words the domain model and its related implementations in the *server* and *client* usually have different life cycles, which must be decoupled to reduce the dependencies between business and software development. Therefore, an integration model, linked to the domain model, should be used on interfaces [9], [22], which decouples their implementations from the domain model. Additionally, the integration model conceals all internal application models and details thus decoupling *server* and *client* from each other, as shown in Figure 3.

An interface itself consists of a set of messages, containing *business objects* and *business events* only [26]. This set of exposed information is naturally restricted due to the responsibility of the *server*, i.e., only the *business objects* or *business events* the *server* is responsible for may be communicated via the interface.

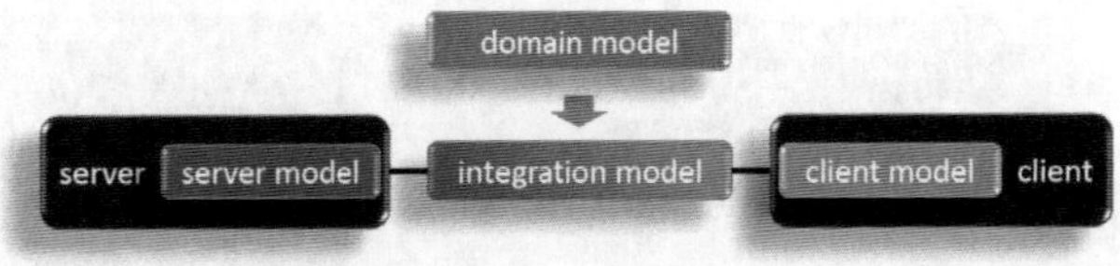

Figure 3. Decoupling the domain model from its implementation using an integration model. Note that different *server* and *client* implementation models are also decoupled in this way [22].

C. Technical aspect

Exchanging information via an interface using *messaging* [9], i.e., by sending and receiving messages, results in specific communication styles depending on the thread behavior of the sender. The resulting communication style should be indicated on the interface using different message types as follows:

- *asynchronous communication*: a message of type *Notification* is sent and the thread resumes execution.
- *synchronous communication*: a message of type *Request* is sent and the thread execution is stopped until a message of type *Reply* has been received.
- *communication supervision*: a message of type *Error* is used to asynchronously report communication errors, that cannot be handeled by the application itself, to the application management. Introducing *Error* messages as an own type emphasizes their semantical difference to *Notifications*.

This set of message types leads to a technical view of an interface. Depending on the functional role of an application, not all message types may be send by all applications. Instead, valid message types sent by an application depend on its functional role with respect to the interface considered.

As depicted in Figure 4, a *server* may send *Notification* and *Reply* messages only. The former message type represents a business event communicated to the environment of the *server*. The *Reply* answers a synchronous *Request* of the *client*. A *server* may not send a *Request* to a *client* due to the functional responsibility of the requested data; doing this would reverse the roles of *server* and *client* and therefore, this *Request* must be part of another interface provided by the former *client*.

The *client* may send *Notifications* and *Requests* to the *server*. Both message types represent accesses to services provided by the *server*. A *Reply* may not be send by a *client* to a *server* because a *client* has no functional responsibility with respect to the interface considered. Again, doing this would reverse the roles of *client* and *server* between both applications. The fourth message type, the it Error message, may be send by all applications in case of communication problems only. This message type is by no means part of a functional interface and send to dedicated communication channels only. In fact, *Error* messages are part of the interface to the application management for supervising ongoing IT operations.

D. Dynamical aspect

An important aspect of an interface is its dynamic behavior describing all valid message sequences on the interface. Since

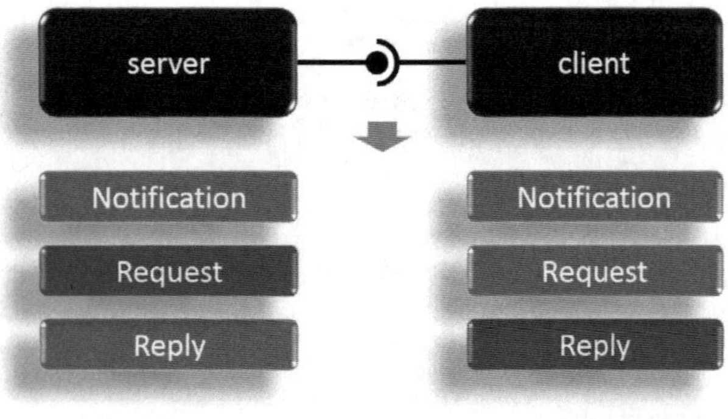

Figure 4. Representation of the message types that a *server* or a *client* may send. Message types depicted in green are allowed to send while red message types may only be received. The *Error* message type has been omitted due to its pure technical nature.

all messages received are processed within a specific context inside the application, there exist important constraints with respect to the message sequence. Thus, a message received out of the defined sequence will not be processed by the application, instead this will result in an error.

Consequently, the dynamic behavior must be described using an appropriate description. Using sequence diagrams of the Unified Modeling Language (UML) [27] is not sufficient for this case, since they describe specific communication examples only. Especially runtime problems, e.g., race conditions, cannot be described holistically using sequence diagrams. Instead, it is strongly recommended to use finite state machines [28], which allow a complete description of the dynamic behavior, as shown in the example of an interface between a container device and a terminal control system depicted in Figure 5.

E. Nonfunctional aspect

Interfaces must be able to provide enough context to execute the desired parts of the business processes within an application since they separate the application from its environment and determine its behavior [4]. Besides the functional and semantical aspects imposed on an interface, this context contains nonfunctional design aspects also, covering robustness, performance and understandability. An application

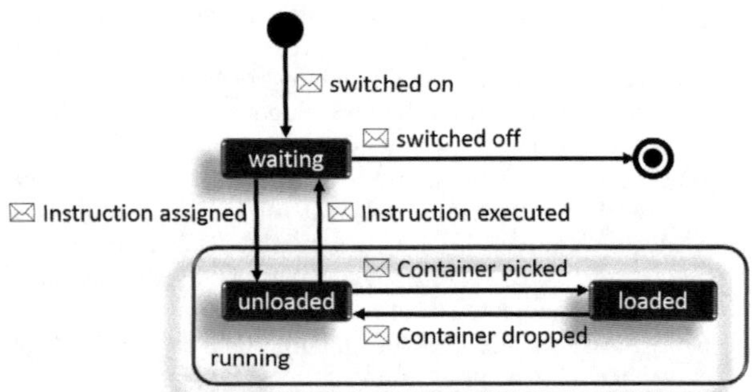

Figure 5. Example of a simplified state machine describing the dynamic behavior of an interface.

will correctly execute the business processes only if these nonfunctional aspects are fully satisfied.

The *robustness* of an interface is crucial with respect to the stability of the overall application landscape. Poorly designed interfaces may propagate internal application errors during runtime, thus causing severe damage within other applications of the application landscape [2], [5].

Robustness of interfaces is achieved by

- *functional coherence*, i.e., assigning a unique functional responsibility to each application according to the underlying domain model thus avoiding inconsistent states of business objects within the application landscape,
- a *non-transactional behavior* between applications [29] thus dropping complex and time consuming coordination problems resulting from the underlying commit protocols [30],
- *integrated content constraints*, i.e., using functional appropriate range restrictions of field values, and
- an *independent field structure* where the content of fields must not depend on the content of other fields within the same message.

Obviously, interfaces must satisfy the required *performance* too. Otherwise, business processes will not work correctly since required business functions may not be executed in time [4]. Using

- a *minimalised interface design*, i.e., a design containing a minimal set of messages only without imposing undue inconvenience for the clients [2] and
- a purely *asynchronous communication* style thus technically decoupling the *client* from the *server* at runtime [31]

covers performance issues at design time already.

Furthermore, well designed interfaces must have a strong and documented relation to the underlying business context thus being easier to learn, remember and use correctly [2], [7]. This will enhance the interface cost efficiency over time due to the enhanced acceptance of the interface within the development teams. This *understandability* can be achieved through

- a functional consistent *message naming schema*, where message names must be functionally meaningful and short to support a clear and understandable integration model on the interface and
- its binding to the application model using an appropriate adapter, see Figure 6 for details.

F. Operational aspect

Usually, each interface requires the usage of a specific infrastructure depending on the used communication technology, e.g., a web server in case of REST over HTTP or a JMS server. To ensure the correct usage of an interface the required infrastructure, its deployment and the communication channel topology must be defined also. The latter one defines the general communication structure, i.e., broadcast or point-to-point communication [9].

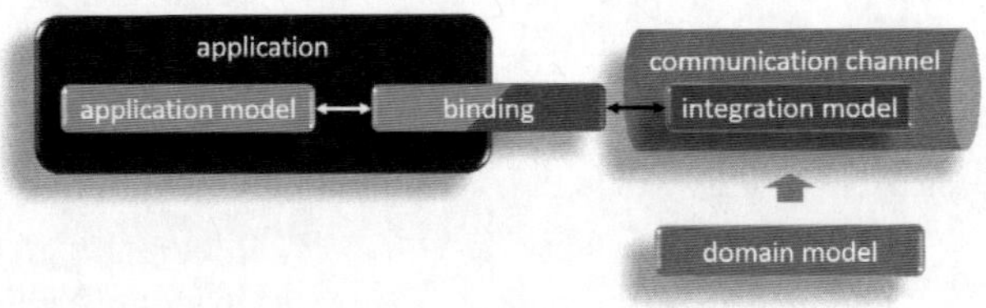

Figure 6. Binding of the integration model to a given application model. Note that the integration model is aligned to the domain model. The required adapter, implementing this binding, can either be a part of the application itself or be realised as a seperate component.

G. Interface components

Given the different aspects presented so far, each of them describing a different important issue with respect to interfaces, the necessary components for a complete interface specification can be derived:

- *message description*: Syntactical descriptions of all messages exchanged over the interface.
- *semantic description*: The meaning of messages on the interface must be specified, i.e., their functional behavior within the comprehensive business process. This description must include the meaning of all individual message fields.
- *dynamic description*: The dynamic behavior of the interface must be fully specified. This specification includes all possible message sequences and the behavior of the applications in case of errors.
- *infrastructure description*: A description of the necessary infrastructure must be provided.
- *quantity description*: The non-functional performance requirements for the interface must be described.

It is important to notice that an interface specification is a signed bilateral contract, which may be changed by mutual agreement of all participating parties only [8]. This contract is represented by the set of artifacts as described above, so none of the artifacts given there may be missed.

IV. Communication Technology

In order to enable communication between applications an appropriate communication technology is necessary. Communication technologies like, e.g., HTTP, FTP, JMS or RMI, have specific transmission properties and often require specific middleware components to fulfill common communication tasks, like, e.g., routing or address resolution [23]. Specific requirements, derived from the typical 24/7 hours mode of operation, guide the selection of appropriate communication technologies.

A. Communication requirements

Large application landscapes often require a set of different communication technologies to satisfy all requirements of IT operations and to fulfill the underlying service level agreements. In order to keep the IT operation costs low, only a few and proven mainstream technologies should be considered for the complete application landscape [8]. Suitable communication technologies typically satisfy an appropriate subset of the following requirements depending on communication properties defined by the enterprise itself.

1) Coupling: The degree of coupling between applications is one of the most important requirements concerning communication technologies. Since modern application landscapes typically involve applications from a wide set of different software vendors, a loose application coupling is usually required [8], since applications

- use different software technologies, e.g., programming languages,
- assume different runtime behaviors, e.g., the number of threads or processes used by an application is completely transparent and independent from all other applications and
- have different life cycles, i.e., they should be replaceable during runtime if they implement the same interface contract without imposing technical interferences to other applications [9].

Loose coupling is directly supported by the communication technology if an asynchronous communication style is used [9], [22]. Furthermore, this requirement usually has a direct impact on maintenance and support costs of an application landscape.

2) Stability: In modern application landscapes things will happen during runtime that cannot be foreseen at development time [5]. Introducing stability into the application landscape reduces the effects of such faults and consequently lowers support costs. Stability is gained by preventing the propagation of failures over application boundaries. A common pattern to achieve this goal is a decoupling of applications during runtime [5], [6], i.e., all applications must technically run completely independ from each other.

3) Flexibility: Applications and middleware can be deployed to different physical or logical machines without having more effort than configuration costs [32], i.e., IP adresses, port numbers etc. are specified in appropriate configuration files. Therefore, the required middleware components of the communication technology have to be flexible enough in order to ensure this arbitrary application distribution. Note that this flexibility usually has a direct impact on maintenance and support costs for application landscapes.

4) Reliability: To minimize support costs for application landscapes the communication must be reliable, i.e., the communication technology has to be able to guarantee the delivery of information. Note that this guarantee usually does not comprise a guaranteed time slot within the information will be delivered to the receiver. Additionally, the requested guarantee of delivery holds for common problems like network breakdown, system breakdown, disc crash etc. only but usually not for disaster scenarios destroying the complete infrastructure. Failing to deliver information to the receiver leads to communication faults that must be cleared by the application management. Consequently, this requirement has a direct impact on the amount of fault clearings.

5) Performance: The communication technology has to be fast enough to handle the predicted information throughput thus guaranteeing the performance specified in the underlying service level agreements. It must also be able to deal with information burst situations during communication. Furthermore, while communicating with another application, the sender should not be delayed by the communication technology, i.e., sending an information is completely decoupled from its transmission. Note that more specific performance requirements depend on individual application requirements and therefore cannot be specified here.

6) Monitoring: To supervise the communication between applications, access points should exist in the communication lines [9]. Using these access points, the application management can

- monitor occurred communication errors,
- monitor the load of the communication channels,
- directly read all information exchanged by the applications for debugging purposes and
- insert test information into the communication channels.

This supports a reduction of the fault clearing time thus reducing the support costs for the application landscape. Additionally, new applications must be integrable into existing IT monitoring tools without further adjustment. In case an application has a technical problem, e.g., a database crash, it should be possible to communicate the problem to the application management using special communication channels [9].

7) Costs: The application communication should be standardized in order to minimize development and operational costs for application integration [8]. It should also be possible to encapsulate most parts of the communication resulting in a minimal code invasion of the application software [9].

In order to minimize the efforts during system integration tests, access to the communication technology should be easily replaceable by mocks [22]. This will minimize software license costs because middleware components of the communication technology must not be used on the various environments used during development and integration testing stages [32].

8) Technical security: If something goes wrong, security has to provide a degree of confidence that the application landscape can remain in a state of normal operation [33]. Communication technology, being one part that ensures the technical security of the application landscape, has to protect the authenticity and integration of all messages exchanged [33]. Additionally, an automated communication recovery is typically required after an application or communication failure in order to minimize the failure recovery time.

B. Selecting a communication technology

Adequate communication technologies have to be selected depending on the communication requirements to be satisfied. These requirements are usually determined by given service level agreements. For example, requirements like *Coupling* and *Stability* typically exclude the use of synchronous communication technologies like RMI [14] or HTTP [11]. Other requirements, e.g., *Performance*, either demand very specialized communication technologies like the Blink Protocol [16] or prevent specific technologies such as shared databases [9].

In contrast, using communication technologies explicitly supporting asynchronous messaging as integration style like, e.g., JMS [13] or AMQP [15] commonly satisfy all requirements. Since messaging is considered to be the best application integration approach [9], it is usually best suited for most integration purposes.

V. Transmission protocol

While the selected communication technology enables exchange of information between applications, further communication services like, e.g.,

- robust communication,
- support of synchronous and asynchronous communication in parallel,
- business process logging,
- support of enterprise integration patterns [9],
- automated reconnect behavior and
- ongoing communication supervision

are typically required in order to support a 24/7 hours maintenance of an application landscape. These communication services are typically not fully provided by the communication technology; instead they must be implemented at the application layer of the OSI model [23], [24]. Consequently, an implementation of these communication services requires an additional transmission protocol layered on top of the communication technology, see Figure 1 for details.

This section introduces such a transmission protocol based on messaging to provide the above mentioned communication services. Using messaging to transmit information between applications requires sending and receiving of structured messages using specific communication channels identified by *destination* names. This messages are exchanged using communication channels addressed by unique destination names. A message consists of a header containing some necessary meta-information to safely transmit the message between applications and a body containing the functional payload data [9].

A. Message header

The meta-information within the header is organized in a set of fields and represents an important part of the transmission protocol. Consequently, a message sender has to use these header fields as described in the following.

1) Message ID: This field contains a unique identification of the message. It is typically provided by the messaging infrastructure itself, see, e.g., [13].

2) Message type: Each message send by an application must belong to one of the four message types *Notification*, *Request*, *Reply* or *Error*, as described in Section III.

3) Message reply to: Generally, using messaging leads to an asynchronous communication behavior between applications. In order to implement synchronous communication, i.e., the sender stops and resumes processing after receiving the reply message, the *Request-Reply* and *Return Address* patterns [9] can be used. A request message, which is always of message type *Request*, has to use this field, where the name of the reply destination must be inserted. The receiver of the request will send its answer to the given reply destination specified in this field.

4) Message correlation ID: In case of synchronous communication, the requester can identify the answer, which always has the message type *Reply*, to his *Request* using the correlation ID. According to the *Correlation Identifier* pattern [9], the sender of the reply must include the original message ID of the request as correlation ID in the reply. The field must not be used in all other cases. Note that the sender of the request must store the message ID of the request in order to compare it to the correlation ID of the *Reply*.

5) Message expiration: This field is used for the *Message Expiration* pattern [9]. If the sender specifies a *time to live* for a message, the messaging infrastructure will deliver the message to the receiver only if it is within the *time to live*. If the *time to live* is expired and the message couldn't be delivered to the receiver, the message will be destroyed in the messaging infrastructure. In case of *Requests*, which usually have a timeout [5], the *time to live* should always be set equal to the timeout, which will decrease the load for the message receiver.

6) Message name: The field message name contains the name of the message. Message names should be meaningful and unique.

7) Message sender: The field message sender contains the name of the sender of the message. This name must be unique within the application landscape and should be as precise as possible. For example, a naming schema could follow an inverse URL like naming style where single parts of the name are separated by capital letters.

8) Error text: The field error text is used for *Error* messages only and contains the exception text, see Section VI for further details.

9) Message version: In case of distributed applications problems always occur while operating different interface versions in parallel. In order to deal with future changes of an interface, the *Format indicator* pattern [9] is used, where each message carries its corresponding interface version number in this field. All applications should have an external editable list of version numbers, called *compatibility list*, for each implemented interface that defines all valid interface versions. The receiver of a message compares the version of a received message with its *compatibility list* and calculates the compatibility state. The following compatibility states exist:

- *true*, if the version of the message is contained in the *compatibility list*
- *false*, in all other cases.

If the compatibility state is true, the message will be processed, otherwise the message will be redirected to an error message channel, as described in detail in Section VI.

Note that a standard downward compatibility behavior as given by some communication technologies like, e.g., HTTP [11] cannot be used at the protocol layer because functional semantics may change significantly between different interface versions thus leading to an incorrect functional behavior. Using an explicit *compatibility list* avoids these semantical problems.

10) Sequence number: Using the patterns *Resequencer* and *Message Sequence* [9], the receiver can get a stream of out-of-sequence messages back into the original sequence. Therefore, the sequence number field can be used, containing a unique sequence number. Each sender generates his own stream of unique sequence numbers; they need not to be unique across different applications. If the range of numbers is exceeded, the sequence will start with the lowest number again.

Note that messaging infrastructures typically guarantee to keep the sequence of all messages sent via a **single** destination only. There is **no** guarantee, however, if multiple destinations between sender and receiver are used in parallel to transmit messages.

11) Trace ID: The field trace ID can be used in distributed systems to trace an activity over individual application boundaries. A common usage of the trace ID is, e.g., for logging purposes within the business processes.

B. Message body

The body of a message contains the functional payload, i.e., its content is the reason why this message has been sent. The content must be a valid structure fulfilling the following issues:

- In order to avoid technical dependencies based on, e.g., compiler issues, only text messages should be used.
- The content of the body should follow a formal document structure like, e.g., the Extensible Markup Language (XML) [34].
- This structure must allow a complete formal syntactical validation of the message, e.g., the XML Schema Definition Language (XSD) [35] in case of XML.
- Only the Universal Time Coordinated (UTC) format may be used for content concerning time. The time format used must follow the international norm ISO 8601 including the time zone designator [36].
- Binary data must be converted using, e.g., a Base64 encoding [37].

For the required encoding, i.e., the transformation between a byte sequence and a unicode string, to transmit a text document, usage of the Universal Character Set Transformation Format (UTF) UTF-8 or UTF-16 is strongly recommended.

VI. Communication Error Handling

During interface operations, failures may occur within the communication of applications. These communication problems can be categorized into *connection problems*, resulting from infrastructure issues in the transport layer, or *communication problems*, resulting from message computation failures in the functional and protocol layers, respectively. Each failure category requires its own error handling procedures, which are described in the following subsections.

A. Connection problems

Connection problems usually result from issues within the communication technology, preventing an application from sending or receiving information and thus interrupting its communication. Consequently, connection errors always represent severe problems, which require immediate activities by the application management. Since the application management can solve connection errors at runtime, applications should support their activities through an automated reconnect behavior to the messaging infrastructure as follows.

Connection failures can occur at any point in time and are signaled by the communication technology to the application. Once this has been done, a configurable timer, called *connection timeout*, must be started by the application. After this *connection timeout* expires, the application must signal the connection error to the application management and disconnect itself from the infrastructure of the communication technology,

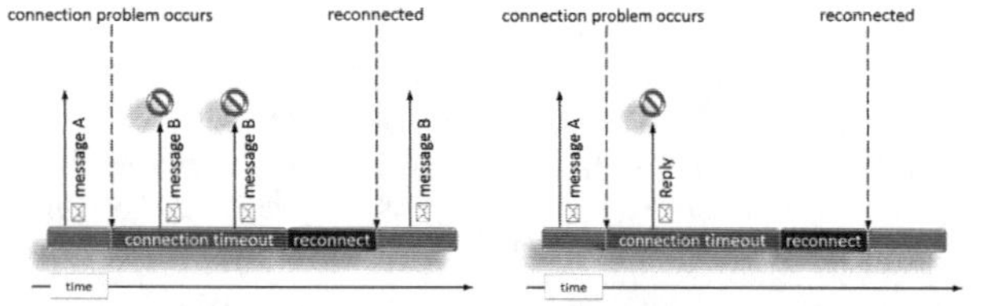

Figure 7. The left figure shows the behavior for *Notification* and *Error* messages, here commonly denoted as messages. Once the connection is broken, the connection timeout starts. If the connection remains broken the application disconnects from the middleware infrastructure, once the connection timeout has been reached. After reestablishing the connection, the message is sent. For *Reply* messages only, as shown in the right figure, nothing happens after the first attempt to send the *Reply* message.

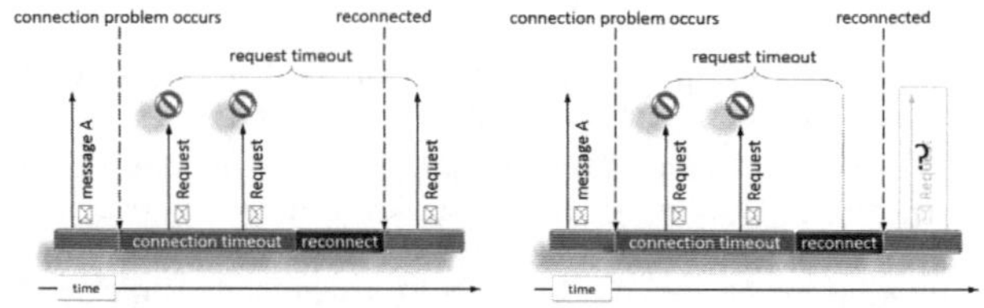

Figure 8. Timeout behavior in case of a *Request*. If the connection is reestablished within the request timeout time, see left figure, the message is sent after reestablishing the connection. If the connection cannot be reestablished within the request timeout, the application decides if the *Request* message will be dropped or resend, as shown in the right figure.

followed by a reconnect attempt to it. The advantage of this behavior, which shall be repeated forever until the connection has been successfully reestablished, is, that changes within the network infrastructure may be executed during application runtime.

The *connection timeout* must be stopped immediately if the connection error has been solved within the time period spanned by the *connection timeout*. No reconnect attempt will occur in this case.

If an application fails to send a message due to connection errors, the following behavior must be adopted by the application, depending on the message type sent:

- *Notification* and *Error*: Periodically retry to send the message until it has been sent successfully.
- *Request*: Periodically retry to send the message until it has been sent successfully or a *request timeout*, see below, has been reached. In the latter case, the application decides all further communication behavior, e.g., if the *Request* message will be dropped or resend.
- *Reply*: Drop the message.

The rationale behind the deviating behavior for *Reply* messages is, that reply destinations may be temporary destinations which may have ceased to exist and thus will never reappear, see, e.g., [13]. Figure 7 visualizes the reconnect behavior in case of *Notification* or *Error* messages on the left side. After the *connection timeout* has been exceeded, the application automatically disconnects from the communication system and tries to reconnect itself to it. Once the connection has been reestablished, the message is send. In contrast, a *Reply* message is dropped once sending the message fails, as shown on the right side of Figure 7.

For *Request* messages, the behavior depends on the relationship between the request timeout, and the time necessary to reestablish the connection, as shown in Figure 8. The *Request* will only be send once the connection has been reestablished if the *request timeout* has not been exceeded.

B. Communication problems

Functional errors resulting from message computation should always be handled by the application itself. All other kinds of exceptions are based on either configuration or programming errors and usually cannot be corrected by the application during runtime. Therefore, this kind of errors must be signaled to the application management.

C. Communication supervision

In order to inform the application management promptly, the protocol layer uses a mechanism based on the *Control Bus* pattern [9]. If necessary, *Error* messages are sent to separate destinations, supervised by the application management.

1) Error message construction: Like other message types, *Error* messages consist of a header and a body section. The header contains a set of header fields as described in Table I, while the body content depends on the cause of the *Error* message. If the latter has been triggered by another message, the body of the *Error* message should contain a copy of the content of the original triggering message. Otherwise, the body of the *Error* message will be empty.

2) Error destinations: All messages that are either

- syntactically incorrect, i.e., those failing the syntactical validation, or
- out-of-sequence, i.e., those received unexpected from the defined message flow of the interface, or
- have an insufficiently defined set of message header fields, or
- have an incompatible version number

must result in an *Error* message sent to a destination called, e.g., *invalid message channel*.

In case of synchronous communication being used between applications, crack propagation due to blocked threads or slow responses must be prevented using a timeout pattern [5]. Whenever a sender sends a *Request* to another application, the sender will wait for a configurable amount of time, denoted *request timeout*, to receive the *Reply*. If the *request timeout* exceeds, the sender converts the *Request* message into an *Error*

TABLE I. Header fields and their valid content for an *Error* message

field name	**field content**
message ID	the message ID
message type	*Error*
message name	*invalid message error* or *timeout message error* or *fatal error*, where the message name used depends on the cause of the error.
message sender	name of the application sending this message
error text	a short and meaningful text describing the error
version	the version number of the interface

message and sends it to a destination called, e.g., *timeout message channel*.

For severe errors that cannot be handled by the application itself, e.g., connection problems or broken database connections, an *Error* message should be sent to a destination called, e.g., *fatal error channel*. Obviously, this can be done in case of *connection problems* only, if the connection to the application management still exists. Note that these kind of failures typically threaten the running state of applications.

D. Communication monitoring

All errors reported to one of the error destinations, i.e., *invalid message channel*, *timeout message channel* or *fatal error channel*, have to be analyzed by the application management to supervise the application landscape. In other words, the error destinations act as part of the *Control Bus* pattern [9].

The required activities of the application management in conjunction with the error destinations is described in the following subsections. For a better overview, a short tabular summary of the most important facts is given at the end of each subsection, consisting of

- the priority necessary to react to an *Error* message,
- the strategy necessary to deal with an *Error* message,
- the environment, i.e., development, test or production stages [32], within most *Error* messages will be produced and
- the information when the *Error* message should be deleted from the error destination.

1) Invalid message channel: Messages sent to this destination mainly occur due to syntactical or dynamic problems, so each message within this destination is important. None of the errors will directly threaten the running state of an application but business processes may degrade depending on their design.

All errors reported to the *invalid message channel* are based on programming or process design errors and cannot be solved during runtime. Instead, they must be delegated to the second level support. Exceptions are *Error* messages due to incompatible interface version numbers. In this case, the application management should first check whether the interface configurations of the involved applications are correct, second, try, if convenient, to up- or downgrade one of the participating applications to a new version that supports the required interface version and third, inform the second level service if none of the before mentioned activities leads to the desired behavior. Once an *Error* message has been analyzed, it should be directly deleted from the *invalid message channel*. It is expected that the main load for the *invalid message channel* occurs within the test stage. Normally, no *Error* messages should be produced in the production stage, otherwise this indicates misbehavior due to unsufficient test cases.

TABLE II. Monitoring of the invalid message channel

summary	
production priority	medium, may effect execution of business processes
evaluation strategy	based on single error messages
main error occurances	test stage
error message deletion	immediately after analysis by application management

2) Timeout message channel: An individual *Error* message within the *timeout message channel* has no further meaning and can be ignored, but the history of the message amount within the *timeout message channel* is very important. The rationale behind this property lies in the unique source of *Error* messages within the *timeout message channel*: in case of synchronous communication the *Request* has not been replied within the *request timeout* by the targeted application. For a single *Error* message this behavior is not problematic, but large amounts of errors indicate either severe load problems within the target application of the *Request* or problems with the communication infrastructure used for sending the *Request* and *Reply*. The running state of the requesting applications is not threatened, but the problem may influence the business processes.

All messages within the *timeout message channel* should be analyzed in real time per targeted application. It is recommended that this analysis should result in a graphical illustration projecting the number of *Error* messages in the *timeout message channel* over time to indicate behavior trends of the targeted applications. If certain thresholds are exceeded, the application management should have a closer look to the targeted application and the corresponding communication infrastructure.

Messages exceeding a configurable amount of time, e.g., one hour, within a *timeout message channel* should be automatically deleted. Failing this will result in resource allocation problems within the corresponding communication infrastructure. It is expected that the main load for the *timeout message channel* occurs in the production stage since these errors typically occur during unexpected load scenarios.

TABLE III. Monitoring of the timeout message channel

summary	
production priority	low, serves as a general health status indicator of applications
evaluation strategy	based on multiple error messages
main error occurances	production stage
error message deletion	after a given time frame of, e.g., one hour

3) Fatal error channel: Errors within this destination can be categorized as either severe programming errors, which must be handled by the second level support or resource errors, e.g., missing table space or wrong port numbers, that can be handled by the application management directly. Once an *Error* message has been analyzed, it should be directly deleted from the *fatal error channel*. It is expected that the load for the *fatal error channel* occurs equally in the test and production stages.

TABLE IV. Monitoring of the fatal error channel

summary	
production priority	high, immediate action necessary
evaluation strategy	based on single error messages
main error occurances	test and production stages
error message deletion	immediately after analysis by application management

Figure 9. The JCA framework can be used in any Java application. A provider specific JMS client has to be included in the application classpath.

VII. Example: Implementation of an Integration Framework

Based on the recommendation for the communication technology given in Section IV, a Java based integration framework has been developed at the Hamburger Hafen und Logistik AG (HHLA) supporting a standardized integration. The framework, which is based on JMS [13] satisfies the transmission protocol and communication error handling requirements described in Sections V and VI, respectively. This section gives an overview about the resulting implementation, which currently guarantees a robust communication within the HHLA production environment since three years.

A. *Communication adapter framework*

The Java Communication Adapter (JCA) framework is organized by two modules, core and gateway, to support the required communication services, see Figure 9 for an overview. It is packaged as Java Archive (JAR) to be easily deployed and reused while integrating applications into the HHLA application landscape. In case of products, which cannot be modified directly, or applications using different programming languages, appropriate adapter have been introduced to technically integrate applications by reusing this framework.

1) Core module: This module encapsulates the transport layer, see Figure 1, i.e., it is responsible for establishing a robust connection to the underlying communication technology. Therefore, the standard transmission protocol JMS [13] has been used, implemented by a JMS provider. The JCA supports all JMS providers that are compatible to the JMS Specification, version 1.1 [13]. It was developed and tested with two different JMS providers, ActiveMQ [38] and SwiftMQ [39], the former one representing an open source implementation and the latter being a commercial product.

As main functionality, the core module of the JCA establishes the connection to the JMS server and extends the standard JMS communication behavior to handle connection and communication problems as described in Section VI.

When *connection* or *communication problems* occur, they are directly reported to the corresponding error message channel, which are supervised by the application management. Broken connections are automatically detached by the core module once the configurable *connection timeout* has been reached and reinitialized immediately, until the connection has been successfully reestablished. Additionally, a thread and timeout handling has been realized to support synchronous and asynchronous communication in parallel via standard JMS. Furthermore, the core module constructs the JMS message itself using the Session.createTextMessage() method of the JMS standard application programming interface and sets the corresponding JMS message header fields *JMSMessageID*, *JMSType*, *JMSReplyTo*, *JMSCorrelationID*, *MessageName*, *MessageSender*, *MessageError*, *MessageVersion* and *TraceID*, according to the message type being send. Note that all header fields starting with *JMS* represent standard JMS header fields that always exist, while all other header fields have to be added using the appropriate message.set<Type>Property() method, where <Type> denotes one of, e.g., String, Long, etc.

When receiving JMS messages, the header fields are read and provided to the gateway module to handle extra communication services like business process logging. All transmitted messages are logged with the message header field *TraceID*, which can be used for error analysation in correlation with the related business process.

2) Gateway module: As shown in Figure 10, the *CommunicationService* is the central interface containing all relevant operations to integrate applications. It offers the following principal communication services:

- Connection handling: *start*, *stop* and *isStarted*
- Create messages: *getMessageFactory*
- Report errors: *reportError*
- Send messages: *sendNotification* and *sendRequest*
- Receive messages: *registerReceiver* and *unregisterReceiver*

The gateway module, encapsulating the protocol layer of Figure 1, extends the functionality of the core module by mapping Java objects onto XML representations and vice versa while sending and receiving messages, respectively. This marshalling and unmarshalling is realized by the Java Architecture for XML Binding (JAXB) framework, which is part of every Java Runtime Environment (JRE) [40]. Additionally, the required message header fields and their content are determined and given to the core module.

The robust communication of the core module is extended within the gateway module by a validation of message header fields and message content. Furthermore, a configurable support of different interface versions has been realized here. Validation errors, i.e., syntactical errors, are directly reported to the supervised *invalid message channel* via the core module. All converted Java objects are logged with the message header field *TraceID*, which, again, can be used for error analyzation in correlation with a business process.

VIII. Interface Design Styles

The main problem to be solved in interface design concerns the intended functional semantic on the interface, i.e., the construction of the functional layer shown in Figure 1. It directly influences the kind of service offered by the *server* and therefore the necessary number and style of all messages.

Looking at existing interfaces, they can be categorized in our experience by their semantic design styles: CRUD based interfaces, use case based interfaces and business process based interfaces, each of them described in detail in the following sections.

A. *CRUD based design*

The Create, Read, Update, Delete (CRUD) based design directly uses the business objects described within the requirements and ignores any given business context. This results in interfaces consisting of a minimal set of messages, representing

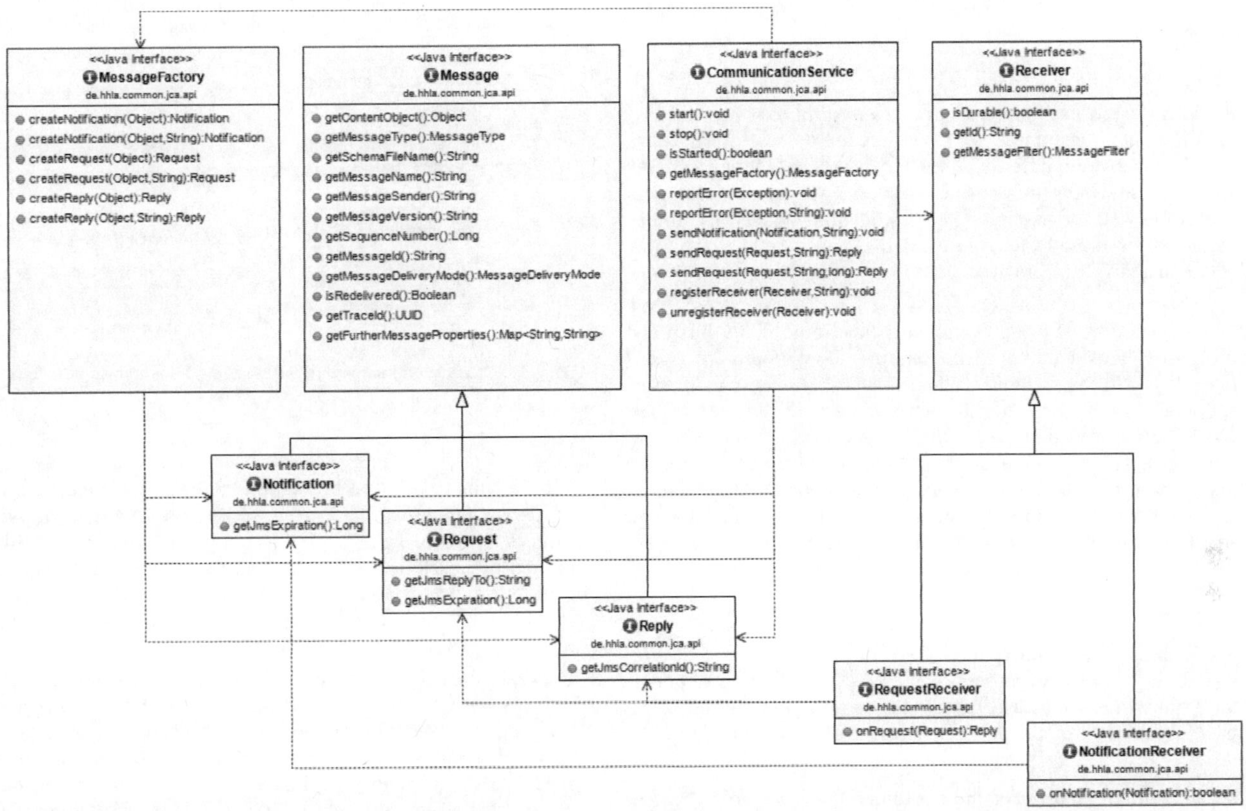

Figure 10. UML class diagramm depicting the main interface structure and methods of the JCA application programming interface (API).

a set of CRUD messages for every business object the *server* is functionally responsible for. Besides the advantages of requiring very little design efforts and being very stable, this interface design style has some important disadvantages.

First, the interface bears absolutely no business context, leading to severe difficulties in understanding the underlying business processes [2]. Second, the read operation demands synchronous communication, which represents an explicit control flow leading to a tight coupling of applications [5], [26] and third, missing business context either leads to a distribution of business functions over the *clients* or to business objects incorporating the results of applied business functions.

B. Use case based design

An interface design based on use cases rests upon requirements formulated from the perspective of the primary actors for individual systems only [41], i.e., the underlying business process is not directly present. Due to the characteristics of use cases, describing non-interrupted interactions with the system [42] that represent the view of the primary actor [41], these requirements are limited to the context of single activities, which are typically independent with respect to each other. A representation of the underlying business process triggering the desired activities is missing and therefore difficult to reconstruct.

These preconditions usually lead to rather fine granular and use case oriented interfaces comprising of a large number of messages, carrying specific use case based information only. Some important consequences arise from this design style. First, all business functions that are identical from the business process point of view, are hard to identify based on a use case analysis only. The absence of a business context leads to an interface design supporting individual use cases, which bear no evident business process semantics. Consequently, these interfaces usually offer a broad range of identical functionalities named differently. Second, the missing business context significantly increases the difficulty to understand the functional behavior of the interface over time [2], leading to serious problems in its usage. As a consequence, further unnecessary messages are often introduced in order to provide some use case specific information. Third, the lower level of abstraction of a use case - compared to the business process - leads to a rather fine granular interface structure. Performance issues may arise with this interface style due to the enforced frequent interface access [9]. And fourth, synchronous communication often arises in order to collect all necessary information to execute the use case, so a control flow arises [26] leading, again, to a tight coupling of applications [5], [31].

Note that using a use case based design must not lead compulsorily to a bad interface design. But given the size of current applications with their numerous use cases and the typical usage of distributed programming teams within industrial projects, the necessary refactoring to introduce an appropriate abstraction on the interface is usually omitted in our experience.

C. Business process based design

This design uses business process descriptions and further requirements formulated with respect to those descriptions, to align between individual business process activities and applications. Using the Business Process Model and Notation (BPMN) [43] and representing applications via pools, interfaces can be directly derived from the exchanged information between individual business activities within the pools.

The resulting interfaces focus on business semantics and directly support objects, events and functions of the business processes, thus leading to a domain model bound to interfaces [7] with the following consequences. Business processes support a high level of abstraction, thus leading to rather coarse granular interfaces with respect to the number of messages. The communication is driven by business events, so asynchronous communication is naturally supported, leading to data flows [26]. Finally, the functionality provided by the *server* within the business processes becomes rather clear, i.e., the business context is represented on the interface.

D. Design example

To explain and clarify the differences between these design styles, the simplified process of loading a truck at a container terminal will serve as an example throughout this section. This process consists of the following steps, executed in the given order:

- *order clearance*: the customer gives an order to the container terminal to load a container on a truck.
- *load clearance*: in order to deliver the container, several clearances must be given, e.g., by customs and the container owner.
- *transport planning*: the container terminal plans the necessary equipment to execute the order.
- *load container*: the container is loaded on the truck using the planned equipment.

Two applications shall be constructed in order to implement the process: the *Administration*, dealing with the administrative parts of the process, and *Operating*, handling the physical transport of the container. An interface between both applications will be designed according to the design style considered, thus showing the differences between the design approaches.

1) CRUD based design: All relevant business objects of the truck loading process are represented in a data model that provides methods to create, read, update and delete the objects. These methods represent the interface of the owning application, i.e., the *server*, and are called by the *clients*, in order to execute the business process. For example, after creating an order using `createOrder()`, the *Administration* calls `createInstruction()` to start the loading of the container on a truck. Subsequently, *Operating* calls `readCustomsClearance()` and `readReleaseOrder()` to check if the container is released to be loaded on a truck. The corresponding return objects must be interpreted within *Operating* to make this decision. If the container has been loaded, *Operating* finally calls `deleteOrder()`, `deleteCustomsClearing()` and `deleteReleaseOrder()` to clear the *Administration*.

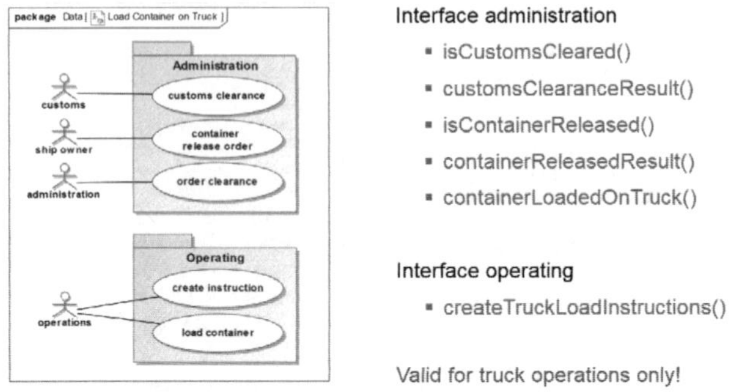

Figure 11. Constructed interface (right) resulting from applying the use case based design approach.

It becomes clear that both applications, i.e., *Administration* and *Operating* must implement some part of the underlying business logic to deal with these type of interfaces. Since the interface style bears no business semantics, the underlying business process cannot be reconstructed easily. Note that the size of the interface directly depends on the number of business objects the server is responsible for.

2) Use case based design: Based on the requirements of the truck loading process, corresponding use cases like order clearance or create instruction can be derived, as shown in Figure 11. Each of these use cases handles a specific functional aspect with respect to its primary actor. The underlying business process is executed through a set of use cases interacting with each other.

For example, if an order has been given, *Administration* calls `createTruckLoadInstructions()` to initiate the container transport. Prior to loading, *Operating* checks the container release status, using `isCustomsCleared()` and `isContainerReleased()`. If the container has been released, it is loaded on truck and *Operating* informs *Administration* via `containerLoadedOnTruck()` that the order has been executed. *Administration* may then clean up its internal data structures.

As depicted on the right side of Figure 11, the resulting interface contains a lot of methods for specific actions, i.e., the level of abstraction is rather low. Consequently the interface is valid for truck operations only and would require a couple of additional methods to incorporate, e.g., vessel and train operations.

Furthermore a use case based interface introduces synchronous communication, as indicated by, e.g., the method pairs `isCustomsCleared()` and `customsClearanceResult()`, leading to a blocking of *Operating* while accessing the information.

3) Business process based design: In this case, the business process itself serves as basis for interface design. Using BPMN, the process of truck loading can be mapped onto the applications as shown on the left side of Figure 12. Due to the given high level of abstraction within the business process, it is valid for all types of carriers, i.e., no further messages are necessary to include vessel and train operations.

Once an order has been given, *Administration* informs *Operating* via `orderPlaced()` that a new order has been

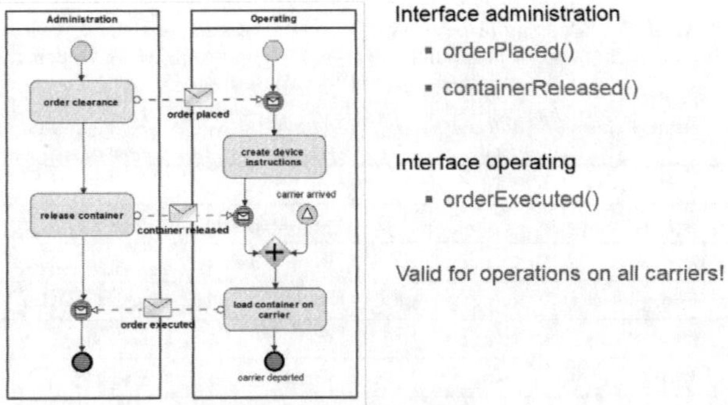

Figure 12. Constructed interface (right) resulting from applying the business process based design approach.

accepted. Within *Operating*, all necessary instructions for container loading will be created. Once the truck has arrived and *Administration* has published via `containerReleased()` that the container is released to be loaded on a truck, the physical moves are executed. Afterwards, `orderExecuted()` informs *Administration*, to clean up its internal data structures.

The dynamic behavior of the interface can be derived directly from the BPMN description, as shown on the left side of Figure 12. The resulting interface is quite small, meaningful and abstract, so it can be easily extended to other carriers. Additionally, the communication between both applications is asynchronous. Note that both applications, *Administration* and *Operating*, do not technically depend on each other, instead they simply publish their information without knowing the receiver, resulting in a data flow [26].

E. Comparison

To give a recommendation for a specific interface design style all design approaches described above have been compared to each other using typical interface design goals like robustness, performance and understandability [2].

1) Robustness: Interfaces are crucial with respect to the stability of the overall application landscape. Poorly designed interfaces may propagate internal application errors during runtime, thus causing damage within other applications [2], [5]. Robustness is achieved by avoiding functional distribution, distributed transactions [6] and semantical ambiguity.

In case of a CRUD interface, the information provided by the interface must be functionally interpreted by the *client* since the *server* informs about changes on business objects only without any functional context. This leads to multiple and distributed implementations of business functions according to the usage of the interface. In contrast, the use case and business process based design styles can both concentrate the business functions within the *server*, so no functional distribution will arise.

In general, distributed technical transactions can be avoided in all three design approaches. But modeling a control flow instead of a data flow bears a higher risk of introducing distributed transactions within the application landscape, due to the usage of synchronous communication. None of the design approaches specifically supports the construction of an efficient message field structure nor prohibits the introduction of content based constraints.

2) Performance: Obviously, interfaces must satisfy the required performance, i.e., they must be able to deal with the given quantity description. Otherwise, the business process will not work correctly since required business functions may not be executed in time. Performance is supported by designing minimal interfaces with respect to the number of messages and avoiding synchronous communication [4], [9].

The more abstract the interface is, the less messages are needed due to the restriction of transmitting core concepts only. With a CRUD based design, the most abstract design is chosen while a use case based design includes relatively less functional abstraction. Asynchronous communication is usually directly supported in the business process based design, while the other two approaches support a rather synchronous communication style. This holds especially for the CRUD based design, where the `read()` operation always enforces synchronous communication.

3) Understandability: Well designed interfaces must have a strong and documented relation to the underlying business context [2], thus ensuring a good usability of the interface. This will enhance the cost efficiency of the interface over time since a much better acceptance of the interface within the development teams will arise because the interface will be easier to learn, remember and use correctly [2].

Understandability is given by a strong functional binding between the domain model and the implementation [7], the usage of business objects and business events as message content [4], [9] and a meaningful message naming schema.

Naturally, a business process based design leads to a direct mapping between interface and business process description thus enriching the interface with a comprehensive business context. On the contrary, a CRUD based design bears no business context at all due to its high level of abstraction.

Although all three approaches directly support the exchange of business objects, differences occur considering the publication of business events. A CRUD based design supports none of them per se, i.e., this approach forces a mapping of business events onto business objects. This will lead to serious problems in understanding the dynamic behavior of the application landscape. Using a business process based design instead, the published business events can be directly derived from the underlying business process. In contrast, a use case based design does not primarily focus on business events but on individual user operations thus obscuring the business context. While the business process and the use case based designs both support message naming schemas providing a rich functional context, a CRUD based design uses only the given names for create, read, update and delete messages.

4) Recommendation: Considering the above mentioned design goals and the important advantage of supporting a direct link between domain model and interface design, the business process based design is the recommended design style for interfaces, leading to the best design compromise.

IX. Example: Integrating an Application Using the Business Process Based Design

The business process based design approach has been used at the HHLA to integrate a new application into an

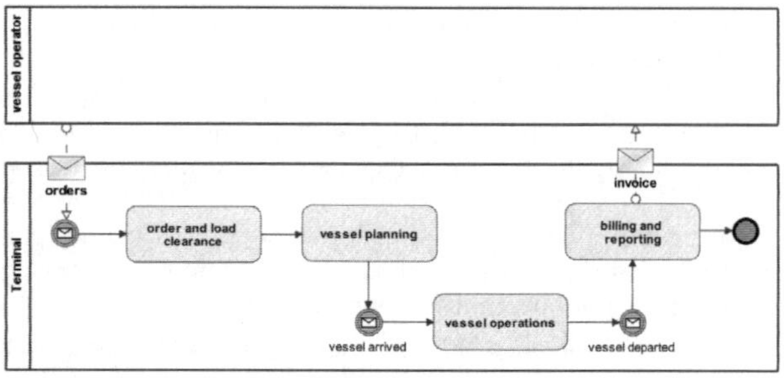

Figure 13. Business process for vessel handling.

TABLE V. Responsibility of applications for business objects.

administrative system	
business object	**description**
carrier order	order to handle a vessel
work instruction	planned instruction to move a container
work queue	planned list of work instructions for a specific device type
vessel geometry	vessel type geometry
...	...
terminal control system	
business object	**description**
container	physical data of a container
carrier	physical data of a carrier, e.g., a vessel
devices	equipment to move a container, e.g., straddle carrier
device instruction	instruction for a specific device to move a container
...	...

existing complex application landscape. This new application will be responsible for the required order management and planning tasks involved with vessel handling processes at a deep sea container terminal. A critical aspect during this integration was the required design of a new interface to an existing terminal control system, which controls all devices and logistical aspects on a container terminal.

Starting with a business process definition at a level showing a rather general process context, i.e. the summary level [41] as depicted in Figure 13, the business process has been further detailed. Using a domain model for HHLA container terminals, this refining leads to all relevant business objects required within this process.

Thereafter, these business objects have been assigned to the administrative system and terminal control system as given in Table V. Being assigned to an application implies that this application acts as a *server* for that specific business object, i.e., only this application is responsible for the business objects entire lifecycle. Consequently, each of the applications has to provide an interface to enable an access to its business objects and events.

The assignment of business objects to applications is usually guarded by the existing functional scope of the applications. In case of ambiguities, i.e., cases where business objects are required by multiple applications, the domain model of the HHLA has been used to determine the *server*. Note that other *clients* may still use caches for these business objects, which have to be updated properly using an appropriate interface of the *server*.

TABLE VI. Mapping of business objects onto existing application objects. To decouple them, an integration model has been introduced. A — denotes a missing object in that application.

business object	integration model	administrative system	terminal control system
carrier order	carrier order	carrier visit	—
work instruction	work instruction	work instruction	transport order
work queue	transport directive	work queue	transport order
vessel geometry	carrier geometry	vessel master data	vessel geometry
container	container	unit	container
carrier	carrier	vessel	vessel
device	device	—	device
device instruction	device instruction	—	order

Once this has been done, an IT alignment took place mapping each business object onto existing application objects. Since applications use different internal objects to represent these business objects, an integration model will be derived, decoupling applications and the domain model from each other. Table VI shows the resulting mapping for the vessel handling process.

Given the integration model, the business process based design approach described in the previous section can be applied. Using BPMN, all applications have been represented as pools with the functional activities being assigned accordingly, see Figure 14 for details. Note that all functional activities of the vessel handling process as well as their sequence have been adapted to the existing functionalities and process sequences within the corresponding applications. Furthermore, one of the given pools directly represents the vessel itself instead of an application. Incorporating the vessel into the BPMN model is helpful in this case since it represents an important physical event source for the whole process.

Looking at Figure 14, nearly all messages functionally required to exchange the necessary information between the administrative system and the terminal control system can be grasped directly from the BPMN description. Table VII summarizes the resulting interfaces of both applications. Note that some messages required for resilience are still missing, e.g., messages that allow a complete download of business objects from the *server* to reset caches located at *clients*.

Finally, individual XML structures using appropriate elements and/or attributes have to be designed for each message. Since most messages contain business objects only, the required information within a message is usually determined by the attributes of the business objects. In case of business events, the information to be carried is usually the event itself enriched with the business object identifier to whom the event applied.

Using the business process based design approach offers a structured approach for designing a functionally complete interface while supporting the nonfunctional aspects given in Section III-E.

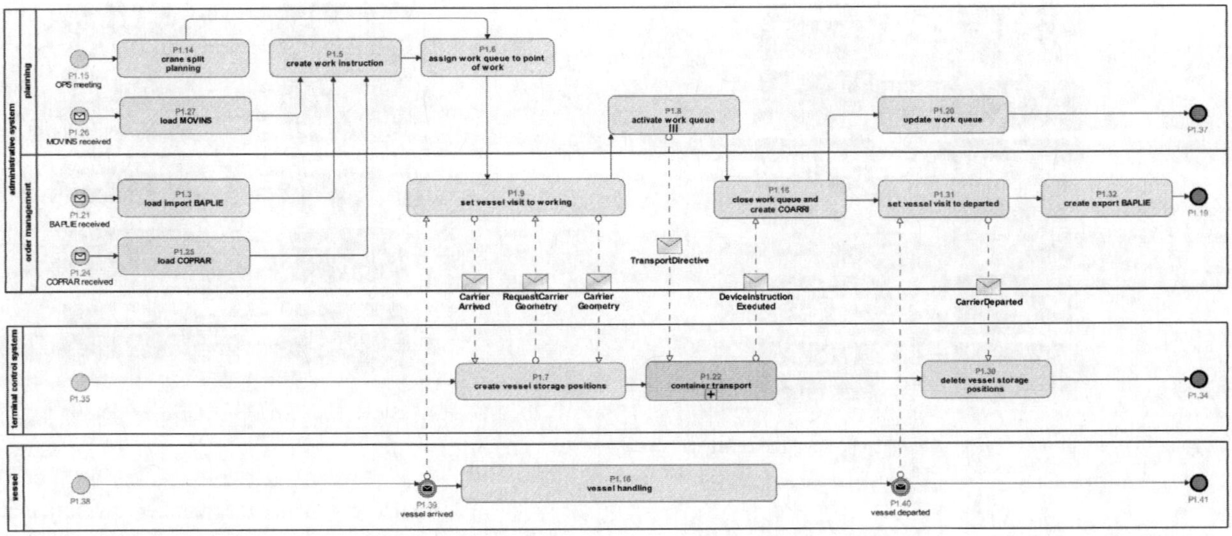

Figure 14. Resulting business process description using the business process based approach. All messages received are UN/EDIFACT messages carrying required order and storage information. Note that the events *vessel arrived* and *vessel departed* will be recorded manually in the administrative system.

TABLE VII. Resulting interfaces using the business process based design approach. All messages have been assigned to an interface according to the application responsibilities for business objects. For each message, its message type and its semantical content is given.

interface of the administrative system		
message name	**message type**	**message content**
RequestCarrierGeometry	Request	requesting vessel geometry
CarrierGeometry	Reply	vessel geometry
TransportDirective	Notification	work queue assigned to a quay crane

interface of the terminal control system		
message name	**message type**	**message content**
CarrierArrived	Notification	business event
DeviceInstructionExecuted	Notification	transport acknowledgement
CarrierDeparted	Notification	business event

X. Interface Operations

Large application landscapes are usually operated in a 24/7 hour mode, requiring appropriate control, maintenance and support by an application management. The application management has to solve upcoming communication failures and supports application updates due to business changes and life cycle management requirements. Updating applications and communication infrastructure components requires deployment into an already running application landscape, resulting in business acceptable downtimes only.

To achieve these goals, interfaces must be versioned and the implementing applications have to be deployed during runtime, using migration patterns as described below.

A. Interface versioning

Every interface specification evolves over time due to syntactic, semantic or dynamic changes on the interface. These changes lead to different versions of the interface specification that are not compatible to each other. Therefore, the implementing applications must implement the correct version of the interface specification. In a complex application landscape, this is a common situation [8].

In order to guarantee a unique identification of a specific interface occurrence over time, each individual interface occurrence must have a version number [1], [8]. Note that any change on an interface leads to a new interface version [8]. This includes syntactical changes in any message, changes within the message sequence flow, i.e., all changes of the dynamic behavior, and changes of the semantic behavior. Even the obviously simple cases of adding either a field to an existing message or introducing a new message to an interface represents a semantical change of the interface. This requires compatibility of the receiving application with the new interface specification version. Otherwise, severe problems may arise, if, e.g., a *client* executes syntactical message checks based on a specific interface version.

B. Migration patterns

Rolling out a new interface version in an application landscape operating 24/7 hours, requires the usage of an appropriate migration pattern.

1) Big bang migration pattern: The simplest approach of an interface migration is *big bang*, where all applications are shutdown, redeployed and restarted at the same time, resulting in

$$1 + c \tag{1}$$

migration steps, where c denotes the number of participating *clients*. In case of a fall-back, the *server* and all *clients* must be redeployed again.

2) Client first migration pattern: Within this pattern, the migration path is dominated by the *clients*. Each *client* will be successively migrated onto a new version that can handle both interface versions in parallel, as shown in Figure 15. In

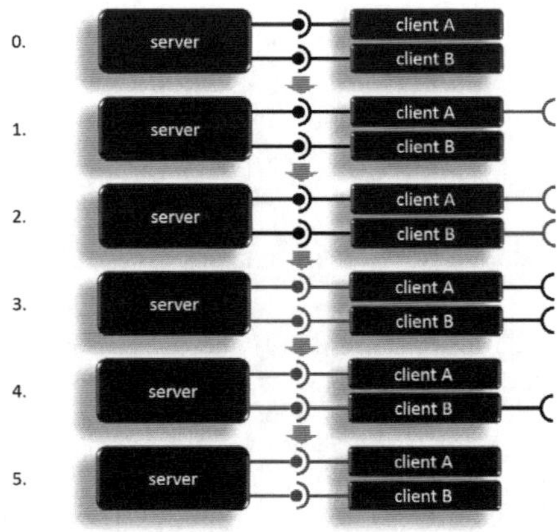

Figure 15. Steps of the *client first migration* pattern. The new interface version is denoted red.

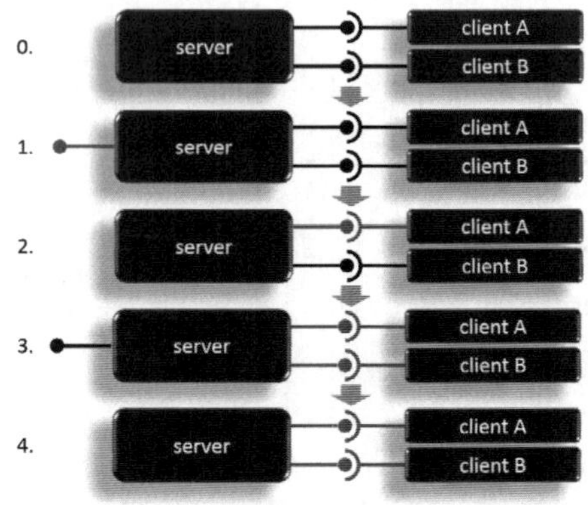

Figure 16. Steps of the *server first migration* pattern.

steps 1 and 2, the *clients* are changed to support additionally the new interface specification version. In step 3, the *server* is merged to the new interface implementation. Steps 4 and 5 are necessary to remove the support of the previous interface specification version from the *clients*. After finishing all *client* migrations, the *server* will be upgraded to support the new interface version. Afterwards, all *clients* will be updated a second time in order to remove the support of the old interface version. During steps one to four of this migration path, the *server* will receive messages with a wrong interface version that must be ignored by the *server*.

The *client first migration* pattern will result in

$$1 + 2 * c \tag{2}$$

deployments, where c denotes the number of *clients* connected to the *server*. An advantage of this migration path is that *clients* can be upgraded independently from each other, i.e., no temporal coupling of the individual *client* migrations exist. The price for this migration behavior is the necessary number of deployments: each *client* must be deployed two times, while the *server* is deployed only once. Furthermore, in case of a failure, the operational safe position of step 2 must be reached again. This is done by falling back with the *server* supporting the old interface version only and all *clients* whose support of the old interface version has been removed so far, requiring

$$1 + c_+ \tag{3}$$

steps, where c_+ denotes the number of *clients* migrated after the *server* migration.

3) Server first migration pattern: In contrast to the *client first migration* approach, the migration path can be reversed resulting in a *server* migration first followed by *client* migrations, see Figure 16. At step 1, the *server* provides support for two interface specification versions. In steps 2 and 3, both *clients* are merged successively. Finally, support of the previous interface specification version is removed from the *server* implementation, resulting in

$$2 + c \tag{4}$$

deployments. Again, c denotes the number of participating *clients*. The advantage of this pattern is, that the number of deployments is

$$(1 + 2 * c) - (2 + c) = c - 1 \tag{5}$$

less than with the *client first migration* pattern. Note that during steps one to three of the migration path both *clients* A and B will receive invalid messages, which must be ignored, due to the concurrent interface version support of the *server*. If a failure on the interface occurs within the migration path, all *clients* upgraded so far must fall back onto the previous interface version using c_+ roll-out steps, where, again, c_+ denotes the number of *clients* migrated after the *server* migration. Thus, the operational safe position of step 1 is reached again.

4) Mixed migration pattern: If the migration of an interface starts as a *client first migration* it could be changed to a *server first migration* at any time. The resulting *mixed migration* pattern is depicted in Figure 17. A *mixed migration* always starts with some *client* migrations followed by the *server* migration. Thereafter the remaining *clients* are migrated, resulting in

$$2 + 2 * c_- + c_+ \tag{6}$$

deployments, where c_- denotes the number of *clients* migrated prior and c_+ the number of *clients* migrated after the *server* migration. Important within this migration path is step 2, where the *server* and all *clients* migrated so far, i.e., c_- *clients*, must be deployed as a big bang. Otherwise, the *server* and these *clients* would communicate using two different interface versions in parallel usually leading to race conditions and doubled messages.

5) Comparison: The main differences between the migration patterns are the number of roll-out and fall-back steps as shown in Table VIII and the required support of multiple interface versions within the applications. Beside the advantages of a lacking necessity to support multiple interface versions and a minimal number of roll-out steps, the *big bang* pattern bears a high risk during fall-back situations where multiple applications must fall-back in parallel. Therefore, this pattern is only recommended if the number of *clients* is very small and a simultaneous fall-back is organizational manageable. Considering the other strategies, the *mixed migration* pattern suffers similar problems due to the required big bang at

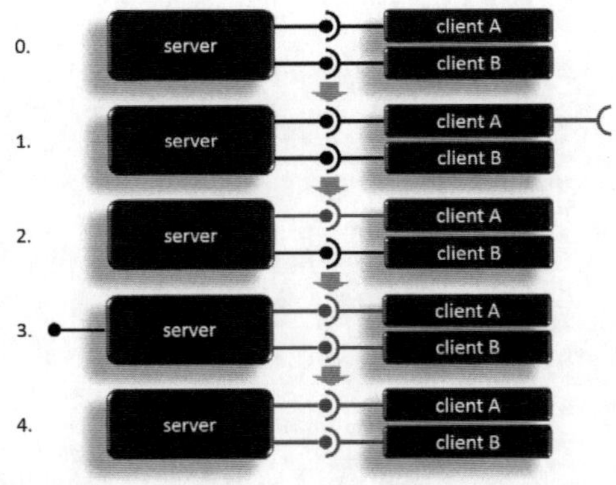

Figure 17. Steps of the *mixed migration* pattern.

migration step 2. Being a more complex pattern than *big bang*, its usage is not recommended. In contrast, *client first migration* and *server first migration* patterns reduce the risk involved with a possible fall-back compared to *big bang* at the cost of some additional roll-out steps. Since the *server first migration* pattern requires less roll-out and fall-back steps than the *client first migration* pattern, it is the recommended roll-out strategy.

XI. Conclusion

Due to the growing distribution of business functionalities, interfaces have become most important while operating applications within an application landscape. Badly designed interfaces have a critical impact on their functional and operational behavior [4]. To overcome these issues, this paper presents a structured and holistic approach to construct interface specifications considering all aspects and requirements of the business domain as well as IT operations.

Depending on the nonfunctional communication requirements to be satisfied to successfully integrate an application, adequate communication technologies have to be selected. Using messaging as integration style typically results in a good integration behavior for applications. In addition, further communication services encapsulated in an appropriate transmission protocol should be offered to deal with integration and error handling issues during operations. As a result, all applications implementing this transmission protocol can communicate in a robust and consistent way. This is a fundamental property for professional application management to support 24/7 hour operations in a large application landscape.

Interface specifications serve as contracts between applications. Thus, it is inevitable to define the artifacts *message description*, *dynamic description*, *semantic description*, *infrastructure description* and *quantity description* to properly describe an interface with respect to these different aspects. In order to construct an interface, different design approaches have been presented and compared to each other. It turns out that the business process based design approach is most likely leading to the best result with respect to robustness, performance and understandability.

Finally, different migration patterns have been presented introducing a new interface version into production stage. Due to the minimal number of required fallback steps in case of a severe error and one additional roll-out step compared to the *big bang* pattern the *server first migration* pattern is recommended, at least for larger application landscapes.

TABLE VIII. Comparison of the migration patterns with respect to the number of migration steps necessary and the number of applications that must be redeployed in case of a fallback.

pattern	**rollout steps**	**application fallbacks**
big bang migration	$1 + c$	$1 + c$
client first migration	$1 + 2 * c$	$1 + c_+$
server first	$2 + c$	c_+
mixed migration	$2 + 2 * c_- + c_+$	c_+

XII. Acknowledgment

The authors would like to thank Andreas Henning for valuable comments.

References

[1] A. Hagemann and G. Krepinsky, "(Inter)facing the Business," in FASSI 2016 - The Second International Conference on Fundamentals and Advances in Software Systems Integration. IARIA, Jul. 2016, pp. 1–7, ISBN: 978-1-61208-497-8.

[2] M. Henning, "API Design Matters," ACM Queue Magazine, vol. 5, 2007.

[3] J. Bloch, "How to Design a Good API and Why it Matters," 2006, URL: http://landawn.com/HowtoDesignaGoodAPIandWhyitMatters.pdf [accessed: 2016-06-08].

[4] R. J. Wieringa, Design Methods for Reactive Systems. Morgan Kaufmann Publishers, 2003, ISBN: 1-55860-755-2.

[5] M. Nygard, Release It!: Design and Deploy Production-Ready Software. O'Reilly, Apr. 2007, ISBN: 978-0978739218.

[6] U. Friedrichsen, "Patterns of Resilience," 2016, URL: http://de.slideshare.net/ufried/patterns-of-resilience [accessed: 2016-06-06].

[7] E. Evans, Domain Driven Design: Tackling Complexity in the Heart of Software. Addison-Wesley, 2004, ISBN: 0-321-12521-5.

[8] B. Bonati, F. Furrer, and S. Murer, Managed Evolution. Springer Verlag, 2011, ISBN: 978-3-642-01632-5.

[9] G. Hohpe and B. Woolf, Enterprise Integration Patterns. Addison-Wesley, 2012, ISBN: 978-0-133-06510-7.

[10] S. Deering and R. Hinden, "Internet Protocol, Version 6 (IPv6) Specification," The Internet Society, Specification, 1998.

[11] R. Fielding and J. Reschke, "Hypertext transfer protocol (http1.1): Message syntax and routing," 2014, URL: https://tools.ietf.org/html/rfc7230\#section-2.6 [accessed: 2017-01-09].

[12] "File Transfer Protocol," 1985, URL: https://tools.ietf.org/html/rfc959 [accessed: 2017-02-13].

[13] M. Happner, R. Burridge, R. Sharma, J. Fialli, and K. Stout, "Java Message Service," Sun microsystems, Specification, 2002.

[14] "Java Remote Method Invocation API," 2016, URL: http://docs.oracle.com/javase/7/docs/technotes/guides/rmi/ [accessed: 2017-18-01].

[15] "Advanced Message Queuing Protocol (AMQP) specification," 2014, URL: http://www.iso.org/iso/home/store/catalogue_tc/catalogue_detail.htm?csnumber=64955 [accessed: 2017-25-01].

[16] "Blink Protocol," 2012, URL: http://blinkprotocol.org/ [accessed: 2016-06-06].

[17] "Financial Information eXchange," 2016, URL: https://en.wikipedia.org/wiki/Financial_Information_eXchange [accessed: 2016-06-06].

[18] "FAST protocol," 2016, URL: https://en.wikipedia.org/wiki/FAST_protocol [accessed: 2016-06-06].

[19] "UN/CEFACT Domains," 2017, URL: https://www2.unece.org/cefact/pages/viewpage.action?pageId=9603195 [accessed: 2017-18-01].

[20] "Service-oriented architecture," 2016, URL: https://en.wikipedia.org/wiki/Service-oriented_architecture [accessed: 2016-06-08].

[21] R. Fielding, "Architectural Styles and the Design of Network-based Software Architectures," dissertation, University of California, Irvine, 2000.

[22] M. Iridon, "Enterprise Integration Modeling," International Journal on Advances in Software, vol. 9, no 1 & 2, 2016, pp. 116–127, ISSN: 1942-2628.

[23] H. Kerner, Rechnernetze nach ISO-OSI, CCITT. H. Kerner, 1989, ISBN: 3-900934-10-X.

[24] "OSI model," 1984, URL: https://en.wikipedia.org/wiki/OSI_model [accessed: 2017-01-26].

[25] "Client-server model," 2016, URL: https://en.wikipedia.org/wiki/Client-server_model [accessed: 2016-03-03].

[26] R. Westphal, "Radikale Objektorientierung - Teil 1: Messaging als Programmiermodell," OBJEKTspektrum, vol. 1/2015, 2015, pp. 63–69.

[27] "OMG Unified Modeling Language," 2017, URL: http://www.omg.org/spec/UML/2.5/PDF/ [accessed: 2017-24-01].

[28] J. Hopcroft, R. Motwani, and J. Ullman, Introduction to Automata Theory, Languages, and Computation. Addison-Wesley, 2001, ISBN: 0-201-44124-1.

[29] U. Friedrichsen, "The promises and perils of microservices," 2017, URL: https://www.slideshare.net/ufried/the-promises-and-perils-of-microservices [accessed: 2017-02-24].

[30] P. Bernstein and E. Newcomer, Principles of Transaction Processing. Elsevier Inc., 2009, ISBN: 978-1-55860-623-4.

[31] U. Friedrichsen, "Watch your communication," 2016, URL: https://www.slideshare.net/ufried/watch-your-communication [accessed: 2017-02-24].

[32] J. Humble and D. Farley, Continous Delivery. Addison-Wesley, 2010, ISBN: 978-0-321-60191-9.

[33] M. Schumacher, E. Fernandez-Buglioni, D. Hybertson, F. Buschmann, and P. Sommerland, Security Patterns, ser. Software Design Patterns. John Wiley & Sons, Ltd, 2005.

[34] "Extensible Markup Language," 2008, URL: https://www.w3.org/TR/2008/REC-xml-20081126/ [accessed: 2017-02-13].

[35] "XML Schema Definition Language," 2012, URL: https://www.w3.org/TR/2012/REC-xmlschema11-1-20120405/ [accessed: 2017-02-13].

[36] "ISO 8601," 2016, URL: https://en.wikipedia.org/wiki/ISO_8601 [accessed: 2016-11-10].

[37] "Base64," 2016, URL: https://en.wikipedia.org/wiki/Base64 [accessed: 2016-11-10].

[38] "ActiveMQ," 2017, URL: http://activemq.apache.org [accessed: 2017-05-25].

[39] "SwiftMQ," 2017, URL: http://www.swiftmq.com [accessed: 2017-05-25].

[40] "Java Language and Virtual Machine Specifications," 2017, URL: http://docs.oracle.com/javase/specs/ [accessed: 2017-05-25].

[41] A. Cockburn, Writing Effective Use Cases. Addison-Wesley, 2001, ISBN: 978-0-201-70225-5.

[42] B. Oestereich, Objektorientierte Softwareentwicklung: Analyse und Design mit der UML 2.0. Oldenbourg, 2004, ISBN: 978-3486272666.

[43] "Information technology – Object Management Group Business Process Model and Notation," 2013, URL: http://www.iso.org/iso/catalogue_detail.htm?csnumber=62652 [accessed: 2017-02-14].

International Journal on Advances in Software, vol 10 no 1 & 2, year 2017, http://www.iariajournals.org/software/

Managing Semantic World Models for eRobotics Applications Two Approaches Based on Object-Relational Mapping and on a Graph Database

Martin Hoppen, Juergen Rossmann, Ann-Marie Stapelbroek, and Sebastian Hiester

Institute for Man-Machine Interaction
RWTH Aachen University
Ahornstrasse 55
Aachen, Germany
Email: {hoppen, rossmann}@mmi.rwth-aachen.de,
{ann-marie.stapelbroek, sebastian.hiester}@rwth-aachen.de

***Abstract*—The main objective of eRobotics is to cope with the complexity in the development and lifecycle of current robotic and mechatronic systems. A key technology for eRobotics applications are Virtual Testbeds, a more holistic approach to 3D simulation that considers the entire system under study within its operational environment modeled in so-called Semantic World Models. Ideally, this complex data should be managed using database technology instead of flat file formats. However, existing related approaches fail to fulfill all the identified requirements. Thus, we present a new database synchronization concept whose basic idea is to use local in-memory simulation databases (SimDB) and synchronize them to a central, external database (ExtDB). In this paper, two new realizations of this concept are presented using two different choices for ExtDB: The first is based on an object-relational mapping approach, the second uses the graph database Neo4j. Both approaches are described in detail, evaluated, and finally compared to each other. In conclusion, both approaches are very well-suited but the actual choice depends the concrete application scenario.**

Keywords–eRobotics; Semantic World Models; Data Management; Object Relational Mapping; Graph Database.

I. INTRODUCTION

The work at hand combines the results from our two previous publications [1] [2] and extends them by a more comprehensive motivation and a comparison of the two approaches.

Current robotic applications are characterized by complex system structures and expensive hardware prototypes. The eRobotics approach [3], a branch of eSystems Engineering like eHealth or eGovernment, is used to cope with these difficulties by combining the usage of electronic media, simulation technology and robotics concepts. It covers not only the development, but the whole lifecycle of robotic systems. The flexibility of eRobotics enables its usage in other fields of application: The modeling and simulation of environmental scenarios (forest, buildings or whole cities), industrial automation applications, and mechatronic systems like satellites in general (Figure 1).

An important method in eRobotics is 3D simulation. According to [4], the term simulation itself can be defined as the "preparation, execution and evaluation of targeted experiments with a simulation model", where a model is defined as a "simplified reproduction of a planned or existing system". Accordingly, a model used in 3D simulations focuses on a system's spatial properties and behavior. The basis of any

Figure 1. Exemplary eRobotics applications: A wood harvester in its operational environment, a distributed city simulation scenario and Virtual Testbed of the International Space Station (ISS).

eRobotics application is a Semantic World Model, a comprehensive 3D model of the system under study itself and its operational environment. It focuses on the problem domain using a domain specific data schema and allows for an inherent interpretation of its meaning. In particular, such models go beyond purely geometric descriptions that are often optimized for rendering only.

Semantic World Models are the basis for so-called Virtual Testbeds (VTBs), a more holistic approach to 3D simulation that considers the entire system under development including its operational environment. In contrast, a standard simulation usually covers and examines only very specific aspects in detail. A VTB, in turn, can be used for various approaches such as simulation-based optimization, reasoning and control.

This can be summarized by the term Simulation-based *X*, with

- *X* = Optimization: The VTB is used during the development phase of the system. By running different simulations with varying system structures and properties the best alternative can be chosen.
- *X* = Reasoning: The VTB is used by the system in live operations, serving as a mental model of the system. This model can be used for optimized decision-making by simulating different action alternatives.
- *X* = Control: A control for a device or process is developed within the VTB (using above mentioned simulation-based optimization). By exchanging the virtual sensors and actuators with their physical counterpart, this control can then be used on the physical device or process, without further implementation or adaption.

An example is given in Figure 2.

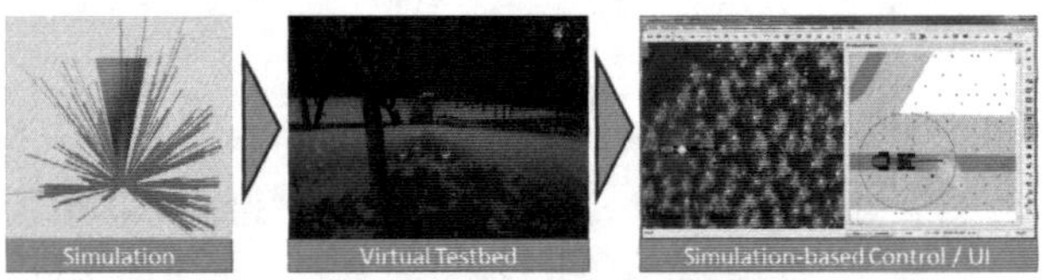

Figure 2. Difference between a simulation (of a single laser scanner), a Virtual Testbed (of a laser scanner equipped wood harvester and its operational environment) and Simulation-based *X* (user interface of a Simulation-based Control approach).

The inherent properties of Semantic World Models are very similar to those of 3D data like Computer-aided Design (CAD) data. Typically, they consist of a huge number of parts with many different types that feature a hierarchical structure with interdependencies. When developing eRobotics applications, this complexity needs to be managed appropriately. For that purpose, instead of widespread flat 3D file formats, the usage of database technology is recommended. Database technology provides many advantages for modern eRobotics applications. Multi-user support with access rights management, safe transactions and concurrency control can allow large development teams or distributed components to corporately work on complex systems. Semantic World Models like environmental models (e.g., forests or cities) or the ISS benefit from database management systems' (DBMS) support for managing huge amounts of data using techniques like (spatial) indexing or distributed databases. Query languages, data independence, and client-server architectures allow for the decoupling of concerns between simulation and data management. Schema support and metadata allow to centrally define a "common language" for (possibly heterogeneous) software components in the development and the whole lifecycle of eRobotics applications.

In particular, five main requirements for a data management approach for eRobotics applications can be identified:

1) Following [5], object-oriented data modeling is optimal to cope with the aforementioned complexity of CAD data and thus of Semantic World Models. Thus, it must be supported by the approach.
2) In eRobotics applications not only the data, but also the processes are complex. They are made manageable by using distributed approaches like distributed simulation, distributed data processing, distributed modeling (collaboration), distributed data acquisition, or distributed control architectures. Thus, a data management approach must also feature a distributed architecture, in particular, to replicate data to different clients, sites or projection screens.
3) For simulation and rendering, Semantic World Model data must be available in memory in every simulation cycle. Thus, the approach must use in-memory technology to keep necessary data available for (live) simulation.
4) Semantic World Models use domain specific data schemata that focus on the problem domain and allow for an inherent interpretation of their meaning. Thus, an appropriate data management approach for eRobotics applications must flexibly adapt to different schemata to make it universally applicable in many scenarios. Examples for such data schemata are CityGML for cities, ForestGML for forest and forestry models, Industrial Foundation Classes (IFC) [6] for building information modeling (BIM) scenarios, Automation Modeling Language (AutomationML) [7] in industrial automation applications, or Systems Modeling Language (SysML) [8] for system specifications.
5) Finally, Simulation-based *X* approaches need to be supported. For *X*=Optimization and *X*=Reasoning, simulation runs need to be recorded and analyzed. Ideally, this can be realized using an integrated versioning or temporal data management that is independent of the specific application schema to make it available to all eRobotics applications. For *X*=Reasoning and *X*=Control, the identical model and thus the identical data management approach must be reusable in live operation.

The rest of this contribution is structured as follows. In the next section, related work is identified representing the state of the art in managing 3D data using database technology. Section III introduces the basic idea of database synchronization that builds the basis for the two approaches presented in Section IV and Section V. In Section VI, both approaches are compared before Section VII gives a conclusion.

II. Related Work

A variety of applications similarly work with 3D data like Augmented Reality applications, collaborative Virtual Environments, applications for city or building modeling and planning, or Product Data Management (PDM) systems, which are particularly used for managing CAD or other CA*x* (e.g., Computer-aided Engineering or Computer-aided Manufacturing) data. Mostly, they use object-oriented data modeling [9] [10] [11] [12] [13] [14] [15] [16] [17] [18] [19] [20] [21] [22] [23]. Among such applications, different motivations for using database technology can be identified:

- Persistence [9] [13] [14] [15] [18] [19] [20] [21] [22] [23] [24]
- Query capabilities [13] [14] [15] [16] [17] [19] [20] [21] [22] [23]
- Multiuser support [10] [13] [14] [15] [16] [18] [20] [21] [22] [23] [25]
- Client-server model [10] [22] [23] [26]
- Large model data [10] [11] [12] [17] [18] [22] [23] [27]
- Access control and rights management [17] [22] [23] [24]
- Internet data provisioning [11] [12] [18] [19] [20] [21] [22] [23] [27]
- Temporal data management / versioning [19] [22] [23]
- Integration of existing databases [28]
- Integration of different data formats [11] [12] [22] [23]

Thus, related applications have similar reasons for the adoption of database technology. In all of them, different approaches are used to integrate databases into the application. Sometimes, databases are used to store additional information (meta information, documents, films, positions, hierarchical structure ...) on scene objects or parts [22] [23] [24] [27] [28] [29] [30] [31] [32] [33] [34] [35] [36] [37]. However, for eRobotics applications, the whole Semantic World Model should be managed using database technology to obtain the referred benefits for all its objects and their properties. This ensures that every aspect is queryable, distributable, and versionable and that the complete application schema is reproduced in the database to enforce it as a common language for all subsystems.

Other systems use a database to store scene data itself, but not all of them with an object-oriented data modeling, which is ideally suited for Semantic World Models. Another important aspect for eRobotics applications is the support for arbitrary application schemata. Many systems use a generic (scene-graph-like) geometric model, in most cases with attributes [11] [17] [18] [19] [20] [26] [27]. In such scenarios, schema flexibility can be achieved to a certain extent by providing import (and export) to different file formats [11] [38] [39] [40]. Some approaches support different or flexible schemata. For example in [26], schema alteration is realized by adding attributes to generic base objects. Other systems support a selection of different static [11] or dynamic [10] [17] schemata. However, most approaches focus on a specific field of application, thus, requiring and supporting only a corresponding fixed schema. This is very common and described in many similar publications presenting applications with a 3D context, for example many from the field of BIM [41] [42] [43] [44] [45] [46] [47]. While PDM systems [22] [23] in principle support arbitrary schemata they are not explicitly reflected within the database schema due to their "black box integration" approach. Similar vaulting-based approaches with a 3D context can be found in other publications [48] [49] [50] [51] [52]. However, to flexibly support various eRobotics applications, arbitrary application schemata of Semantic World Models need to be explicitly supported. Most scenarios provide a distributed architecture in terms of multiuser support, a client-server model, or access control and rights management. However, only some build it on a Distributed-Database-like approach [10] [18] [25] with client-side databases. The latter is favorable for eRobotics applications, e.g., to provide schema flexibility or a query interface on client-side, as well. Finally, some approaches support temporal data management or versioning [19] [22] [23] [38] [39] [40] [41] [43] [44] [48] [52] [53] [54] [55]. In most cases, these approaches require special schema structures and many are based on file vaulting. To be flexibly used in eRobotics applications, however, it needs to be available for arbitrary application schemata.

Thus, especially due to deviant motivations, there is no single approach fulfilling all the requirements identified for managing Semantic World Models in eRobotics applications. This was the motivation for the development of our basic concept of database synchronization presented in the next section.

III. Database Synchronization Concept

Based on the requirements described above and as previously shown in [56] [57], we developed a new database synchronization concept ideally suited for eRobotics applications. Its basic idea is to combine and synchronize two types of databases (Figure 3): Each 3D simulation system uses a local database (dubbed SimDB) as its core data management component. This database is an active, in-memory database whose main purpose is to cache the shared Semantic World Model and to build the basis for its runtime execution. All instances of SimDB are synchronized to an external database (dubbed ExtDB). It centrally manages the shared model, provides a persistence layer, can be used for versioning and serves as a communication hub for the distributed system.

Figure 3. Basic idea of the database synchronization approach for eRobotics applications that synchronizes databases on four levels.

The synchronization component between each pair of ExtDB and SimDB performs a synchronization on four different levels:

1) On schema level, the schema is synchronized from ExtDB to every SimDB to make the whole distributed system "speak the same language".
2) On data level, instance data is replicated on demand from ExtDB to SimDB and kept in sync to make the shared Semantic World Model available to the 3D simulation systems.
3) On a semantic level, where necessary, native data in application specific schemata (e.g., SEDRIS [58]) is selectively translated to allow for an interpretation by the simulation system.
4) On a versioning level, a temporal database is used for ExtDB to synchronize snapshots to SimDB and to make the history of changes to the Semantic World Model persistent.

The question which arises now is, which database technology is best used when implementing this concept. For SimDB, we successfully utilize the simulation database VSD (Versatile Simulation Database) of the 3D Simulation System VEROSIM (Virtual Environments and Robotic Simulation [59]). VEROSIM was originally developed as a virtual reality and robot simulation system. Due to its flexible nature, it has become the basis for the development of various eRobotics applications in the fields of industrial automation, space robotics and environmental modeling. All its rendering and simulation techniques are based on VSD, an object-oriented, in-memory database. Similar to the common scene-graph, VSD builds a graph-like structure by means of objects and references in between. However, unlike scene-graphs, it does not only support a fixed set of generic node types. VSD rather provides means to freely configure a schema for its objects. By offering views on its contents, time-critical components like rendering and simulation can still quickly access their respective part of interest without repetitively traversing the whole graph. A VSD schema describes the structure as well as the behavior of its objects. That is, the simulation logic is not externally applied to the Semantic World Model but is in fact part of the objects it comprises. For that reason, VSD can be called an active database. Last but not least, VEROSIM and VSD are based on C++ and provide a proprietary meta system.

In VSD, objects are called instances and are characterized by properties. Such properties can either be value properties (Val-Properties) with basic or complex data types or reference properties. The latter model $1 : 1$ (Ref-Properties) or $1 : n$ (RefList-Properties) directed relationships between instances. Furthermore, these relationships can be marked to *contain* target instances using an *autodelete* flag allowing to model UML (Unified Modeling Language) composite aggregations.

VSD comprises a meta information system providing access to its schema and also to specify its schema. So-called meta instances describe an instance's class (name, inheritance, etc.) and so-called meta properties its properties (name, type, etc.). Figure 4 shows VSD's data model.

For ExtDB, we currently use a generic, third-party object-relational mapper (OR mapper) called SupportGIS-Java (SGJ) [60] in combination with standard relational back-ends (mostly PostgreSQL [61]). SGJ's main purpose and field of application

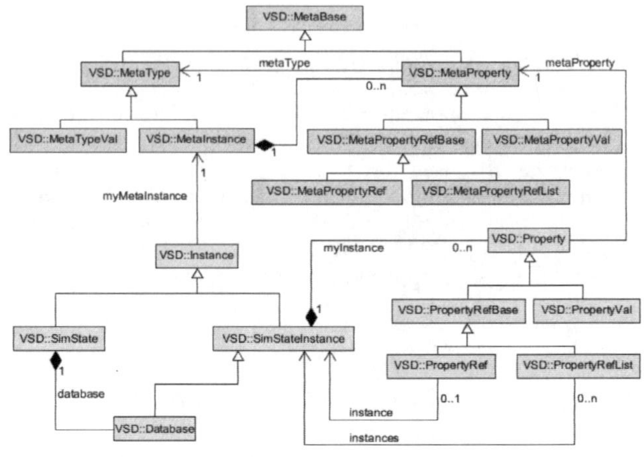

Figure 4. VSD data model (top: metadata, bottom: instance data).

is managing geodata for GIS (Geographic Information System). Thus, an import principle is its adherence to international standards like GML (Geography Markup Language [62]). SGJ flexibly supports arbitrary object-oriented application schemata by using a generic base schema within the back-end. This base schema is used to flexibly store a description of the respective application schema in terms of management table entries and generic data tables. This flexibility motivated our usage of SGJ in many different eRobotics applications.

However, a drawback of this current solution is the need for an additional translation layer between SimDB, the synchronization interface and ExtDB (Figure 5). To persist a new VSD instance, it firstly has to be translated into an object of the SGJ API (Application Programming Interface). This object representation is then translated into a relational representation. The same (in reverse order) applies to loading data into VSD.

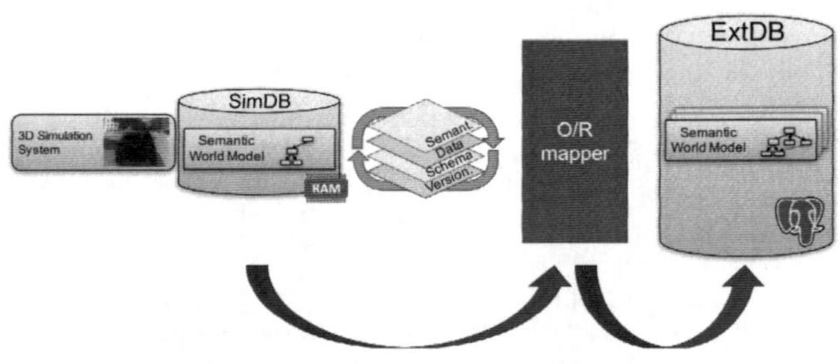

Figure 5. Drawback of the current SGJ-based solution: An additional translation layer between SimDB and ExtDB.

Thus, we evaluated alternative choices for ExtDB in two student projects. The first is an OR mapper solution directly built into the synchronization component and, thus, omitting the additional layer currently imposed by SGJ. In the prototype it is also combined with a PostgreSQL back-end. The main motivation for using an OR mapper is the same: The prevalence, matureness and well-defined theoretical basis of relational database management systems (RDBMS) lead to an extensive software availability but also to wide user acceptance especially in business and industry. The OR mapper-based approach is presented in the next section. The second approach uses graph database technology, namely the graph database Neo4j [63] [64]. The study was mainly motivated by VSD's graph database like structure and the drawbacks of OR mapper solutions subsumed by the well-known object-relational impedance mismatch. This second approach is presented in Section V.

IV. Direct Object-Relational Mapping Approach

The most widespread database paradigm is the relational data model. If relational databases should be used as a persistence layer for object-oriented 3D simulation systems, a mapping has to be defined bridging the differences between both paradigms. These differences are summarized as the object-relational impedance mismatch. The term object-relational mapping (OR mapping) describes the process of mapping the objects of an application (here, a 3D simulation system) to table entries of a relational database and vice versa. A manual mapping between the object-oriented concept and the relational database model is complex and error-prone so that object-relational mappers (OR mappers) are used. An OR mapper is a tool that builds a translation layer between application logic and relational database to perform a semi-automatic object-relational mapping.

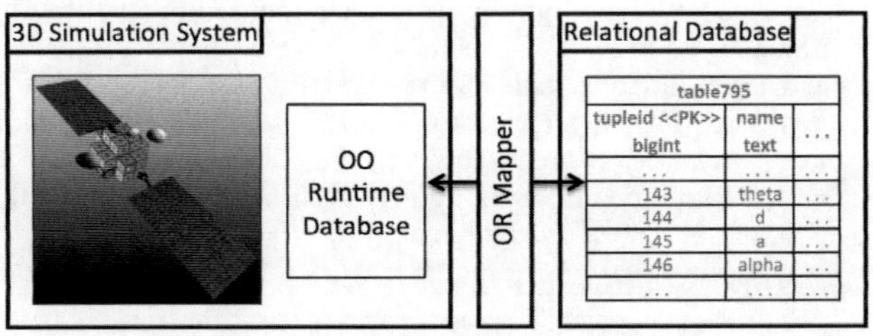

Figure 6. OR mapping for a 3D simulation system with an object-oriented runtime database (data: [65]).

In this section, we present an OR mapper for 3D simulation systems with an object-oriented runtime database and a meta information system, see Figure 6. The work was conducted as a student project and is based on our previous work as introduced above. A prototypical implementation is based on the 3D simulation system VEROSIM and PostgreSQL as an RDBMS. However, the underlying approach itself provides database independence allowing the usage of other RDBMSs. A key aspect of the presented OR mapping is the schema mapping that is built during a schema synchronization. The introduced concept considers both forward and reverse mapping. Furthermore, the OR mapper supports change tracking and resynchronization of changes. The OR mapper provides an eager and a lazy loading strategy. The prototype is evaluated using simulation models for industrial automation and space robotics (Figure 16).

A. State of the Art

Some RDBMSs provide additional object-relational features. For example, PostgreSQL supports some object-oriented extensions like user defined types or inheritance. However, these features are not provided uniformly by all RDBMSs contradicting the desired database independence. Therefore, the OR mapping is realized with standard relational concepts only.

There are several references in literature dealing with the differences between object-oriented concepts and the relational data model. To solve the object-relational impedance mismatch and successfully generate an OR mapper, it is important to consider the properties of both paradigms and the consequent problems. For example, one main idea of object-orientation is inheritance [66]. However, the relational data model does not feature any comparable concept. Thus, rules have to be defined how inheritance can be mapped onto table structures. Further differences between both paradigms that contribute to the object-relational impedance mismatch are polymorphism, data types, identity, data encapsulation, and relationships.

The following subsections summarize the state-of-the-art of theoretical mapping strategies for inheritance, relationships and polymorphism.

1) Inheritance: The approaches to map objects onto tables differ in to how many tables one object is mapped. Most authors name three standard mapping strategies for inheritance. They are illustrated in Figure 8 regarding the exemplary inheritance hierarchy from Figure 7.

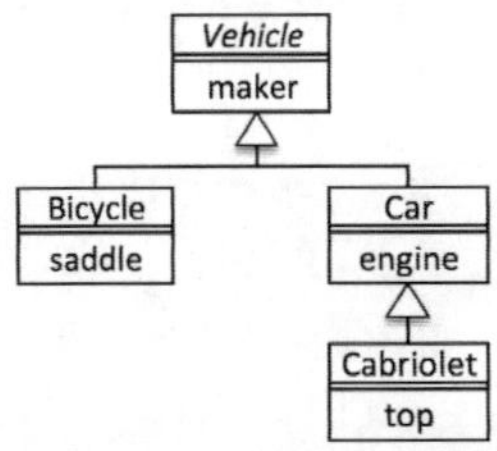

Figure 7. Exemplary inheritance hierarchy (adapted from [67, p. 62f]).

The first strategy is named *Single Table Inheritance* [67] and maps all classes of one inheritance hierarchy to one table, see Figure 8(a). A discriminator field is used to denote the type of each tuple [68]. An advantage is that all data is stored in one table preventing joins and allowing simple updates [67, p. 63]. Unfortunately, this strategy leads to a total denormalization, which is contrary to the concept of relational databases [68].

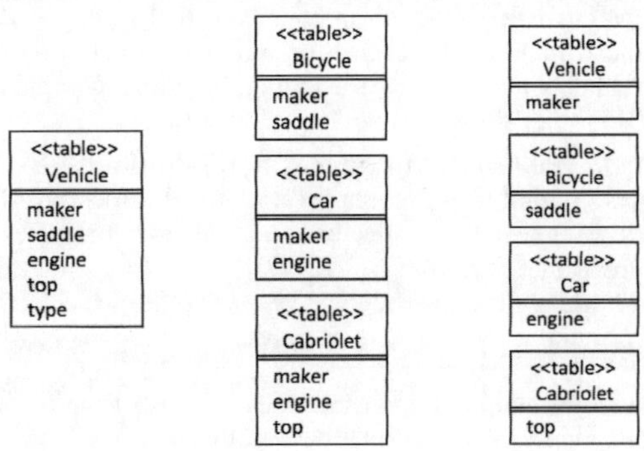

(a) Single Table Inheritance. (b) Concrete Table Inheritance. (c) Class Table Inheritance.

Figure 8. Standard mapping strategies for inheritance (adapted from [67, p. 62f]).

The *Concrete Table Inheritance* [67] strategy maps each concrete class to one table, see Figure 8(b). This mapping requires only few joins to retrieve all data for one object. A disadvantage is that schema changes in base classes are laborious and error-prone [67, p. 62f].

The third standard mapping strategy for inheritance is named *Class Table Inheritance* [67] and uses one table for each class of the hierarchy, see Figure 8(c). It is the easiest approach to map objects onto tables [67, p. 62] and uses a normalized schema [68]. However, due to the use of foreign keys, this approach realizes an *is-a* relationship as a *has-a* relationship [68]. Thus, multiple joins are necessary if all data of one object is required. This aspect can have an effect on performance [67, p. 62f] [69, p. 7].

Another possibility to map objects onto tables not mentioned in every reference on OR mapping is the generic approach [70]. It differs from the strategies mentioned above as it has no predefined structure. Figure 9 shows an exemplary set-up, which can be extended as required. The approach is particularly suitable for small amounts of data because it maps one object to multiple tables. It is advantageous if a highly flexible structure is required. Due to the generic table structure, elements can easily be added or rearranged [70].

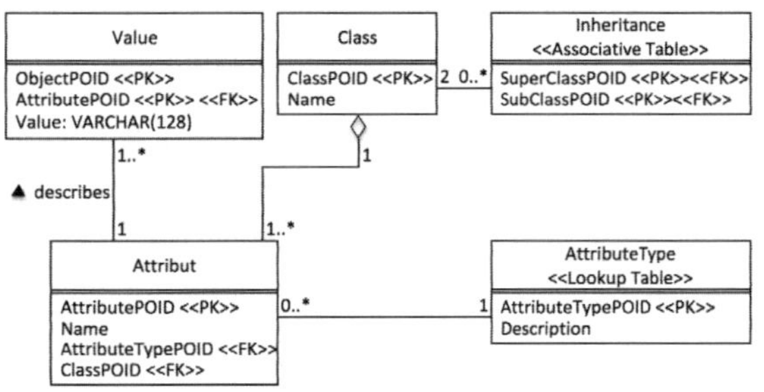

Figure 9. Map classes to generic table structure (adapted from [70, Chapter 2.4]).

In conclusion, there is no single perfect approach to map objects onto tables yielding an optimal result in all situations. Instead, a decision has to be made from case to case depending on the most important properties. For this purpose, the three standard mapping strategies for inheritance can also be combined, however, to the disadvantage of more complexity [67, p. 63].

2) Relationships: In contrast to relationships between two objects, which can be unidirectional, relationships between tables in a relational database are always bidirectional. In unidirectional relationships, associated objects do not know if and when they are referenced by another object [69]. Due to the mandatory mapping of unidirectional onto bidirectional relationships, information hiding cannot be preserved regardless of the relationship's cardinality, i.e., 1:1 (one-to-one), $1{:}n$ (one-to-many) or $n{:}m$ (many-to-many) relationships.

1:1 relationships can simply be mapped onto tables using a foreign key. To map $1{:}n$ relationships, structures have to be reversed [70] [67, p. 58f]. In case of $n{:}m$ relationships, additional tables are mandatory: A so-called association table is used to link the participating tables [70] [67, p. 60]. It is also possible to map an $n{:}m$ relationship using multiple foreign keys in both tables if constant values for n and m are known [70].

Several references describe the aforementioned mapping strategies for relationships. Besides, [71] describes an approach using an additional table regardless of the cardinality. Thus, objects can be mapped onto tables regardless of their relationships. Following [71], one disadvantage of the aforementioned approaches is the violation of the object-oriented principle of information hiding and abstraction. Furthermore, tables are cluttered by foreign key columns, which reduce maintainability and performance. The authors prove (by a performance test) that their own approach shows no performance degradation [71, p. 1446f].

3) Polymorphism: Polymorphism is an essential concept in object-orientation. However, relational databases do not have any feature to reference entries of different tables by one foreign key column. The target table and column have to be explicitly defined for each foreign key constraint. It is not possible to define a foreign key that references more than one table [72, p. 89]. Thus, a mapping is required to map polymorphic associations onto a relational database. Following [72], [73], there are three mapping approaches for polymorphic associations.

The first approach is named *Exclusive Arcs* and uses a separate foreign key column for each table that can be referenced by the polymorphic association, see Figure 10. This approach requires NULL values for foreign key columns. For each tuple, at most one of the foreign key columns may be unequal to NULL. Due to foreign key constraints, referential integrity can be ensured. However, the administrative effort for the aforementioned NULL rule is high. An advantage of this approach is that queries can easily be formulated.

Owner					
ID<<PK>>	Name	Prename	Car<<FK>>	Cabriolet<<FK>>	Bicycle<<FK>>
1234	Müller	Hans	101	*null*	*null*
2456	Müller	Lieschen	112	*null*	*null*
5634	Meier	Ernst	*null*	*null*	87

Car		
ID<<PK>>	Color	...
101	black	...
112	red	...

Bicycle		
ID<<PK>>	Model	...
87	racer	...

Figure 10. Mapping of polymorphic associations using *Exclusive Arcs*.

Another approach is named *Reverse the Relationship* and is shown in Figure 11. It uses an intermediate table with two foreign key columns like the aforementioned approach for $n{:}m$ relationships. Such an intermediate table has to be defined for each possible type (table) that can be referenced by the polymorphic association [72] [73]. The application has to ensure that only one entry of all subordinate tables is assigned to the entry of the superordinate table [72, p. 96ff].

Owner		
ID<<PK>>	Name	Prename
1234	Müller	Hans
2456	Müller	Lieschen
5634	Meier	Ernst

Cars	
Owner<<FK>>	Car<<FK>>
1234	101
2456	112

Car		
ID<<PK>>	Color	...
101	black	...
112	red	...

Bicycles	
Owner<<FK>>	Bicycle<<FK>>
5634	87

Bicycle		
ID<<PK>>	Model	...
87	racer	...

Figure 11. Mapping of polymorphic associations using *Reverse the Relationship*.

The third approach uses a super table (or "base table") and is named *Base Parent Table*. It is based on the basic idea of polymorphism where subtypes can be referenced using a common, often abstract supertype. In most cases, these supertypes themselves are not mapped to the relational database. The strategy uses a table to represent a supertype for all its subtypes' tables as shown in Figure 12.

Owner			
ID<<PK>>	Name	Prename	Vehicle<<FK>>
1234	Müller	Hans	101
2456	Müller	Lieschen	112
5634	Meier	Ernst	87

Vehicles
ID<<PK>>
101
112
87

Car		
ID<<PK,FK>>	Color	...
101	black	...
112	red	...

Bicycle		
ID<<PK,FK>>	Model	...
87	racer	...

Figure 12. Mapping of polymorphic associations using *Base Parent Table*.

Such a base table only consists of one column containing a primary key value. The assigned subordinate entry has the same primary key value as the entry of the base table. Thus, an unambiguous assignment is possible. This approach has the big advantage that base tables do not have to be considered in queries. They are only used to ensure referential integrity [72, p. 100ff].

4) Existing OR Mappers: For a long time, differences between both the object-oriented and relational paradigm were bridged by simple protocols like Java Database Connectivity (JDBC) and Open Database Connectivity (ODBC), which provide a general interface to different relational databases. These interfaces have the disadvantage that the programmer itself is responsible for data exchange between objects and tables. Due to the mixing of SQL statements and object-oriented commands, this usually leads to complex program code that is not easily maintained [68].

OR mappers are used to realize a simpler and smarter mapping between objects and table entries on the one side and a clear separation between the object-oriented and relational layer on the other side. Thus, the application can be developed independently of the mapping and the database. As a consequence, different development teams can be deployed [68].

There are several tools for OR mapping with different features and documentation. Examples are Hibernate (Java), NHibernate (.NET), ADO.NET Entity Framework (.NET), LINQ to SQL (.NET), Doctrine (PHP), ODB (C++), LiteSQL (C++), and QxOrm (C++). Not every existing mapper features all three standard mapping strategies for inheritance. Another main difference is how the mapping approach can be specified. In particular, OR mappers like Hibernate [74] and NHibernate [75] recommend an XML-based mapping while mappers like ODB [76] and QxORM [77] recommend the opposite.

The applicability of an OR mapper depends on the utilized application. In the presented scenario, this is the 3D simulation system VEROSIM. Thus, an OR mapping is required that maps data of a runtime database like VSD onto a relational database. None of the existing OR mappers support a direct mapping of a runtime database's meta information system. They only map object-oriented classes and objects of a specific programming language. Similarly, the SGJ-based approach used in our previous work maps a relational database to a generic object interface that is subsequently mapped to VSD. Thus, if one of these mappers is used, a second mapping is required to map between the meta information system and the object-oriented layer of the OR mapper (see Figure 5).

Based on meta instances, any VSD instance can be classified during runtime. This is a key advantage for the OR mapping with regard to the generation and maintenance of all mappings. Thus, the decision was made to develop a new OR mapper. This allows the OR mapping to be tailored to the requirements of runtime simulation databases like VSD.

B. Approach

A basic decision criterion for OR mapping is the definition of the database schema. Given an existing object-oriented schema, *forward mapping* is used to derive a relational database schema. In contrast, if the initial situation is a given relational database schema, *reverse mapping* is used to derive an object-oriented schema. As already mentioned, database independence is a key aspect of OR mapping. In reverse mapping, this aspect is omitted as a specific database schema of a particular RDBMS is used as the basis for the mapping [68]. The focus of the presented OR mapper is forward mapping to map existing model data of the 3D simulation system onto an arbitrary relational database. Nevertheless, reverse mapping is supported in the concept as well to use the 3D simulation system for other existing databases (see the upper path in Figure 13).

The designed forward mapping of the presented OR mapper is briefly described in the following paragraph and the overall structure of the OR mapper is shown in Figure 13.

First of all, the database schema has to be generated to be able to store object-oriented simulation data in the relational database. Subsequently, a schema synchronization defines a schema mapping between the object-oriented and the relational schema. More details on this are given in [57]. The schema mapping defines, which meta instance is mapped to which table. Based on this mapping, initial simulation model data can be stored. *Generate Schema Based on Meta Information* and *Export Model Data in Database* are performed only once and can be seen as the initialization of the OR mapping. Subsequently, model data can be loaded from the relational database and updated within the simulation database. A change tracking mechanism keeps track of changes within the simulation database and allows for their resynchronization to the relational database.

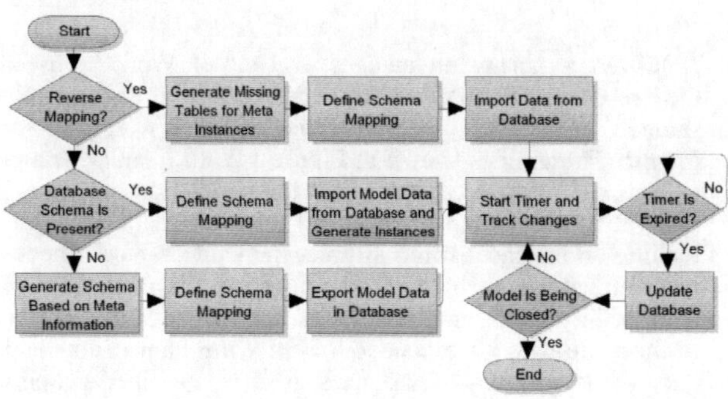

Figure 13. Sequence diagram of the presented OR mapping approach.

In most cases, structural aspects are associated with OR mapping. Behavioral and architectural aspects are often considered secondarily although they are not less important [67, p. 58]. All three aspects should be regarded when developing an OR mapper.

Architectural aspects define the communication between business logic and database. The basic principle is not to mix up the business logic with SQL statements, but rather to use separate classes for database access. These can be classified in four strategies: *Row Data Gateway*, *Table Data Gateway*, *Active Record* and *Data Mapper*. To completely isolate business logic, [67] recommends a Data Mapper. Although this is the most complex strategy, it is used for the developed OR mapper to realize an independent layer between the 3D simulation system and the selected relational database. As a result, both systems can independently be extended. Furthermore, Data Mapper is especially well suited for complex structures [67, p. 49f].

Behavioral aspects define how data can be loaded from or saved to the relational database. With only a few instances to manage, it is easy to keep track of loaded, modified or removed instances and to synchronize these changes with the database. The more instances must be managed, the more complex this process gets. In addition, if various users or processes can access the database, it is even more complex. Here, it has to be ensured that a loaded instance contains valid and consistent data. Following [67], the pattern *Unit of Work* is indispensable to solve this behavioral and concurrency problem, see Figure 14. A Unit of Work can be seen as a control for OR mapping. It registers all loaded, removed or newly created instances as well as changes. A central concept of the Unit of Work is that it aggregates all changes and synchronizes them in their entirety rather than letting the application call separate stored procedures. Alternatives to a central Unit of Work are to immediately synchronize changes or to set dirty flags for each changed object [67, p. 54f].

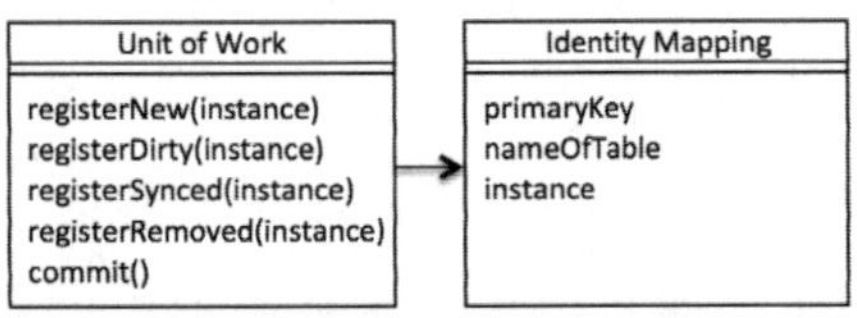

Figure 14. Combination of the patterns *Unit of Work* and *Identity Mapping* (adapted from [67]).

Given its many advantages, a Unit of Work is used in the presented OR mapper. To avoid repetitive loading of the same instances, the Unit of Work is combined with the pattern *Identity Mapping* as shown in Figure 14. An Identity Mapping records each instance loaded into the simulation database and maps it to the related tuple in the relational database. Before loading an instance from its tuple, the Unit of Work checks if there already is an Identity Mapping for this instance, which is especially important for lazy loading [67, p. 55f]. Compared to literature [67] we extended the dirty mechanism. Instead of only registering whole instances as dirty, modified properties are registered as well. This allows to synchronize changes more efficiently.

The fundamentals of structural aspects are described in Section IV-A. To minimize the overall number of joins, the Concrete Table Inheritance strategy was chosen for mapping inheritance. Furthermore, two strategies are selected to map relationships. 1:1 relationships are mapped to simple foreign key columns whereas $1{:}n$ relationships are mapped to association tables. However, this is only possible for monomorphic associations. For the polymorphic case, the strategies described in Subsection IV-A3 have to be evaluated. Due to the high administrative effort, Exclusive Arcs is inapplicable. The other two strategies are compared regarding the formulation of queries. Base Parent Table allows for simpler queries. However, the theoretical mapping of this strategy (Figure 12) does not fit in combination with the aforementioned selected mappings for inheritance and monomorphic associations. In practice, a subordinated instance can be referenced by both a monomorphic and a polymorphic association of superordinated instances. As a consequence, the foreign key constraint could be violated. So the theoretical mapping of Base Parent Table is adapted to fit in combination with the aforementioned selected mappings for inheritance and monomorphic associations as shown in Figure 15. As an advantage, both the base table and the additional foreign key column do not need to be considered in queries. They are only used to ensure referential integrity.

Owner			
ID<<PK>>	Name	Prename	Vehicle<<FK>>
1234	Müller	Hans	101
2456	Müller	Lieschen	112
5634	Meier	Ernst	87

Vehicles
ID<<PK>>
101
112
87

Car		
ID<<PK>>	Color	base_Vehicle<<FK>>
101	black	101
112	red	112

Space in Bike Station		
ID<<PK>>	Space Number	Bicycle<<FK>>
307	1	87
308	2	89

Bicycle		
ID<<PK>>	Model	base_Vehicle<<FK>>
87	racer	87
89	e-bike	*null*

Figure 15. Adapted *Base Parent Table* mapping of polymorphic associations.

Another important part of an OR mapper is data type mapping. Data types of the object-oriented data model can differ from those of the relational data model. Thus, a data type mapping has to be defined. The developed OR mapper comprises an interface to use a dynamic data type mapping, which can be adapted for each database and its related data types. This is one main aspect of the supported database independence. Furthermore, the utilized Qt framework [78] (QSqlDatabase) allows for a vendor-independent database communication. Altogether, the developed OR mapper can easily support different RDBMSs.

After schema synchronization, model data can be loaded from the relational database populating the simulation database with corresponding instances. A so-called *eager loading strategy* is used to immediately load and generate all model instances. The Unit of Work generates an identity mapping for each loaded instance. This provides an unambiguous mapping between each loaded instance and the corresponding tuple in the relational database. Furthermore, a so-called *lazy loading strategy* is specified for selectively loading model data from the database. It is based on the ghost strategy presented in [67, p. 227ff]. Here, typically necessary information, like primary key and table name, is determined for all tuples from all tables regardless whether the instance is loaded or not. Ghost instances are generated containing only this partially loaded data [67, p. 227ff]. The presented OR mapper uses a *Ghost Identity Mapping* (Figure 14). The advantage of this modified approach is that only "complete" instances are present in the 3D simulation system's runtime database.

C. Evaluation

As mentioned before, schema generation and synchronization work independently of the selected simulation model. All required structures are defined during schema generation. In the evaluated configuration of the 3D simulation system VEROSIM, 910 tables, 1,222 foreign key columns, and 2,456 association tables are generated to map all meta instances and 1:1 as well as 1:n relationships. The schema generation takes about 200 seconds on a local PostgreSQL 9.4 installation. The required schema mapping is built up during schema synchronization and takes about 2.7 seconds.

Due to its flexibility, the OR mapper can be used for any simulation model. The prototype is evaluated using two exemplary models from two different fields of application: industrial automation and space robotics. Given the current functional range of the presented prototype, further tests do not appear to provide any additional insights.

Figure 16(a) shows the first model from the field of industrial robotics. The robot model contains only a few objects so that only 173 primary keys have to be generated to map all objects to table entries. It takes about 0.43 seconds to store the whole robot into the relational database and about 4.7 seconds to load it.

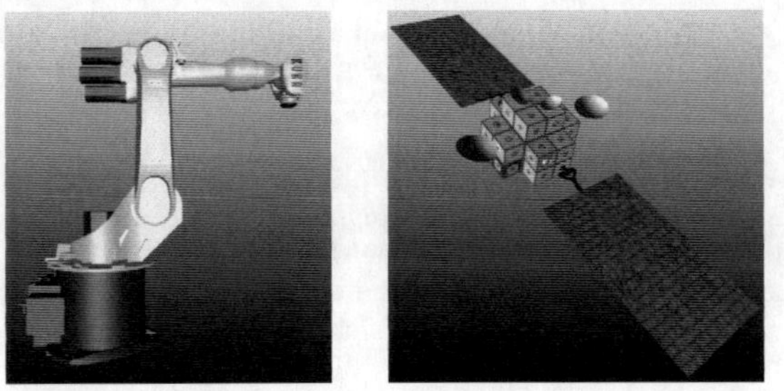

(a) Industrial robot simulation model.

(b) Modular satellite simulation model (data: [65]).

Figure 16. Evaluated simulation models.

The second model (Figure 16(b)) is a modular satellite. In comparison, it contains much more objects so that 19,463 primary keys are generated to map all objects to table entries. In this case, it takes about 22 seconds to store all objects of the satellite and about 7.1 seconds to load all of them from the relational database.

An overview of the performance values compared to the proprietary VEROSIM MOD file format is given in Table I. The results are about factor two slower for loading data, which is acceptable for a first prototype. However, the overhead for writing data is especially larger for the more complex satellite model. This can mainly be explained by the structures described in Subsection IV-B that have to be build up in the relational database. This process is far more complex than linearly writing out model data to the (highly optimized) MOD file format. Yet again, the optimization of the prototype might improve these results.

As mentioned in Subsection IV-A4, a comparable interface to existing ORM solutions would be less efficient as well as more complex and time-consuming to realize due to the necessary second mapping. Thus, we refrain from performing such comparisons.

TABLE I. LOADING AND SAVING TIMES OF THE ORM-BASED PROTOTYPE COMPARED TO PROPRIETARY VEROSIM MOD FILE FORMAT.

	ORM		File	
	Robot	Satellite	Robot	Satellite
Loading	$4.7s$	$7.1s$	$2.5s$	$3.5s$
Saving	$0.4s$	$22s$	$0.5s$	$1.0s$

V. GRAPH DATABASE APPROACH

Currently, relational databases are dominating the market. Due to different problems with scalability and effective processing of big data with relational databases the field of NoSQL ("Not only SQL") databases has emerged [79]. In this context, the approach of graph databases (GDBs) has become popular. GDBs save their data in the nodes and edges of a mathematical graph, in particular, to manage highly linked information. As such, they are ideally suited for 3D simulation models. As mentioned above, like in CAD, such 3D data usually comprises a huge number of parts of many different types (mostly, each with only few instances), structured hierarchically with interdependencies. This recommends a graph-like data structure. For the same reason, the scene graph is a common approach to manage 3D data at runtime.

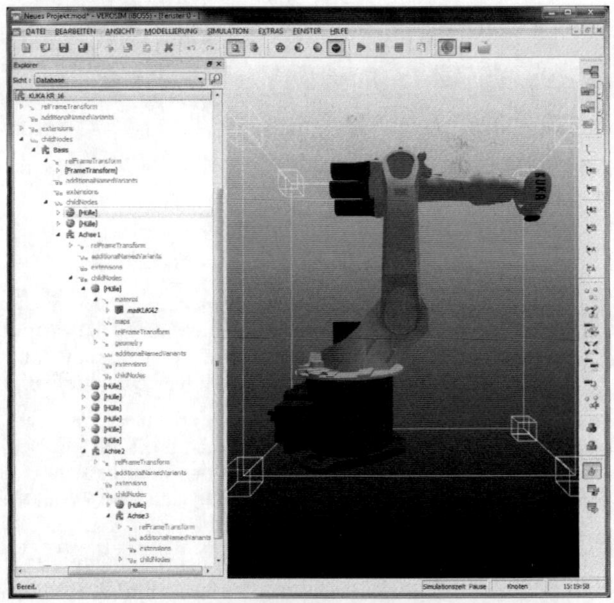

Figure 17. Robot model (from Figure 24) loaded from Neo4j into the in-memory simulation database VSD.

In this section, we present an approach for a synchronization interface between a GDB and a 3D simulation database, i.e., the runtime database of a 3D simulation system. The applied data mapping strategy is bidirectional and in part incremental. The approach was developed in the context of a student project and is based on our previous work. Its feasibility is shown with a prototypical implementation using the GDB Neo4j and the 3D simulation system VEROSIM and its VSD database (Figure 17).

A. State of the Art

In this section, the necessary basics for our work are presented.

1) Graph Database Basics: The idea of a GDB relies on the mathematical graph theory. Information is saved in the nodes (or vertices) and edges (or relationships) of a graph as shown in Figure 18. A graph is a tuple $G = (V, E)$, where V describes the set of nodes and E the set of edges, i.e., $v_i \in V$ and $e_{i,j} = (v_i, v_j) \in E$ [80]. To specify records, properties of nodes and (depending on the GDB) even relationships can be described by key-value pairs [63]. An important aspect of GDBs is the fact that all relationships are directly stored with the nodes so that there is no need to infer them as in relational databases using foreign keys and joins. Hence, read operations on highly connected data can be performed very fast. During a read access, the graph is traversed along paths so that the individual data records (nodes and edges) can be read in situ and do not have to be searched globally. Therefore, the execution time depends only on the traversal's depth [79].

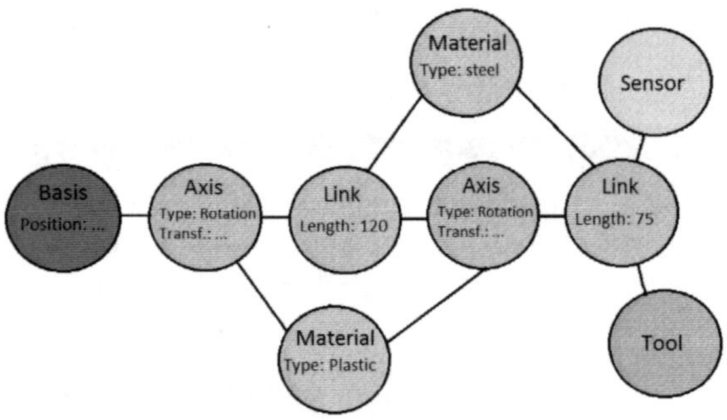

Figure 18. Graph database of a robot model.

GDBs also provide standard database features like security, recovery from hard- or software failures, concurrency control for parallel access, or methods for data integrity and reliability.

In contrast to flat files, using a (graph) database, data can be modified with a query language. Such languages are a powerful tool to manipulate the database content so that the data is not only stored persistently and securely but can also be handled simply.

2) Neo4j: Neo4j is a GDB implemented in Java. It can be run in server or embedded mode. Figure 19 shows its data model. Central elements are nodes and relationships containing the stored records. These records are described by an arbitrary number of properties (key-value pairs). Neo4j offers the concept of *labels* and *types* to divide the graph in logical substructures. A node is extendible with several labels characterizing the node's classification. Similarly, a relationship is identified by a type (exactly one). Besides the classification of the data, this also improves reading performance as just a part of the graph must be traversed to find the desired record [63] [64]. Apart from that, Neo4j is schemaless, i.e., it does not require any metadata definition before inserting actual user data.

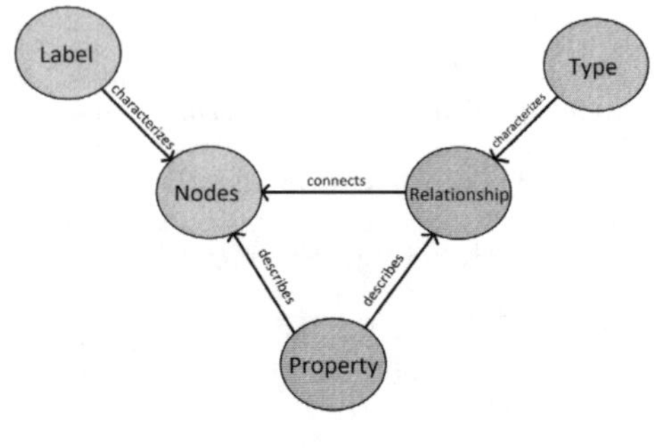

Figure 19. Neo4j data model.

All Neo4j accesses are processed in ACID (Atomicity, Consistency, Isolation, Durability) compliant transactions guaranteeing the reliability, consistency and durability of the database content [79]. Accesses are either performed with Neo4j's own query language called Cypher or using its Java API.

3) Other Graph Databases: Besides Neo4j, there are many other GDBs in the market. They differ in their conceptual structure and application area.

DEX is a GDB based on the labeled and directed attributed multigraph model. All nodes and edges are classified (labeled), edges are directed, nodes can be extended with properties (attributes), and edges can be connected with more than two nodes (multigraph) [81]. The graph is represented by bitmaps and other secondary structures. DEX has been designed for high performance and scalable graph scenarios. The good performance is achieved by the bitmap-based structure and the indexing of all attributes, which are efficiently processed by the C++ kernel [82].

Trinity [83] [84] is a memory-based graph store with many database features like concurrency or ACID-conform transactions. The graph storage is distributed among multiple well connected machines in a globally addressable memory address space yielding big data support. A unified declarative language provides data manipulation and message passing between the different machines. The great advantage of Trinity is the fast access to large data records. It is based on a multigraph model, which can exceed one billion nodes. Since there is no strict database schema, Trinity can flexibly be adapted to many data sets.

HypergraphDB stores its data in a directed multigraph, whose implementation is based on BerkeleyDB. All graph elements are called atoms. Every atom is characterized by its atom arity indicating the number of linked atoms. The arity determines an atom's type: An arity larger than zero yields an edge atom, or else, a node atom. Each atom has a typed value containing the user data [85].

InfoGrid is a framework specialized in the development of REpresentational State Transfer (REST)-full web applications. One part of this framework is a proprietary GDB used for data management. The graph's nodes are called MeshObjects, which are classified by one or more so-called EntityTypes, properties, and their linked relationships. MeshObjects not only contain the user data but also manage events relevant to the node [86].

Infinite Graph is a GDB based on an object-oriented concept. All nodes and edges are derived from two basic Java classes. Thus, the database schema is represented by user-defined classes. Besides data management, Infinite Graph provides a visualization tool [87]. Since the database can be distributed on multiple machines working in parallel, Infinite Graph can achieve a high data throughput. To manage concurrency, a lock server handles the different lock requests [82].

AllegroGraph [88] provides a REST protocol architecture. With this interface, the user has full control of the database including indexing, query and session management. All transactions satisfy ACID conditions.

Despite this wide range of GDBs, for the following reasons, we decide to use Neo4j in our approach:

- In many tests it proves to process data fast and efficiently,
- it can handle more than one billion nodes – even enough for extremely large 3D simulation models – which could be useful in coming stages of extension,
- Neo4j is a full native GDB so that traversal and other graph operations can be performed efficiently,
- Neo4j provides a comprehensive and powerful query language (e.g., for efficient partial loading strategies in future versions of the presented prototype),
- directed edges allow to model object interdependencies more accurately, however, without disadvantages in traversal performance,
- properties on relationships allow for a more flexible modeling (e.g., to distinguish between shared and composite aggregation relationships),
- finally, Neo4j is currently the most prevalent GDB in the market indicating it to be especially well explored and developed. Hence, it provides the best prospects of success.

Note that while we choose Neo4j for the reasons given above, the presented concepts are mostly independent of the choice of the particular GDB.

B. Concept

In this section, we describe the fundamental concept and the required features of our synchronization component's prototype. Its implementation using Neo4j and VSD is described in Subsection V-C.

1) Structure Mapping: An essential question when synchronizing two databases is: How do we map the different data structures? Depending on the database paradigm, entities with attributes and relationships (connecting two or more entities) are represented differently. For example, a relational database uses relations, attributes and foreign keys while a GDB uses nodes, relationships and properties.

1) **Schema Mapping:** Before synchronizing user data, a generic schema mapping is performed mapping the metadata of one database to the other as described in [57]. This is performed once on system startup. For example, when performed between a relational and an object-oriented database, each table of the former might be mapped to a corresponding class of the latter (columns and class attributes accordingly).
2) **Schemaless Approach:** When a schemaless database is involved, a different approach has to be applied. Here, metadata from a non-schemaless database must be mapped onto the user data of the schemaless one. For example, class names from an object-oriented database are mapped onto node labels of a schemaless GDB.

For the schemaless Neo4j, in our prototype, we chose the second approach.

2) Object Mapper: Another key aspect of the concept is the object mapper. It maps objects from one database to an equivalent counterpart in the other database. For example, an object from an object-oriented database is mapped to a corresponding node in the GDB. The mapping is based on the counterparts' identities and includes a transfer of all property (or attribute) values in between. Based on these mappings, individual object or property changes can be tracked and resynchronized. Summarized the mapping is bidirectional and in part incremental.

3) Transactions: Any changes (insert, update, delete) to the data are tracked and stored in transactions, which can be processed independently. By executing these transactions, data is (re)synchronized on object level. During the accumulation (and before the execution) of such transactions, the operations stored within can be filtered for redundancies. For example, a transaction for creating a new object followed by a transaction for deleting the very same object can both be discarded.

C. Prototype

This section gives an insight into the prototypical implementation of the interface between VSD and Neo4j. The prototype should have the ability to save simulation data from VSD in Neo4j and to load it back into VSD. Initially, when storing a simulation model in Neo4j, VSD's contents are archived once. Subsequently, changes in VSD are tracked and updated to Neo4j individually. That is, when a VSD instance has been changed just the changes are transferred as mentioned above. In the current version of the interface, only changes within VSD are tracked for resynchronization. Thus, Neo4j serves as database back end, which can store simulation models persistently.

The prototype is realized in a C++ based VEROSIM plugin, which uses Neo4j's Java API in embedded mode in order to communicate with Neo4j.

1) Data Mapping: In the context of this work, synchronization represents data transfer from one database to another. However, the structure of one database's data elements often differs from those of another. Thus, it becomes necessary to map these different structures on each other. Figure 20 shows our intuitive approach.

Single VSD instances are mapped to single Neo4j nodes and references (Ref/List-Properties) from one instance to another are represented by relationships between the corresponding nodes. The relationship is orientated to the referenced node's direction. Furthermore, we transfer the Val-Properties of a VSD instance to Neo4j node properties.

As mentioned above, a basic difference between VSD and Neo4j is that the former comprises metadata describing (and prescribing) a schema while the latter is schemaless. VSD metadata contains important information for the simulation and

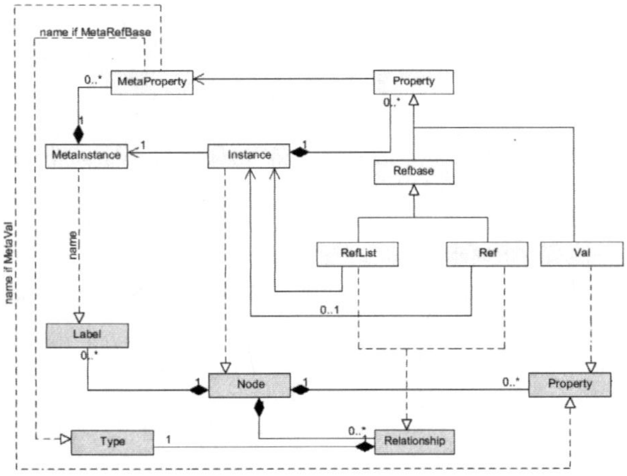

Figure 20. Data mapping of the synchronization component (top: VSD data model, bottom: Neo4j data model).

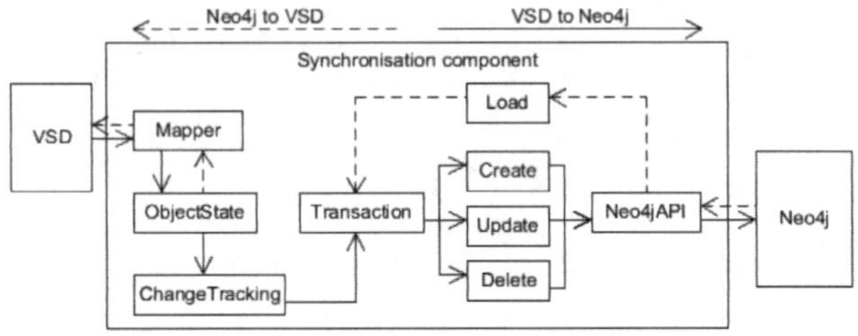

Figure 21. Synchronization component.

VSD-Id	Neo4j-Id	State	Pending-Transactions
...			
6049	0	SYNCED	-
6050	1	PENDING_UPDATE	Update-Transaction1, Update-Transaction2
6051	2	PENDING_DELETE	Delete-Transaction
...			

Figure 22. Exemplary list of object states of the mapper.

is indispensable for a correct data mapping. Thus, it is essential to transfer this informations as well. We store VSD metadata on Neo4j's object level:

1) A VSD instance's class name is mapped to its Neo4j node's label,
2) a VSD Ref/List-Property's name is mapped to its Neo4j relationship's type, and
3) a VSD Val-Property's name is mapped to its Neo4j property's key.

Val-Property values are handled depending on their data type. If the type corresponds to one of Neo4j's supported basic types (e.g., integer, float, string, boolean, etc.) the value will be transfered directly. More complex data structures (e.g., mathematical vectors, etc.) are serialized to a binary representation and transfered as such.

To store additional meta information about VSD Ref/List-Properties, we take advantage of Neo4j's feature to add properties to relationships. Currently, every relationship gets a boolean property with the key *autodelete* as introduced above. Additionally, a RefList-Property entry's order is stored as an index in a relationship property.

2) Synchronization Component: Figure 21 depicts the structure of the synchronization component (based on [89]). Its core is the (object) mapper managing mappings between pairs of VSD instances and Neo4j nodes. Each mapping is stored in form of a so-called ObjectState (OS) holding all relevant information. The OS contains both objects' ids, all collected (but not executed) transactions and the state of the relation between the two. This state indicates whether the pair is synchronous, i.e., equal, or whether one of them has been changed and differs from its counterpart. An exemplary list of object states of the mapper is given in Figure 22.

Each change to a VSD instance is encapsulated in a transaction stored in the appropriate OS. Subsequently, they can be executed. Depending on the change's type, a create, update, or delete transaction is generated. Furthermore, a separate load transaction is used to load Neo4j contents into VSD. Each transaction comprises all type specific information necessary for its execution. For example, a create transaction contains the names and values of all Val-Properties, the class name, and information on Ref/List-Properties like target ids, reference names and *autodelete* values.

The last part of the synchronization component is the Neo4jAPI, which interacts with Neo4j's Java API.

VSD to Neo4j: VSD is an active database. One aspect of this activity is that changes to its instances are notified to registered components like the synchronization component presented in this work. Notifications include all relevant information about the modification like the instance's id or the changed property. The synchronization component encapsulates this information in an appropriate transaction. Using the instance id, the mapper is able to identify the corresponding OS and retrieve the mapping's state. A change tracking mechanism is used to filter redundant transactions as mentioned above (more details are given in Section V-C3).

When the user or some automatic mechanism (e.g., a timer) triggers a resynchronization, all collected transactions are executed modifying Neo4j's contents accordingly.

Neo4j to VSD: When loading a Neo4j database's contents to VSD, the Neo4jAPI traverses the graph and generates a load transaction for each visited node. All data is read from Neo4j before entries are stored in the mapper. Load transactions contain the respective node's id, all its property keys and values and the ids of adjacent nodes of outgoing relationships and their respective properties (*autodelete* and index for RefList-Properties). Subsequently, the synchronization component executes all load transactions. For each, a new VSD instance with appropriate properties is created and its id is stored in an OS with the corresponding node's id.

3) Change Tracking: As mentioned above, when collecting transactions, newly created ones may cancel out older ones. A change tracking mechanism performs the necessary filtering of such redundant transactions.

Change tracking is based on the current state of the considered OS. Depending on the incoming transaction's type, the state changes and the list of collected transactions is updated.

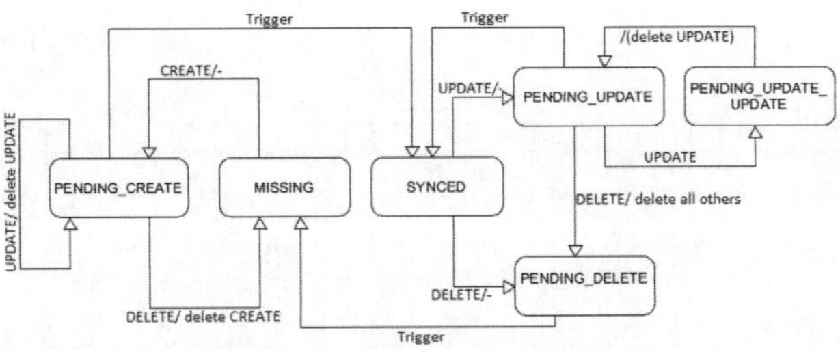

Figure 23. State machine of the change tracking mechanism.

Change tracking is modeled as a state machine as depicted in Figure 23. Here, the input (triggering state transitions) is represented by the incoming transaction type and the output (emitted during state transitions) describes the transaction list's modification. The initial state of any OS for a newly created VSD instance is the *MISSING* state as there is no corresponding Neo4j node. This intermediate state is left as soon as the corresponding create transaction is generated and the state changes to *PENDING_CREATE*. If this VSD instance is deleted before the transaction of type create has been executed, both transactions (create and delete) are removed and the whole OS is deleted. Else, upon a resynchronization trigger, a corresponding Neo4j node is generated, the state changes to *SYNCED*, and all executed transactions are removed from the list. The *SYNCED* state means that a Neo4j node and its VSD instance counterpart are in sync. It is reached every time a resynchronization was performed and is left when the VSD instance is modified (*PENDING_UPDATE*) or deleted (*PENDING_DELETE*).

In *PENDING_UPDATE* state, the changed property of an additional update transaction is compared to existing update transactions to avoid multiple updates of the same property. If two transactions modify the same property only one of them needs to be stored. This is represented by the intermediate *PENDING_UPDATE_UPDATE* state.

D. Evaluation

Finally, the interface's effectiveness and performance have been evaluated using the same two simulation models of an industrial robot and a satellite as used in the OR mapping approach. As above, given the current functional range of the presented prototype, further tests do not appear to provide more insights. Initially, both models are stored in a Neo4j database and, subsequently, loaded back into an (empty) VSD. The robot model yields 170 Neo4j nodes and 209 relationships. The more complex satellite about 20,000 nodes and 25,000 relationships. The highly connected nature of the 3D simulation data is apparent making a GDB ideally suited for its storage.

Figures 24 and 17 give an impression of the interface's effectiveness. Figure 24 shows an excerpt of the robot model data within Neo4j. Figure 17 shows the same data loaded into the VSD in-memory simulation database. The data mapping operates generically, i.e., independent from the actual data, making the whole synchronization component very flexible. The interface can synchronize arbitrary VSD contents to a Neo4j database.

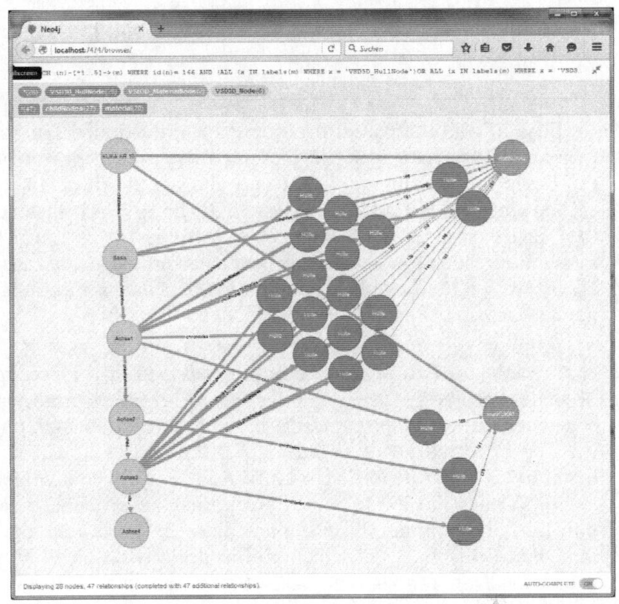

Figure 24. 3D simulation model data (excerpt) of an industrial robot stored within Neo4j.

TABLE II. LOADING AND SAVING TIMES OF THE NEO4J-BASED PROTOTYPE.

	Neo4j		File	
	Robot	Satellite	Robot	Satellite
Loading	0.14	3.99	0.1	2.8
Saving	2.63	10.53	1.8	9.9

In Subsection V-C, we present the interface's functionality to selectively resynchronize changes to VSD instances. This feature has been tested by changing some VSD properties (e.g., name or position of a component). In the Neo4j browser, we verified that these modifications were transferred correctly. Inversely, changes to node properties from the Neo4j browser show up in VEROSIM when the model is reloaded. This also shows the advantage of selectively modifying data within a database in contrast to a file-based approach.

Another important aspect of the evaluation is the interface's performance. Here, the initial storage of a simulation model into Neo4j and the loading of a whole simulation model from Neo4j were examined and compared to saving and loading models to and from the native VEROSIM file format. Results are given in Table II. The access operations to the GDB are only somewhat slower than the native file operations. For a prototypical implementation from a student project, these results are very promising. First of all, compared to the highly optimized code for reading and writing the native file format, the current prototype is only optimized to a certain degree. Furthermore, the more high-level database access operations will always remain a little more complex than simple, sequential file reading or writing. Yet, the additional benefit from a full-fledged database (providing security, multi-user support, etc.) more than compensates for this small drawback.

Altogether, this shows that a GDB like Neo4j is well suited

for highly connected 3D simulation model data and can be handled fast.

VI. Comparison

First of all, compared to our previous solution using the generic OR mapper SGJ, the presented two prototypes avoid the usage of an additional layer between the synchronization component and ExtDB, i.e., PostgreSQL and Neo4j. Instead, they realize a direct database access. Besides fewer transformations (presumably, leading to better performance) this also allows for a more flexible adaptation to the needs of eRobotics applications and Semantic World Models.

From a performance point of view – as far as this is comparable for two prototypes both developed in the context of student projects – the results for the Neo4j-based prototype are better than those of the ORM-based approach. In fact, this was our expected result as the graph paradigm obviously fits better to the structure of Semantic World Models. The complex mapping rules needed to properly represent inheritance, relationships and polymorphism to overcome the object-relational impedance mismatch take their toll, especially when writing data. However, further optimization of these first prototypes might change these differences.

Regarding the implementation of schemata, in both cases, special structures within the relational or graph database are necessary that have to be interpreted by the respective synchronization component. Other applications accessing these databases must have knowledge about this "encoding" – especially when writing data. The schemaless Neo4j obviously has drawbacks as opposed to the ORM-based approach. In the latter, many object-oriented schema structures from VSD can be mapped to their relational counterparts (e.g., attributes). This allows to secure more structural requirements on the side of ExtDB rather than the synchronization interface.

Another important aspect is the dissemination of the two systems. While the graph database paradigm might be more suited for storing Semantic World Model data, RDBMSs are far more pervasive. Thus, it is easier to find stable DBMSs, tool or query language (SQL vs. Cypher) support, or even specialized developers and administrators. Finally, customer acceptance is also a key decision criterion. Many users of eRobotics applications in business and industry already use a DBMS in their enterprise. Mostly, these are well-established relational solutions like Oracle, Microsoft SQL Server, MySQL or PostgreSQL – and mostly they want to keep using these solutions for different reasons (existing infrastructure, existing maintenance contracts, existing personnel etc.).

Finally, by being based on the general database synchronization concept presented in Section III, both approaches fulfill most of the five requirement for data management for eRobotics applications:

1) both map VSD's object-oriented data to either PostgreSQL or Neo4j,
2) both realize a distributed architecture by synchronizing the local VSD to a central PostgreSQL or Neo4j,
3) both integrate the in-memory database VSD as a cache for the shared Semantic World Model in PostgreSQL or Neo4j,
4) both flexibly adapt to different schemata by mapping them appropriately to PostgreSQL or Neo4j structures,
5) and both DBMS allow for a usage in simulation as well as live operation scenarios. However, regarding temporal data management, in both cases, further research needs to be conducted for a realization using PostgreSQL or Neo4j.

TABLE III. Comparison chart of the two presented approaches.

	ORM	Neo4j
Additional transformations	no	no
Impedance mismatch	yes	no
Native schema support	yes	no
Encoding of OO schema	complex	straightforward
Dissemination of DBMS	high	low
Fulfillment of 5 main requirements	all	all
Prototype performance	limited	good

Table III gives an overview.

Thus, while both approaches are applicable for eRobotics applications, each has its advantages and drawbacks.

VII. Conclusion and Future Work

In this paper, we give an introduction to eRobotics applications and define their requirements for data management. We present the various benefits from using database technology to manage the underlying Semantic World Models instead of using flat file formats. Furthermore, we show how existing approaches for database integration into applications with a 3D context do not provide a sufficiently comprehensive and flexible solution to fulfill all these requirements. This motivated the development of our new database synchronization concept for eRobotics applications. Its basic idea is to use local in-memory simulation databases (SimDB) and to synchronize them to a central, external back-end database (ExtDB). This concept has previously been realized using a generic OR mapper with the drawback of an additional translation layer. Thus, in this paper and based on this concept, two new direct approaches are presented omitting this additional layer. The first is an integrated OR mapping approach, directly mapping the schema and data from SimDB to a central relational ExtDB without an intermediate representation. The second uses a graph database for ExtDB, benefiting from the graph-like structure of Semantic World Models. For both cases, the state of the art (theory and existing solutions) is analyzed, based on which the approaches are developed. The respective evaluations and the final comparison show the basic suitability and practical feasibility of both prototypes for the management of eRobotics applications' Semantic World Models. While the graph database approach is advantageous in terms of performance the OR mapping approach is more suited to integrate into existing corporate infrastructures. Thus, the decision for a database paradigm for ExtDB depends on the concrete application scenario.

In future, both prototypes might receive more development and optimization. For the direct OR mapper, data type mapping can be extended by more specialized data types and further RDBMSs can be combined with the prototype. Furthermore, the currently generated structures within the relational database do not contain explicit information on the inheritance relationships as they are not needed by the simulation system itself (they can be retrieved from its meta information system). However, to allow third party applications to interpret the data, inheritance structures would be of interest. Another aspect to investigate is the mapping of queries and operations. For the former, an object-based query language meeting VSD's demands, e.g., XQuery or (a variation of) Java Persistence Query Language (JPQL) or Hibernate Query Language (HQL), needs to be mapped to proper SQL queries. Further performance optimizations and, with an extended functional range of the mapper, evaluations beyond the results from the student project could be performed, as well. Finally, we could examine further applications, e.g., from other fields like forestry. For the Neo4j-based approach, also further performance optimizations and evaluations beyond the results from the student project could be performed. For instance, better traversal algorithms might improve loading speed. Another idea is to use Neo4j's batch inserter in contrast to the transactional structure to reduce resynchronization time. Furthermore, Neo4j might be used as a central database in a distributed simulation scenario with several VEROSIMs and VSDs. Here, an equivalent notification mechanism is needed for Neo4j to be able to track modifications in the central database. Finally, apart from the two presented approaches, further database paradigms like in-memory databases (e.g., SAP HANA, H2 or Redis) could be examined as candidates for ExtDB.

References

[1] A.-M. Stapelbroek, M. Hoppen, and J. Rossmann, "Object-Relational Mapping in 3D Simulation," in DBKDA 2016, The 8th International Conference on Advances in Databases, Knowledge, and Data Applications, Lisbon, Portugal, 2016.

[2] M. Hoppen, J. Rossmann, and S. Hiester, "Managing 3D Simulation Models with the Graph Database Neo4j," in GraphSM 2016, The 3rd International Workshop on Large-scale Graph Storage and Management, Lisbon, Portugal, 2016.

[3] J. Rossmann, M. Schluse, M. Rast, and L. Atorf, "eRobotics Combining Electronic Media and Simulation Technology to Develop (Not Only) Robotics Applications," in E-Systems for the 21st Century: Concept, Developments, and Applications, S. Kadry and A. El Hami, Eds. Apple Academic Press, 2015.

[4] Verein Deutscher Ingenieure (VDI), "VDI 3633 - Simulation of systems in materials handling, logistics and production - Fundamentals," Düsseldorf, 2013, URL: https://www.vdi.de/richtlinie/entwurf_vdi_3633-simulation_von_logistik_materialfluss_und_produktionssystemen_begriffe/ [retrieved: 2017.05.17].

[5] R. Elmasri and S. B. Navathe, Database Systems: Models, Languages, Design, And Application Programming, 6th ed. Prentice Hall International, 2010.

[6] buildingSMART Internatioinal, "Industry Foundation Classes (IFC)," URL: http://www.buildingsmart-tech.org/specifications/ifc-releases/summary [retrieved: 2017.05.17].

[7] A. e.V., "AutomationML," URL: https://www.automationml.org [retrieved: 2017.05.17].

[8] SysML Open Source Specification Project, "SysML Specification," URL: http://www.sysml.org/sysml-specifications/ [retrieved: 2017.05.17].

[9] S. Julier, Y. Baillot, M. Lanzagorta, D. Brown, and L. Rosenblum, "Bars: Battlefield augmented reality system," in NATO Symposium on Information Processing Techniques for Military Systems, 2000, pp. 9–11.

[10] D. Schmalstieg et al., "Managing complex augmented reality models," IEEE Computer Graphics and Applications, vol. 27, no. 4, 2007, pp. 48–57.

[11] J. Haist and V. Coors, "The W3DS-Interface of Cityserver3D," in European Spatial Data Research (EuroSDR) u.a.: Next Generation 3D City Models. Workshop Papers : Participant's Edition, Kolbe and Gröger, Eds., Bonn, 2005, pp. 63–67.

[12] J. Haist, R. Schnuck, and T. Reitz, "Usage of persistence framework technologies for 3D geodata servers," in AGILE 2006, 9th AGILE Conference on Geographical Information Science. Shaping the future of Geographic Information Science in Europe, 2006, pp. 43 – 50.

[13] Y. Masunaga and C. Watanabe, "Design and implementation of a multi-modal user interface of the Virtual World Database system (VWDB)," in Proceedings Seventh International Conference on Database Systems for Advanced Applications. DASFAA 2001. IEEE Comput. Soc, 2001, pp. 294–301.

[14] Y. Masunaga, C. Watanabe, A. Osugi, and K. Satoh, "A New Database Technology for Cyberspace Applications," in Nontraditional Database Systems, Y. Kambayashi, M. Kitsuregawa, A. Makinouchi, S. Uemura, K. Tanaka, and Y. Masunaga, Eds. London: Taylor & Francis, 2002, ch. 1, pp. 1–14.

[15] C. Watanabe and Y. Masunaga, "VWDB2: A Network Virtual Reality System with a Database Function for a Shared Work Environment," in Information Systems and Databases, K. Tanaka, Ed., Tokyo, Japan, 2002, pp. 190–196.

[16] K. Kaku, H. Minami, T. Tomii, and H. Nasu, "Proposal of Virtual Space Browser Enables Retrieval and Action with Semantics which is Shared by Multi Users," in 21st International Conference on Data Engineering Workshops (ICDEW'05). IEEE, apr 2005, pp. 1259–1259.

[17] M. Kamiura, H. Oisol, K. Tajima, and K. Tanaka, "Spatial views and LOD-based access control in VRML-object databases," in Worldwide Computing and Its Applications, ser. Lecture Notes in Computer Science, T. Masuda, Y. Masunaga, and M. Tsukamoto, Eds. Springer Berlin / Heidelberg, 1997, vol. 1274, pp. 210–225.

[18] E. V. Schweber, "SQL3D - Escape from VRML Island," 1998, URL: http://www.infomaniacs.com/SQL3D/SQL3D-Escape-From-VRML-Island.htm [retrieved: 2017.05.17].

[19] A. Vakaloudis and B. Theodoulidis, "Spatiotemporal Database Connection to VRML," in Proceedings of the 9th UK Electronic Imaging & the Visual Arts Conference, EVA '98, Cambridge, 1998.

[20] K. Walczak, "Dynamic Database Modeling of 3D Multimedia Content," in Interactive 3D Multimedia Content, W. Cellary and K. Walczak, Eds. London: Springer London, 2012, ch. 4, pp. 55–102.

[21] K. Walczak and W. Cellary, "Building database applications of virtual reality with X-VRML," in Proceeding of the seventh international conference on 3D Web technology - Web3D '02. New York, New York, USA: ACM Press, feb 2002, pp. 111–120.

[22] U. Sendler, The PLM Compendium: Reference book of Product Lifecycle Management (orig.: Das PLM-Kompendium: Referenzbuch des Produkt-Lebenszyklus-Managements). Berlin: Springer, 2009.

[23] Verein Deutscher Ingenieure (VDI), "VDI 2219 - Information technology in product development Introduction and economics of EDM/PDM Systems (Issue German/English)," Düsseldorf, 2002.

[24] T. Manoharan, H. Taylor, and P. Gardiner, "A collaborative analysis tool for visualisation and interaction with spatial data," in Proceedings of the seventh international conference on 3D Web technology. ACM, 2002, pp. 75–83.

[25] H. Takemura, Y. Kitamura, J. Ohya, and F. Kishino, "Distributed Processing Architecture for Virtual Space Teleconferencing," in Proc. of ICAT, vol. 93, 1993, pp. 27–32.

[26] G. Van Maren, R. Germs, and F. Jansen, "Integrating 3D-GIS and Virtual Reality Design and implementation of the Karma VI system," in Proceedings of the Spatial Information Research Centre's 10th Colloquium. University of Otago, New Zealand, 1998, pp. 16–19.

[27] B. Damer et al., "Data-Driven Virtual Environment Assembly and Operation," in Virtual Ironbird Workshop, 2004, p. 1.

[28] C. Borgatti, M. Felicori, M. Mauri, L. Calori, A. Guidazzoli, S. Pescarin, T. Diamanti, M. Liguori, and L. Valentini, "Databases and virtual environments: a good match for communicating complex cultural sites," in ACM SIGGRAPH 2004 Educators program. ACM, 2004, p. 30.

[29] H. Richards-Rissetto, F. Remondino, G. Agugiaro, J. Von Schwerin, J. Robertsson, and G. Girardi, "Kinect and 3D GIS in archaeology," in Proceedings of the 2012 18th International Conference on Virtual Systems and Multimedia, VSMM 2012: Virtual Systems in the Information Society, 2012, pp. 331–337.

[30] M. Forte and G. Kurillo, "Cyberarchaeology: Experimenting with

teleimmersive archaeology," in 2010 16th International Conference on Virtual Systems and Multimedia, VSMM 2010, 2010, pp. 155–162.

[31] A. Guarnieri, F. Pirotti, and A. Vettore, "Cultural heritage interactive 3D models on the web: An approach using open source and free software," Journal of Cultural Heritage, vol. 11, no. 3, 2010, pp. 350–353.

[32] M. F. Shiratuddin and W. Thabet, "Utilizing a 3D game engine to develop a virtual design review system," Journal of Information Technology in Construction (ITcon), vol. 16, no. Special Issue Use of Gaming Technology in Architecture, Engineering and Construction, 2011, pp. 39–68.

[33] S. Wang, Z. Mao, C. Zeng, H. Gong, S. Li, and B. Chen, "A new method of virtual reality based on Unity3D," in 2010 18th International Conference on Geoinformatics, 2010, pp. 1–5.

[34] Y. Zhao et al., "The research and development of 3D urban geographic information system with Unity3D," in Geoinformatics (GEOINFORMATICS), 2013 21st International Conference on, 2013, pp. 1–4.

[35] D. Pacheco and S. Wierenga, "Spatializing experience: a framework for the geolocalization, visualization and exploration of historical data using VR/AR technologies," in Proceedings of the 2014 Virtual Reality International Conference, 2014.

[36] A. Martina and A. Bottino, "Using Virtual Environments as a Visual Interface for Accessing Cultural Database Contents," in International Conference of Information Science and Computer Applications (ICISCA 2012), Bali, Indonesia, 2012, pp. 1–6.

[37] T. Guan, B. Ren, and D. Zhong, "The Method of Unity3D-Based 3D Dynamic Interactive Query of High Arch Dam Construction Information," Applied Mechanics and Materials, vol. 256-259, 2012, pp. 2918–2922.

[38] T. Scully, J. Doboš, T. Sturm, and Y. Jung, "3drepo. io: building the next generation Web3D repository with AngularJS and X3DOM," in Proceedings of the 20th International Conference on 3D Web Technology, 2015.

[39] Z. Wang, H. Cai, and F. Bu, "Nonlinear Revision Control for Web-Based 3D Scene Editor," in Virtual Reality and Visualization (ICVRV), 2014 International Conference on, 2014, pp. 73–80.

[40] J. Doboš and A. Steed, "Revision Control Framework for 3D Assets," in Eurographics 2012 - Posters, Cagliari, Sardinia, Italy, 2012, p. 3.

[41] J. Beetz, L. van Berlo, R. de Laat, and P. van den Helm, "bimserver.org - An Open Source IFC Model Server," in Proceedings of the CIB W78 2010: 27th International Conference, no. Weise 2006, Cairo, Egypt, 2010, pp. 16–18.

[42] H.-s. Kang and G. Lee, "Development of an object-relational IFC server," in ICCEM/ICCPM, 2009.

[43] S. Malaikrisanachalee and H. Vathananukij, "Integration of java-based BIM with spatial database," International Journal of Civil Engineering, vol. 9, no. 1, 2011, pp. 17–22.

[44] V. Tarandi, "The BIM Collaboration Hub: A model server based on IFC and PLCS for Virtual Enterprise Collaboration," in Proceedings of the CIB W78-W102 2011: International Conference, Sophia Antipolis, France, 2011, pp. 26–28.

[45] M. Nour, "Using Bounding Volumes for BIM based electronic code checking for Buildings in Egypt," American Journal of Engineering Research (AJER), vol. 5, no. 4, 2016, pp. 91–98.

[46] B. Domínguez-Martín, "Methods to process low-level CAD plans and creative Building Information Models (BIM)," Doctoral Thesis, University of Jaén, 2014.

[47] S. Hoerster and K. Menzel, "BIM based classification of building performance data for advanced analysis," in Proceedings of International Conference CISBAT 2015 Future Buildings and Districts Sustainability from Nano to Urban Scale, 2015, pp. 993–998.

[48] H. Eisenmann, J. Fuchs, D. De Wilde, and V. Basso, "ESA Virtual Spacecraft Design," in 5th International Workshop on Systems and Concurrent Engineering for Space Applications, 2012.

[49] M. Mahdjoub, D. Monticolo, S. Gomes, and J. Sagot, "A collaborative design for usability approach supported by virtual reality and a multi-agent system embedded in a PLM environment," Computer-Aided Design, vol. 42, no. 5, 2010, pp. 402–413.

[50] M. Roberts, N. Ducheneaut, and T. F. Smith, "The "3d Wiki": Blending virtual worlds and Web architecture for remote collaboration," in 2010 IEEE International Conference on Multimedia and Expo, ICME 2010, 2010, pp. 1166–1171.

[51] M. Fang, X. Yan, Y. Wenhui, and C. Sen, "The Storage and Management of Distributed Massive 3D Models based on G/S Mode," in Lecture Notes in Information Technology, vol. 10, 2012.

[52] D. Iliescu, I. Ciocan, and I. Mateias, "Assisted management of product data: A PDM application proposal," in Proceedings of the 18th International Conference on System Theory, Control and Computing, Sinaia, Romania, 2014.

[53] C. Shahabi, F. Banaei-Kashani, A. Khoshgozaran, L. Nocera, and S. X. S. Xing, "GeoDec: A Framework to Visualize and Query Geospatial Data for Decision-Making," IEEE Multimedia, vol. 17, no. 3, 2010, pp. 14–23.

[54] M. Lobur, O. Matviykiv, A. Kernytskyy, and R. Dobosz, "Presentation of the heat simulation model with use of relational data model," 2011 11th International Conference The Experience of Designing and Application of CAD Systems in Microelectronics CADSM, 2011, pp. 228–229.

[55] A. Stadler, C. Nagel, G. König, and T. H. Kolbe, "Making interoperability persistent : A 3D geo database based on CityGML," 3D Geo-Information Sciences, 2009, pp. 175–192.

[56] M. Hoppen and J. Rossmann, "A novel distributed database synchronization approach with an application to 3d simulation," IARIA International Journal on Advances in Software, vol. 7, no. 3 and 4, December 2014, pp. 601–616.

[57] M. Hoppen, M. Schluse, J. Rossmann, and B. Weitzig, "Database-Driven Distributed 3D Simulation," in Proceedings of the 2012 Winter Simulation Conference, 2012, pp. 1–12.

[58] SEDRIS Associates & Partners, "SEDRIS," 2013, URL: http://www.sedris.org [retrieved: 2017.05.17].

[59] J. Rossmann, M. Schluse, C. Schlette, and R. Waspe, "A New Approach to 3D Simulation Technology as Enabling Technology for eRobotics," in 1st International Simulation Tools Conference & EXPO 2013, SIMEX'2013, J. F. M. Van Impe and F. Logist, Eds., Brussels, Belgium, 2013, pp. 39–46.

[60] CPA Geo-Information, "CPA SupportGIS Java (SGJ)," URL: http://www.supportgis.de [retrieved: 2017.05.17].

[61] The PostgreSQL Global Development Group, "PostgreSQL: About," 2015, URL: http://www.postgresql.org/about/ [retrieved: 2017.05.17].

[62] Open Geospatial Consortium (OGC), "Geography Markup Language (GML)," URL: http://www.opengeospatial.org/standards/gml [retrieved: 2017.05.17].

[63] M. Hunger, Neo4j 2.0 A graph database for everyone (orig.: Neo4j 2.0 Eine Graphdatenbank für alle), 1st ed. entwickler.press, 2014.

[64] Neo4j Team, "The Neo4j Manual v2.2.5," 2015, URL: http://neo4j.com/docs/stable/ [retrieved: 2017.05.17].

[65] J. Weise et al., "An Intelligent Building Blocks Concept for On-Orbit-Satellite Servcing," in Proceedings of International Symposium on Artificial Intelligence, Robotics and Automation in Space (i-SAIRAS), 2012, pp. 1–8.

[66] D. J. Armstrong, "The Quarks of Object-Oriented Development," Communications of the ACM, vol. 49, no. 2, 2006, pp. 123–128.

[67] M. Fowler, Patterns of Enterprise Application Architecture, 1st ed. Addison Wesley, 2002.

[68] A. Schatten, "O/R Mappers and Alternatives (orig.: O/R Mapper und Alternativen)," 2008, URL: http://www.heise.de/developer/artikel/O-R-Mapper-und-Alternativen-227060.html [retrieved: 2017.05.17].

[69] T. Neward, "The Vietnam of Computer Science," 2006, URL: http://www.odbms.org/2006/01/the-vietnam-of-computer-science/ [retrieved: 2017.05.17].

[70] S. W. Ambler, "Mapping Objects to Relational Databases: O/R Mapping In Detail," 2013, URL: http://www.agiledata.org/essays/mappingObjects.html [retrieved: 2017.05.17].

[71] F. Lodhi and M. A. Ghazali, "Design of a Simple and Effective Object-to-Relational Mapping Technique," in Proceedings of the 2007 ACM symposium on Applied computing. ACM, 2007, pp. 1445–1449.

[72] B. Karwin, SQL Antipatterns: Avoiding the Pitfalls of Database Programming, 1st ed. Railegh, N.C.: Pragmatic Bookshelf, 2010.

[73] ——, "Practical Object Oriented Models in Sql," 2009, URL: http://de.slideshare.net/billkarwin/practical-object-oriented-models-in-sql [retrieved: 2017.05.17].

[74] Hibernate, HIBERNATE–Relational Persistence for Idiomatic Java, 2015, URL: http://docs.jboss.org/hibernate/orm/5.0/manual/en-US/html/index.html [retrieved: 2017.05.17].

[75] NHibernate Community, NHibernate–Relational Persistence for Idiomatic .NET, 2015, URL: http://nhibernate.info/doc/nhibernate-reference/index.html [retrieved: 2017.05.17].

[76] Code Synthesis Tools CC, ODB: C++ Object-Relational Mapping (ORM), 2015, URL: http://www.codesynthesis.com/products/odb/ [retrieved: 2017.05.17].

[77] L. Marty, QxOrm (the engine) + QxEntityEditor (the graphic editor) = the best solution to manage your data in C++/Qt !, 2015, URL: http://www.qxorm.com/qxorm_en/home.html [retrieved: 2017.05.17].

[78] The Qt Company, "Qt Documentation," 2016, URL: http://doc.qt.io/qt-5/index.html [retrieved: 2017.05.17].

[79] I. Robinson, J. Webber, and E. Eifrem, Graph Databases-New Opportunities For Connected Data, 2nd ed. O'Reilly, 2015.

[80] R. Diestel, Graph Theory, 2nd ed. Springer, 2000.

[81] N. Martinez-Bazan, S. Gomez-Villamor, and F. Escale-Claveras, "Dex: A high-performance graph database management system," in Data Engineering Workshops (ICDEW), 2011 IEEE 27th International Conference on, April 2011, pp. 124–127.

[82] R. Kumar Kaliyar, "Graph databases: A survey," in Computing, Communication Automation (ICCCA), 2015 International Conference on, May 2015, pp. 785–790.

[83] Microsoft, "Graph engine 1.0 preview released," 2016, URL: http://research.microsoft.com/en-us/projects/trinity/ [retrieved: 2017.05.17].

[84] B. Shao, H. Wang, and Y. Li, "Trinity: A distributed graph engine on a memory cloud," in Proceedings of the 2013 ACM SIGMOD International Conference on Management of Data. ACM, 2013, pp. 505–516.

[85] B. Iordanov, "HyperGraphDB: A Generalized Graph Database," in Web-Age information management. Springer, 2010, pp. 25–36.

[86] InfoGrid Team, "Infogrid: The web graph database," 2016, URL: http://infogrid.org/trac/ [retrieved: 2017.05.17].

[87] J. Peilee, "A survey on graph databases," 2011, URL: https://jasperpeilee.wordpress.com/2011/11/25/a-survey-on-graph-databases/ [retrieved: 2017.05.17].

[88] "Allegrograph," 2016, URL: http://franz.com/agraph/allegrograph/ [retrieved: 2017.05.17].

[89] M. Hoppen and J. Rossmann, "A Database Synchronization Approach for 3D Simulation Systems," in DBKDA 2014, The 6th International Conference on Advances in Databases, Knowledge, and Data Applications, A. Schmidt, K. Nitta, and J. S. Iztok Savnik, Eds., Chamonix, France, 2014, pp. 84–91.

A Cost-Benefit Analysis of Accessibility Testing in Agile Software Development

Results from a Multiple Case Study

Aleksander Bai
Norwegian Computing Center,
Oslo, Norway
Email: aleksander.bai@nr.no

Heidi Camilla Mork
Kantega AS,
Oslo, Norway
Email: heidi.mork@kantega.no

Viktoria Stray
University of Oslo,
Oslo, Norway
Email: stray@ifi.uio.no

***Abstract*—It is important to include accessibility testing in software development to ensure that the software developed is usable by as many people as possible, independent of their capabilities. Few guidelines exist on how to integrate accessibility testing in an agile process, and how to select testing methods from a cost-benefit point of view. The end result is that many development teams do not include accessibility testing, since they do not know how to prioritize the different testing methods within a tight budget. In this paper, we present an evaluation of nine accessibility testing methods that fits in an agile software development process. We discuss the cost of each method with regards to resources and knowledge requirements, and based on a cost-benefit analysis, we present an optimal combination of these methods in terms of cost and issues discovered. Finally, we describe how accessibility testing methods can be incorporated into an agile process by using the agile accessibility spiral.**

Keywords*—*Accessibility testing; Agile software development; Cost-benefit analysis; Usability;

I. INTRODUCTION

Accessibility testing in software development is testing the software to ensure that it is usable by as many people as possibly, independent of their capabilities. The past decade have seen an increased interest in integrating usability in the software development process. However, far to little attention has been paid to the field of accessibility, and how to incorporate accessibility testing in software development. Earlier we have described a cost-benefit approach for selecting accessibility testing methods [1]. In this paper, we further investigate and develop this approach with an additional case study.

There is an increased focus on accessibility from legislation and the United Nations with "Convention on the Rights of Persons with Disabilities" [2]. While usability focus on the quality and ease of use for a product, accessibility focus on letting people with the widest range of capabilities be able to use a product [3]. However, both definitions are overlapping and within the spirit of universal design: the design of products and services to be usable by all people, to the greatest extent possible [4].

Studies show that doing usability testing is costly and can take around 8-13% of the project's total budget [5]. Much of the cost goes to recruiting participants and evaluators in addition to the man-hours required for conducting and evaluating the results [6]. For accessibility testing, the cost can be even higher than usability testing, since recruitment and accommodation of participants usually have more requirements.

However, by not doing accessibility testing at all or by postponing testing until the end of the project, the cost can be extremely high, and it might not even be possible to do accessibility adjustments at a late stage [7] [8]. Many studies show that software that is hard to use, or have features that are hard to understand, make users find better alternatives [9]. There might also be legal requirements to provide accessibility, like in the European Union and in the US.

Our approach is targeted towards agile software development, since it has become the mainstream development methodology [10]. According to a recent survey [11], more than 70% of developers work in agile software projects. Agile software development emphasise delivery of working software in short development iterations [12], active customer engagement [10], frequent communication through daily stand-up meetings [13] and integration of development and testing [14]. All these principles make it feasible to integrate accessibility testing in the whole development process.

We argue that developers, testers and designers in agile software teams can take more responsibility for accessibility testing, and thus lower the total testing cost of the project and at the same time deliver a better product that is both more usable and accessible. Jurca et al. [15] found that one of the major problems with integration of Agile methods and User-centered design (UCD) was that interaction designers are often overworked and distributed across several projects. Thus, it is beneficial that developers and testers in agile software teams also take responsibility for accessibility testing.

During our evaluations, we have investigated different accessibility testing techniques, and we discuss the cost-benefit aspect of these in an agile development process. We argue that accessibility testing does not necessarily require a high cost. We describe where in the process the methods can be used and how they can be combined in optimal ways. Consequently, the impact from accessibility testing towards the end of the project will be minimized, and thus reduce the cost of retrofitting [7]. Our suggested approach is not a substitute for doing user testing, but an addition, incorporated into the agile development process, to reduce the overall cost and increase the usability and accessibility of the software.

The remainder of this paper is organized as follows. Section II summarizes related work, and Section III gives an overview of accessibility testing methods. Section IV describes the evaluation setup and the two case studies, and the results from the studies are presented in Section V. Section VI reports our cost-benefit analysis of the accessibility testing methods and Section VII discusses the results and implications. We have presented limitations in Section VIII, before we summarize and conclude in Section IX.

II. Related Work

Zimmermann and Vanderheiden [16] have proposed a method for integrating accessible design and testing in the development of software applications, both iterative and non-iterative processes. However, the proposed method's main focus is on how to gather accessibility requirements and does not contain much details on how to actual perform testing in an iterative process. There has been some focus on integrating an agile development process with usability testing [17], and in recent years, there has been an increasing interest in Agile UX (User Experience) [18]. Bonacin et al. [19] propose how to incorporate accessibility and usability testing into an agile process, but do not discuss which accessibility testing methods that are optimal to use or how to combine them in an efficient setup. Horton and Sloan [20] have proposed a accessible user experience framework for organizations on how to integrating accessibility in the design and development process.

There has been research on how to conduct a cost-benefit analysis of universal design of ICT [21], but there is a lack of case studies to verify the concepts. The research focus has also primarily been on the overall effect of universal design, and not the testing methods.

A recent systematic review of usability testing methods for software development processes [9] requests more research into evaluating the different testing methods and how they affect the testing outcome. To the best of our knowledge, there are no evaluations of accessibility testing methods in an agile process, and there are no studies of which accessibility testing methods that are most effective compared to resources and knowledge available in a agile team. We address the latter issue in this paper by showing a cost-benefit approach on how to select accessibility testing methods in an agile process.

Most agile team members have good knowledge and focus on both testing and usability, but it is much rarer to consider accessibility as part of the development cycle. This is probably caused by little knowledge and experience with accessibility testing, cost and time constraints associated with accessibility testing, and available resources to perform accessibility testing. According to [22], who surveyed participants involved in web development projects, only 20% consider accessibility aspects in their projects and nearly half said that they do not use any accessibility evaluation methods.

III. Background

Nowadays there is a widespread application of agile methods in software projects. Agile software development is a set of principles for developing software iteratively, in order to react rapidly and flexible to changing requirements [12]. Agile development teams have given more attention to the importance of usability the last decade, and interaction designers are often part of the agile teams. User-centered design (UCD) is a design process where the needs, requirements and capabilities of the end-users are considered throughout the entire design- and development life cycle. The integration of agile principles with those from UCD is called Agile-UX. In recent years, there has been an increasing interest in Agile UX [18], but little attention has been paid to the field of accessibility.

Accessibility is often divided into two parts; *technical accessibility* and *usable accessibility* [23]. Technical accessibility is to follow good technical standards when developing software, like giving alternate text to images or use the correct heading tag. Usable accessibility is to ensure that the solution is usable to the widest range of users as possible in the sense that users can understand, navigate and interact with the solution. Software can be technical accessible but still not usable if the user does not understand how to interact with the system in order to solve a task. Note that there is rarely a clean separation between technical and usable accessibility and the issues are often overlapping.

There are several methods for testing usability [9] and accessibility [16] in software development: automated checkers, guidelines, expert walkthrough, interviews and user testing, to name a few. The different testing methods uncover different kinds of issues. Automated checkers cover technical accessibility, whereas methods closer to user testing cover more of the usable accessibility.

Automated checkers are tools that a developer or tester can run to get an evaluation of issues regarding the technical accessibility. There are numerous alternatives out there [24], like the NetBeans accessibility module [25] that integrate directly into the developer's tools, or tools that can be used as a step in continuous integration. However, automated checkers only check issues that can be detected programmatically, i.e., issues related to technical accessibility.

There are many different tools, kits or wearables that a person can use to simulation various types of disabilities. The motivation is to let a person experience an impairment so the person might be able to gain some insight into the issues that an impairment might have with a certain design or solution [26]. It is important to note that the intention of a simulation kit is not to simulate the disability in itself, which is highly criticized [27]. Simulation with wearables, also refered to as screening techniques [28], will uncover issues mainly in the area of usable accessibility, but it will also find issues with technical accessibility, for instance low color contrast between text and background.

Testing with assistive technology like a screen reader or computers' high contrast mode will make issues with the technical accessibility very obvious as assistive technology is highly dependant of proper coding to function properly.

Checklists and guidelines provide the evaluator with a set of instructions and criteria to evaluate, and the WCAG (Web Content Accessibility Guidelines) 2.0 standard [29] is the de facto choice. Checklists cover both technical and usable accessibility.

Persona walkthrough or persona testing approach [30],

is where an expert simulates or play-acts a persona while carrying out tasks. The more knowledge the expert has about the disability that a particular persona has, the easier it is to do a realistic and credible acting while testing the solution. A persona walkthrough will usually cover usable accessibility.

There are many approaches on how to group accessibility testing methods [31], and we have chosen to group the testing methods into five groups as shown in Table I. The table shows different groups of testing methods with an indication of whether the group mainly discovers technical or usable accessibility issues, or issues of both types.

TABLE I. ACCESSIBILITY TESTING GROUPS.

#	*Group*	*Technical accessibility*	*Usable accessibility*
1	Automated checkers	x	
2	Checklist and guidelines	x	x
3	Simulation kits		x
4	Assistive technology	x	
5	Walkthrough		x

The best approach for accessibility testing is user evaluation, since the actual users are involved and the testers does not have to do any approximation of impairments or mental states [32] [33]. However, it is also an expensive method because it requires much planning, recruitment and management [6]. It is also particular important to find as many problems as possible before involving users. Examples of user evaluation involve user testing, interview and focus groups. The focus of our study was to investigate testing methods that members of an agile team can use themselves during the various phases of the development process. User testing is therefore outside the scope of this paper.

IV. CASE STUDIES

To conduct a cost-benefit study, we at least need to consider resources requirements of the methods, including knowledge requirements. We also need to consider what kind of issues the different accessibility testing methods can discover, and how the test methods differ from each other. A further goal is to investigate where in an agile development process the different accessibility test methods might be most valuable.

We conducted two case studies with two different software solutions. After the first case study we performed a cost-benefit analysis, and the result of this analysis was used to suggest which methods to use and when to apply the different methods in an agile development process. In the second case study we wanted to further investigate the most valuable testing methods found in the cost-benefit analysis from the first case.

In each case we did a selection of accessibility testing methods, where each selected method was tested by at least two persons, and the results were aggregated. One person performing one test method is called an *evaluation*. Each evaluation had a coordinator who wrote down the issues reported by the tester, and the coordinator also made notes when difficulties, that were not verbally expressed, were observed. The registered issues were then classified as critical, cognitive, both or none of them. We defined a *critical issue* as an issue that prevents the participant from continuing or completing a task; e.g., difficult to read images or text because of poor contrast or resolution. A *cognitive issue* was an issue caused by confusing or missing information for the given context; e.g., not understanding the purpose of a screen or not understanding how to operate a controller. A problem can thus belong to both the critical and cognitive category, as it was often the case. The number of issues for each of the testing methods, together with the number or critical and cognitive issues, formed the basis for further analysis.

For the case studies, we selected methods from all the groups in Table I. From Group 1 we used the WAVE Web Accessibility Evaluation Tool [34], which is an online tool that evaluates the website of any given available URL. The user provides the URL and the tool gives a report on the errors on the web page. We selected the WCAG (Web Content Accessibility Guidelines) 2.0 standard [29] and the VATLab checklist [35] from Group 2. From Group 3 we used Cambridge inclusive design glasses [36] for simulating reduced vision, and the Cambridge inclusive design gloves [36] to simulate dexterity reduction. The gloves are typically used for testing a physical product, but they were included in the first case since there was a card reader involved. From Group 4, we used the screen reader NVDA [37] and the built-in high contrast mode in Windows. We used dyslexia and old male for persona walkthrough from Group 5.

In the first case study we had two participants with the necessary knowledge and experience to do persona walkthrough with one persona as old male and one with dyslexia.

The total set of methods used in the case studies is shown in Table II.

TABLE II. SELECTED METHODS FOR CASE STUDIES.

	Method	*Case A*	*Case B*
M1	Automated checker		x
M2	Simulation kit reduced vision	x	x
M3	Simulation kit reduced dexterity	x	
M4	Assistive technology screen reader	x	x
M5	Assistive technology high contrast	x	x
M6	Manual WCAG	x	x
M7	VATLab checklist	x	x
M8	Persona dyslexia	x	
M9	Persona old male	x	

The different testing methods vary in how much resources and knowledge it takes to use them. In each case study we categorized the methods as either *low*, *medium* or *high* in required amount of resources and knowledge. In terms of resources, *low* means that none or little prerequisites (tools, setup, administration) are required to conduct the method; *medium* means that some prerequisites are required, and they are relatively cheap (under $1000); *high* means that the method requires considerable investments in terms of setup, purchase, administration or maintenance. In terms of knowledge, *low* means that no or very little prior knowledge is required; *medium* require some prior knowledge, either technical (usage, commands) or domain (knowledge or experience with the impairment); *high* means that extensive or expert training is required to conduct the evaluation. These categories will be used for the cost-benefit analysis in Section VI.

A. Case A: e-ID

The solution used for evaluation in case A was a pilot for electronic identification, developed during the EU project FutureID [38]. The pilot uses a software certificate or an ID card with a card reader for the authentication process. The pilot uses both a Java client and a web front end, and consists of around ten different user interfaces with varying complexity.

1) Selected Methods: We used eight of the methods from Table II and labelled them with the categories *low*, *medium* and *high* with regard to the requirements of resources and knowledge.

Almost all methods are labelled as *low* with regard to resources. The only methods with prerequisites were the simulation kits because some hardware must be purchased ahead of testing. This is usually a one-time purchase, but it must also be stored and assembled before usage, so we think it qualifies as medium resource demanding compared to the others.

Most of the methods require very little prior knowledge. Method M4 involves using a screen reader, which requires knowledge on how to operate it, but almost everyone can learn how to use a screen reader in a reasonable amount of time, and therefore we labelled it *medium*. However, our level of using screen readers cannot compare with the expert level of people that use screen readers daily and are dependent on them.

The persona walkthrough is informal and relatively quick to do but is heavily dependent on the selected personas and the experience that the expert has with the particular type of disability. The persona walkthrough methods require expert knowledge, and is thus marked with *high* knowledge requirements. However, there are few resource requirements for persona walkthrough methods, and this is why they are labeled with *low* for resource requirements.

Table III gives the summary of the selected methods, and more details can be found in [1].

TABLE III. OVERVIEW THE SELECTED METHODS

Method	*Resources requirements*	*Knowledge requirements*
M2	Medium	Low
M3	Medium	Low
M4	Low	Medium
M5	Low	Low
M6	Low	Low
M7	Low	Low
M8	Low	High
M9	Low	High

2) Participants: Five different participants performed the evaluations, where the participants' knowledge on accessibility testing ranged from beginner to expert. All the participants had technological background, their age ranged from 35 to 61, and there were both males and females in the group. Two of the participants where recruited based on their experience with persona testing and their knowledge on dyslexia and aging. The participants performed a total of 17 evaluations.

TABLE IV. PARTICIPANTS P1 – P5 AND THE METHODS THEY EVALUATED

Method	P1	P2	P3	P4	P5
M2	x	x	x		
M3	x	x			
M4	x	x			
M5	x	x			
M6	x	x			
M7	x	x			
M8				x	x
M9				x	x

3) Procedures: All the evaluations were conducted on the same machine with the same setup to ensure an equal test environment. A short initial test was conducted before the evaluations started, in order to verify that the overall setup, the scenarios, and the ordering of them were best possible. The goal of all the scenarios was to successfully log into the solution. Each participant performed five different scenarios in the same order:

1) Invalid digital certificate
2) Valid digital certificate
3) Invalid smart card
4) Valid smart card, but incorrect PIN code
5) Valid smart card and correct PIN code

The participants were unaware that they were given invalid certificate, invalid smart card and invalid PIN (Personal Identification Number) code. The scenarios were also executed in the listed order to avoid biasing the participants as they should gradually progress a little further in the login process. Each method took under two hours to complete for a single participant for all the scenarios.

B. Case B: pension

The solution used for evaluation in Case B is a Norwegian public available website, Norsk Pensjon [39], used by citizens to get an overview of their personal pension schemes. The key functionality of the website is a calculator where one can estimate future pension payments based on parameters like current salary and the expected year of retirement. The company behind the website is concerned with universal design and accessibility. The website has recently been evaluated by accessibility experts, and there is a plan to improve the site accordingly. The website is developed by the IT consultancy company Kantega, and current members of the development team were participants in the evaluation. The focus of this second case was to further verify the results of the first Case A and see how the testing methods worked for participants in agile teams. An important aspect with Case B was to evaluate the key findings from case A in real environments with actual developers and testers.

1) Selected Methods: The methods for this second case was chosen based on the cost-benefit analysis of the first case and the agile accessibility spiral [1] that fits in an agile development process. We also chose to include an automated checker that were not included in Case A, since automated tools in general require fewer resources than other methods. We hypothesised that an automated checker could be a natural first choice for any agile team, even though they only discover issues that are detectable programmatically. The selected tool, WAVE [34] is free to use, and thus *low* in required resources. WAWE gives reports with explanations to the operator, hence very little prior knowledge is required and we labelled it *low*.

We used the Cambridge inclusive design glasses [36] to simulate reduced vision, but we did not test with the simulation kit for reduced dexterity since no extra device, like a card reader, was involved. The testing methods assistive technologies screen reader and high contrast were also selected. All these methods were labelled with the same knowledge and resource requirements as in Case A. We also included the manual WCAG evaluation and the VATLab chekclist, based on how they scored in Case A. However, we experienced that the checklists were more difficult to use than expected, and we therefore decided to label them as medium in knowledge requirements in Case B. We chose to not include persona testing in this second case since none of the participants or teams had experience with this type of testing.

TABLE V. OVERVIEW OF THE SIX METHODS

Method	*Resource requirements*	*Knowledge requirements*
M1	Low	Low
M2	Medium	Low
M4	Low	Medium
M5	Low	Low
M6	Low	Medium
M7	Low	Medium

2) Participants: There were in total six participants. The participants were a designer and a developer of the current development team for the website, along with other developers and technologists. Their age ranged from 25 to 37, and there were both males and females in the group. The participants performed a total of 22 evaluations.

TABLE VI. PARTICIPANTS P1 – P6 AND THE METHODS THEY EVALUATED

Method	P1	P2	P3	P4	P5	P6
M1	x	x	x	x		
M2	x	x	x	x		
M4	x	x	x	x		
M5			x	x		
M6	x	x	x	x	x	x
M7			x		x	

3) Procedures: The evaluations with methods from the simulation group were conducted with a coordinator, and one or two observers who registered issues. The participants performed five scenarios in the same order:

1) Calculate the pension payment at age 80 if you retire at age 63 and currently have a salary of 500 000 NOK
2) Send the payment plan by email in the case where you retire at age 70 and have a salary of 500 000 NOK
3) Find the estimated payment at age 68 if you take partial retirement at age 66 with 50% work position and you want to take out 40% of the pension. You have a salary of 500 000 NOK and take full retirement from age 70
4) Find the payment at age 70 given in percentage of your current salary, when you retire at age 63 and have a salary of 500 000 NOK
5) Find information about contractual pension (AFP)

The scenarios were ordered so that it gradually revealed more of the functionality in the solution. After completing an evaluation, the participant was asked how it was to perform the evaluation and to reflect on the use of the test method.

The selected methods from the checklist group, manual WCAG and VATLab checklist, were conducted individually and remotely by the participants. The participants received a checklist with success criteria to meet, together with instructions to mark a criteria in the checklist as failed if they could find an example which did not meet the criteria, otherwise mark it as passed. If the criteria was evaluated as not applicable or relevant for the solution, the criteria was marked n/a.

V. EVALUATION RESULTS

The evaluation results from the case studies in Section IV are presented here, together with a comparison on how the testing methods performed in the two cases.

A. Results from Case A

As can be seen from Table VII, a high number of critical issues were discovered with most of the methods. It should be noted that a critical issue might only be critical in the context of a given disability. For instance, incorrect HTML tags can be critical for blindness, but may not be relevant for impairments like reduced dexterity. However, for the solution as a whole, all critical issues are equally relevant since an issue might exclude some users if nothing is done to improve the problem.

TABLE VII. ISSUES FOUND IN CASE A.

Method	*Issues*	*Critical*	*Cognitive*
M2	54	14	9
M3	4	0	0
M4	33	26	0
M5	10	4	0
M6	32	7	5
M7	19	17	0
M8	34	15	15
M9	27	13	9
	213	96	38

The simulation kit methods (M2, M3) found a lower percentage (25.9%) of critical issues compared to the other methods. The main reason was that most of the issues reported by these methods were visual problems that were annoying at best, and in some cases problematic, but not marked as critical since it did not hinder further progress. Of the critical issues discovered with simulation kits, almost all were also marked as cognitive. Note that a relative few number of issues were found when simulating reduced dexterity, and we believe this is mainly because the application did not require much motoric precision. This is of course very dependent on the software that is evaluated.

Manual WCAG (M6) also reported relative few critical issues (21.9%), and this was mostly because the WCAG evaluations criteria are high level. For instance did a single criteria in WCAG cause over 17 critical issues to be reported in the screen reader method (M4) since it has a much finer granularity. The WCAG evaluations also reported few cognitive issues for the same reason.

The screen reader testing method (M4) identified the most critical issues (78.8%), and many of the issues were related to poor compatibility with screen readers. We suspect that more issues could be found if there had not been so many critical problems that made further investigations in many cases impossible. High contrast testing method (M5) did not find many issues, and even fewer critical issues, and this is mainly because contrast was not a big problem in the solution. VATLab checklist (M7) found a very high number of critical issues, and this is because the focus is on compatibility with screen readers, and as already explained the support for screen readers was poor.

Persona testing methods (M8, M9) found the most cognitive issues, and this is not unexpected since the persona used in the evaluations focused on usability and understanding the context. Most of the issues reported by persona testing were directly related to the participant not understanding the context of a page and what was expected from the participant. A high number of the cognitive issues were also marked as critical since it is impossible for the participant to complete his task, and this explains the high number of critical issues discovered by persona testing.

B. *Results from Case B*

The results from Case A guided us in choosing the methods to investigate further in Case B. We chose automated checker, simulation kit reduced vision, screen reader, high contrast and checklists, as can be seen in Table VIII. Also here it must be noted that a critical issue might only be critical in the context of a given disability. This is discussed further in Section VIII.

TABLE VIII. ISSUES FOUND IN CASE B.

Method	*Issues*	*Critical*	*Cognitive*
M1	27	0	0
M2	58	8	17
M4	16	7	5
M5	16	2	5
M6	25	5	6
M7	15	8	0
	157	30	33

All methods found a reasonable amount of issues, but relatively few critical issues, at least compared to what was found in Case A. This was partly expected since the solution used in Case B were in production and less complex than the solution in Case A. However, more cognitive issues were found in Case B. In Case A, only 17.8% of the issues reported was considered cognitive while 21.0% of the issues in Case B were considered cognitive. This is probably because the domain (pension) in Case B was more complex than Case A (login), and thus more cognitive issues were found. It should be noted that few of the cognitive issues were marked as also being critical.

The simulation kit with reduced vision (M2) found considerably more issues compared to the rest, and this is mainly because of visual problems that were annoying, but not critical since it did not prevent progression. This testing method also found most cognitive issues, and this is because reduced vision caused the tester to miss or misunderstand important information.

WCAG (M6) found many issues and managed to identify a large number of cognitive issues in addition to some critical. WCAG in Case B found considerably more cognitive issues than in Case A, and this was partly due to a revaluation of the WCAG checkpoints as explained in Section IV, but also because correct delivery of content and error messages are even more critical in a complex domain such as pension.

The automated checker (M1) found many issues, but none that were considered critical or cognitive. This is because the identified issues were only trivial issues like minor contrast problems and not fundamental problems. It was also a problem that the automated checker could not be used for a solution that uses a secure connection and two-factor authentication, and could thus only be used on the static pages and not the more complex pages. We suspect more issues would be found otherwise, but not necessarily more critical or cognitive.

Both the screen reader (M4) testing method and high contrast (M5) method found a reasonable amount of issues, but of very different types. The screen reader testing method revealed poor support for screen readers, while the high contrast found issues connected to poor contrast mode in essential images in the solution. The VATLab checklist (M7) found many of the same issues as the screen read method.

In Case B, external experts had evaluated the accessibility of the solution. The findings from the experts and the findings from our case study with internal developers and testers showed that we found more or less the same type of issues. This further indicates that doing internal accessibility testing is crucial and worth the investment.

C. *Comparison of both cases*

Four of the testing methods were the same for Case A and B, and it is interesting to see which of these four methods that identified most issues in total, most critical issues and most cognitive issues. A heat map of the issues found is shown in Figure 1, where green indicate high percentage and red indicate low percentage.

	Total	Critical	Cognitive
M2	40,3 %	22,4 %	55,3 %
M4	17,6 %	33,7 %	10,6 %
M5	9,4 %	6,1 %	10,6 %
M6	20,5 %	12,2 %	23,4 %
M7	12,2 %	25,5 %	0,0 %

FIGURE 1. HEAT MAP OF ERRORS FOUND WITH SHARED METHODS IN BOTH CASES.

It is apparent from the heat map in Figure 1 that the testing method simulation kit with reduced vision (M2) identified most issues in both case studies. This method also found most cognitive issues, which might be unexpected at first glance. However, many cognitive issues are linked to poor descriptions or lack of explanations, and this often makes it even harder for the person to understand the purpose of a particular step or page. The WCAG testing method (M6) also found many cognitive issues, but had more trouble finding critical issues. This is most likely because most of the WCAG criteria are high level and too general.

A high coverage of critical issues was found by the screen reader testing method (M4) and the VATLab checklist (M7) in both cases, and this is not unexpected since both try to find problems with screen reader support. As both test cases show, if a solution is not created with screen readers in mind, then the solution is usually not possible to use properly with a screen reader and thus many critical issues are identified.

The high contrast testing method (M5) found generally few issues, and also few critical or cognitive. It is worth mentioning that most of the issues found with high contrast were also found by other methods (over 75%).

	Total	Critical	Cognitive
Automated tools	7,3 %	0,0 %	0,0 %
Checklists	24,6 %	29,4 %	15,5 %
Assistive Technology	20,3 %	31,0 %	14,1 %
Simulation kit	31,4 %	17,5 %	36,6 %
Expert walkthrough	16,5 %	22,2 %	33,8 %

FIGURE 2. HEAT MAP OF ERRORS FOUND WITH THE VARIOUS TESTING METHOD GROUPS.

Figure 2 shows a heat map of testing method groups for both cases. The heat map supports the notion that some testing method groups are better at finding critical issues, while others are better at finding cognitive issues. As can be seen from Figure 2 both simulation kit and expert walkthrough have a high discovery rate for cognitive issues, while checklists and assistive technology testing methods have a high discovery rate for critical issues.

D. Testing time usage

During the evaluations, we noted the time used per tester, and the average time per testing method can be found in Table IX. The numbers in Table IX is the average for both Case A and B, and as the table shows, most methods use between 20 and 60 minutes, with the exception of method 3 and 5. The reason for such low numbers for M3 is because the solution was not very depended on dexterity as explained in Section V. Method M5 also gave very quick test times, mostly because it was fairly obvious what was standing out and what was difficult to see with a high contrast mode.

The used time recorded is depending both on scenario, experience and solution that is being tested. Some testing methods were not tested with scenarios, like automated checker (M1), WCAG (M6) or VATLab checklist (M7), but used in an open exploratory testing approach. We saw on average higher testing times for most methods in Case A compared to Case B, and this is most likely because Case A was more complex with more pages than Case B. However, the average time per testing method is representative for both cases. More important is that the relative difference between the methods were similar for both cases.

TABLE IX. AVERAGE TIME PER METHOD.

Method	*Time*	*Issues Case A*	*Issues Case B*
M1	$\approx$ 20 min	-	27
M2	$\approx$ 45 min	54	58
M3	$\approx$ 10 min	4	-
M4	$\approx$ 30 min	33	16
M5	$\approx$ 10 min	10	16
M6	$\approx$ 60 min	32	25
M7	$\approx$ 45 min	19	15
M8	$\approx$ 60 min	34	-
M9	$\approx$ 60 min	27	-

It is interesting to see the number of issues found compared to average time used per method. This is shown in the two columns to the right in Table IX. In general, more issues are found with a longer average testing time per method, but there are exceptions like the screen reader testing method (M4) that finds many issues in a short amount of time. This is also very apparent for the automated checker (M1) which finds many issues in a very short amount of time. However, most of those issues are more trivial as explained in the previous sections.

VI. COST BENEFIT ANALYSIS

Based on the evaluation results in Section V, we performed a cost-benefit analysis (CBA) of which combinations of accessibility testing methods that identified most issues with regards to resources and knowledge. The motivation for doing a CBA is to get a more objective evaluation of the different testing methods, so it is easier to decide when to include a testing method in the process. CBA is a systematic approach for comparing strengths and weaknesses for different options [40]. It is a well-known technique used in many fields [41], but to our knowledge we are the only ones that have used it for comparing accessibility testing methods [1].

In order to do a CBA we must first create a cost function. We have defined the cost function to be the product of resources and knowledge (explained in III) where $resources$ and $knowledge \in \{1, 2, 3\}$ and *low* corresponds to 1, *medium* to 2 and *high* to 3. This makes sense since both variables contribute equally to the cost of executing a testing method. We argue that the most beneficial accessibility testing methods are those that find a high number of issues, and also many critical and cognitive issues. We can then define the benefit function as the sum of found, critical and cognitive issues. Based on the definition of cost and benefit we can then define the cost-benefit relationship accordingly:

$$CB = \frac{1}{\sqrt{n}} \frac{total^2 + critical^2 + cognitive^2}{resources \times knowledge} \quad (1)$$

Where $total$ is the total number of issues for n methods, $cognitive$ is the total number of cognitive issues for n method, $critical$ is the total number of critical issues for n method and n is the number of methods. We have included squared

TABLE X. COST BENEFIT RESULTS CASE A.

#	Methods	Cost	Issues	Critical	Cognitive
1	M2, M4, M6, M7	6	64.8%	66.7%	36.8%
2	M2, M4, M6	5	55.9%	49.0%	36.8%
3	M2, M6	3	40.4%	21.9%	36.8%
4	M2, M6, M7	4	49.3%	39.6%	36.8%
5	M2, M4, M6-M8	9	80.8%	82.3%	76.3%
6	M2, M4, M6, M8	8	71.8%	64.6%	76.3%
7	M2, M4, M5-M7	7	69.4%	70.8%	36.8%
8	M2, M4, M6-M9	12	93.4%	95.8%	100%
9	M2, M4, M7	5	49.8%	59.4%	23.7%
10	M2, M4, M6, M7, M9	9	77.5%	80.0%	60.5%
...					
20	M2, M4-M9	13	98.1%	100.0%	100.0%
...					
52	M2-M9	15	100.0%	100.0%	100.0%
...					
254	M3, M5	3	6.6%	4.2%	0.0%
255	M3	2	1.9%	0.0%	0.0%

weighting of both cognitive and critical issues since we argue that these issues are more important to discover than minor issues. We used $\sqrt{n}$ instead of n as a penalty for the number of evaluations, since using only n gave a too big penalty when using multiple methods.

A. Analysis from Case A

For Case A we calculated *CB* for all permutations of the different accessibility testing methods to identify the combinations that give most benefit compared to cost. The top results in addition to some selected results are shown in Table X, ordered by *CB*.

Combining all methods (except M3) gives a very high coverage (almost 100%), but comes at a high cost, as shown with #20. The *CB* found 19 better alternatives when considering the costs. The optimal combination of methods that maximize benefit compared to cost is using methods M7, M6, M4 and M2 (#1). This combination has a relatively low cost and discovered almost 65% of all issues in addition to a high number of both critical and cognitive issues (66.7% and 36.8%).

It is not surprising that if more methods are combined then the results are better, but at a higher cost, as for instance shown with combination #5 and #8 in Table X. However, a combination of two methods (#3) gives reasonable good results of discovering around 40% of the known issues, and a large number of both critical and cognitive issues (21.9% and 36.8%).

With a small increase in cost using three testing methods, around 50% of all issues were discovered, as shown with combination #2 and #4. Combination #2 finds 55.9% of all issues, and almost half the known critical issues. It is also worth noting that this testing method combination uses three different accessibility testing method groups (simulation kit, assistive technology and checklist) to discover many different issues.

The first method combination that discover over 80% of known issues is combination #5. This is also the first combination where the persona testing method (M8, M9) is included, but the consequence is high cost. This is the first method combination that requires expert knowledge by including the persona testing method. It is impossible to achieve a very high discovery rate for Case A without including one of the persona testing evaluations, but the downside is that the cost for persona testing is much higher than the rest.

TABLE XI. COST BENEFIT RESULTS CASE B.

#	Methods	Cost	Issues	Critical	Cognitive
1	M2	2	36.9%	26.6%	51.5%
2	M1, M2	3	54.1%	26.6%	51.5%
3	M1, M2, M5	4	64.3%	33.3%	66.6%
4	M1, M2, M6	5	70.0%	43.3%	69.7%
5	M2, M5	3	47.1%	33.3%	66.6%
6	M1, M2, M5, M6	6	80.3%	50.0%	84.8%
7	M2, M5	4	52.9%	43.3%	69.7%
8	M1, M2, M4	5	64.3%	50.0%	66.6%
9	M2, M5, M6	5	63.1%	50.0%	84.8%
10	M1, M2, M4, M5	6	74.5%	56.6%	81.9%
...					
18	M1, M2, M4-M7	10	100.0%	100.0%	100.0%
...					

As shown in Table VII, the method simulation kit with reduced dexterity (M3) reported a low number of issues, and this is why there are few combinations in Table X that includes M3. The first method that includes M3 is #53, and here all the methods are included. The two last combinations (#254 and #255) are also based on M3, and this clearly shows that testing method M3 was not very useful for accessibility testing in Case A.

B. Analysis from Case B

For Case B we also calculated *CB* for all testing method permutations to identify the combinations that gives most benefit compared to cost. The top 10 results in addition to the result which use all the methods are shown in Table XI ordered by *CB*.

The optimal approach based on Case B is to use only method M2, which is the disability kit with reduced vision. This has a very low cost, but does not give a high discovery of issues (36.9%). By including more methods, the discovery of issues increases, but naturally so does the cost, as in Case A. It is not until combination #18 that all methods are combined to give a 100% coverage at a high cost.

If only two methods are combined as shown in combination #2, over half the known issues are found (54.1%), but few critical issues are identified. The best combination to find over half the critical issues is with combination #6, where four testing methods are combined to discover 80.3% of known issues and 50.0% of known critical issues. Note that all top 10 results discover at least 51.5% of known cognitive issues.

VATLab checklist (M7) is not part of any top 10 combinations, and this is because of a low ratio of found issues versus cost. This is very different from Case A where the M7 method was part of top 10 multiple times. However, in both Case A and Case B almost the same number of issues were identified, but in Case A many more critical issues were identified compared to Case B.

From Table XI we can also see that the general cost is much lower compared to Table X, and this is because persona testing methods (M8, M9) were not part of Case B. Persona testing has a very high cost in terms of knowledge requirements, and that is the main reason for higher costs in Case A.

C. Comparison of both cases

From X and XI we see that some methods are prioritized in both top 10 results. Both simulation kit with reduced vision (M2), WCAG (M6) and screen reader (M4) testing methods are the most popular testing methods according to the *CB* analysis. Two testing methods are a little more difficult to compare since we have upgraded the knowledge requirement from Case A to B. This includes WCAG (M6) and VATLab checklist (M7) as indicated in Table V. Because of this, we have calculated the *CB* for Case A with the updated knowledge requirement values from Table V to get better comparison data.

In Table XII the best combination for Case A and Case B is presented. The updated calculation for Case A is also included (A updated). The best combination is determined by counting the occurrences of the testing methods in the top 10 results. In general all methods are part of the best combinations, with the exception of simulation kit with reduced dexterity (M3), but the ordering is a little different depending on the original Case A or the updated Case A.

TABLE XII. COMBINATION OF CASE A AND B.

Case	*Best combination*
A + B	M2, M6, M4, M7, M1/M5, M8, M9
A updated + B	M2, M4/M6, M1/M5/M8, M7, M9

Simulation kit with reduced vision (M2) is the clear winner in both case studies, while WCAG (M6) and screen reader (M4) battle for second place. The other testing methods (M1, M5, M7, M8) compete for the remaining 4th to 7th places while M9 is in the last place for both A and B.

VII. DISCUSSION

Based on the results in Section VI we found that the combination of several methods gives good results compared to the investment. Our CBA from Case A and Case B shows that the testing methods simulation kit with reduced vision, WCAG and screen reader gives good results in both cases with a moderate cost, and yet, the combination of these methods discover a large number of issues with the solutions we evaluated. In addition, the automated checker from Case B showed good issue discovery with very little resource and knowledge requirements, while persona testing from Case A showed great issue discovery, particular for finding cognitive issues, but with high knowledge requirement. Based on an overall assessment from both cases, these five methods gives the best combination of methods. However, the results do not say anything about when to apply the different methods during a development process.

In Figure 3 we have illustrated how to prioritize the different accessibility testing methods in an agile development process, and we call this the *agile accessibility spiral* [1]. The circular layers represent the testing methods, and start from the center with simulation kit using reduced vision and expand outwards to show the priority of the testing methods. The outer layers illustrate an agile process that covers four common activities (design, development, test, review) in successive iterations. The activities are not necessarily clearly separated as shown in the illustration, and they often happen in parallel. The motivation behind the *agile accessibility spiral* is that the different testing methods can be included in all activities in an agile process. The total cost increases as more testing methods are included during testing, but the number of issues discovered also increases, as indicated with the spiral arrow circling outwards from the center.

We have primarily based the ordering of the accessibility testing methods in the spiral on Table XII, but with some exceptions. Testing accessibility using simulation kit with reduced vision is the only method which is always part of top ten results in both cases, and is thus a natural first choice as a testing method. Not only does the method discover most issues, but it is also low on knowledge requirements. Furhermore, the method is exciting to use according to the testers that were part of both studies. Or, as one designer said:

> "I greatly appreciated using the glasses because they made me *feel* the error."

The statement is also supported by the results in Section VI. Finally, the simulation kit for reduced vision is a method that can be performed many times without affecting the bias of the tester, since it is a wearable gadget that is used by the tester and not so much a mental testing approach.

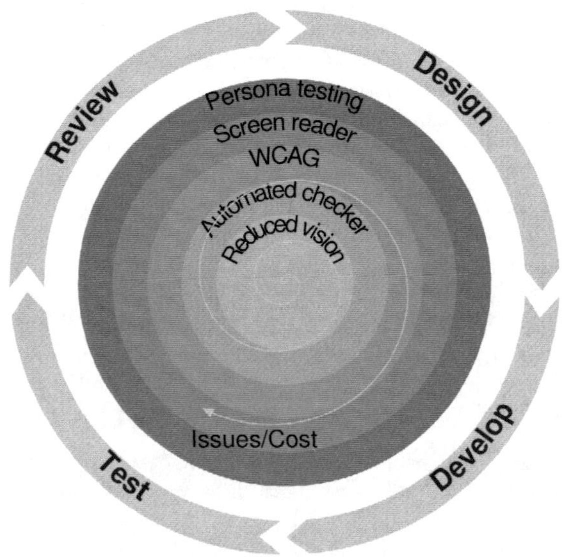

FIGURE 3. AGILE ACCESSIBILITY SPIRAL.

The second accessibility testing method that should be used is the automated checker, since this require very little investment or prior knowledge. Some automated checkers can also be part of the developer IDE or build cycle, and we argue that using an automated checker should be prioritized after simulating reduced vision. Automated checker was only part of the top 10 results 6 times, but both the low average testing time and low requirements (resources and knowledge) are strong indications that the testing method could be done before both the WCAG and screen reader testing methods. Feedback from the tester during the case studies support that automated checker is something they prefer over most methods, and one developer summarized the first two testing method in this manner:

> "I think the automated checker revealed most errors, and I liked that tool the most because it was quick and easy to use. For example, it quickly revealed the high number of contrast errors. That said, it was not until I had the glasses on that I actually understood how severe the errors were. So maybe it is best to use WAVE to reveal the errors and then the glasses to feel them on the body."

Checklists like WCAG is part of the top 10 a total of 13 times, and we therefore place this method as the third testing method in the *agile accessibility spiral*. It should be noted that VATLab checklist was part of top 10 a total of 3 times, but the method had much overlap with other methods (over 75%), and we therefore decided to drop the VATLab checklist from the *agile accessibility spiral*. We argue that WCAG covers most of the VATLab criteria, but discovers more issues and is thus a natural choice. In addition, WCAG is an international standard and legislation that most developers and testers are familiar with.

However, we found that the use of WCAG and VATLAB checklists were perceived as tedious and somewhat difficult, and this is another reason why we place WCAG as the third method instead of the second testing method. One developer commented:

> "I found the WCAG guidelines cumbersome to use. The success criteria was not very explanatory which made it hard for me to take an objective decision whether the criteria was fulfilled or not. I also found it too time-consuming, I would much rather use automated tests or glasses."

Our findings are similar to Farrelly [42], who found that WCAG was perceived by web developers as overwhelming, confusing and with an obtuse and too technical language. While Freire et al. [22] found in their study that nearly 40% of the web developers did not have any knowledge about the WCAG, our findings suggest that developers have knowledge of the guidelines, but that it is too difficult and tiresome to use them regularly.

Screen reader is part of top ten a total of 11 times, and is an obvious choice as the fourth testing method. As Figure 2 shows, this method discovers the highest amount of critical errors of all the methods. The last testing method in the spiral is persona testing, which should be performed less often since the cost is quite high, but also because it is a mental process which might be biased if performed too often by the same person. However, if the team has experience with persona testing or is willing to invest in training, then persona testing is a very good accessibility testing method that we strongly recommend.

We have not included more methods in Figure 3, since these five methods cover over 82.7% of known issues as shown in Table VII and Table VIII. As a minimum at least two different testing method should be included during testing [43].

A. *Use of the testing methods*

We argue that it is important to do accessibility testing at early stages in the development of a user story to avoid costly adjustment at a later stage [7]. It is well worth the investment to make sure that a solution works well for both screen readers and for people with reduced vision, since this will benefit all end-users [9].

During the up-front analysis and design, sketches and wire-frames are created by hand or by tools. The motivation of making these sketches is to create something visual that can be discussed and explained to developers, testers and product owners. There are limited accessibility testing methods that can be used on such sketches, but we argue that both simulation kit with reduced vision and high contrast testing method may be used with success. It will, of course, depend on the quality of the sketches, but bad contrast and use of too small font sizes are typical issues that will be discovered with these methods. Besides, some elements of the WCAG checklist can be used for assessing logic, flow and common general errors. One designer expressed interest for doing accessibility testing early on:

> "I would probably have used the glasses once a week, and I would also have used them early in the projects. For example, if I were deciding on fonts and colours I would put the glasses on to check how someone with reduced vision would experience the solution."

Once a prototype is implemented, then more testing methods can be used naturally. The idea behind a prototype is to verify concepts of sketches and maybe try different interactions or ideas. In addition to the testing methods that can be applied during the design, elements from VATLab checklist and persona testing can be used. It depends on how good the prototype is, but some parts of the VATLab checklist can be used to test for screen reader support, and persona testing can be used to identify cognitive issues already in the prototype stage. An automated checker can be used at a prototype, depending on the product, to detect design issues like poor color contrast.

While simulation kits for reduced vision can be used early in the development and testing of a user story, other testing methods,for example screen readers and persona testing, need a more stable version of the code in place before the methods can be used successfully. The reason for this is that screen readers require elements to be marked so that the screen readers can find the required information. Persona testing is most suitable at the end of an implementation of a user story, since entire features should have been implemented for this testing method, and the testers should use the real software product.

B. Implications for practice

Our findings have implications for software organizations wanting to build more usable and accessible software. Practitioners can use the agile accessibility spiral to assess the appropriate tools to test accessibility early and frequently in the agile development cycle.

While there exist many accessibility testing methods, they are not that known to agile team members. Companies should strive to inform their employees about what techniques they can use and how to use them during the development cycle. A survey on accessibility awareness among web development project members [22] finds that the main reasons for not considering accessibility issues in the development process were the lack of formal requirements from the organization, lack of customer requirements and lack of training.

Based on the evaluation results and the cost-benefit analysis, we strongly suggest that all agile software projects buy glasses for simulating reduced vision and make them easily available for their employees to get hold of. Using the glasses was undoubtedly the tool that revealed the most errors, and additionally it was an eye-opener for many of the developers. However, while all participants claimed they would use the glasses if they had them at their desk, they said they would not order them themselves. This barrier for use must be removed by the project leaders. Both designers and developers should use automated checkers, such as WAVE, as early as possible in the projects and as often as possible. Use of automated checkers to quickly get an overview of errors and then using the glasses to get a feeling of how the errors would be perceived by a person with reduced vision creates new insights and the iterative use of these two methods complement each other.

In order to make software as accessible as possible, all members of an agile software team should have basic knowledge of accessibility testing and universal design, and norms and practices should be incorporated into the development process to ensure that the software developed is accessible. Norms are an integral aspect of how agile teams work [44], and promoting the right norms in the team may influence how developers think of accessibility testing. For example, promoting norms that simulation kits are frequently used and that accessibility issues are discussed in team meetings.

Our findings suggest that checking for accessibility issues with the use of automated checkers and simulation kits will make developers and designers in agile projects more positive towards continuous accessibility testing than the use of manual guidelines. Use of guidelines and checklists was perceived as tedious and boring.

VIII. Limitations

We only covered a limited selection of possible methods and tools for accessibility testing in our study, and other methods could prove to be more beneficial. We have, however, selected methods from a wide range with respect to what they cover of technical and usable accessibility.

The cost-benefit analysis was calculated based on the requirements in resources and knowledge of each method. The classification of methods as low, medium or high in demands for resource and knowledge could be further validated. One should also consider other factors contributing to cost in the analysis. For example, the amount of time spent in performing a test method is a cost. Besides, satisfaction and ease of use could also be possible beneficial criteria to include.

The categorization of issues as critical or cognitive is subjectively performed by the authors and future research should try to standardize the classification of issues. However, each evaluation was observed and reported by at least two, sometimes three, observers and most of the testing methods where used in both case studies. These conditions should result in a reduced number of errors.

Our study of accessibility testing methods was limited in number of participants and the size of the evaluated applications. Hence, future work should explore the different accessibility testing methods for other software solutions. Additionally, more studies should be performed to validate the cost-benefit relationships and the *agile accessibility spiral*.

IX. Conclusion

In this study, we investigated methods for accessibility testing in agile projects. Based on evaluations from two case studies and a cost-benefit analysis we proposed the *agile accessibility spiral*. We included five of the tested methods in the spiral. The cost and knowledge of testing methods increase from the center of the spiral and outwards, but the discovery of issues also increases when moving outwards from the center. We recommend to choose methods from the center and gradually apply more testing methods.

The different testing methods should be adjusted to the software solution and the expertise of the team, so they fit into the agile process. The more knowledge and experience an agile team gains, the smaller the circles in the *agile accessibility spiral* will become. We argue that developers and testers can contribute more with accessibility testing to deliver a better end product as shown with our two case studies. We also believe they will be more positive towards testing for accessibility with the use of simulation kits for reduced vision and automated checkers instead of only using guidelines such as WCAG.

More research on evaluations of accessibility testing should be carried out, and it would be interesting to evaluate other testing methods than those used in this study and incorporate them into the *agile accessibility spiral*. Further work should also investigate whether other factors such as time, satisfaction and ease of use should be included in the cost-benefit analysis.

References

[1] A. Bai, H. C. Mork, and V. Stray, "A Cost-benefit Evaluation of Accessibility Testing in Agile Software Development," in ICSEA 2016 : The Eleventh International Conference on Software Engineering Advances, 2016, pp. 62–67.

[2] United Nations. Convention on the Rights of Persons with Disabilities. [Online]. Available: https://www.un.org/development/desa/disabilities/convention-on-the-rights-of-persons-with-disabilities.html [Accessed: 2017-05-26].
[3] H. Petrie and N. Bevan, "The evaluation of accessibility, usability and user experience," The universal access handbook, 2009, pp. 10–20.
[4] R. Mace, "What is universal design," The Center for Universal Design at North Carolina State University. Retrieved Retrieved, vol. 19, 1997, p. 2004.
[5] J. Nielsen, "Return on investment for usability," Jakob Nielsen's Alertbox, January, vol. 7, 2003.
[6] L. C. Cheng and M. Mustafa, "A reference to usability inspection methods," in International Colloquium of Art and Design Education Research (i-CADER 2014). Springer, 2015, pp. 407–419.
[7] M.-L. Sánchez-Gordón and L. Moreno, "Toward an integration of web accessibility into testing processes," Procedia Computer Science, vol. 27, 2014, pp. 281–291.
[8] B. Haskins, B. Dick, J. Stecklein, R. Lovell, G. Moroney, and J. Dabney, "Error Cost Escalation Through the Project Life Cycle," in Incose - Annual Conference Symposium Proceedings- Cd Rom Edition; 2004, 2004.
[9] F. Paz and J. A. Pow-Sang, "A systematic mapping review of usability evaluation methods for software development process," International Journal of Software Engineering and Its Applications, vol. 10, no. 1, 2016, pp. 165–178.
[10] T. Dingsøyr, S. Nerur, V. Balijepally, and N. B. Moe, "A decade of agile methodologies: Towards explaining agile software development," Journal of Systems and Software, vol. 85, no. 6, 2012, pp. 1213 – 1221.
[11] V. Stray, N. B. Moe, and G. R. Bergersen, "Are daily stand-up meetings valuable? A survey of developers in software teams," in Agile Processes in Software Engineering and Extreme Programming: 18th International Conference, XP 2017, Cologne, Germany, May 22-26, 2017, Proceedings, H. Baumeister, H. Lichter, and M. Riebisch, Eds. Cham: Springer International Publishing, 2017, pp. 274–281. [Online]. Available: http://dx.doi.org/10.1007/978-3-319-57633-6_20 [Accessed: 2017-06-01].
[12] K. Schwaber and M. Beedle, "Agile Software Development with Scrum". Upper Saddle River, NJ: Prentice Hall, 2002.
[13] V. Stray, D. I. K. Sjøberg, and T. Dybå, "The daily stand-up meeting: A grounded theory study," Journal of Systems and Software, vol. 85, 2016, pp. 101 – 124.
[14] J. Highsmith and A. Cockburn, "Agile software development: The business of innovation," Computer, vol. 34, no. 9, 2002, pp. 120 – 127.
[15] G. Jurca, T. D. Hellmann, and F. Maurer, "Integrating agile and user-centered design: a systematic mapping and review of evaluation and validation studies of agile-ux," in Agile Conference (AGILE), 2014. IEEE, 2014, pp. 24–32.
[16] G. Zimmermann and G. Vanderheiden, "Accessible design and testing in the application development process: considerations for an integrated approach," Universal Access in the Information Society, vol. 7, no. 1-2, 2008, pp. 117–128.
[17] J. C. Lee and D. S. McCrickard, "Towards extreme (ly) usable software: Exploring tensions between usability and agile software development," in Agile Conference (AGILE), 2007. IEEE, 2007, pp. 59–71.
[18] D. Salah, R. F. Paige, and P. Cairns, "A systematic literature review for agile development processes and user centred design integration," in Proceedings of the 18th International Conference on Evaluation and Assessment in Software Engineering, ser. EASE '14. New York, NY, USA: ACM, 2014, pp. 5:1–5:10. [Online]. Available: http://doi.acm.org/10.1145/2601248.2601276 [Accessed: 2017-03-01].
[19] R. Bonacin, M. C. C. Baranauskas, and M. A. Rodrigues, "An agile process model for inclusive software development," in Enterprise information systems. Springer, 2009, pp. 807–818.
[20] S. Horton and D. Sloan, "Accessibility in practice: a process-driven approach to accessibility," in Inclusive Designing. Springer, 2014, pp. 105–115.
[21] T. Halbach and K. Fuglerud, "On assessing the costs and benefits of universal design of ict." Studies in health technology and informatics, vol. 229, 2016, p. 662.
[22] A. P. Freire, C. M. Russo, and R. P. M. Fortes, "A survey on the accessibility awareness of people involved in web development projects in Brazil," in Proceedings of the 2008 international cross-disciplinary conference on Web accessibility. ACM, 2008, pp. 87–96.
[23] C. Paddison and P. Englefield, "Applying heuristics to accessibility inspections," in Interacting with Computers, vol. 16, no. 3, 2004, pp. 507–521.
[24] Web accessibility evaluation tools list. [Online]. Available: https://www.w3.org/WAI/ER/tools/ [Accessed: 2017-02-01].
[25] NetBeans. Accessibility Checker. [Online]. Available: http://plugins.netbeans.org/plugin/7577/accessibility-checker [Accessed: 2017-05-26].
[26] C. Cardoso and P. J. Clarkson, "Simulation in user-centred design: helping designers to empathise with atypical users," Journal of Engineering Design, vol. 23, no. 1, 2012, pp. 1–22.
[27] A. M. Silverman, J. D. Gwinn, and L. Van Boven, "Stumbling in their shoes disability simulations reduce judged capabilities of disabled people," Social Psychological and Personality Science, vol. 6, no. 4, 2015, pp. 464–471.
[28] S. L. Henry, "Just ask: integrating accessibility throughout design". Lulu. com, 2007.
[29] W3C. Web Content Accessibility Guidelines. [Online]. Available: https://www.w3.org/TR/WCAG20/ [Accessed: 2017-03-01].
[30] T. Schulz and K. S. Fuglerud, "Creating Personas with Disabilities," in Computers Helping People with Special Needs, ser. Lecture Notes in Computer Science, K. Miesenberger, A. Karshmer, P. Penaz, and W. Zagler, Eds., vol. 7383. Linz, Austria: Springer Berlin / Heidelberg, 2012, pp. 145–152.
[31] A. Bai, H. C. Mork, T. Schulz, and K. S. Fuglerud, "Evaluation of accessibility testing methods. which methods uncover what type of problems?" Studies in health technology and informatics, vol. 229, 2016, p. 506.
[32] J. S. Dumas and J. Redish, "A practical guide to usability testing". Intellect Books, 1999.
[33] R. G. Bias and D. J. Mayhew, "Cost-justifying usability: An update for the Internet age". Elsevier, 2005.
[34] Wave web accessibility evaluation tool. [Online]. Available: http://wave.webaim.org/ [Accessed: 2017-02-01].
[35] K. S. Fuglerud, S. E. Skotkjerra, and T. Halbach. (2015) Håndbok i testing av websider med hjelpe-middel-program-vare, Virtuell hjelpe-middellab.
[36] Cambridge. Inclusive Design Toolkit. [Online]. Available: http://www.inclusivedesigntoolkit.com [Accessed: 2017-02-01].
[37] NV Access. NVDA Screen Reader. [Online]. Available: https://www.nvaccess.org/ [Accessed: 2017-02-01].
[38] Futureid. [Online]. Available: http://www.futureid.eu/ [Accessed: 2017-03-01].
[39] Norsk pensjon. [Online]. Available: https://www.norskpensjon.no/ [Accessed: 2017-03-01].
[40] M. M. Mantei and T. J. Teorey, "Cost/benefit analysis for incorporating human factors in the software lifecycle," Communications of the ACM, vol. 31, no. 4, 1988, pp. 428–439.
[41] A. E. Boardman, D. H. Greenberg, A. R. Vining, and D. L. Weimer, "Cost-benefit analysis: concepts and practice," 2006.
[42] G. Farrelly, "Practitioner barriers to diffusion and implementation of web accessibility," Technology and Disability, vol. 23, no. 4, 2011, pp. 223–232.
[43] K. S. Fuglerud, "Inclusive design of ICT: The challenge of diversity". Dissertation for the Degree of PhD, University of Oslo, Faculty of Humanitites, 2014.
[44] V. Stray, T. E. Fægri, and N. B. Moe, "Exploring norms in agile software teams," in Proceedings of the International Conference on Product-Focused Software Process Improvement. Springer International Publishing, 2016, pp. 458–467.

On the Effort Required by Function Point Measurement Phases

Luigi Lavazza
Dipartimento di Scienze Teoriche e Applicate
Università degli Studi dell'Insubria
Varese, Italy
email: luigi.lavazza@uninsubria.it

Abstract— **Function Point Analysis is widely used, especially to quantify the size of applications in the early stages of development, when effort estimates are needed. However, the measurement process is often too long or too expensive, or it requires more knowledge than available when development effort estimates are due. To overcome these problems, early size estimation methods have been proposed, to get approximate estimates of Function Point measures. In general, early estimation methods adopt measurement processes that are simplified with respect to the standard process, in that one or more phases are skipped. Early estimation methods are considered effective; however there is little evidence of the actual savings that they can guarantee. To this end, it is necessary to know the relative cost of each phase of the standard Function Point measurement process. This paper presents the results of two surveys concerning the relative amount of effort required by the phases of the standard Function Point measurement process. The analysis of the collected data can be used to assess the expected savings that early estimation methods make possible.**

Keywords- functional size measurement; Function Point Analysis; IFPUG Function Points; Simple Function Point; measurement process; cost of measurement; measurement effort.

I. INTRODUCTION

Knowing the relative cost of the phases that compose Function Point Analysis (FPA) is of great importance for software project managers [1].

FPA [2][3][4][5] is widely used. Among the reasons for the success of FPA is that it can provide measures of size in the early stages of software development, when they are most needed for cost estimation.

However, FPA performed by a certified Function Point (FP) consultant proceeds at a relatively slow pace: between 400 and 600 FP per day, according to Capers Jones [6], between 200 and 300 FP per day according to experts from Total Metrics [7]. Consequently, measuring the size of a moderately large application can take too long, if cost estimation is needed urgently. Also, the cost of measurement can be often considered excessive by software developers. In addition, cost estimates may be needed when requirements have not yet been specified in detail and completely.

To overcome these problems, early estimation methods (EEM's) have been proposed: these methods provide approximate estimated values of FP measures. Instead of going through the standard FP measurement process, EEM's provide estimates based on a little number of parameters that can be collect in a short time and with little effort. Most EEM's estimates are obtained via statistical models and contain unavoidable estimation errors. A list of EEM's can be found in [8] and [20].

The goal of the work presented here is to assess the cost of the measurement activities in terms of the effort required. However, as mentioned in the introduction, there is little agreement on the effort needed to carry out FP measurement: for instance, Capers Jones [6] and Total Metrics [7] provide quite different evaluations. Therefore, it appears more feasible to pursue an evaluation of the *relative* effort required by the measurement phases (i.e., the fraction of the total measurement effort dedicated to each phase). In this way, we can assess how much we save –in terms of measurement effort, hence ultimately of money– by skipping a measurement phase, i.e., by not performing one of the activities of the standard measurement process. In fact, if a manager knows that applying the standard measurement process in her organization takes X PersonHours per FP, and a simplified measurement process allows for saving 30% of the effort, she can easily conclude that in her organization the application of the simplified process will take 0.7X PersonHours. Of course, our manager should also take into account that Early Estimation Methods provide *estimates* of the actual measures, that is, the savings are usually associated to a loss of accuracy (not dealt with in this paper: interested readers can find some evaluations in [20]).

To estimate the relative effort required to carry out each phase of the FP measurement process, we made two surveys. Both surveys involved collecting opinions from expert measurers concerning the relative effort required by measurement phases. The first survey was carried out completely on-line, using a web-based questionnaire management system. The second one was carried out at a conference: the questions were illustrated to the audience and answers were provided on paper at the end of the conference.

The paper is structured as follows. Section II reports a few basic concepts of FPA. Section III describes how the first survey was carried out and illustrates the results of the survey. Section IV is similar to Section III, but it is dedicated to the second survey. In Section V we discuss how the results given in Sections III and IV can be used to assess the savings that can be obtained by using EMM's. Section VI discusses the threats to the validity of this study. Section VII accounts for related work. Finally, Section VIII draws conclusions and briefly sketches future work.

II. Function Point Analysis Concepts

FPA aims at providing a measure of the size of the functional specifications of a given software application.

A. *The model of the software being measured according to FPA*

FPA addresses functional specifications that are represented according to a specific model. The model of functional specifications used by FPA is given in Figure 1. Briefly, Logical files are the data processed by the application, and transactions are the operations available to users. The size measure in FP is computed as a weighted sum of the number of Logical files and Transactions. The weight of logical data files is computed based on the Record Elements Types (RET), i.e., subgroups of data belonging to a data file, and Data Element Types (DET), i.e., the elementary pieces of data; besides, the weight depends on whether the data file is within the boundaries of the application, i.e., it is an Internal Logic File (ILF) or it is outside such boundaries, i.e., it is an External Interface File (EIF). The weight of transactions is computed based on the Logical files involved –see the FTR (File Type Referenced) association in Figure 1– and the DET used for I/O; besides, the weight depends on the "main intent" of the transaction. In fact, depending on the main intent, transactions are classified as External Inputs (EI), External Outputs (EO) or External Queries (EQ).

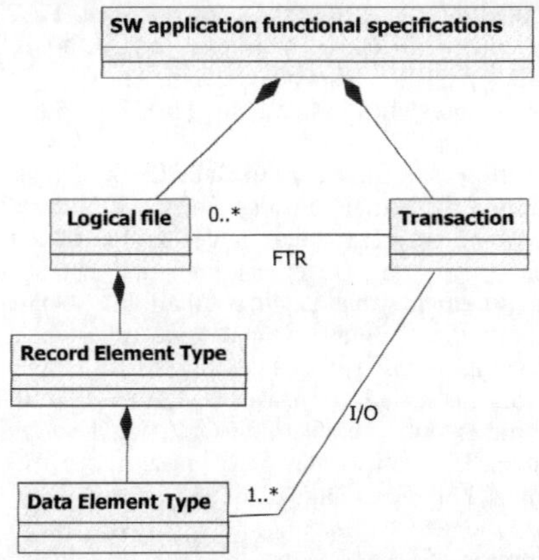

Figure 1. The model of software used in FPA.

B. *The FPA measurement process*

According to the International Function Point User Group (IFPUG) measurement manual [4][5], the measurement process includes the following phases:

1. Gathering the available documentation concerning functional user requirements;
2. Identifying application boundaries and determining the measurement goal and scope;
3. Identifying Elementary Processes (Transactions) and Logical Data Files;
4. Classifying transactions as EI, EO or EQ; classifying files as ILF or EIF; identifying RET, DET, FTR and determining complexity;
5. Calculating the functional size;
6. Documenting and presenting the measurement.

C. *Early Estimation methods*

EEM's tend to skip as many as possible of the steps listed above. The idea is straightforward: the less phases have to be performed, the faster and cheaper is the process. However, some activities –e. g., those involved in phases 1 and 2– are preparatory of the real measurement and cannot be skipped. Similarly, phase 6 can hardly be avoided. In any case, it should be noted that the simplification of the measurement process can affect phases 1 and 6 as well: on the one hand, a simplified process requires less documentation concerning the functional specifications of the application; on the other hand, documenting and presenting a simplified measurement is easier and faster than documenting the full-fledged measurement.

As a final observation, the extent of phase 6 depends on the context and the goal of measurement: for instance, if an organization is measuring the size of the application to be developed for internal purposes, the documentation can be kept to a minimum; on the contrary, if the functional size measures have to be used in a bid or in establishing the price of a contract, the documentation to be produced has usually to be quite detailed, and the presentation of the measures and measurement has also to be accurate.

In conclusion, EEM's address mainly phases 4 and 5. However, there is hardly any evidence of how much you save if you skip or simplify any of these phases. On the contrary, some evidence exists that by simplifying the measurement process, some measurement error is introduced [20].

D. *Other functional size measurement methods*

Besides IFPUG function points, several other methods have been proposed. These are treated as follows, in this paper:

- NESMA (Netherlands Software Metrics Association) function points [10] have become essentially equivalent to IFPUG Function Points. Therefore, the analysis presented in the paper applies to NESMA FP measurement as well.
- The Simple Function Point (SiFP) method [16][17][26][27] adopts a model of the software to be measured that is greatly simplified with respect to the model given in Figure 1. Hence, the measurement is similarly simplified: it requires only that transactions and logical data files are identified; then the functional size is computed as follows:

$$Size = 4.7\ \#UGEP + 7\ \#UGDG \quad (1)$$

where #UGEP is the number of transactions (UGEP is for Unspecified Generic Elementary Process) and #UGDG is the number of logical data files (UGDG is for Unspecified Generic Data Group). Although it adopts a simplified measurement process, the SiFP method is not an EEM method: it is a proper functional size measurement method, which provides a proper measure (expressed in SiFP) [18], not an approximate estimate of the size expressed in IFPUG FP. The outcomes of our analysis can be used to evaluate the effort required for the SiFP process in comparison with the IFPUG measurement process.

- Other methods (like the COSMIC method [29], MKII Function Points [30] of FISMA [28]) are not considered in this paper, and the results we present are not applicable to these methods.

As a final remark, we remind that Function Point can be adjusted or not adjusted. In this paper we consider only unadjusted Function Points. This is consistent with the choice of the International Standardization Organization, which standardized unadjusted FP, not adjusted FP.

III. THE FIRST SURVEY

As mentioned in the introduction, the study reported here is based on two surveys. In this section we report about the first survey.

A. *The survey*

The investigation described here was performed via a questionnaire, which was filled by people that are experienced in IFPUG Function Point measurement.

The questionnaire was published on the kwiksurveys site [21]. The questionnaire was publicized via several channels:

- An invitation to fill out the questionnaire was sent to the Italian Software Measurement Association (www.gufpi-isma.org);
- A similar invitation was sent to the Nesma association [22];
- Finally, a question was published on ResearchGate [23], and experts were redirected to the questionnaire URL.

The questionnaire is reported in Appendix A. It can be noticed that the questionnaire targets both the IFPUG [4][5] and the Nesma [10] measurement processes. In fact, according to Nesma, *"[Since 1994,] owing to [...] the intensive cooperation between the Nesma and the IFPUG, the counting guidelines of the NESMA and the IFPUG continuously came closer and closer. [...] With the publication of IFPUG CPM 4.2 (2004) the last major differences between IFPUG and NESMA disappeared."* Therefore, mixing data concerning the current IFPUG and Nesma measurement processes is perfectly safe, and the results found apply equally well to both measurement methods.

The questionnaire was published in November 2014, and answers were collected until April 2015.

B. *The Results of the survey*

31 answers were collected. Even if the number is not very large, it is nonetheless sufficient to get a reasonably reliable assessment of the relative effort required by FP measurement activities.

Of the respondents, 21 are certified Function Point Specialist (CFPS), and 4 are certified Function Point Practitioner (CFPP). Only 6 have no certification; however, of these, 2 use NESMA Function Points, therefore it is reasonable that they do not need an IFPUG certification.

The experience of the respondents is also quite reassuring: 20 respondents have been using FP measurement for over 10 years; only two for less than 5 years.

It should be noted that the questionnaire does not ask for a specific percentage for each phase; instead, it asks to specify in what range the actual percentage of effort belongs. This choice was due to two reasons: 1) the free version of the questionnaire provided by kwiksurveys does not support the collection of numeric values, and 2) it is unlikely that a respondent knows the exact fraction of effort that is spent in each phase, while it is much more probable that he/she can indicate the correct range.

The collected data concerning the relative effort required by each measurement phase are given in Table VI in Appendix A.

When information is collected via questionnaires, it is always possible that some respondents do not provide correct data. Therefore, before proceeding to the analysis of the collected data, it is necessary to remove unreliable answers from the dataset. In our case, the following problems were detected:

1) The sum of the efforts spent in each phase must be 100%. Having asked for ranges, we expect that the sum of the lower bounds of the ranges is ≤ 100% (but close to 100%) and that the sum of the upper bounds is ≥ 100% (but close to 100%). Respondents 12, 23 and 31 do not satisfy these conditions: total effort is in [27%, 60%] range for respondent 12, in [200%, 230%] range for respondent 23 and in [12%, 45%] range for respondent 31. These are clearly worthless indications, therefore they have been excluded from the dataset.
2) Among the remaining respondents, it is easy to spot a few outliers. Respondent 19 declared a fraction of effort for phase 6 (Documenting and presenting the measurement) that is almost half the total effort and more than double than the other respondents'. Respondent 27 declared an abnormally large amount of effort dedicated to phase 1 (Gathering the available documentation concerning functional requirements): such a large effort may be required in specific contexts, but is not representative of the general case (as other respondents clearly show). To preserve the representativeness of the data, the answers provided by the mentioned respondents have been excluded from the dataset.
3) Respondents 4 and 5 declared that they use EEM's. Their answers were removed from the dataset, since we are interested in the relative effort for the phases of the *standard* measurement process.

The answers provided by respondents concerning each measurement phases are summarized in Figure 2, where the boxplots of relative effort –expressed as a percentage– are given (diamond-shaped points indicate the mean values).

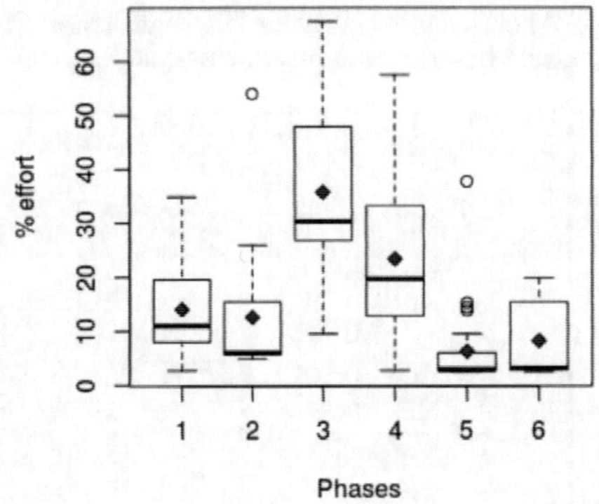

Figure 2. Distribution of relative phase efforts for the first survey dataset.

To analyze the data in Table VI, the following procedure was adopted:

1) Let ML_{ij} and MU_{ij} be the minimum and maximum relative effort for phase i indicated by respondent j. First of all, we computed for every phase i and for every respondent j, $M_{ij} = (ML_{ij} + MU_{ij})/2$: M_{ij} is the most likely effort for phase i according to respondent j.
2) For every respondent j, we computed $T_j = \Sigma_{i=1,6} M_{ij}$. Of course, we would like that $T_j = 100\%$, that is, the sum of the relative effort spent for each phase should be the total effort spent for measurement. In general it was not so. Thus, we normalized each phase effort: we computed $WM_{ij} = 100\ M_{ij}/T_j$. So, $\Sigma_{i=1,6} WM_{ij} = 100\%$.
3) For every phase i, we computed $M_i = (\Sigma_{j\in J} WM_{ij})/|J|$, where J is the set of respondents. M_i is the average effort indicated by respondents for phase i.

The resulting values (expressed as percentages) are given in Table I.

TABLE I. MEAN AND MEDIAN VALUES OF (NORMALIZED) PHASE RELATIVE EFFORTS

Phase	1	2	3	4	5	6
Mean	14.0	12.5	35.8	23.3	6.2	8.2

The results of the analyses provide some useful indications concerning the relative effort required by the phases of FP measurement, performed according to the IFPUG or Nesma process.

The fact that more than half the effort is concentrated in phases 3 and 4 also appears to confirm the reliability of results. In fact, it is popular wisdom that most measurement effort is required by the analysis of data and processes, which is concentrated in phases 3 and 4.

C. *An issue with survey one*

In Figure 2 it can be observed that the percentage effort data have fairly large variance only for phases 3 and 4. This suggests that some measurers dedicate to phase 3 only the minimum effort that is needed to identify transactions and data files, so that phase 4 requires a substantial amount of work; on the contrary, some measurers probably perform some amount of analysis of transactions and data already in phase 3, so that the effort for phase 3 increases, while the effort for phase 4 decreases, because part of the analysis needed to assign complexity levels to transactions and data files has already been done.

The fact that some activities of phase 4 can be anticipated into phase 3 is critical for our analysis, since we know that most EEM's allow for simplifying or skipping altogether phase 4, while phase 3 cannot be simplified much, in general. As a consequence, the results of survey one can be regarded as non-conclusive. For this reason we performed a second survey, which is described in the following section.

IV. THE SECOND SURVEY

A. *The survey*

The second survey (whose details are given in Appendix B) was carried out during a meeting of the GUFPI-ISMA (the Italian Function Points User Group – Italian Software Measurement Association), which took place in Rome in December 2016. The questionnaire was first explained to the participants, then the respondents compiled the questionnaire (on paper) and handed it to the author.

The collected answers concerning the relative (percentage) effort for IFPUG Function Point measurement are given in Table VII in Appendix B. Note that respondents were invited to express a specific percentage of the total effort for each phase, rather than a range, as in survey one.

We collected 37 answers. Of the respondents, 36 are certified Function Point Specialist (CFPS) and one is a certified Function Point Practitioner (CFPP). On average, the respondents have over 10 year experience and count over 7000 FP per year. Therefore, the respondents are extremely well qualified, and we can regard their answers as exceptionally reliable in representing current IFPUG measurement practices.

B. *The results of the survey*

Table II reports the mean relative effort per phase according to respondents. Note that –unlike in the first survey– no normalization was necessary, so we could compute the statistics given in Table II directly from the collected data.

TABLE II. STATISTICS OF PHASE RELATIVE EFFORT

Phase	1	2	3	4	5	6
Mean	16.9	10.2	23.3	31.5	8.1	10.0

Figure 3 shows the distributions of the relative effort dedicated to each phase according to respondents. It can be seen that the opinions concerning the amount of effort that should be dedicated to phases 3 and 4 vary widely. In fact, for both phases 3 and 4 the distance between the minimum and the maximum evaluations is 40% (quite a large variation indeed).

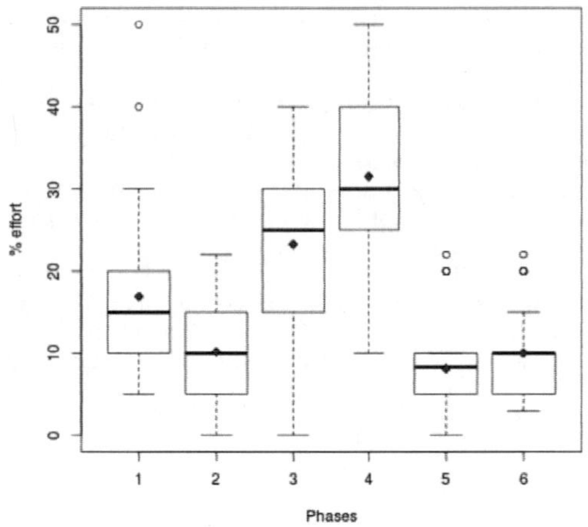

Figure 3. Distribution of relative phase efforts for the second survey dataset.

Figure 3 suggests that there is little agreement on how to perform the FP measurement process. This is confirmed by the visual analysis of raw data (see Table VII in Appendix B). In fact, it seems that some respondents prefer to start measuring after a relatively lightweight analysis of requirements, which results in longer and/or more difficult activities in phases 3 and/or 4: for instance, respondent 9 spends only 5% of the measurement effort in phase 1, thus causing the effort for phases 3 and 4 to increase substantially (in fact, phases 3 and 4 together require 85% of the total measurement effort). On the contrary, some respondents perform a thorough analysis of requirements in phase 1, so that the following phases become simpler and require less work: for instance, respondent 10 spends 50% of the measurement effort in phase 1, then phases 3 and 4 together require only 20% of the total effort.

In practice, it appears that there is not a unique way of implementing the IFPUG measurement process: rather some measurers prefer to collect all the required information in advance, so that the actual measurement phases are facilitated; on the contrary, some other measurers prefer to collect only the minimum information necessary to start; then they explore details when needed, during the measurement phases (phases 3 and 4).

This observation suggested to partition the dataset into two datasets, corresponding to the two approaches described above: in the first dataset we put the data that indicate heavyweight phase 1, in the second dataset we put the data concerning processes characterized by lightweight phase 1.

The data in Table VII suggest to use 15% as the threshold that can be used to partition the data concerning phase 1.

Figure 4 shows the distributions of the relative effort dedicated to measurement phases, when phase 1 is heavyweight (i.e., it consumes more than 15% of the total effort). Table III reports the mean effort per phase when the process is characterized by heavyweight phase 1.

It is easy to see that the mean effort for phases 3 and 4 decreases sensibly (as expected, since most work is done in phase 1). The variability of phase 3 also decreases sensibly, while the variability of phase 4 remains quite large.

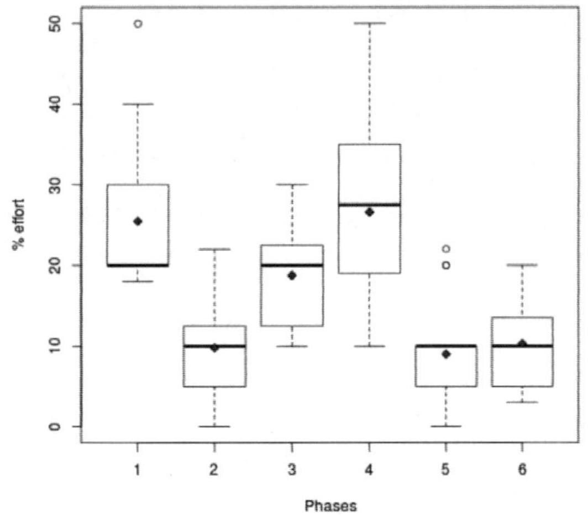

Figure 4. Distribution of phase efforts for the second survey dataset (only "heavyweight" data collection).

TABLE III. MEAN RELATIVE EFFORT PER PHASE, WHEN PAHSE 1 IS 'HEAVYWEIGHT'

Phase	1	2	3	4	5	6
Mean	25.5	9.8	18.8	26.6	9.0	10.3

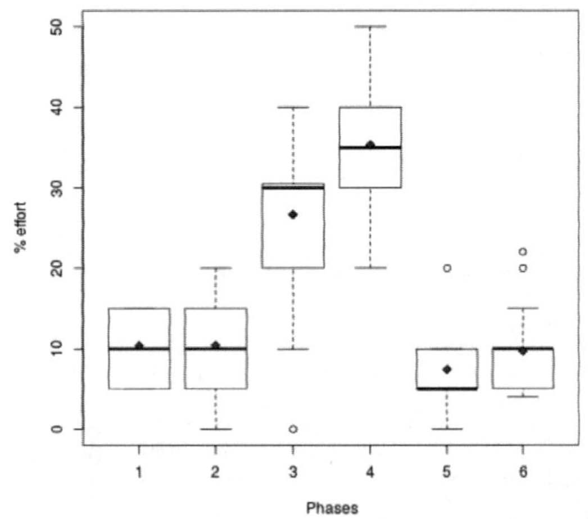

Figure 5. Distribution of phase efforts for the second survey dataset (only "lightweight" data collection)

Figure 5 shows the distributions of the relative phase effort, when phase 1 is lightweight (i.e., it consumes no more than 15% of the total effort). Table IV reports the mean effort per phase when the process is characterized by lightweight phase 1.

It is easy to see that the mean effort for phases 3 and 4 increases (as expected, since little preparatory work is done in phase 1). The variability of phase 3 and 4 decrease, although not much.

TABLE IV. STATISTICS OF PHASE RELATIVE EFFORTS, WHEN PAHSE 1 IS 'HEAVYWEIGHT'

Phase	1	2	3	4	5	6
Mean	10.4	10.4	26.7	35.3	7.4	9.7

V. AN ASSESSMENT OF POSSIBLE SAVINGS

The standard Function Point measurement process according to the IFPUG counting manual can be represented as in Figure 6. Actually, the process in Figure 6 is an abstraction of what really happens in practice, since it ignores loops. For instance, it happens quite frequently that while analyzing a transaction to determine its complexity the need to collect more information concerning the transaction arises, so that the measurer has to go back to the documentation gathering phase.

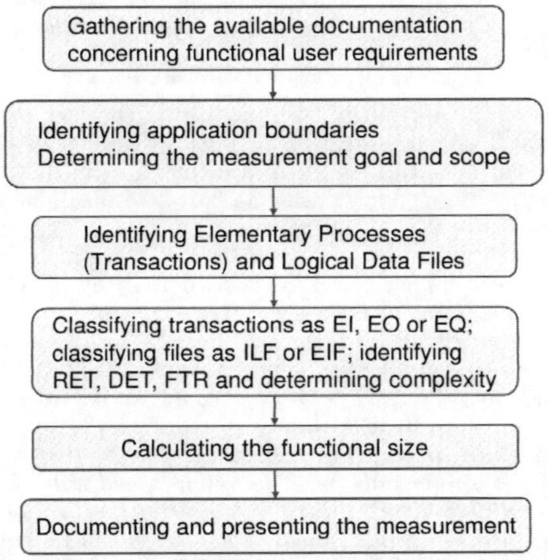

Figure 6. A schematic representation of the FP measurement process.

Now, the most popular EEM's simplify the phase that involves classifying transactions and data files and determining their complexity to a great extent. Among such methods are the NESMA estimated [9][12][13], Early&Quick Function Point [11], simplified Function Point [15] (not to be confused with the Simple Function Point method), and ISBSG average weights (which assigns to each basic functional component the average weight that type of component has in the ISBSG (International Software Benchmarking Standards Group) dataset [14]). For instance, the NESMA estimated method only requires that transactions are classified into EI, EO and EQ, and logical data files are classified into ILF and EIF, but no weighting is required; thus there is little need to analyze the details of transactions and data files, which is definitely the most effort consuming activity in this phase.

When the SiFP method is used, the phase that involves classifying transactions and data files and determining their complexity is skipped altogether, since the SiFP method does neither require that transactions are classified into EI, EO and EQ, nor that data files are classified as ILF or EIF.

Moreover, with both EEM's and SiFP the first and the last two phases are also greatly simplified:

- Since the methods require less details, there is less information to be gathered.
- Computing the size measures is often straightforward with early estimation methods. With SiFP, it amounts to computing formula (1), so there is actually no work to do.
- Documenting the measurement is simpler, since there is less to document (e.g., when there is no notion of complexity, one does not need to document the characteristics of transactions and data that determine their complexity).

According to the findings reported in Sections III and IV, we can (very roughly) estimate the possible savings that can be achieved via EEM's and with the SiFP measurement method.

In Table V, we compute the savings that in principle can be achieved for each phase:

- In column "Est. % savings" we have the percentage of phase effort that can be possibly saved. This is a subjective estimation, based on the considerations reported above.
- In column "1st survey M_i" the average weighted relative effort for each phase (as in Table I) is given.
- In column "2nd survey M_i" the average relative effort for each phase (as in Table II) is given.
- In the rightmost column, the approximate potential saving is computed. Since the mean efforts resulting from the two surveys are different, we often provide a range (form the most pessimistic to the most optimistic hypothesis). So, concerning phase 1, for instance, we can possibly save 50% of the effort, which is between 14.0% (according to the first survey) and 16.9% (according to the second survey). Thus, we have a minimum saving of 50%×14.0%=7% and a maximum saving 50%×16.9%=8.45%: accordingly, we provide an approximate evaluation that the likely saving will be in the 7-8% range.

TABLE V. POTENTIAL SAVINGS WITH EEM'S

Phase	Est. % savings	1st survey M_i	2nd survey M_i	Likely savings (approx.)
1	50%	14.0%	16.9%	7–8 %
2	0%	12.5%	10.2%	0 %
3	0%	35.8%	23.3%	0 %
4	80-100%	23.3%	31.5%	18–30 %
5	90%	6.2%	8.1%	5–7 %
6	50%	8.2%	10.0%	4–5 %
Total	–	100.0%	100.0%	**34–50 %**

Of course, the evaluations given in Table V are based on averages, thus the reader is advised that in specific cases the actual savings could be somewhat different.

Anyway, we have to note that the savings described above are *potential* savings, that is, it largely depends on the specific situations if the possible savings are actually achieved or not. For instance, if an organization represents requirements via UML diagrams, the first phase of the measurement process is greatly eased, since extracting the information required for functional measurement from UML diagrams [24][25] is fairly easy; so phase 1 will require a smaller relative effort, hence savings on phase 1 will not be very large, in absolute terms.

Finally, let us consider the answers provided during the second survey to the question concerning the relative effort required by EEM's. In fact, in the second survey, measurers who use EEM's were invited to directly indicate what is the effort required for measurement when an EEM is used instead of the standard IFPUG process. The frequency of answers is given in Figure 7, where the effort for measurement using EEM's is expressed as the percentage of the effort required using the standard process. Note that Figure 7 illustrates data concerning the spent effort: to derive the amount of savings you have to subtract the percentage effort from 100%: for instance, when the effort spent with EEM's is 40% of the effort required by the standard process, you save 60% of the effort.

The picture shows that most respondents stated that with EEM's the measurement of FP requires 60% of the effort required by the standard IFPUG process (i.e., they save 40%). It is also apparent that we received only 7 answers, therefore we cannot draw general conclusions. Anyway, it is noticeable that these answers are consistent with our computation of the potential savings:

- The most frequent answer indicates 40% savings, and 40% is mid-way in the 34%-50% range of expected potential savings.
- The collected answers indicate saving in the 30%-60% range: they are consistent with our expected potential savings, with just one respondent that is more pessimistic (having indicated that savings amount to 30%) and one respondent that is more optimist (having indicated that savings can amount to 70%).

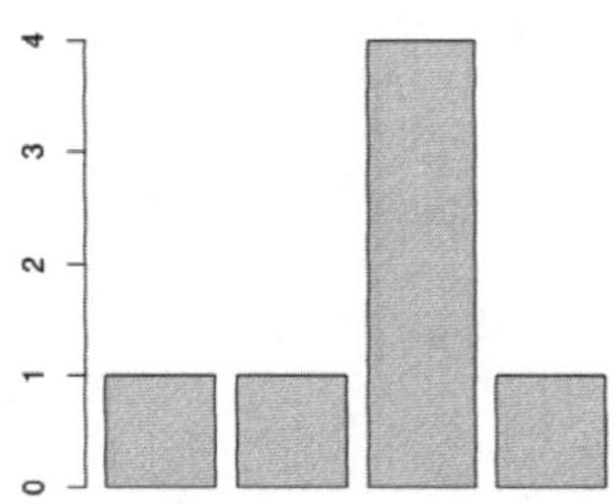

Figure 7. Frequency of answers concerning the relative effort required by EEM's

VI. Threats to Validity

A first threat to the validity of the study is due to the number of datapoints that were collected. Although it was possible to collect less than 40 datapoints in each survey, we strived to guarantee the representativeness of the collected data by eliminating outliers, as well as data that appear incorrect. In any case, the size of the datasets that was finally analyzed is not smaller than many datasets used for empirical software engineering studies.

Concerning the statistical analyses that were performed in this study, they are so simple that it is unlikely that any serious threat to statistically validity actually applies.

Most respondents to the first survey are from Italy, four are form the Netherlands and the remaining ones are from Brazil, Switzerland and Belgium. All the respondents to the second survey are from Italy. The lack of geographic dispersion could be a limit for the generalizability of results. However, most respondents are certified Function Point Specialists (CFPS) or certified Function Point Practitioners (CFPP), thus we can assume that they all follow the process specified in the official manuals [4][5][9][10] (or at least they should be trying to follow such process). Hence, our results should be applicable to all the measurements performed according to the standard counting practices.

VII. Related Work

There is not much literature concerning the cost of functional size measurement. A couple of documents report about the total cost of FP measurement [6][7], but none provides information concerning how the total effort is spread among the various measurement phases.

Some indications are provided by the proposers of EEM's. For instance, it was reported that "*the E&Q size estimation technique has been proved in practice to be quite effective, providing a response within ± 10% of the real size in most real cases, while the savings in time (and costs) can be between 50% and 90% (depending on the comprised aggregation level) with respect to corresponding standard measurement procedures.*" [19]

It was also reported that "*the results found with NESMA estimated fall within a reach of -6% to +15% of the corresponding result found with a NESMA detailed approach, and NESMA estimated FSM is performed 1,5 times as fast as a NESMA detailed FSM.*" [13]

These evaluations are probably optimistic to some extent. However, they are not precise enough to be used for decision making: for instance, it is not clear if the reported savings are evaluated with respect to the whole measurement process or only with respect to the core part (phases 3-5).

VIII. Conclusions

The measurement processes of IFPUG and Nesma FP require a quite detailed analysis of the transactions that the measured software application is expected to provide and of the data it has to manage. Under given circumstances, practitioner may actually consider the standard process excessively expensive or time consuming. To overcome this problem, EEM's have been proposed: via these methods it is possible to obtain faster and cheaper approximate measure estimates.

With similar purposes, but with a different approach, the SiFP method proposes a full-fledged functional size measure that can be used as an alternative to Function Point. The SiFP method –like EEM's– greatly simplifies the functional measurement process.

In any case, managers who have to choose whether to perform a standard IFPUG measurement or an approximate IFPUG FP estimation or a Simple Function Point measurement need to know how much measurement effort can be actually saved.

Since we know which measurement phases are skipped or simplified with EEM's or the SiFP method, to evaluate the possible savings we need to know the relative effort required by the measurement phases that compose the standard IFPUG measurement process. To this end, questionnaires were proposed to professional measurers, in two distinct surveys, and the collected answers were analyzed.

The results of the analysis –given in Sections III and IV illustrate the relative effort required by each phase of the measurement process according to professional measurers.

Considering the overall measurement process, our analysis shows that potential savings are in the 34%-50% range, with respect to the effort required to carry out the standard IFPUG process.

As a final remark, it is interesting to note that both in the first and in the second surveys we found large variations in the effort dedicated to some phases. This indicates that –even though the IFPUG certified measurers are expected to carry out a well-defined standard process– in practice there are a few activities that in some cases are "extended" so to ease the following ones, while in other cases they are performed "minimally," so that more work is demanded to the following phases. Therefore, when evaluating the amount of savings that can be achieved, an organization should first understand what flavor of measurement process they implement, because this determines where the biggest opportunities for savings are located. For instance, when an organization that puts a lot of effort in phase 1 decides to use an EEM, they should reduce the amount of analysis performed in phase 1, otherwise they end up collecting more information than is actually used to get measure estimates via the chosen EEM.

Future work includes:

- Extending the dataset, especially with answers from non-European countries, to make the dataset representative of a larger community of IFPUG users.
- If possible, collecting real effort data from the field, instead of subjective indications provided by measurers. This would make it possible to analyze not only the relative effort, but also the actual effort (in PersonHours, for instance) required by each measurement phase.
- Characterizing the contexts in which measurement is performed, to support the empirical evaluation of the dependency of the relative effort required by measurement phases on the context, and to explore the effects of lightweight or heavyweight activities concerning requirements documentation gathering.

ACKNOWLEDGMENT

The work presented here has been partly supported by the "Fondo di Ricerca d'Ateneo" of the Università degli Studi dell'Insubria.

REFERENCES

[1] L.Lavazza, "An Investigation on the Relative Cost of Function Point Analysis Phases" The 11th Int. Conf. on Software Engineering Advances – ICSEA, 2016.

[2] A. J. Albrecht, "Measuring Application Development Productivity", Joint SHARE/GUIDE/IBM Application Development Symposium, pp 83–92, 1979.

[3] A. J. Albrecht and J. E. Gaffney, "Software function, lines of code and development effort prediction: a software science validation", IEEE Trans. on Software Eng., vol. 9, pp. 639–648, 1983.

[4] International Function Point Users Group, "Function Point Counting Practices Manual - Release 4.3.1", 2010.

[5] IFPUG, "Function Point Counting Practices Manual Release 4.3.1", 2010.

[6] C. Jones, "A new business model for function point metrics", http://concepts.gilb.com/dl185, 2008. Last access June 12th, 2016.

[7] "Methods for Software Sizing – How to Decide which Method to Use", Total Metrics, www.totalmetrics.com/function-point-resources/downloads/R185_Why-use-Function-Points.pdf, August 2007. Last access June 12th, 2016.

[8] L. Santillo, "Easy Function Points – 'Smart' Approximation Technique for the IFPUG and COSMIC Methods", IWSM-MENSURA, pp. 137–142, 2012.

[9] ISO/IEC, ISO/IEC 24750:2005, Software Engineering "NESMA Functional Size Measurement Method, Version 2.1, Definitions and counting guidelines for the application of Function Point Analysis. International Organization for Standardization, Geneva, 2005.

[10] NESMA, "Counting Practice Manual, Version 2.1", 2004.

[11] "Early & Quick Function Points for IFPUG methods v. 3.1 Reference Manual 1.1", April 2012.

[12] nesma, Early Function Point Analysis, July 15, 2015, http://nesma.org/freedocs/early-function-point-analysis/ Last access June 12th, 2016.

[13] H. S. van Heeringen, E. W. M. van Gorp, and T. G. Prins, Functional size measurement accuracy versus costs is it really worth it? Software Measurement European Forum, May 2009.

[14] ISBSG, Worldwide Software Development–the Benchmark, International Software Benchmarking Standards Group. http://isbsg.org/software-project-data/

[15] R. Meli and L. Santillo, Function Point Estimation Methods: a Comparative Overview, FESMA conference, pp. 2009.

[16] L. Lavazza and R. Meli. "An Evaluation of Simple Function Point as a Replacement of IFPUG Function Point." IWSM-MENSURA 2014. IEEE, pp. 196–206, 2014.

[17] F. Ferrucci, C. Gravino, and L. Lavazza, "Assessing Simple Function Points for Effort Estimation: an Empirical Study", 31st ACM Symposium on Applied Computing – SAC 2016, Pisa, April 4-8, pp. 1428–1433, 2016.

[18] Simple Function Point Association, Simple Function Point - Functional Size Measurement Method Reference Manual v01.01, March 2014, http://www.sifpa.org/en/sifp-method/manual.htm. Last access June 12th, 2016.

[19] L. Santillo, M. Conte, and R. Meli. "Early & Quick function point: sizing more with less." 11th IEEE International Symposium on Software Metrics, 2005. IEEE, 2005.

[20] L. Lavazza and G. Liu, An Empirical Evaluation of Simplified Function Point Measurement Processes, Int. Journal on Advances in Software, vol. 6, n. 1-2, pp. 1-13, 2013.

[21] Kwiksurveys site, https://kwiksurveys.com/s.asp?sid=aazttngx1iibno6450647#/ Last accessed June 12th, 2016.

[22] nesma association, www.nesma.org. Last accessed June 12th, 2016.

[23] ResearchGate, http://www.researchgate.net/ Last accessed June 12th, 2016.

[24] L. Lavazza, V. Del Bianco, and C. Garavaglia. "Model-based functional size measurement." Proceedings of the Second ACM-IEEE International Symposium on Empirical Software Engineering and Measurement. ACM, 2008.

[25] L. Lavazza, and G. Robiolo. "Introducing the evaluation of complexity in functional size measurement: a UML-based approach." Proceedings of the 2010 ACM-IEEE International Symposium on Empirical Software Engineering and Measurement. ACM, 2010.

[26] R. Meli. "Simple function point: a new functional size measurement method fully compliant with IFPUG 4. x." Software Measurement European Forum. 2011.

[27] A. Z. Abualkishik, F. Ferrucci, C. Gravino, L. Lavazza, G. Liu, R. Meli, G. Robiolo. "A Study on the Statistical Convertibility of IFPUG Function Point, COSMIC Function Point and Simple Function Point." Information and Software Technology, 2017.

[28] FiSMA - Finnish Software Measurement Association, FiSMA FSM Method 1.1 (2004).

[29] COSMIC – Common Software Measurement International Consortium, The COSMIC Functional Size Measurement Method – Version 4.0.1 Measurement Manual (The COSMIC Implementation Guide for ISO/IEC 19761: 2003) (2016).

[30] C. Symons, Function point analysis: difficulties and improvements, IEEE Transactions on Software Engineering 14 (1988) 2–11.

APPENDIX A – DETAILS OF THE FIRST SURVEY

A survey about the relative effort required by the phases of Functional Size Measurement

A. *The questionnaire*

The questionnaire was structured in two sections, described below.

1) *About you.*

Question	Possible answers
Are you a certified Function Point Specialist (CFPS)?	Yes/No
Are you a certified Function Point Practitioner (CFPP)?	Yes/No
How many years of experience do have in FP counting?	Less than 5 Between 5 and 10 More than 10
How many FP per year do you count on average?	No more than 200 Between 200 and 1000 Between 1000 and 5000 More than 5000

2) *Relative effort required by the phases of functional size measurement*

According to your experience, what is the relative effort required by the phases of functional size measurement? Please, specify how big is the percentage effort for each phase, according to your experience. Please note that here we consider the measurement performed at the beginning of the project, based on functional user requirements.

Thanks a lot for your answers! If you have any additional comment or remark, or if you want to be informed on the results of the survey, please send an email to: luigi.lavazza@uninsubria.it

Question	Possible answers
Phase 1: gathering the available documentation concerning functional user requirements	0-5%, 6-10%, 11-15%, 16-20%, 21-25%, 26-30%, 31-35%, 36-40%, 41-45%, 46-50%, 51-55%, 56-60%, 61-65%, 66-70%, 71-75%, 76-80%, 81-85%, 86-90%, 91-95%, 96-100%
Phase 2: Identifying application boundaries	0-5%, 6-10%, 11-15%, 16-20%, 21-25%, 26-30%, 31-35%, 36-40%, 41-45%, 46-50%, 51-55%, 56-60%, 61-65%, 66-70%, 71-75%, 76-80%, 81-85%, 86-90%, 91-95%, 96-100%
Phase 3: Determining the measurement goal and scope	0-5%, 6-10%, 11-15%, 16-20%, 21-25%, 26-30%, 31-35%, 36-40%, 41-45%, 46-50%, 51-55%, 56-60%, 61-65%, 66-70%, 71-75%, 76-80%, 81-85%, 86-90%, 91-95%, 96-100%
Phase 4: Identifying Elementary Processes (Transactions) and Logical Data Files	0-5%, 6-10%, 11-15%, 16-20%, 21-25%, 26-30%, 31-35%, 36-40%, 41-45%, 46-50%, 51-55%, 56-60%, 61-65%, 66-70%, 71-75%, 76-80%, 81-85%, 86-90%, 91-95%, 96-100%
Phase 5: Classifying transactions as EI, EO or EQ; classifying files as ILF or EIF; identifying RET, DET, FTR and determining complexity	0-5%, 6-10%, 11-15%, 16-20%, 21-25%, 26-30%, 31-35%, 36-40%, 41-45%, 46-50%, 51-55%, 56-60%, 61-65%, 66-70%, 71-75%, 76-80%, 81-85%, 86-90%, 91-95%, 96-100%
Phase 6: Calculating the functional size	0-5%, 6-10%, 11-15%, 16-20%, 21-25%, 26-30%, 31-35%, 36-40%, 41-45%, 46-50%, 51-55%, 56-60%, 61-65%, 66-70%, 71-75%, 76-80%, 81-85%, 86-90%, 91-95%, 96-100%
Phase 7: Documenting and presenting the measurement	0-5%, 6-10%, 11-15%, 16-20%, 21-25%, 26-30%, 31-35%, 36-40%, 41-45%, 46-50%, 51-55%, 56-60%, 61-65%, 66-70%, 71-75%, 76-80%, 81-85%, 86-90%, 91-95%, 96-100%
Please, specify what measurement method the given data you gave apply to	IFPUG NESMA Other
Please, specify if the given data take into account some type of simplification	No simplification Nesma estimated Nesma indicative Early & Quick FP Other

It should be noted that in the first survey phase 2 was split into two distinct activities: Identifying application boundaries and Determining the measurement goal and scope, which were labeled phase 2 and phase 3, respectively. Anyway, in the paper we have considered phases 2 and 3 together, as we did in the second survey.

B. *Answers*

Collected answers are in Table VI.

TABLE VI. ANSWERS CONCERNING RELATIVE PHASE COSTS (FIRST SURVEY)

Respondent	Phase 1	Phase 2	Phase 3	Phase 4	Phase 5	Phase 6	Phase 7
1	11-15%	0-5%	0-5%	26-30%	36-40%	0-5%	16-20%
2	16-20%	6-10%	0-5%	36-40%	6-10%	0-5%	16-20%
3	6-10%	0-5%	0-5%	6-10%	46-50%	0-5%	11-15%
4	0-5%	0-5%	0-5%	66-70%	0-5%	0-5%	0-5%
5	0-5%	6-10%	6-10%	36-40%	16-20%	0-5%	0-5%
6	0-5%	0-5%	46-50%	31-35%	0-5%	0-5%	0-5%
7	6-10%	6-10%	0-5%	21-25%	26-30%	0-5%	11-15%
8	26-30%	11-15%	6-10%	11-15%	11-15%	0-5%	11-15%
9	16-20%	0-5%	0-5%	21-25%	21-25%	0-5%	11-15%
10	0-5%	0-5%	0-5%	46-50%	31-35%	0-5%	0-5%
11	31-35%	0-5%	0-5%	21-25%	16-20%	11-15%	0-5%
12	0-5%	0-5%	0-5%	16-20%	0-5%	0-5%	11-15%
13	0-5%	0-5%	0-5%	21-25%	46-50%	0-5%	0-5%
14	0-5%	0-5%	0-5%	41-45%	26-30%	0-5%	0-5%
15	11-15%	6-10%	0-5%	36-40%	11-15%	0-5%	0-5%
16	6-10%	0-5%	0-5%	51-55%	16-20%	0-5%	0-5%
17	6-10%	6-10%	0-5%	26-30%	6-10%	36-40%	6-10%
18	0-5%	0-5%	0-5%	36-40%	36-40%	0-5%	0-5%
19	6-10%	6-10%	0-5%	11-15%	11-15%	0-5%	41-45%
20	31-35%	16-20%	6-10%	26-30%	11-15%	0-5%	0-5%
21	16-20%	6-10%	6-10%	16-20%	11-15%	6-10%	16-20%
22	16-20%	0-5%	0-5%	61-65%	0-5%	0-5%	0-5%
23	0-5%	56-60%	16-20%	66-70%	51-55%	0-5%	11-15%
24	6-10%	6-10%	11-15%	26-30%	11-15%	11-15%	0-5%
25	11-15%	6-10%	0-5%	21-25%	21-25%	11-15%	6-10%
26	6-10%	0-5%	0-5%	41-45%	21-25%	0-5%	6-10%
27	41-45%	6-10%	0-5%	6-10%	6-10%	6-10%	11-15%
28	6-10%	16-20%	6-10%	31-35%	11-15%	0-5%	16-20%
29	11-15%	0-5%	0-5%	66-70%	11-15%	0-5%	0-5%
30	21-25%	0-5%	0-5%	21-25%	21-25%	6-10%	0-5%
31	0-5%	0-5%	0-5%	6-10%	6-10%	0-5%	0-5%

APPENDIX B – DETAILS OF THE SECOND SURVEY

C. *The questionnaire*

The questionnaire is illustrated below.

About yourself

Are you a certified Function Point Specialist (CFPS)?	☐ Yes ☐ No
Are you a certified Function Point Practitioner (CFPP)?	☐ Yes ☐ No
For how many year have you been counting Function Points?	
How many Function Points do you count per year, approximately?	

Did you participate in the survey published on kwiksurveys? ☐Yes ☐No

According to your experience, what is the percentage cost of every phase in the measurement process?
We are considering measures carried out at the beginning of the project, based on Functional Requirements, for new software development projects.

Phase	Description	% cost (using the IFPUG process)	% cost (using an approximate estimation method ________)
1	Collection of documentation concerning functional requirements		
2	Identifying application boundaries and determining the measurement scope		
3	Identifying elementary processes (transactions) and logical files		
4	Classifying transactions into EI, EO, EQ; Classifying data files into ILF and EIF; determining function complexity		
5	Computation of functional size		
6	Documentation and presentation of measures		
Total	**Please check that the sum of phases' costs is 100%!**	**100%**	**100%**

D. Answers

Collected answers are in Table VII.

TABLE VII. ANSWERS CONCERNING RELATIVE PHASE COSTS (SECOND SURVEY)

Respondent	Phase1	Phase2	Phase3	Phase4	Phase5	Phase6
1	15	10	40	20	5	10
2	5	15	30	30	5	15
3	15	10	20	25	20	10
4	15	20	20	35	5	5
5	10	20	0	50	10	10
6	10	10	35	20	5	20
7	5	10	30	40	5	10
8	5	3	15	45	10	22
9	5	0	35	50	0	10
10	50	10	10	10	10	10
11	20	15	20	40	2	3
12	20	5	15	50	5	5
13	20	10	20	20	10	20
14	5	5	40	40	5	5
15	20	0	10	35	20	15
16	40	5	30	20	0	5
17	30	5	30	30	0	5
18	20	20	20	30	5	5
19	20	10	30	25	5	10
20	20	22	10	18	10	20
21	18	15	15	18	22	12
22	15	5	30	35	5	10
23	15	5	30	35	5	10
24	20	10	15	35	10	10
25	30	5	20	30	10	5
26	8.3	8.3	30.5	36.3	8.3	8.3
27	15	8	30	40	3	4
28	15	10	25	35	10	5
29	10	10	10	50	10	10
30	10	15	15	40	10	10
31	30	10	20	20	10	10
32	20	5	25	35	5	10
33	5	20	30	30	10	5
34	10	20	30	30	5	5
35	30	10	10	10	20	20
36	10	10	30	30	10	10
37	15	5	35	25	10	10

Specification of Requirements Using Unified Modeling Language and Petri Nets

Radek Kočí and Vladimír Janoušek

Brno University of Technology, Faculty of Information Technology,
IT4Innovations Centre of Excellence
Czech Republic
email: {koci,janousek}@fit.vutbr.cz

***Abstract*—One of the major problems the software engineering is dealing with is the correct specification and implementation of requirements to the system being developed. A lot of design methods use models of the Unified Modeling Language for requirements specification and further design of the system. To validate the specification, the executable form of models has to be obtained or the prototype has to be developed. This may cause errors in the transformation or implementation process, which results in incorrect validation. The approach presented in this work focuses on formal requirement modeling combining the classic models for requirements specification (use case diagrams and class diagrams) with models having a formal basis (Petri Nets). Created models can be used in all development stages including requirements specification, verification, and implementation. All design and validation steps are carries on the same models, which avoids mistakes caused by model implementation.**

Keywords–Object Oriented Petri Nets; Use Cases; requirement specification; requirement implementation.

I. INTRODUCTION

This work is based on the paper [1], which is extended of detailed explanation of modeling requirements and behavior of software systems using formal models. This work is part of the *Simulation Driven Development* (SDD) approach [2] and combines basic models of the most used modeling language Unified Modeling Language (UML) [3][4] and the formalism of Object-Oriented Petri Nets (OOPN) [5].

The fundamental problem associated with software development is an identification, specification and subsequent implementation of the system requirements [6]. Many design methods have no formal definitions and depend on intuitive approach to requirements specification and design. It results in troubles with correct specification of system requirements and their realization. The second problem is a rather complicated way to verify designed concepts through models under realistic conditions. Designers either have to implement a prototype or transform the models into executable form, which can be tested. All changes that result from testing are difficult to transfer back to models that become useless.

Formal techniques allow to specify system requirements and the solution in a clear, unambiguous way. Nevertheless, there is a gap between the features that formal approaches may offer and how they are actually utilized in the area of system design. This gap is a result of two arguments. First, it is a belief that formal approaches are hard to understanding and therefore to use. Second, the formal specification is not suitable for testing because of its non-executable form. Utilization of formal approaches, such as the formalism of OOPN, addresses mentioned disadvantage. Their formal nature combined with graphic representation of models allows them to be used by designers who have minimal knowledge of the formal background. Models described by these formalisms can be simulated as well as integrated into real conditions. All changes in the validation process are entered directly into the model, and it is therefore not necessary to implement or transform models.

To model domain concepts of the system being developed the class diagrams from UML are usually used [7]. Similarly, to specify user requirements the use case diagrams from UML are used. The concept of modeling requirements presented in this paper is based on mentioned UML models and the formalism of OOPN, which is used for behavior specifications. The goal is to combine the advantages of intuitive approach to system modeling with the precise specification of requirements and the detailed description of realization. The concept is demonstrated on a simple case study.

The paper is organized as follows. Section II deals with related work. Section III summarizes the concept of software system modeling and introduces the simple case study. The question of user requirements modeling using use case diagrams is discussed in Section IV. It introduces our extension to use case diagrams by one special relationship. Section V deals with behavior modeling and compares an usage of statecharts from UML and the formalism of OOPN. Modeling use case relationships is discussed in Section VI. Use cases and their behavior described by the formalism of OOPN create the architectural form of modeled system. Mapping use cases, nets, and classes is introduced in Section VII. The summary and future work is described in Section VIII.

II. RELATED WORK

One of the major criticisms of UML is the inability to precisely describe all aspects of the designed system including integrity constraints [8]. The clear understanding, automated transformations, and simulation of models are complicated. One approach to addressing the problem is to introduce the constraints on the model elements. An example is Object Constraint Language (OCL) [9], which allows to precisely specify the semantics of the model elements. Another approach works with modified UML models that can be executed and, therefore, validated by simulation. An example is the Executable UML (xUML) language [4] used by the Model Driven Architecture (MDA) methodology [10], or Foundational Subset for xUML [11][12] associated with Action Language (Alf) [13].

These methods are faced with a problem of model testing. Models have to be transformed into executable form, whereas the validation of proposed requirements through these models in real conditions is complicated. Transferring changes made during testing back to higher abstraction models is difficult, sometimes impossible. It is a problem because the models become useless over the development time.

Similar work based on ideas of model-driven development deals with gaps between different development phases and focuses on the usage of conceptual models during the simulation model development process—these techniques are called *model continuity* [14][15]. While it works with simulation models during design phases, the approach proposed in this paper focuses on *live models* that can be used in the deployed system.

III. Modeling of Software Systems

To specify the system being designed, a wide range of languages and formalisms can be adopted. The most commonly used means is UML language, which concentrates experiences of other languages used in the past to modeling requirements and behavior of systems. UML, however, fails to capture the essential features of one model. It is necessary to work with different views, but there is no mechanism for easy portability between those views. The basic diagrams are use case diagrams and class diagrams, which are supplemented by other diagrams as necessary. Use case diagrams model the options, how the system can be used, whereas use cases are specified by diagrams of activities or interaction diagrams. Class diagrams are a fundamental domain model and are linked with already mentioned interaction diagrams. The behavior of individual classes can be specified, e.g., by a state diagram.

A. Case Study

We will demonstrate basic principles and problems of user requirements modeling on the simplified example of robotic system. The example works with a robot, which is controlled by the algorithm. Users can handle algorithms for controlling the robot (he/she can choose one algorithm for handling and start or stop the algorithm).

B. Domain modeling

Domain model captures the system concepts, as they are identified and understood during the process of requirements analysis. The domain concepts are modeled by class diagram containing conceptual classes and their relationships. The domain model is the initial model for modeling the functional requirements and creation of design models. It is one of the first models when creating software.

Initial analysis of presented case study suggests that we must be able to work with concepts *User*, *Algorithm*, and *Robot*. Thus, we can create the initial domain model, which is shown in Fig. 1. There is a one-to-N association (1..N) between

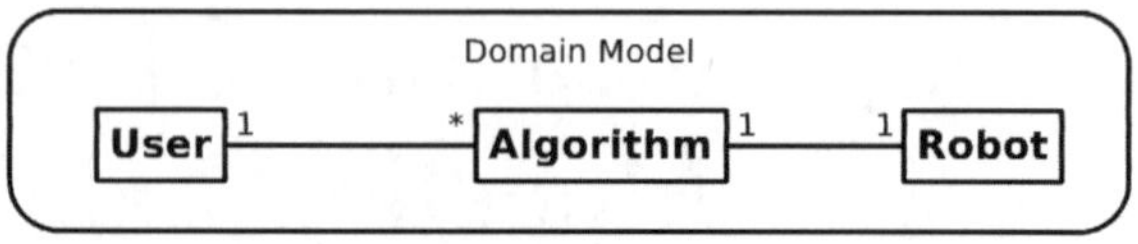

Figure 1. Domain model of the case study.

User and *Algorithm*, since a user may work with multiple algorithms. One particular algorithm controls only one specific robot, so there is a one-to-one association between *Algorithm* and *Robot*.

C. User Requirements Modeling

The use case diagrams are used for modeling of user requirements. The aim is to identify users of the system, the system requirements and how the user can work with requests. The basic elements are therefore *users*, their *role*, and *activities*. Roles are modeled as *actors* and activities are modeled by individual *use cases*. The use case diagram of our example is shown in Fig. 2.

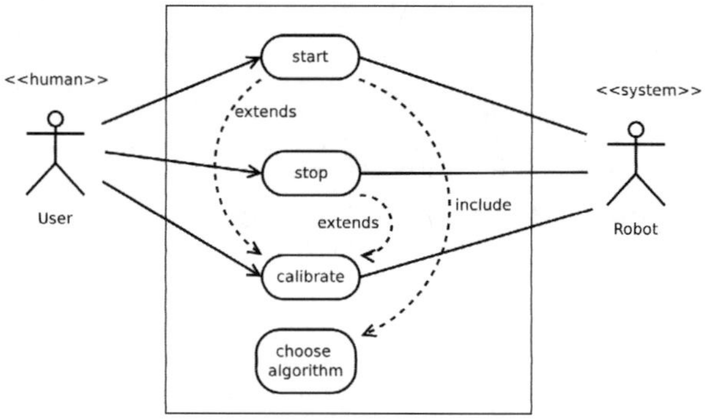

Figure 2. First Use Case Diagram for the robotic system.

The diagram shows actors (roles) *User* and *Robot* and use cases *Start* algorithm, *Stop* algorithm, *Choose* algorithm, and *Calibrate* the system. Roles represent the interface between the system and its surrounding and define operations allowed for that role.

D. Behavior Modeling

Behavior models deal with functional requirements. They model *scenarios*, i.e., specific behaviors and interactions of individual use cases. For that purpose, various types of description are used—structured text, activity diagrams, state diagrams etc. Generally, they are models enabling to capture work-flow supplemented by communications. Scenarios of individual cases are modeled by activity diagrams, state diagrams, or interaction diagrams. However, the formal models and formal languages, such as *Petri nets*, can be used as well. An important feature is the interconnection of use case diagrams and scenarios modeled using specific diagrams, since both types of models represent different view of the developed system.

IV. Modeling User Requirements

This section detail examines the concept of use cases in system design. Use case diagrams (UCDs) are used in the process of software system design for modeling user requirements. The system is considered as a black-box, where only external features are taken into account. The objective of UCDs is identify system users, user requirements, and how the user interacts with the system. The model consists of *actors* and *use cases*. Actor generates an external stimulus of the system and, generally, it represents a kind of users working with the system. Use case models a sequence of interactions between actors and software system. For a description of the interactions, plain text is usually used. The text describes inputs from actors and reactions of the system. Use case defines *what* the system is to do and pays no attention to a question *how* the system would implement modeled requirements.

A. Actor

Actor is an external entity working with the software system, so that actor is not part of the system, but it is a generator of input stimulus and data for the system. Actor models a group of real users, whereas all members of the group are working with the system in the same way. Therefore, actor represents *a role* of the user in which can appear in the system. One real user can appear in the system in more roles. Let us consider the example of conference system with actors *Author* and *Reviewer*. These actors model two roles, each of them defines a set of functions (use cases) the user can initiate or can participate on. The real user can either be author or reviewer, or can work with the system in both roles (the user usually stands in just one role at the time).

Now, let us consider another example of the garage gate handling system. The system consists of actuators (garage gate), sensors (driving sensor, card scanner), and control software. It is closed autonomous system with which two groups of real users can work—*Driver* and *Reception clerk*. The driver comes to the garage gate, applies a card to the scanner, and the system opens the gate. If the user does not have a card, he can ask reception clerk, who opens the gate. From system point of view, actuators, sensors, and control software are internal parts of the system. From the software engineering point of view, actuators and sensors are *external* elements that are controlled by the system, or from which it receives information.

We can ask a question whether we can model these external elements using the actor concept. Actors represent human users in many information systems (*human actors*). But, they can also be used to model other subsystems such as sensors or devices (*system actors*) because of they really represent external entity. The system has to communicate with these subsystems, nevertheless, they need not to be part of the modeled software system. There are systems where this form of actors is more important than users [16]. They concern especially embedded or autonomous systems that intensively cooperate with input–output devices, such as sensors, actuators, etc. These actors represent the surroundings in which the system operates.

It will be useful to define specific categories of actors based on their merit, whose semantics differ from conventional apprehension of the term *actor* in use case diagrams. The categorization follows:

- *real user* (stereotype *human*) – models a real user, or more precisely his/her role in the system, which is concerned in interactions with the system
- sensor, actuator, *device* in general (stereotype *device*) – model a system element, which provides stimulus to control software or receives commands
- *system* (stereotype *system*) – other system (or subsystem) with which the modeled system cooperates

B. Use Case

An important part of functional requirements analysis is to identify sequences of interaction between actors and modeled system. Each such a sequence covers different functional requirement on the system. The sequence of interactions is modeled by *use cases*. The use case describes a main sequence of interactions and is invoked (its execution starts) by input stimulus from the *actor*. The main sequence can be supplemented by alternative sequences describing less commonly used interactions. Their invocation depends on specified conditions, e.g., wrong information input or abnormal system state. Each sequence (the main or alternative one) is called *scenario*. Scenario is a complete implementation of one specific sequence of interactions within the use case.

C. Relationships Between Use Cases

Among the different use cases you can use two defined relationships, *include* and *extend*. The aim of these relations is to maximize extensibility and reusability of use cases if the model becomes too complex. A secondary effect of using of these relationships is to emphasize the dependence of the individual use case scenarios, structuring too long scenarios to more lower level use cases, or highlighting selected activities.

1) Relationship extend: Relationship *extend* reflects alternative scenarios for basic use case. In cases where the specification of a use case is too complicated and contains many different scenarios, it is possible to model a chosen alternative for new use case, which is called *extension use case*. This use case then extends the basic use case that defines a location (point of extension) in the sequence of interactions and conditions under which the extension use case is invoked. The relationship *extend* is illustrated in Fig. 2. The use case *calibrate* has to stop the running algorithm first, then to calibrate the system and, finally, to start it. Use cases *start* and *stop* can thus expand the base case scenario *calibrate*.

2) Relationship include: Relationship *include* reflects the scenarios that can be shared by more than one use case. Common sequence can be extracted from the original use cases and modeled by a new use case, which we will call *inclusion use case*. Such use case can then be used in various basic use cases that determine the location (point of insertion) in the sequence of interactions for inclusion. The relationship *include* is illustrated in Fig. 2. Now, we adjust the original sequence of interactions with the use case *start*, which will need to select the algorithm to be executed first. Use case *start* thus includes the use case *choose algorithm*.

3) Generalization use cases: The activities related to interactions between the software system and a robot were not highlighted yet. One possibility is to define *inclusion use case* describing these interactions, i.e., the algorithm. However, this method supposes only one algorithm, which contradicts the specified option to choose algorithm. Second possibility is to define *extension use cases*, everyone for various algorithms. The disadvantage of this solution is its ambiguity; there is no obvious the problem and the appropriate solution.

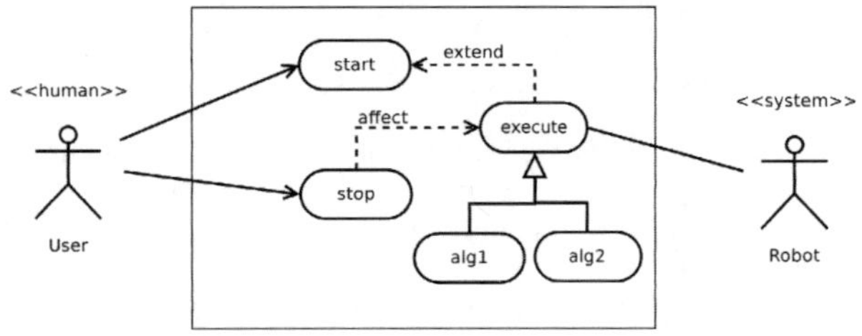

Figure 3. Specialization of the use case *execute* and the relationship affect.

Use case diagram offers the possibility to generalize cases. This feature is similar to the generalization (inheritance) in an object-oriented environment. In the context of the use case diagrams, generalization primarily reflects the interchangeability of the base-case for derived cases. Although there are methods that consider generalization as abstruse [17] and recommend replacing it with relation *extend*, generalization has a unique importance in interpreting the use case diagram. Relation *extend* allows to invoke more extension use cases, whereas generalization clearly expresses the idea that case *start* works with one of cases *execute* (the model is shown in Fig. 3). The model can also be easily extended without having to modify already existing cases.

4) Use Case Diagram Extension: The present example shows one situation that is not captured in the diagram and use case diagrams do not provide resources for its proper modeling. This is the case *stop*, which affects the use case *execute* (or possibly derived cases), but does not form its basis (the case *execute* is neither part of it nor its extension). Nevertheless, its execution affects the sequence of interactions, which is modeled by use case *execute* (it stops its activity). In the classical chart this situation would only be described in the specification of individual cases, however, we introduce a simple extension *affect*, as shown in Fig. 3. Relation *affect* represents a situation, where the base use case execution has a direct impact on other, dependent use case. This relation is useful to model synchronization between cases in such a system, which suppose autonomous activities modeled by use cases.

D. Problems associated with modeling relationships

The disadvantage of the use of relationships between use cases is the ability to determine the nature of addiction without detailed knowledge of the specification. If we analyze the model in Fig. 2, we find that the relations *extend* are not used correctly and can lead to more complications in the design model. The example assumes that when you start the algorithm, the user must always choose the algorithm, which is in connection with the case *calibrate* inappropriate (the algorithm is already selected, just for a moment it was suspended). Moreover, it is not a user interaction, it is therefore preferable to model the suspension and starting the algorithm directly as the activity of the case *calibrate* without using the relation *extend*.

V. Behavior Modeling

Use case specification format is not prescribed and can have a variety of expressive and modeling means, e.g., plain text, structured text, or any of the models. UML offers, among others, the activity and state diagrams. These charts allow precise description based on modeling elements with clear semantics. In this section, we will outline UML based way how to specify the use case *alg1* (one of the possible algorithms for controlling the robot; see Fig. 3).

A. State Diagram

Let us walk through an example of use case *alg1* specification using state diagram. We will discuss only part of the model shown in Fig. 4.

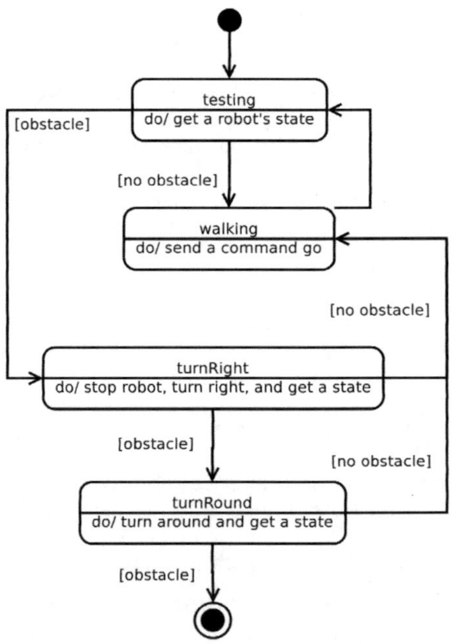

Figure 4. Statechart modeling the use case *Algorithm1* (*alg1*).

The model captures system sub-states, system activities carried out in those states and transitions between states. Execution of transition is conditioned, conditions include activities that are carried out to change the system state (in this example it is not used). States are modeled as elements that can contain internal activities performed by the system or a particular object, which is in this state. Simultaneously, it declares response to external events, i.e., its method of operation depending on the system state. The transition is modeled by edge, whose execution may depend on a condition or external events. An example might be a possibility to stop the algorithm in any state. We will now analyze the model. When activated, the system will move from the initial state (bulging black full circle) into a state called *testing*. Activity performed in this state is the acquisition of the robot state, i.e., testing that the robot is facing an obstacle. Based on the information obtained, the system moves into one of the states *walking* (the road is clear and the condition *no obstacle* is met) or *turnRight* (the road is not clear, the condition *obstacle* is met).

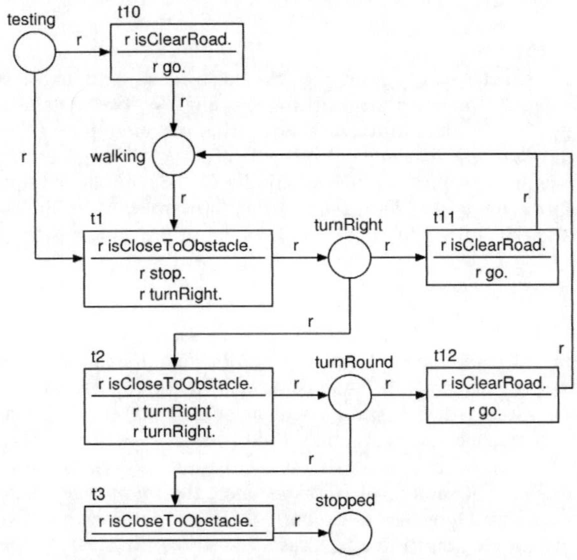

Figure 5. Petri net modeling the use case *Algorithm1* (*alg1*).

These charts allow to describe functional requirements of use case diagrams but their validation is problematic because of impossibility to check models either by formal means or by simulation. Of course, there are tools and methods [4][18] that allow to simulate modified UML diagrams. Nevertheless, there is still a strict border between *design* and *implementation* phases. Another way is to use some of the formal models. In this section, we introduce Object Oriented Petri Nets (OOPN) for specifying *use case*, i.e., interactions between the system and the actors. Let us walk through the previous example of use case *alg1* shown in Fig. 5.

B. Object Oriented Petri Nets

By comparison OOPN model (see Fig. 5) and the state diagram (see Fig. 4) we find a fundamental difference in the way of the states and transitions declaration. The system state is represented by places of the OOPN formalism. System is in a particular state if an appropriate place contains a *token*. Actions taken in a particular state is modeled as part of the transition whose execution is conditioned by a presence of tokens in that state. The transition is modeled as an element that moves the tokens between places. Except the input places, the transition firing is conditioned by a *guard*. The guard contains conditions or synchronous ports. The transition can be fired only if the guard is evaluated as true. If the transition fires, it executes the guard, which can have a side effect, e.g., the executed synchronous port can change a state of the other case.

The model (see Fig. 5) consists of states *testing*, *walking*, and *turnRight* that are represented by places. State *turnRight* is only temporal and the activity goes through these ones to the one of stable states (e.g., *walking*). Control flow is modeled by the sequence of transitions, where each transition execution is conditioned by events representing the state of the robot. Let us take one example for all, the state *testing* and linked transitions *t10* and *t1*. The transition *t1* is fireable, if the condition (modeled by the synchronous port) *isCloseToObstacle* is met. When firing this transition, actions to stop the robot (*stop*) and to turn right (*turnRight*) are performed and the system moves to the state of *turnRight*. The transition *t10* is fireable, if the condition (synchronous port) *isClearRoad* is met. When firing this transition, the action to go straight (*go*) is performed and the system moves into the state *walking*.

Both testing condition and messaging represent the interaction of the system with the robot. The robot moves the control flow as *token*, which allows interaction at the appropriate point of control flow and at the same time defines the state of its location in one of the places. To achieve correct behavior, it is useful to define type constraints on tokens (see $\geq \{Robot\}$; it means the token should be of a type *Robot*). Even as, it clearly shows *which* actor (and derived actors) interacts in those scenarios.

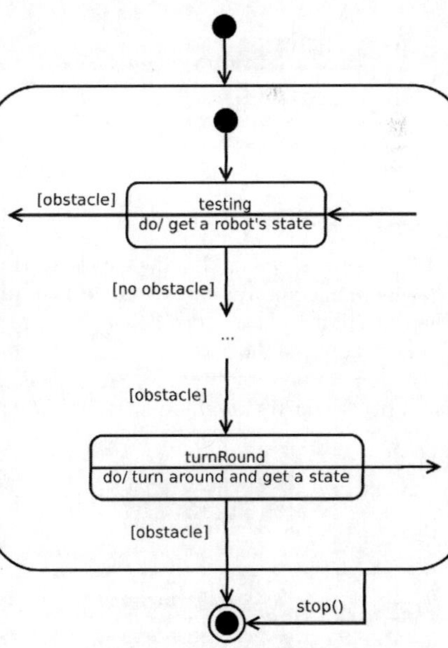

Figure 6. Composite state manipulation in statecharts.

To make decision about moving between states, obtaining data is not separated from state testing. If we look at the state *testing* in Fig. 5, we see that obtaining information and state testing are modeled in the transition guard by calling predicates or synchronous ports over the actor *Robot*.

C. Modeling Alternative Scenarios in State Diagram

Modeling alternative scenarios, i.e., scenarios that supplement the basic scenario, will be described on the case of *stopping algorithm*. It can be modeled by transition that responds to an external event *stop*. Since the transitions of the same type had to be included in every state offers a state diagram for these situations *composite state*, which introduces a certain hierarchy in the modeling phase diagrams. Each folded state is defined by the states and transitions again, there is a possibility to define a transition from a folded condition, which is interpreted as a transition from any state of the folded state. The example is shown in Fig. 6.

D. Modeling Alternative Scenarios in OOPN

Alternative scenarios, i.e., scenarios that supplement the basic scenario, are modeled by synchronous ports (perhaps even methods) to handle a response to an external event. We show a variant of the suspension of the algorithm, i.e., removal of the token from the current state and restoring algorithm, i.e., return the token back to the correct place. We introduce a new state (place) *paused* representing suspended algorithm. Because the formalism of OOPN does not have a mechanism for working with composite states, we should declare auxiliary transitions or ports for each state we want to manipulate with.

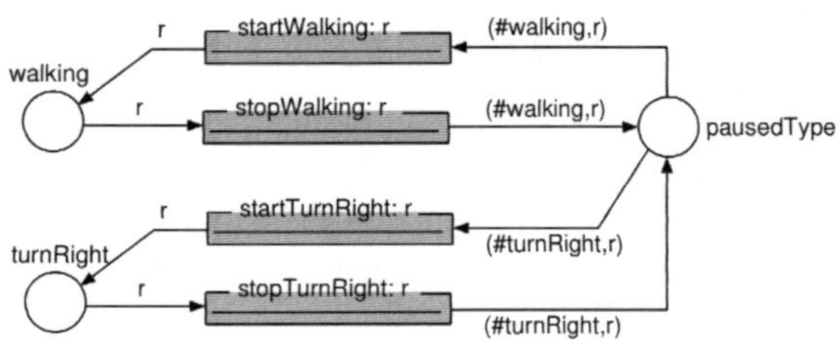

Figure 7. Composite state manipulation in OOPN.

Part of the use case model having established responses to external events *pause* and *resume* is shown in Fig. 7. We have to define an auxiliary place *pausedType* to store information about original placing of the token. For example, the composite synchronous port *pause* is fireable, if at least one of the synchronous ports *stopWalking* and *stopTurnRight* is fireable.

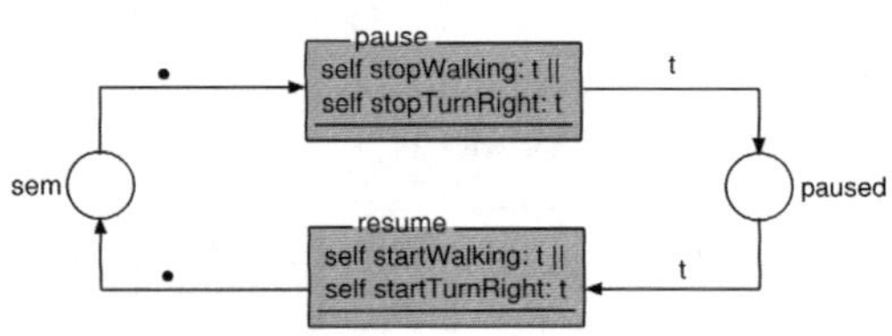

Figure 8. Composite state manipulation in OOPN.

This way of modeling is clear, however, confusing for readability. Furthermore, to work with a larger set of states is almost unusable. Nevertheless, there is the same pattern for each state, so that the concept of collective work with the states is introduced. It wraps the syntax of the original net. This will improve the readability of the model, while preserving

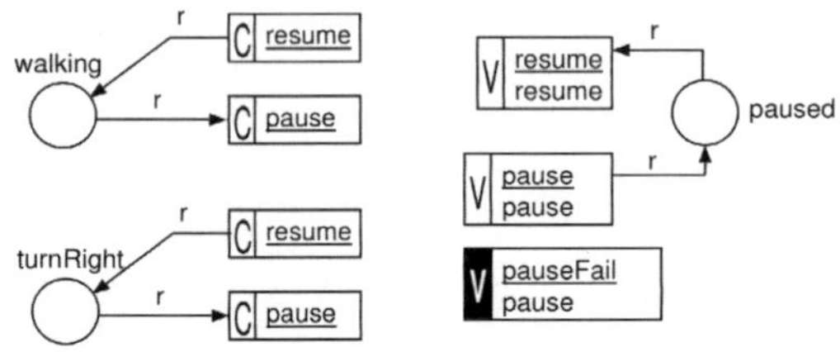

Figure 9. Composite state manipulation in OOPN.

the exactness of modeling by Petri nets including testing models. The example is shown in Fig. 9. The synchronous port is divided into two parts—the *common* part (*C-part*) and the *variable-join* part (*V-part*). The *C-part* represents all synchronous ports, which should be called from the composite port. The *V-part* represents a way how to work with the *C-part*—it is fireable, if at least one item of the *C-part* is fireable.

E. Modeling Roles

Until now we have neglected the essence of the token that provides interaction with the actors and defines the system state by its position. As mentioned, actor represents *role* of the user or device (i.e., a real actor), which can hold in the system. One real actor may hold multiple roles, can thus be modeled by various actors. Actor defines a subset of use cases allowed for such a role. For instance, the *robot* is not allowed to choose algorithm to execute, so its model does not contain any interaction to that use case.

A role is modeled as a use case and it behavior by Petri nets. Interactions between use cases and actors are synchronized through *synchronous ports* that test conditions, convey the necessary data and can initiate an alternative scenario for both sides. Use case can then send instructions through messages too.

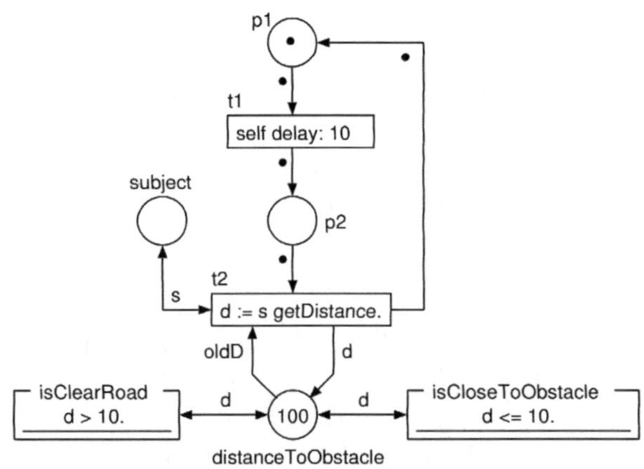

Figure 10. Petri net specification of the role *Robot*.

In our example, we will model the secondary role *Robot*, whose basic model is shown in Fig. 10. Scenarios of the *execute* use cases are synchronized using synchronous ports *isCloseToObstacle* and *isClearRoad* whose definition is simple—to test the distance to the nearest obstacle, which is stored in the place *distanceToObstacle*. Its content is periodically refreshed with a new value coming through the common place *distance*. The net can define methods for controlling a real actor too.

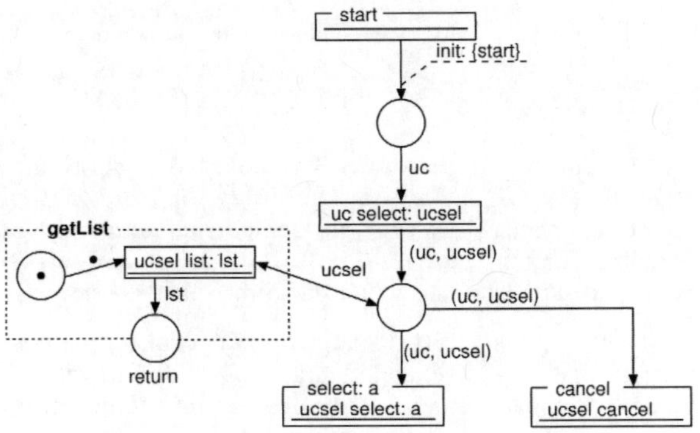

Figure 11. Petri net specification of the role *User*.

Model of the next role *User* is shown in Fig. 11. The primary actor defines stimuli (modeled as synchronous ports and methods) that can perform a real actor. Their execution is always conditioned by an actor workflow and a net of currently synchronized use case. Model shows the workflow of the use case *start*, which starts by calling a synchronous port *start*. It invocates the use case *start* (the syntactically simpler notation is used, it is semantically identical to invocation shown in Fig. 12). Using the method *getList* is possible to obtain a list of algorithms. Allowed actions can be executed by one of the defined synchronous ports *select:* and *cancel*.

VI. Relationships Modeling

We turn now to a method of modeling the relationships between use cases. As we have already defined, we distinguish relations *include*, *extend*, *affect*, and *generalization*.

A. Common Net and Common Places

Modeling the workflow that includes multiple separate synchronized nets may need to share a single network to other networks. For this purpose, the synchronous ports are used. Nevertheless, it can be difficult to read the basic model of the flow of events, because of the need for explicit modeling synchronous ports for data manipulation. Therefore, we introduce the concept of *common net* and *common place*. It is not a new concept, only the syntactic coating certain patterns using synchronous ports.

Each model has defined its initial class that also defines the common net represented by the class *Common* that for each running model has exactly one instance identified by the name *common*. The initial class initiates execution of the simulation and, simultaneously, provides a means for accessing common places. Content of the common places is is available through standard mechanisms (e.g., synchronous ports). Difference to the ordinary usage lies in the fact that access mechanisms are hidden and access to the common places from other nets is modeled by *mapping*—the place marked as common in the other net is mapped onto common place defined in the common net.

B. Modeling the include relationship

We will continue our example and create models of use cases *start* and *choose algorithm*, which is *inclusion case* to the case *start*. Case *start* is activated by actor *user*, connected by a mutual interaction. Actor *user* is the primary actor, so it generates stimulus to that the case has to respond. It implies a method of modeling events in the sequence of interactions. Responses to actor's requirements have to be modeled as an external event, i.e., using a synchronous port. Another significant issue is a place of inclusion into the basic sequence of interactions and invocation activities of the integrated case.

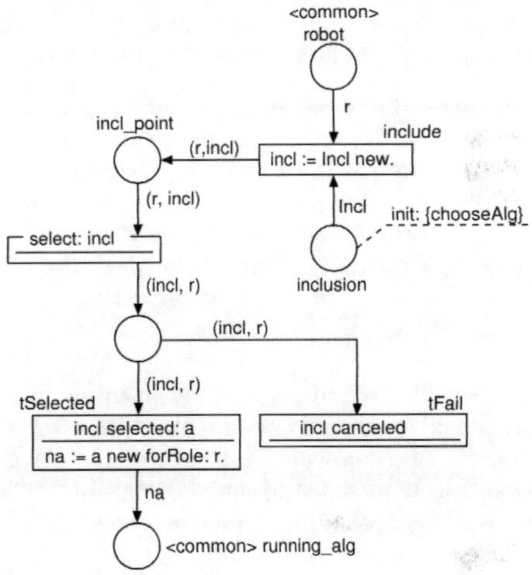

Figure 12. Petri net specification of the use case *start*.

The model of use case *start* is shown in Fig. 12. The inclusion use case is stored in a place *inclusion* and the insertion point is modeled by internal event (transition) *include* with a link to a place *incl_point*. Invoking the use case corresponds to instantiate the appropriate net (see the calling *new* in the transition *include*). The following external event (synchronous port) *select:* initiates the interaction of the actor *user* with integrated activity. The event binds the inclusion case to the free variable *incl*, and simultaneously stores it to an auxiliary place. Conditional branching is modeled by internal activities (transitions) *tSelected* and *tFail*. Their execution is subject to a state of inclusion case, which is tested by synchronous ports in guards. In case of success (transition *tSelected*), the synchronous port *selected:* binds the selected algorithm to the free variable *a* and stores it to the common place *running_alg*.

The use case *choose algorithm* specification is shown in Fig. 13. The basic sequence (to obtain algorithm list and select one of them) is supplemented with an alternative sequence (the user does not select any algorithm) and a condition (empty list corresponds to the situation when a user selects no algorithm). Inclusion case is viewed from stimuli generation point of view as secondary element; its activities are synchronized by basic case or actor, which works to the base case. Synchronization

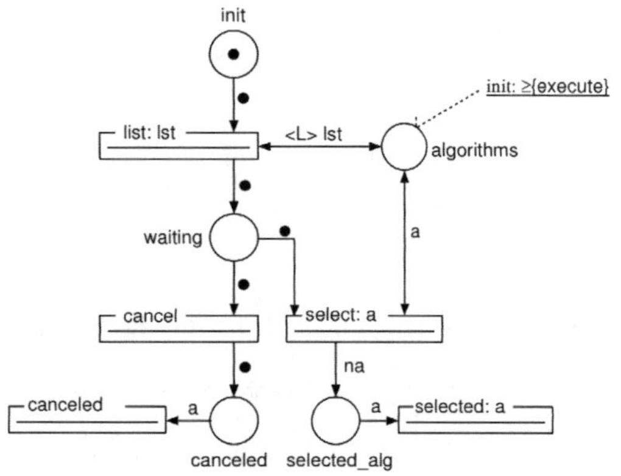

Figure 13. Petri net specification of the use case *choose algorithm*.

points are therefore modeled as external events, i.e., using synchronous ports. The case does not work with any secondary actor, so that to define the status of the net is sufficient type-free token (modeled as dot). The first external event is to obtain a list of algorithms (synchronous port *list:*); the variable *lst* binds the entire content of the place *algorithms*. This place is initialized by a set of cases (nets) derived from the case (net) *execute*. Now, the case waits for actor decision, which may be two. A user selects either no algorithm (external event *cancel*), or select a specific algorithm from the list, which has to match the algorithm from the place *algorithms* (external event *select:*). Token location into one of the places *canceled* or *selected_alg* represents possible states after a sequence of interactions. These conditions can be tested by synchronous ports *unselected* and *selected:*.

C. Modeling the extend relationship

Relation *extend* exists between cases *start* and *execute*, where *execute* is the extension use case. This relationship expresses the possibility of execution of the algorithm, provided that some algorithm was chosen. Since this is an alternative, it is expressed by branches beginning transition *tSelected*, as we can see in Fig. 12. The transition *tSelected* represents the insertion point of the extension of the basic sequence of interactions.

D. Modeling the affect relationship

Relationship *affect* exists between cases *stop* and *execute*, where *stop* influences the sequence of interactions of the case *execute*, respectively any inherited cases. Petri nets model for this use case is shown in Fig. 14. The activity begins from the common place *running_alg* and branches in three variants (transitions *t1*, *t2*, and *t3*). Branch *t1* says *no algorithm is running*; common place *running_alg* is empty. Because OOPN do not have inhibitors, the negative predicate *empty* is used to test conditions, which is feasible, if it is impossible to bind any object to the variable *a*.

Branch *t2* says *the algorithm is running*; the common place *running_alg* contains an active algorithm. Synchronous port *pause* (see Fig. 9) called on the running algorithm is evaluated

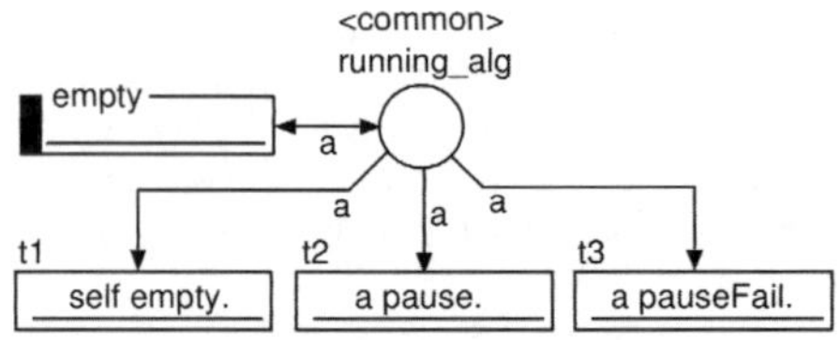

Figure 14. Petri net specification of the use case *stop*.

as true and when performed, it moves the algorithm into *stopped* state. Branch *t3* says *the algorithm is not running*; the common place *running_alg* contains an active algorithm. Synchronous port *pauseFail* called on the running algorithm is evaluated as true and when perform, it has no side effect.

This model is purely declarative. We declare three possible variants that may arise, and simultaneously declare target individual options to be done. Only one variant can be performed at a time. We can define other activities related to these variants. We can see that it does not invoke the use case *execute*, i.e., there is no instantiating a net, but this activity is affected. It is therefore not appropriate to model this situation with the relations *include* or *extend*. After all, it is appropriate to model that relationship.

E. Modeling the generalization relationship

The generalization of use cases does not have the same meaning like the generalization of classes in object-oriented architectural modeling. Special (inherited) case does not develop or modify the basic case, the relationship demonstrates only that fact, that it is possible to use any inherited case instead of the base case. Modeling of the generalization relationship in Petri nets reduces to express the possibility of working at a point defining the relationship *include* or *extend* to some case *c*, with all cases inherited from case *c*. In our example, this situation is shown on the use case model *choose algorithm* (Fig. 13). The place *algorithm* contains all possible algorithms that can be provided, i.e., nets inherited from base use case *execute*. Wherever the case *executed* is used in the model, it is possible to use any inherited case.

VII. Architecture Model

The presented concept of modeling assumes mapping use cases and roles to individual nets. Each net is part of a class, usually defined as the object net and in some cases as the method net. This section introduces the class diagram of the case study, which encapsulates designed nets.

A. Initial Class

Each model has defined its initial class that also defines the *common net* in the form of an object net. The initial class initiates execution of the simulation and, simultaneously, provides a means for accessing common places.

The example uses two common places *robot* and *running_alg*. The place *robot* stores information about the role of robot the whole system works with. The role is initialized by the creation of initial object, as shown in the initial object

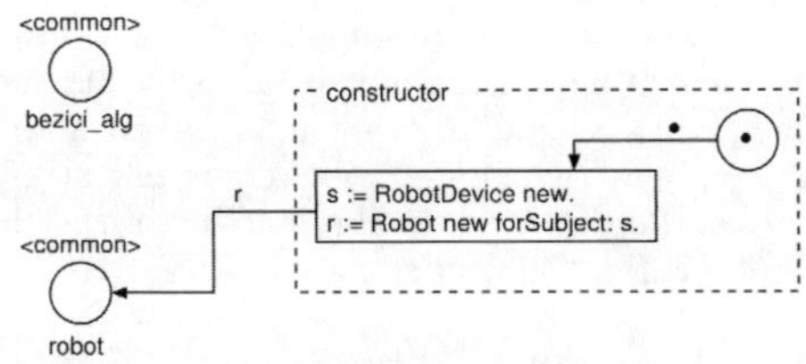

Figure 15. The initial class.

net. As the initialization is done only once, immediately the net is created, this part can be regarded as a constructor (see Fig. 15). The role is working with equipment whose interface is represented by the class *RobotDevice*. At this moment we do not resolve how this class is implemented (Petri nets or domain language). The currently selected algorithm is inserted into place *running_alg* by the activity *Start*.

B. Modeling Real Actors

Real actor can hold many roles that are modeled by actors in the system. Each of these roles always has a common base, which is a representation of the real actor, whether a user, system, or device. The model has to capture this fact. For terminological reasons, in order to remove potential confusion of terms *actor* and *real actor*, we denote a real actor by the term *subject*. The subject is basically an interface to a real form of the actor or to stored data. Therefore, it can be modeled in different ways that can be synchronized with Petri nets. Due to the nature of the used nets, there can be used Petri nets, other kind of formalism, or programming language.

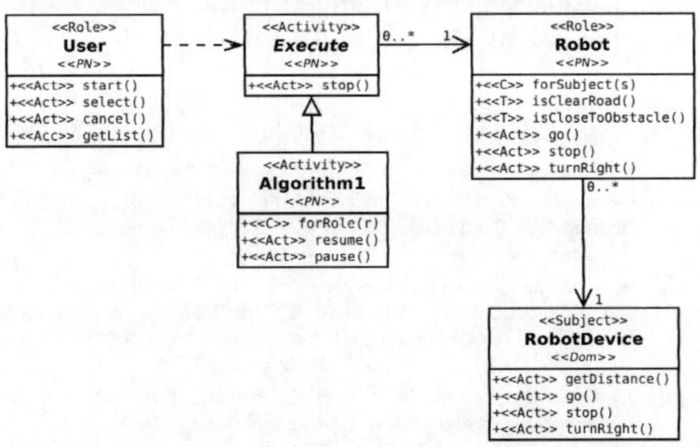

Figure 16. The basic class diagram.

The subject of the role *Robot* is modeled by the class *RobotDevice*. Its operations are implemented by methods in the supported language (in our case it is Smalltalk). This class represents the interface to the real robot, which is controlled by our application. The specific implementation is not important for demonstration of the modeling principles, therefore we do not mention it here.

The subject of the actor *User* can be modeled as a Smalltalk class, whose object can access OOPN objects directly [19][20]. The following pseudo-code shows a simple example of accessing model from the subject implemented in programming language. First, it asks a common net to get a role of user, then invokes synchronous port *start*, a method *getList*, and finally select first algorithm from the list.

```
usr ← common.newUser();
usr.asPort.start();
lst ← usr.getList();
usr.asPort.select(lst.at(1));
```

C. Mapping Petri Nets and Classes

Class diagram of the architecture model is shown in Fig. 16. Classes represent elements of different levels, therefore each class is marked by stereotypes for distinction. Stereotype *Activity* denotes the class representing a use case, the stereotype *Role* denotes the class representing a role and stereotype *Subject* denotes the class representing the subject. Each class can be modeled (described) by different formalism, the next stereotype distinguishes variant formalism. In our example, the formalism of Petri nets (stereotype *PN*) and Smalltalk language (stereotype *Dom*) are used.

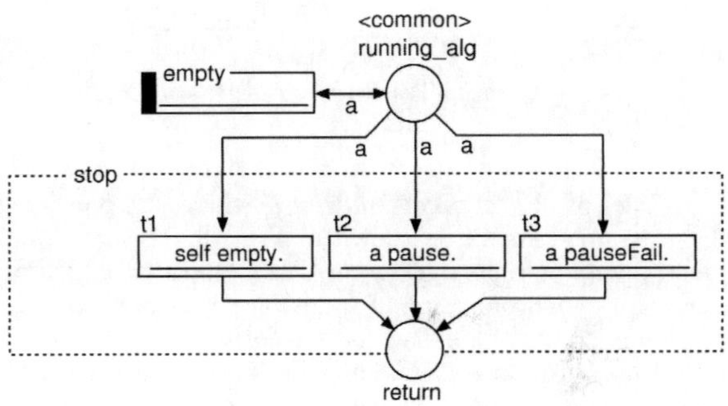

Figure 17. Model of the method net *Execute.stop*.

Class diagram shows the interface of individual elements and the knowledge about other elements. This is indicated by the arrows at the associations. The model shows that *User* is aware of the existence of the activity *Execute* (corresponding with the use case *Execute* in Fig. 3) and its derived activities (classes). The activity *Algorithm1* is created (instantiated) by a user stimulus (this part is not captured). The activity *Algorithm1* is aware of the existence of role *Robot* (it may not be in reverse order), and the role of *Robot* knows about the existence of a subject *RobotDevice* (it may not be in reverse order). The interface operations utilizes stereotypes that correspond to the interface definition. Two kinds of relationships between classes are suggested—the association and the usage. The association expresses a condition where an instance of a class depends on the instance of the second class; dependent instance always contains a reference to the second instance (is part of the place and is often represented by a control token). An example is the association between class *Algorithm1* and the class *Robot*. The usage expresses a condition where the dependent instance may not contain a reference to the second instance, but it can be got through a common place. An example is the usage of the classes *Algorithm1* by the class *User*.

D. Class Execute

The method net *Execute.stop* is shown in Fig. 17. The net is invoked by sending the message *stop*, which corresponds with the use case *Stop*. The method net works with the common place *running_alg* and uses the negative predicate *empty* from the object net.

E. Class Algorithm1

Class *User* represents the role *User*, which enables basic operations with the system *start*, *select*, *cancel*, and *getList*. The operation *start* initiates the use case *Start*.

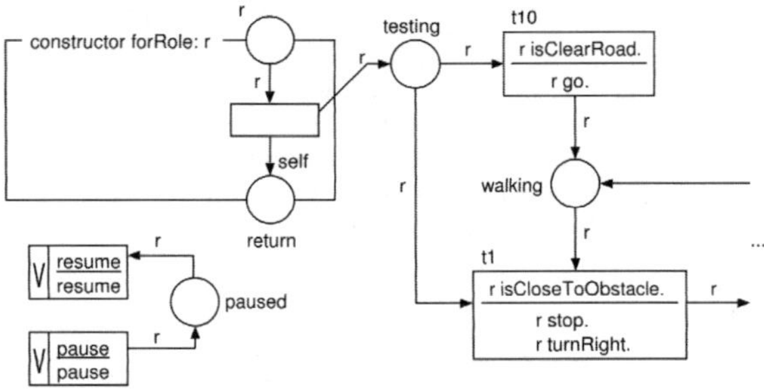

Figure 18. Part of the class *Algorithm1*.

Model of the activity *Algorithm1*, which is represented by the class *Algorithm1*, is shown in Fig. 18. This net communicates with a secondary actor *Robot* through synchronous ports (for synchronization of states) and message passing (for providing commands). The class *Algorithm1* offers the operation *forRole* for activity initialization of the group *constructor* (stereotype *C*) and two operations to stop and resume (*pause* and *resume*) of the group *actions* (stereotype *Act*). If we map classes to OOPN model, we can see that the operation *forRole* is modeled as constructor and both operations *pause* and *resume* is modeled as synchronous ports.

F. Class Robot

The class *Robot* has the constructor *forSubject*, three operations of an *action* group (*go*, *stop* and *turnRight*) and two operations from the *test* group (*isClearRoad* and *isCloseToObstacle*). The operations *stop*, *go*, and *turnRight* can be realized by synchronous ports or methods, depending on the selected communication channel and the internal architecture of the model.

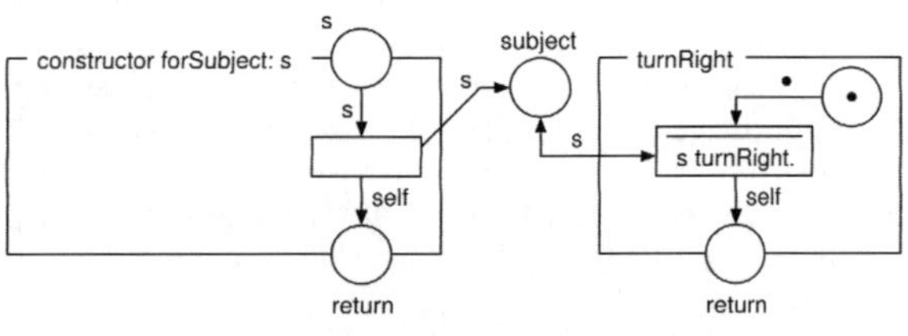

Figure 19. Method nets of the class *Robot*.

Fig. 19 shows the perhaps implementation of the operation *turnRight*, which delegates the execution on the subject. The other operations *go* and *stop* are modeled in a similar way. The subject, with which the role communicates, is stored in the place *subject*. Constructor that initializes the role by inserting the correct subject is shown in Fig. 19.

VIII. Conclusion

The paper presented the concept of modeling software system requirements, which combines commonly used models from UML, such as use case and diagrams, with Petri nets that are not commonly used in the requirements specification. Relationships between actors, use cases, and Petri nets have been introduced. Use case diagrams are used for the initial specification of user requirements while Petri nets serve for use case scenario descriptions allowing to model and validate requirement specifications in real conditions. This approach does not need to transform models or implement requirements in a programming language and prevents the validation process from mistakes caused by model transformations.

At present, we have developed the tool supporting presented approach. In the future, we will focus on the tool completion, a possibility to interconnect model with other formalisms or languages, and feasibility study for different kinds of usage.

Acknowledgment

This work was supported by the internal BUT project FIT-S-17-4014 and The Ministry of Education, Youth and Sports of the Czech Republic from the National Programme of Sustainability (NPU II); project IT4Innovations excellence in science - LQ1602.

References

[1] R. Kočí and V. Janoušek, "Modeling System Requirements Using Use Cases and Petri Nets," in ThinkMind ICSEA 2016, The Eleventh International Conference on Software Engineering Advances. Xpert Publishing Services, 2016, pp. 160–165.

[2] R. Kočí and V. Janoušek, "Modeling and Simulation-Based Design Using Object-Oriented Petri Nets: A Case Study," in Proceeding of the International Workshop on Petri Nets and Software Engineering 2012, vol. 851. CEUR, 2012, pp. 253–266.

[3] J. Rumbaugh, I. Jacobson, and G. Booch, The Unified Modeling Language Reference Manual. Addison-Wesley, 1999.

[4] C. Raistrick, P. Francis, J. Wright, C. Carter, and I. Wilkie, Model Driven Architecture with Executable UML. Cambridge University Press, 2004.

[5] M. Češka, V. Janoušek, and T. Vojnar, "Modelling, Prototyping, and Verifying Concurrent and Distributed Applications Using Object-Oriented Petri Nets," Kybernetes: The International Journal of Systems and Cybernetics, vol. 2002, no. 9, 2002.

[6] K. Wiegers and J. Beatty, Software Requirements. Microsoft Press, 2014.

[7] N. Daoust, Requirements Modeling for Bussiness Analysts. Technics Publications, LLC, 2012.

[8] E. Seidewitz, "UML with meaning: executable modeling in foundational UML and the Alf action language," in HILT '14 Proceedings of the 2014 ACM SIGAda annual conference on High integrity language technology, 2014, pp. 61–68.

[9] J. Warmer and A. Kleppe, The Object Constraint Language: Getting your models ready for MDA. Longman Publishing, 2003.

[10] R. France and B. Rumpe, "Model-driven development of complex software: A research roadmap," in International Conference on Software Engineering, ICSE, 2010.

[11] Object Management Group, "Semantics of a Foundational Subset for Executable UML Models (fUML). OMG Document Number: formal/2013-08-06," http://www.omg.org/spec/FUML/1.1, OMG Document Number: formal/2013-08-06, 2013.

[12] S. Mijatov, P. Langer, T. Mayerhofer, and G. Kappel, "A framework for testing uml activities based on fuml," in Proc. of 10th Int. Workshop on Model Driven Engineering, Verification, and Validation, vol. 1069, 2013.

[13] Object Management Group, "Action Language for Foundational UML (Alf). OMG Document Number: formal/2013-09-01," http://www.omg.org/spec/ALF/1.0.1, OMG Document Number: formal/2013-09-01, 2013.

[14] D. Cetinkaya, A. V. Dai, and M. D. Seck, ACM Transactions on Modeling and Computer Simulation, vol. 25, no. 3, 2015.

[15] X. Hu, "A Simulation-Based Software Development Methodology for Distributed Real-Time Systems," Ph.D. dissertation, The University of Arizona, USA, 2004.

[16] H. Gomaa, Real-Time Software Design for Embedded Systems. Cambridge University Press, 2016.

[17] H. Gomma, Designing Software Product Lines with UML: From Use Cases to Pattern-Based Software Architecture. Addison-Wesley Professional, 2004.

[18] D. S. Frankel, Model Driven Architecture: Applying MDA to Enterprise Computing, ser. 17 (MS-17). John Wiley & Sons, 2003.

[19] R. Kočí and V. Janoušek, "Formal Models in Software Development and Deployment: A Case Study," International Journal on Advances in Software, vol. 7, no. 1, 2014, pp. 266–276.

[20] R. Kočí and V. Janoušek, "The Object Oriented Petri Net Component Model," in The Tenth International Conference on Software Engineering Advances. Xpert Publishing Services, 2015, pp. 309–315.

Predicting Candidate Uptake on Individual Online Vacancies and Vacancy Portfolios

Corné de Ruijt[†‡], Sandjai Bhulai [†], Bram L. Gorissen [†], Han Rusman[‡] and Leon Willemsens[‡]

[†]Faculty of Sciences
Vrije Universiteit Amsterdam
Amsterdam, the Netherlands
Email: {s.bhulai, b.l.gorissen }@vu.nl
[‡]Endouble
The Netherlands
Email: {Corne, Han, Leon}@endouble.com

***Abstract*—The internet has undoubtedly had an substantial effect on how organizations and job seekers behave on the labor market, which has been beneficial for both job seekers and organizations. However, despite these benefits, it also comes with difficulties. Organizations might observe both applicant excess and applicant shortage on their vacancies. The problem of either applicant excess or shortage has been addressed by previous studies, which frequently conclude that this problem is inherent to the process of online recruitment. The usage of analytical techniques might reveal new insight into how organizations can account for this problem. This paper therefore studies how the number of job-applications on online vacancies in a particular week, which is referred to as the application rate, can be predicted and controlled. To answer this question, a dataset originating from a large Dutch organization was used. This dataset contains recruitment outcomes over a period of three years and just over 5,000 unique vacancies. This study trained multiple machine learning models on predicting the application rate. Furthermore, it analyses the predictability of the total number of weekly applications over the entire vacancy portfolio, and how both the application rate and the total number of applications is affected by the usage of online marketing campaigns.**

Keywords*–*Recruitment analytics; HR analytics; Corporate career website; Predicting application rate

I. INTRODUCTION

This paper explores how online vacancies attract job seekers and how this process might be predicted and controlled. It thereby extends previous work [1], by discussing in more depth the predictability of the total number of weekly job applications over an organization's entire vacancy portfolio. Furthermore, this paper puts more emphasis on the effect of online marketing campaigns on the number of applications per vacancy per week, a metric that is further referred to as the application rate.

The internet has undoubtedly had an substantial effect on how organizations attract and select job seekers, and how job seekers search for new job opportunities. Already in 2003, 94% of the Global 500 companies reported having a corporate career website (CCW) [2]. Furthermore, there is a steady growth in the percentage of unemployed job seekers using the internet in different countries [3].

These results are not without reason: online recruitment has the potential for organizations to lower cost, shorten recruitment lead times, and attract a wider range of applicants [4], [5]. With employee turnover cost being easily over 150% of the departing employee's salary, lowering recruitment cost could have a substantial positive financial impact [6][p. 88]. Furthermore, the usage of the internet also has a positive effect on job seekers: job seekers using the internet are less likely to become unemployed, and can expect a larger growth in terms of their wage [7].

The internet also comes with difficulties. One of these is the excess of applicants, many of which being unsuited or poorly suited for the job they apply to [5], [8]. The ease of using the internet to apply apparently removes some barriers for job seekers to also apply to jobs they might be less suited for. On the other hand, some organizations find more difficulties in attracting sufficient candidates to their corporate career website, in particular organizations with a less well-known employer brand [9].

For that reason, this paper studies the predictability and controlability of the application rate. A dataset originating from a large Dutch organization, describing recruitment outcomes over a period of three years and just over 5,000 unique vacancies is considered. We study both the predictability of the total number of applications over all vacancies in the vacancy portfolio in a particular week, as well as the predictability of the total number of applications per vacancy per week, i.e., the application rate.

This paper has the following structure: in Section II, previous research on the effectiveness of corporate career websites is discussed, as well as methods to overcome the problem of an excess in the number of applications. Section III discusses how data was obtained and prepared for this study. Section IV discusses results from preliminary data analysis, whereas Section V reviews the machine learning methods used to make accurate predictions over the application rate. Section VI shows the results that were obtained from running different machine learning models in an attempt to predict the application rate. Finally, Section VII provides short summary of this research combined with its conclusions, whereas Section VIII discusses ideas for further research.

II. RELATED WORK

Although to our knowledge no previous studies have considered predicting and controlling the application rate using data describing historic recruitment outcomes, previous research has studied how applicant shortage and excess can be controlled via other means. Firstly, by studying the effectiveness of corporate career websites as a whole, i.e., not per vacancy, using questionnaires. Secondly, by considering the usage of machine learning in the applicant selection process in order to manage applicant excess, rather than using machine learning to attract or repulse job seekers to apply in the first place. This section will discuss results from both research perspectives.

A. *Effectiveness of corporate career websites*

Maurer and Liu [9] introduced a model that describes how corporate career websites influence job seekers in their decision to apply. In their model, Maurer and Liu define three inputs that affect job seekers in their usage of the recruitment website. The first input are job seekers' characteristics, such as his/her search query, motivation, current job, and knowledge. The second input, influence emphasized routes, defines how the job seeker navigates through the website. The third input are source features: features and content that are actually on the website. To analyze the influence emphasized routes (input 2), the elaboration likelihood model of persuasive communication [10] is used. The elaboration likelihood model defines two types of cues that can attract job seekers' attention. Central cues are cues that trigger the job seeker's careful thought and consideration. Vacancies that offer more salary or offer improved working conditions might persuade the job seeker to apply. Peripheral cues are cues that attract job seekers by raising an emotional response, such as employee testimonials.

Using this model, decisions can be made in the website design to attract a certain audience. Maurer and Liu argue that job seekers with a low level of search motivation or experience are more influenced by peripheral cues than central cues, the opposite holds for high levels of search motivation and experience. Furthermore, to attract job seekers, web designers should consider that the effectiveness of an application as a function of the amount of information is U-shaped. Hence, more information is not always better. Information richness should also be considered from different dimensions including active control (the ability to maintain control over the environment and information received), reciprocal communication (speed and direction of communication), vividness degree (auditory or visual channels used), and vividness depth (quality of information). Maurer and Liu stress that although online recruitment is more unbounded in the information that can be presented, potential excesses should be well managed.

Parry and Tyson [8] performed a longitudinal study to the usage of internet recruitment methods and the perception towards internet recruitment by employers. The study conducted seven surveys in the period from 1999 until 2006, where 16,000 employers were contacted per e-mail. Also, the study conducted fifteen semi-structured interviews with individuals from different industries, organization sizes, and geographical locations. Five interviews were held with providers of online recruitment technology. The study revealed four best practices that companies could exercise to increase the effectiveness of their internet recruitment practices. First, while prominent brands automatically attract job seekers to the organization's recruitment website, this is more difficult for organizations that are less known within the job seekers' audience. Hence, these organizations should use tools such as job boards and advertising channels to drive traffic towards the organization's recruitment website. Second, for prominent brands the large number of applicants is rather a burden than a blessing. Processing all these applicants can take a significant amount of time and resources. Therefore, these companies should consider using automated initial screening to already filter out those applicants who are unsuited for the job. Third, data from candidates can be saved in a talent pool. Finally, companies should attempt to make the job description and company description realistic. Unrealistic descriptions might generate traffic to the recruitment website, but also contain job seekers that in reality have a bad person-job or person-organization fit.

In another study, Braddy et al. [11] instructed 48 undergraduate students to explore a pair of corporate career websites. Afterwards, the participants were asked which of the two was most strongly associated with each of the following nine cultural dimensions: innovative, emphasis on rewards, supportiveness, outcome orientation, attention to detail, team orientation, aggressiveness, decisiveness and diversity. Based on this information, the researchers were able to identify which website content was associated with which cultural dimension. For example: explicitly mentioning that risk taking is encouraged was found to associate with an innovative culture, where stating the awards won in the past and the plans for company growth is associated with aggressiveness. The researchers also found that explicitly stating the companies culture was the most cited reason for associating a culture with an organization. Furthermore, website design features were found highly important for conveying perceptions of innovation, attention to detail, team orientation and diversity. Stating relevant organizational policies seemed instrumental for conveying perceptions of rewards, supportiveness and diversity.

Ton et al. [12] asked 100 Hong Kong students to complete four assignments on two Chinese job boards, namely creating an account, creating a resume, conduct a job search, and complete a job application. The job boards had an a priori high service level and low service level respectively. The service quality of the two websites was measured over the dimensions: overall service quality, time spent on the website, mental workload, general service quality, accuracy and efficiency, interface, maneuvering speed, and additional support. The latter five dimensions were measured via a questionnaire. The study found that the total time spent on the website was significantly less for the job board having the a priori high service level. The mental workload was significantly higher for the a priori low service level website, which could be caused by the job seeker having to put more effort in searching and interpreting information on the low quality website. The research concludes that general service quality, accuracy/efficiency and interface were most highly correlated with the overall service quality ratings.

Sylva and Mol [13] considered 1,360 applicants that applied for different positions within a multinational financial organization having more than 100,000 employees. Data was gathered by a questionnaire that appeared right after someone applied online during a period of two months. The collected data included demographical data, perceptions of the online application process and system and the perceived fairness. The researchers found that applicants were generally favorable towards the web-based procedure. Efficiency, user-friendliness, process fairness, and internet selection image were found as main determinants of applicant satisfaction. Candidates being external or highly familiar with the usage of the internet were more positive about the recruitment system.

Jansen and Jansen [14] study job search related queries that were filled into search engines Excite and MSN. From the analyzed queries, 45% was based on location, 17% on industry, 11% on skill set, 8.9% on specific job sites, 7.3% on government and 2.2% on temporal jobs. Furthermore, the search queries were generally long and specific, whereas the actual session duration was relatively short. The words used in the queries also changed over time.

B. Recruitment analytics for managing application excess

Internet recruitment has caused an excess of information spread to both recruiters and job seekers, based on which many studies conclude that these problems are inherent to internet recruitment, i.e., these problems are a natural consequence of internet recruitment and cannot be avoided. However, recent developments in machine learning are increasingly applied to the recruitment process in order to automate parts of this process [15]. For example, [16] found that by fast-tracking candidates who score highly in their pre-selection algorithm through some parts of the selection process, the time to hire can significantly be reduced without negatively impacting the overall quality of hired candidates. Besides automating parts of the selection process, previous research has also focused on automating other recruitment related tasks, such as CV parsing [17].

Although automated (pre-)selection and CV parsing automate part of the recruitment activities, they are more a workaround than an actual solution to the problem of applicant excess. More specifically, by analyzing how the quantity and quality of applications is affected by the online channel and message used by the vacancy, recruitment has the opportunity to control the quality and quantity of applicants before the job seeker applies. This not only may decrease the total number of applications, but also reduce the number of rejected applicants. Interestingly, previous research has not used the increasing amounts of data stored by recruitment departments themselves [18] to study the effect of online recruitment channels and ways of communication on the quality and quantity of applicants.

III. Data Gathering and Preparation

This section will give a short overview of how data was gathered for this study, which data was gathered, and how the data was prepared for further analysis.

A. Data gathering

To investigate whether the number applications can accurately be predicted and controlled, a dataset was gathered from a large Dutch company which employs over 30,000 people. This data was gathered over the period 2013-08-26 until 2015-12-31 and contained 5,036 unique vacancies.

The dataset was gathered from three systems: first, from an application tracking system (ATS), in which vacancy characteristics are stored such as work location, required education level, and working hours. Second, data was gathered from the corporate career website's Google Analytics account: how many job seekers visited the corporate career website per week, how frequently job seekers followed different paths from the website's landing page to the application submit page (the web page visited by applicants after submitting an application), and whether job seekers visited the website via a paid hyperlink, which was part of an online marketing campaign. The latter was used to determine which vacancies had been used in online marketing campaigns. Third, the number of weekly tweets the recruitment department published via their recruitment Twitter account was gathered, along with whether certain vacancies were referred to in a tweet via a hyperlink.

Combining these three data sources (ATS, Google Analytics, and Twitter) yields for each vacancy v and time period t, whether v was used in online marketing campaigns, and how many job seekers navigated from the landing page to the vacancys submit page during time period t. A measurement per vacancy per week is for simplicity denoted as per vacancy-week. This dataset was extended with time related data such as the recruitment lead time at time t, and application rates of a vacancy in weeks prior to week t.

The dataset was split into a test- and training set. The training set contained all values between 2013-08-26 and 2015-09-31, whereas the test set contained all values between 2015-10-01 and 2015-12-31. Note that this split was made only on date: it is possible that a vacancy exists both in the training set and in the test set. The split was chosen for two reasons: first, at the time of splitting the dataset there was no prior knowledge of possible time dependency in the data. A growing popularity of an employer brand might for example cause all vacancies to attract more applicants over time. If the application rate would include this time dependency, then validating the predictive model on the last period of the total dataset would produce the most realistic evaluation. Second, three months is the maximum period for which it is safe to assume that the vacancy portfolio over that period is known.

B. Data preparation

1) Clustering of categorical variables: To improve the quality of the data set, multiple operations were performed. Attributes related to work location and job title contained many possible categorical values, which was not practical for analysis. To reduce the number of categorical values, the locations were clustered based on similarities in their application rate probability density.

Let $N_{h,k}^{(l)}$ be the number of times application rate $h = 1, 2, \ldots, H$ was found for categorical value $k = 1, 2, \ldots, K$, which is a category of attribute $l = 1, 2, \ldots, L$. Furthermore, let $N_k^{(l)}$ be the number of times categorical value k of attribute l occurs in the dataset. Then $X_{h,k}^{(l)} = \frac{N_{h,k}^{(l)}}{N_k^{(l)}}$ is the element of the $H \times K$ matrix $X^{(l)}$ at position (h, k). A single row of $X^{(l)}$ gives the marginal application rate probabilities for categorical value i. Similar marginal probabilities were clustered using a K-means clustering algorithm by Hartigan and Wong [19].

To find the right number of clusters, the Akaike Information Criteria: $AIC = SS + 2CK$, was used for $C = 1, \ldots, 10$ clusters, where SS is the sum of squared Euclidean distance between the observations $i = 1, \ldots, n$ and the centroid to which it is assigned to, and K is defined as earlier. If a cluster had fewer than 100 observations, we assigned the categorical values of that cluster to the cluster which mean application rate was closest to the overall mean application rate.

Besides location attributes, the job title had even more unique values, which made the usage of the probability density unpractical. As an alternative, similar job titles were identified and clustered manually.

2) Low variance removal, normalization and dummification: In order to identify attributes having a small variance, the frequency cut off from the *nearZeroVar* function of the caret package was used [20]. Since all predictors are either binary, categorical, or discrete, it was possible to apply this procedure to all predictors. Let $N_{(z)}^{(l)}$ be the zth order statistic of $N_1^{(l)}, \ldots N_K^{(l)}$, with $N_k^{(l)}$ defined as in III-B1, then we have frequency ratio:

$$F_l = \frac{N_{(K)}^{(l)}}{N_{(K-1)}^{(l)}}. \quad (1)$$

Thus, F_l gives the ratio of the most frequent and second most frequent value of attribute l. Attributes were removed from the data set if $F_l > 19$.

During the last data preparation step, categorical attributes were dummified into binary vectors. Numerical attributes were normalized using:

$$\tilde{x}_{il} = \frac{x_{il} - \bar{x}_l}{s(x_l)}. \quad (2)$$

Here $\bar{x}_l$ and $s(x_l)$ are the mean and standard deviation over the values $i = 1, 2, \ldots, n$ of attribute l respectively.

IV. Results Exploratory Data Analysis

This section discusses two subjects. First, it will discuss the probability distribution of the application rate, which affected further modeling considerations that will be discussed in Section V. Second, it discusses the predictability of the total number of weekly applicants over the entire vacancy portfolio, using other website traffic indicators, time, characteristics of the vacancy portfolio, and the usage online marketing campaigns as predictors.

A. The application rate

When considering possible probability distributions of the application rate, a Poisson distribution would come first to mind. This follows from assuming that each vacancy has a large population of potential applicants, who each have a small probability of applying in a given week. However, as Fig. 1 suggests, the Poisson distribution does not seem to fit the data well: the application rate's distribution is more zero inflated and overdispersed than a Poisson distribution. Dependent on the nature of the vacancy, a log-normal or negative binomial distribution is more appropriate. The distribution also confirms previous research stating that some vacancies can attract a large number of applications [8]. In fact, 10% of the rates account for 53% of all applications.

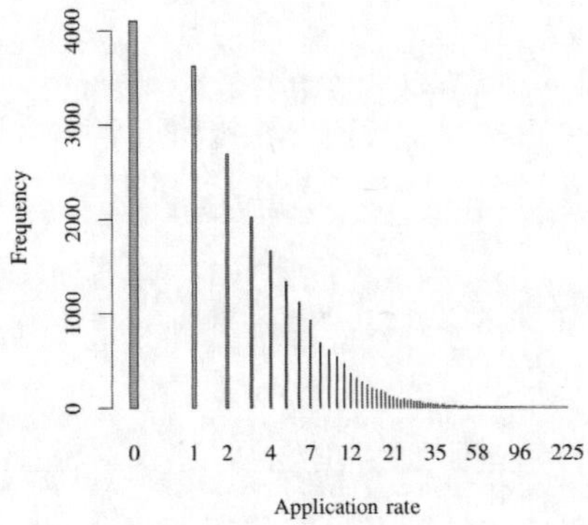

Figure 1. Histogram application rate

B. Total number of applications vs sessions and number of vacancies

Besides considering the distribution of the application rate, also the predictability of the total number of applications per week was considered. In particular its dependency on the total number of sessions on the website, number of vacancies in the vacancy portfolio, usage of online marketing campaigns, and time.

Fig. 2 shows a scatter plot of the total number of weekly sessions against the total number of weekly applications, whereas Fig. 3 shows the size of the vacancy portfolio compared to the total number of applications. From these figures it can be derived that, without considering their interaction or taking into account other covariates, increasing the number of sessions or increasing the size of the vacancy portfolio has a positive effect on the total number of applications (R^2 of 0.67 and 0.51 for the number of sessions and number of applications respectively).

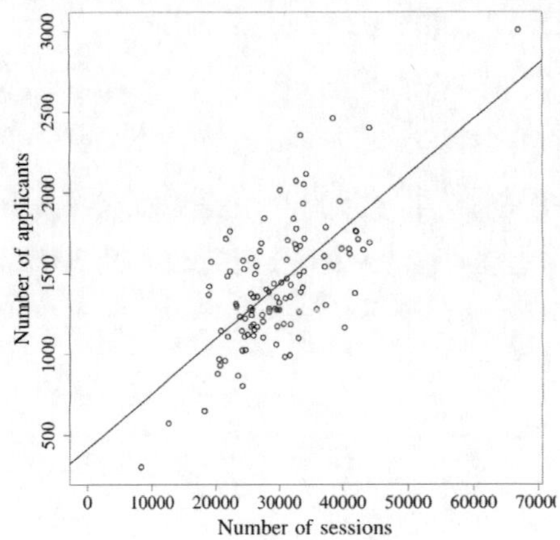

Figure 2. Sessions vs applications

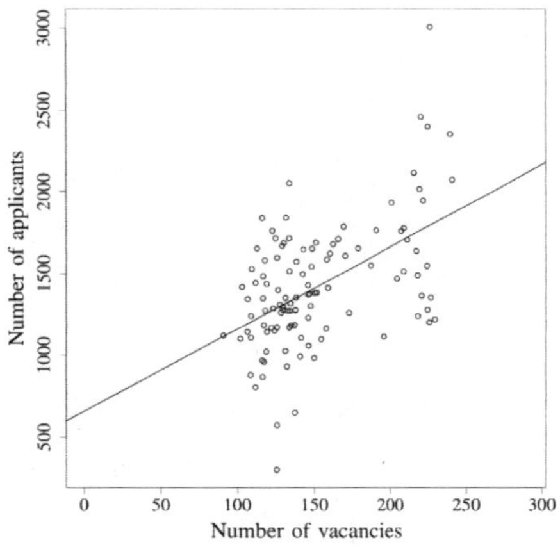

Figure 3. vacancies vs applications

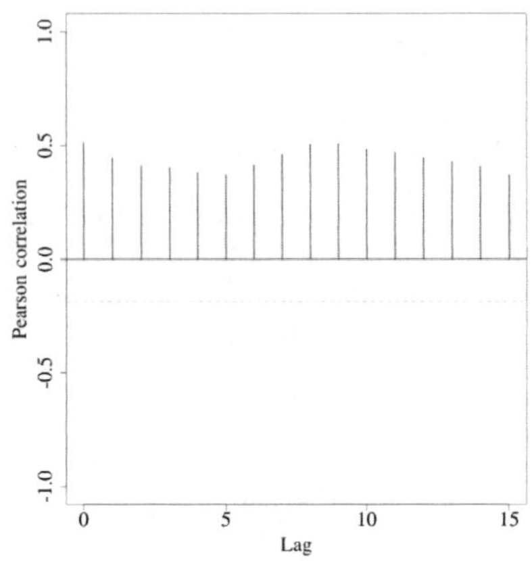

Figure 5. Cross correlation vacancies and applications

Fig. 4 shows the cross-correlation at different lags between the weekly sessions and weekly applicants, the blue lines represent the 5% significance level. The figure indicates that this cross-correlation peaks at lag zero (with a Pearson correlation of 0.67), after which it rapidly drops and becomes insignificant after 2 weeks. Hence, the job seekers are most likely to apply within the same week they first visit the website.

When considering the cross-correlation between the weekly size of the vacancy portfolio and the number of applications (Fig. 5), we obtain a rather different result. Again, the cross correlation peaks at lag zero (Pearson correlation of 0.51). However, it remains more or less constant before lag 0.

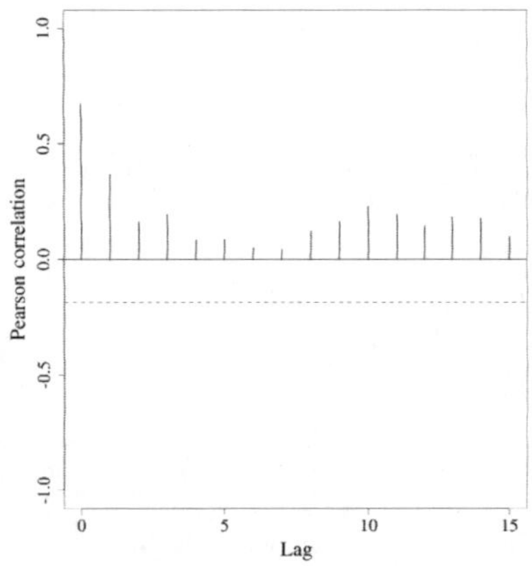

Figure 4. Cross-correlation sessions and applications

Table I shows the number of sessions that originated from a certain source, and used a certain device. Since visitors to the corporate career website can originate from many different sources, only the top four sources causing most traffic were considered, whereas smaller sources were combined in an 'other' category. What becomes most apparent is that only a small number of sources contributes to the number of sessions: the top three sources (Google, Indeed, and the corporate site) account for 71% of all traffic.

TABLE I. SOURCE AND DEVICE OF SESSIONS

Source-device	Sessions
Google desktop	634982
Indeed desktop	612637
Corporate site desktop	509441
Other desktop	328395
Google mobile	291040
Direct desktop	284256
Direct mobile	196089
Direct tablet	57666

C. *Predicting the weekly number of applications*

From Section IV, we already found that the correlation between the total number of vacancies online in a particular week is significantly correlated with the total number of applications. Therefore, a logical follow-up question would be how the total number of weekly applications depends on vacancy portfolio characteristics and the used online marketing campaigns. Here, the vacancy portfolio's characteristics are determined by counting the number of vacancies online having certain characteristics, such as vacancies having the same work location or the same job title.

Since the number of observations for the total number of weekly applications was relatively small, especially compared to the number of covariates, a multiple linear regression model was used without interaction terms. Furthermore, to remove non-predictive variables, a backwards AIC algorithm was applied. This algorithm iteratively removes those attributes from the linear regression model resulting in the largest reduction in the AIC value. The algorithm terminates if removing attributes does not result in a smaller AIC value. The resulting model is shown in Table II, which has an R^2 value of 0.62. From the table it can be observed that especially an increase in the number of vacancies related to certain locations has a positive effect on the total number of applications.

We also observe a negative effect of Google Adwords campaigns and twitter references. It is however difficult to draw solid conclusions from this observation for two reasons. First, the campaigns were frequently used in combination with each other, which makes it difficult to identify the effect of a single campaign. This can easily be seen from their correlation, 0.88 for Google Adwords and Facebook campaigns, and from the condition indices and variance decomposition proportions [21]. The largest condition index (91.68) has, for the number of Facebook and the number of Google campaigns, variance decomposition proportions of 0.636 and 0.620, which are larger than the threshold value for collinearity of 0.5. A possible remedy for this collinearity is to add more characteristics of the campaigns to the data set, such as the profiles used in a Facebook campaign. This was however not considered in this study. Second, online campaigns were most frequently used on vacancies receiving a small number of applications, hence the usage of online marketing campaigns could have been more of a response to a small number of applications rather than that it determines a small number of applications.

TABLE II. Summary linear regression model for predicting number of weekly applications

Coefficient	Estimate	Std. Error	t-value	p-value
Intercept	368.36	222.07	1.66	0.1005
Vacancies	6.47	2.01	3.22	0.0018
Business unit A	-50.55	13.83	-3.65	0.0004
Business unit B	-27.77	8.27	-3.36	0.0011
Business unit C	-32.61	15.43	-2.11	0.0373
Location 1	59.15	18.06	3.27	0.0015
Location 2	27.97	8.24	3.39	0.0010
Job category 1	72.74	18.65	3.90	0.0002
Job category 2	38.89	13.58	2.86	0.0052
Job category 3	2.22	2.38	0.93	0.3537
Location 4	-31.15	8.65	-3.60	0.0005
Location 5	-27.50	17.60	-1.56	0.1215
Location 6	-27.39	8.35	-3.28	0.0015
# Facebook campaigns	18.48	4.61	4.01	0.0001
# Google Adwords campaigns	-9.12	3.38	-2.70	0.0083
# Twitter references	-17.41	12.04	-1.45	0.1517

When considering the residuals of the linear regression model over time (Fig. 6), a Box-Pierce test showed that these residuals were correlated. However, when examining the autocorrelation and partial autocorrelation functions, this correlation turns out to be small: both the autocorrelation and partial autocorrelation show a maximum absolute correlation of 0.21, at lag one and two respectively. Therefore, for simplicity, it was found acceptable to assume that the residuals were uncorrelated. As a result it was assumed that the total number of applications per week was independent of the date of the measurement.

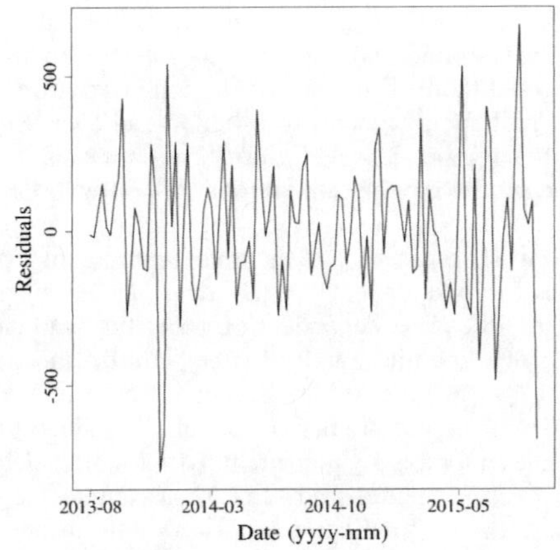

Figure 6. Errors over time

D. Best sources

In Section IV-B, we already considered which source-device combinations contributed most to the number of sessions (Table I). A related question is how the source-device combination contribute to the number of weekly applications. Again a linear regression model without interaction terms was used, combined with the backwards AIC algorithm to remove attributes which did not contribute to the model.

TABLE III. SUMMARY LINEAR REGRESSION MODEL FOR PREDICTING NUMBER OF WEEKLY APPLICANTS

Coefficient	Estimate	Std. Error	t-value	p-value
Direct mobile	0.34	0.06	4.92	0.0000
Corporate site desktop	0.27	0.06	4.93	0.0000
Direct desktop	0.19	0.05	3.99	0.0001
Other desktop	0.07	0.01	5.58	0.0000
Google mobile	0.06	0.02	2.57	0.0116
Direct tablet	-2.00	0.42	-4.73	0.0000

The result is shown in Table III. Interestingly, the source-device combinations causing most traffic to the website did not produce most applications. Where visitors originating from Google on a desktop produced most traffic to the website, changes in direct traffic on either desktop, mobile, or tablet, and traffic from the corporate website were the main drivers for changes in the number of weekly applications. This observation seems intuitive: job seekers will use a search engine the first time they visit a career website, but after that the browser will have stored the vacancy's URL such that the job seeker can easily return to the web page directly.

V. METHODS

This section gives an overview of the methods that were used to predict the application rate. Also, it will describe how the predictive quality of the different methods were compared, and how the effect of online marketing campaigns was computed.

A. Method selection

To determine which methods would be most suited to predict the application rate, six considerations were taken. First, since the application rate is count data, its prediction is considered to be a regression problem. Second, exploratory data analysis found that the data is more zero inflated and overdispersed than a Poisson distribution. Therefore, predictive models which incorporate zero inflation and overdispersion are preferred. Third, during exploratory data analysis it was found that when predicting the total number of applications per week, the residuals of this model were only slightly correlated. As a result, it was assumed that the total number of applications per week is independent of the date of the measurement. Though it still can be dependent on other time indicators, such as the current recruitment lead time. Fourth, the dataset still contained a large number of attributes, some of which might not be useful for the predictive model. To reduce the number of attributes, methods which included variable selection were preferred. Fifth, since a grid search was applied to find good model parameters, methods which were able to produce good results within reasonable time were preferred (i.e., methods that took more than 1 hour to compute a single predictive model using a 1.6 GHz dual-core Intel Core i5 processor were disregarded). Sixth, methods which have been applied successfully in other regression application were preferred.

Based on these criteria, seven methods were identified: Linear elastic net, Poisson elastic net, Tweedie elastic net, Classification And Regression Trees (CART), random forest (RF), Support Vector Regression (SVR), and Artificial Neural Networks (ANN). For convenience, we write the application rate as $\mathbf{y} = (y_1, \ldots, y_N)$, with N the total number of observations, and the covariate matrix as $X = (\mathbf{x}_1, \ldots, \mathbf{x}_N)$. All methods were only executed on the training set.

1) Linear elastic net: Linear elastic net is a method which attempts to minimize the sum of squared errors, plus a linear combination of the lasso and ridge penalty. Let $SSE(\lambda, \boldsymbol{\beta}, \alpha)$ be the regularized sum of squared errors, with λ the weight of the regularization terms, α the convex combination parameter for ridge vs lasso regularization, and $\boldsymbol{\beta}$ the vector of main effects. $SSE(\lambda, \boldsymbol{\beta}, \alpha)$ is given by:

$$\begin{aligned} SSE(\lambda, \boldsymbol{\beta}, \alpha) = \; & \tfrac{1}{2N} \textstyle\sum_{i=1}^{N} (y_i - \beta_0 - x_i^T \boldsymbol{\beta})^2 \\ & + \lambda \left[(1-\alpha) \tfrac{1}{2} ||\boldsymbol{\beta}||^2 + \alpha ||\boldsymbol{\beta}||_1 \right]. \end{aligned} \tag{3}$$

To minimize (3), the glmnet R package was utilized, which applies a coordinate descent algorithm to estimate $\boldsymbol{\beta}$ [22]. To determine good values for λ and α, a grid search was applied. For λ, $K = 100$ uniformly spread values between $\lambda_{\max} = \frac{\max_l |\langle \mathbf{x}_l, \mathbf{y} \rangle|}{N\alpha}$, where $\mathbf{x}_l$ is the lth column of matrix X, and $\langle \mathbf{x}_l, \mathbf{y} \rangle$ is the inner product between vectors $\mathbf{x}_l$ and $\mathbf{y}$. For $\lambda_{\min}$ we take $\lambda_{\min} = 10^{-3} \lambda_{\max}$. To find a good value for α, values from 0 up to 1 with increasing steps of 0.2 were used.

2) Poisson elastic net: Poisson elastic net is a combination of a generalized linear regression model and elastic net using the link function $g(\mu_i) = \log(\mu_i)$, where $\mu_i = \mathbb{E}(y_i | \mathbf{x}_i)$. Instead of using the sum of squared errors, the log-likelihood is used to estimate $\boldsymbol{\beta}$. Let ALL be the regularized adjusted log-likelihood, then $\boldsymbol{\beta}$ is found by maximizing (4):

$$\begin{aligned} ALL(\lambda, \boldsymbol{\beta}, \alpha) = & \tfrac{1}{2N} \textstyle\sum_{i=1}^{N} \left[y_i \mathbf{x}_i^T \boldsymbol{\beta} - \exp\left(\mathbf{x}_i^T \boldsymbol{\beta}\right) \right] \\ & - \lambda \left[(1-\alpha) \tfrac{1}{2} ||\boldsymbol{\beta}||^2 + \alpha ||\boldsymbol{\beta}||_1 \right]. \end{aligned} \tag{4}$$

To maximize (4), again the glmnet R package was used. In case of Poisson regression, glmnet iteratively creates a second order Taylor expansion of (4) without the penalty, using current estimates for $\boldsymbol{\beta}$. This Taylor expansion is then used in a coordinate descent algorithm to update $\boldsymbol{\beta}$ [22], [23]. To find appropriate values for λ and α, the same grid search as for linear elastic net was applied.

3) Tweedie elastic net: To incorporate the fact that the application rate is more zero inflated and overdispersed than a Poisson distribution, the Tweedie compound Poisson model was used. The Tweedie compound Poisson model can be represented by $Y = \sum_{m=1}^{M} X_m$, where Y is the response vector, M a Poisson random variable, and X_m are i.i.d. Gamma distributed with parameters α and γ. The regularized negative log-likelihood is given by (5) [24]:

$$\begin{aligned} NLL(\lambda, \boldsymbol{\beta}, \alpha) = \; & \textstyle\sum_{i=1}^{N} \Bigg[\frac{y_i \exp\left[-(\rho-1)(\mathbf{x}_i^T \boldsymbol{\beta})\right]}{\rho - 1} \\ & + \frac{\exp\left[(2-\rho)(\mathbf{x}_i^T \boldsymbol{\beta})\right]}{2-\rho} \Bigg] \\ & + \lambda \left[(1-\alpha) \tfrac{1}{2} ||\boldsymbol{\beta}||_2 + \alpha ||\boldsymbol{\beta}||_1 \right]. \end{aligned} \tag{5}$$

To minimize (5), the HDTweedie R package was used. This method applies an iterative reweighted least squares (IRLS) algorithm combined with a blockwise majorization descent (BMD) [24]. To find appropriate values for λ, the standard procedure from HDTweedie was used. This method first computes $\lambda_{\max}$ such that $\boldsymbol{\beta} = 0$, and then sets $\lambda_{\min} = 0.001 \lambda_{\max}$. The other $K - 2$ values for λ are found by projecting them uniformly on a log-scale on the range $[\lambda_{\min}, \lambda_{\max}]$. For α the values from 0.1 to 0.9 with an increase of 0.2 were used. Furthermore, $\rho = 1.5$ was used.

4) Classification And Regression Trees: To construct a regression tree the rpart implementation in R was used [25]. This implementation first constructs a binary tree by maximizing $SS_T - (SS_R + SS_L)$ in each node, where SS_T is the sum of squared errors of the entire tree, and SS_R and SS_L are the sum of squared errors of the left and right branch respectively. The tree constructions stops when further splits would violate a constraint on the minimum number of observations in each node.

Second, the constructed tree is split into m sub-trees. Let $R(T)$ be the risk of tree T, which is the sum of squared errors in the terminal nodes of T. CART computes the risk of each sub-tree, which is defined by $R_\alpha(T) = R(T) + \alpha |T|$, using K-fold cross validation. The term $\alpha |T|$ is an additional penalty on the size of the tree. The final tree is the sub-tree which minimizes the average sum of squared errors over the K-fold cross validation. The method described here is referred to as the "ANOVA" method.

Alternatively, rpart also has the option to maximize the deviance $D_T - (D_L + D_R)$, where D is the within node deviance, assuming that the response originates from a Poisson distribution. Both the Poisson and ANOVA methods have been applied to the dataset. To find an appropriate value for α, a grid search was applied using $\alpha \in \{0.001, 0.01, 0.1, 0.3\}$, both for the ANOVA and Poisson models.

5) Random forest: A random forest model was produced using the RandomForest package in R [26]. RandomForest constructs T unpruned regression trees T_i, where in each split only d randomly chosen predictors are considered. A prediction $\hat{y}_i$ is then created by $\hat{y}_i = \frac{1}{T}\sum_{i=1}^{T} T_i(x)$, thus the average over all trees. To find the appropriate number of trees, a grid search was applied using 50, 100, and 500 trees. Furthermore, at each split, $d = 61$ randomly sampled attributes were considered.

6) Support Vector Regression: Support Vector Regression is the regression alternative for Support Vector Machines. Given the linear regression problem: $y_i = \mathbf{w}^T\mathbf{x}_i + b + \epsilon$, SVR attempts to find the flattest hyperplane $\mathbf{w}^T\mathbf{x}_i + b$ such that, for all data points $i = 1, \ldots, N$; we have $|y_i - (\mathbf{w}^T\mathbf{x}_i + b)| < \epsilon$. Also incorporating slack variables ζ_i^+ and ζ_i^-, the problem can be described as (6):

$$\begin{aligned} \min \quad & \tfrac{1}{2}||\mathbf{w}||^2 + C\sum_{i=1}^{n}(\zeta_i^+ + \zeta_i^-) \\ \text{s.t.} \quad & y_i - \mathbf{w}^T\mathbf{x}_i - b \leq \epsilon + \zeta_i^+, \quad i = 1, \ldots, N \\ & \mathbf{w}^T\mathbf{x}_i + b - y_i \leq \epsilon + \zeta_i^-, \quad i = 1, \ldots, N \\ & \zeta_i^+, \zeta_i^- \geq 0. \end{aligned} \tag{6}$$

Since the solution to (6) only depends on inner products between vectors $\mathbf{x}_i$, the problem can be transformed into a higher dimension without much extra computation using kernels [27]. For the computation of the SVR, the R kernlab package was used [28]. Although in this study initially both a linear kernel (hence no kernel) and the RBF kernel: $\kappa(\mathbf{x}_i, \mathbf{x}_j) = \exp\left(-\frac{||\mathbf{x}_i - \mathbf{x}_j||^2}{2\sigma^2}\right)$ were considered, not using a kernel surprisingly had a large negative effect on the runtime and was therefore discarded. To find appropriate values for ϵ and C a grid search was applied using: $\epsilon \in \{0.01, 0.1, 1\}$ and $C \in \{1, 10\}$.

7) Artificial Neural Networks: In this study we considered a feed-forward Artificial Neural Network with a single hidden layer. To find the weights the nnet R package was used, which utilizes an L-BFGS algorithm to find the appropriate weights [29], [30]. A grid search was applied to find an appropriate number of units in the hidden layer. During the grid search, 1, 5, 10, 30, and 50 hidden units were considered.

B. Method evaluation

To evaluate the quality of predictive models, two scenarios were distinguished. The first scenario assumes that application rates in weeks prior to the predicting period are known, which is comparable with predicting one week ahead. The second scenario assumes these application rates to be absent, and is more comparable with predicting 2 to 12 weeks ahead. These two scenarios are indicated by including PAR (Previous Application Rates) and excluding PAR respectively.

To evaluate the quality of the predictions two error measures are used: the root mean squared error: $RMSE = \sqrt{\frac{1}{N}\sum_{i=1}^{N}(\hat{y}_i - y_i)^2}$, where $\hat{y}_i$ is the predicted value for actual y_i. Second, the determination coefficient: $R^2 = 1 - \frac{SS_{res}}{SS_{tot}}$, with $SS_{res} = \sum_{i=1}^{N}(\hat{y}_i - y_i)^2$, the residual sum of squares, and $SS_{tot} = \sum_{i=1}^{N}(y_i - \bar{y})^2$, the total sum of squares. A 10-fold cross validation was applied to obtain accurate estimates for the quality of the predictions over the training set in both scenarios. Furthermore, a final prediction over the test set was made using the model showing the best results over the training set to estimate out of sample performance.

C. Effect of online campaigns

To gain more insight into how an increase in the usage of online marketing campaigns might affect the number of applications, two procedures were applied: one for binary indicators of online campaigns, and one for numeric indicators. We first consider the binary indicators, let:

$$z_{ij} = \begin{cases} 1 & \text{if campaign } j \text{ is used for measurement } i \\ 0 & \text{otherwise} \end{cases} \tag{7}$$

and $\alpha_{ij} = \alpha_j = \mathbb{P}(z_{ij} = 1)$ be the probability that a vacancy in some week is stimulated by online campaign $j \in J$ in the training set, with J the set of all campaigns. Then for each online marketing campaign j we iterate over:

$$\alpha_j^{(k)} = 10^{-2}(k-1), \quad k = 1, \ldots, K \tag{8}$$

while keeping $\alpha_r^{(k)} = 0$ for $r \in J \setminus \{j\}$, and we compute how the best performing predictive model predicts the application rate for this increasing probability. Hence, we iterate from not using the campaign for any vacancy ($k = 1$), to using the campaign for each vacancy ($k = K$). Note that $\alpha_j^{(k)}$ does not depend on the observation i, i.e., all observations i have the same probability of being used in marketing campaign j. For K we chose $K = 101$.

For numeric indicators, of which there was only one: the number of tweets, a similar procedure was applied. In this procedure we again iterate over $\alpha_j^{(k)}$, $k = 1, \ldots, 101$. However, we now impute the usage of this campaign by computing

$$C_j^{(k)} = \left[C_{\min} + \frac{(C_{\max} - C_{\min})}{\alpha_j^{(k)}}\right] z_{ij}^{(k)} \tag{9}$$

where $C_j^{(k)}$ is the frequency campaign j is used in iteration k. $z_{ij}^{(k)}$ are samples from a Bernoulli distribution with probability $\alpha_j^{(k)}$, and $C_{\min}$ and $C_{\max}$ are the minimum and maximum number of times campaign j has been used in the training set for an individual vacancy in an arbitrary week.

VI. Results Predicting the Application Rate

The following section compares the predictive ability of the methods discussed in Section V. Furthermore, it will give an overview of the variables that provided most predictive value, and discuss the effect of increasing online marketing efforts on the application rate.

A. Method comparison

Table IV shows the best results per model when applying a 10-fold cross validation on the training set. The table indicates that random forest produced the best results, both when predicting with and without PAR. Table IV also indicates that multiple methods, such as artificial neural networks without PAR, Poisson elastic net, and Tweedie elastic net with PAR, did not produce accurate results. Furthermore, Table IV indicates that the added value of including previous application rates into the model is relatively small. Hence, the predictive model would only produce slightly better results when predicting short term (1 week), in comparison with predicting long term (2 to 12 weeks).

TABLE IV. RESULTS 10-FOLD CROSS VALIDATION

Method	Best $RMSE$ including PAR	Best R^2 including PAR	Best $RMSE$ excluding PAR	Best R^2 excluding PAR
Linear elastic net	11.82	0.35	11.87	0.34
Poisson elastic net	15.53	0	NA	NA
CART ANOVA	10.72	0.46	11.12	0.42
CART Poisson	10.17	0.52	10.75	0.46
random forest	9.38	0.59	9.93	0.54
Tweedie elastic net	13.86	0.03	11.62	0.37
SVR	10.58	0.46	11.28	0.41
ANN	11.14	0.42	17.35	0

The $RMSE$ in Table IV is largely influenced by some large application rates, which are difficult to predict. This can also be concluded from the errors of the RF model on the test set (Fig. 7). In fact, 90% of the errors are smaller than 9.63, and the average absolute error over this 90% is 2.43. Also interesting is that adding more trees to the RF model only had a small impact on the predictive quality of the model (Table V).

TABLE V. RESULTS 10-FOLD CROSS VALIDATION FOR DIFFERENT NUMBER OF TREES

Trees	$RMSE$ **including PAR**	$RMSE$ **excluding PAR**	R^2 **including PAR**	R^2 **excluding PAR**
50	9.50	9.97	0.58	0.53
100	9.40	9.98	0.59	0.53
500	9.38	9.93	0.59	0.54

B. Test set evaluation

Since RF produced the most promising results in a 10-fold cross validation, this model was evaluated on the test set. The results are shown in Table VI, whereas the distribution of the error in the test set is shown in Fig. 7. The quality of the prediction was slightly worse than the average error obtained from 10-fold cross validation. Furthermore, just as in the training set, few vacancies with large application rates account for most of the $RMSE$.

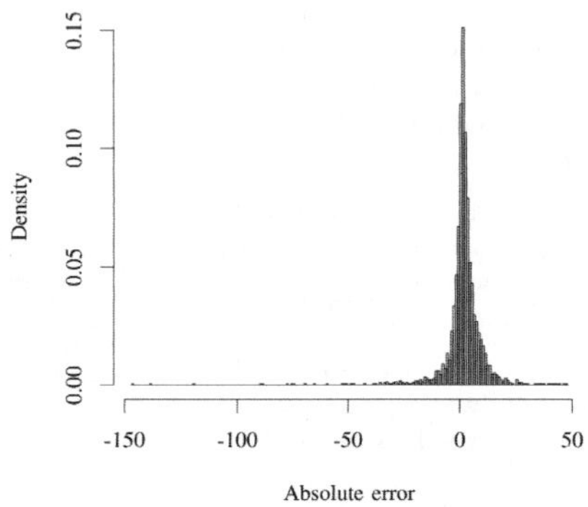

Figure 7. Test set error with PAR

TABLE VI. RESULTS APPLYING RANDOM FOREST ON TEST SET

Performance metric	Value including PAR	Value excluding PAR
MAE	5.25	6.35
MSE	100.44	123.99
RMSE	10.02	11.13
Residual mean	1.53	1.81
Residual sd	9.90	10.98
R^2	0.44	0.32

C. Variable importance

To determine the importance of different variables in the model, the standard method from the R RandomForest package was used [26]. For regression problems, as opposed to classification problems, this method computes the reduction in residual sum of squares when splitting on a certain variable. This amount is summed over all trees to obtain the impurity, which provides an overall picture of the decrease in residual sum of squares of a variable. Table VII shows the ten most important variables found in the model for the case of including PAR.

TABLE VII. VARIABLE IMPORTANCE

Top including PAR	**Impurity** $(\cdot 10^5)$
Application rate 1 week ago	5.65
Job category 1	4.94
Current vacancy lead time	4.38
Job type 1	1.75
Application rate 2 weeks ago	1.49
Job type 2	0.91
Min. hours in contract	0.85
Job type 3	0.80
Job type 4	0.67
Business Unit C	0.62

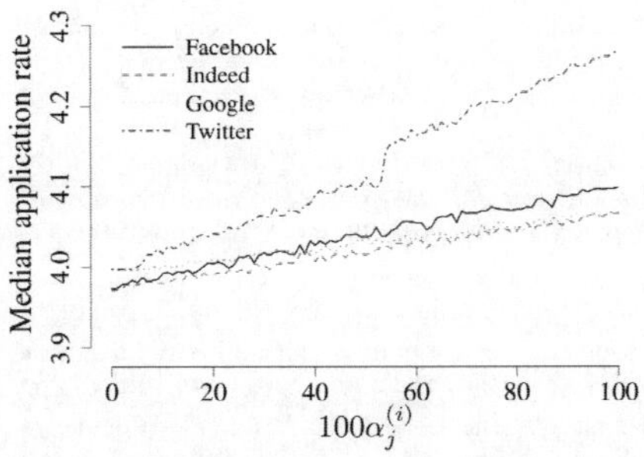

Figure 8. Effect of using online campaigns

From Table VII it can be observed that there is some overlap with the variable importance found when predicting the total weekly number of applications (Table II). In particular, both tables include the factors job category 1 and business unit C. Table VII also shows the importance of time related variables such as the current vacancy lead time and previous application rates of the vacancy, indicating that the application rate of a vacancy is time dependent. Another interesting observation is that the effect of online marketing campaigns in this figure is missing, meaning that their effect is smaller than the effect of the variables in the table.

To obtain more insight into the effect of online marketing campaigns we follow the procedure described in Section V-C, which resulted in Fig. 8. To avoid that some large application rates would have a large influence on the found effect of online campaigns, we consider the median application rate instead of the mean. The figure shows that all campaigns had a positive effect on the median application rate, though this effect is quite small. Especially an increasing usage of Twitter shows a positive effect on the application rate. However, since the campaign data was not obtained in an experimental set-up, it is difficult to draw firm conclusions.

VII. CONCLUSION

This paper considered the predictability of the number of weekly applicants per vacancy on a corporate career website, also referred to as the application rate. Being able to predict and influence this metric can be important to recruitment departments: it provides information about how to either prevent applicant excess from online platforms, or how the number of online applications could be increased. In order to study the predictability of the application rate, a dataset from a large Dutch organization employing over 30,000 employees was considered, which was collected from the organization's Applicant Tracking System (ATS), Google Analytics account and Twitter.

From the preliminary data analysis, which was mainly focused on predicting the total number of weekly applications and determining the distribution of the application rate, we found that the total number of applications could be predicted quite well from characteristics of the vacancy portfolio and the usage of online marketing campaigns ($R^2 = 0.62$). Interestingly, the number of vacancies referenced by Google Adwords campaigns and Twitter was found to have a negative effect on the total number of applications. However, it is difficult to make clear conclusions based on this observation. Marketing campaigns were found to be highly correlated with each other, and may suffer from reverse causality: they are most frequently used for vacancies which are already under-performing.

When focusing on the probability distribution of the application rate, we found that its distribution is more zero-inflated and overdispersed than what would be expected from a Poisson distribution. A negative binomial or log-normal distribution was found to be a better fit. In an attempt to predict the application rate, multiple machine learning algorithms were used, including linear elastic net, Poisson elastic net, Tweedie elastic net, CART, random forest, Support Vector Regression, and feed-forward Artificial Neural Networks. Predictors included characteristics of the vacancy (e.g., location, work hours, etc.), usage of online marketing campaigns, number of competing vacancies on the same corporate career website, and vacancy lead time up to the time of prediction.

In a comparison between the different machine learning algorithms, random forest showed the best results. Time related attributes, such as the application rates in prior weeks and the vacancy lead time, contributed most to the quality of the predictions. Of the online campaigns, Twitter was found to have the most positive effect on the application rate.

From this analysis a few conclusions can be made. First, even though the predictions are quite accurate in most situations, i.e., have an error of less than five applicants, some vacancies can attract a large number of job seekers (> 50), which the model is unable to predict. On the other hand, both the predictions and insights into the variability of these predictions are helpful to manage the expectations recruiters and hiring managers might have when publishing a vacancy. In particular, recruiters should manage vacancies expecting a large number of applications carefully to avoid excess of applications, especially when applicant excess does not improve the quality of the hire. Also, recruiters could consider how attractive vacancies can be used to market less attractive vacancies, for example, by generalizing the vacancy such that it may refers to both popular and less popular job positions.

Second, we found that the effect of online marketing campaigns on the application rate is positive, though quite small. Furthermore, it is likely that there exists reverse causality between online marketing campaigns and the application rate: online marketing campaigns were only used on already under performing vacancies. Therefore, we were not able to draw a firm conclusion on the effect of online marketing campaigns on the application rate.

VIII. FURTHER WORK

The research presented here can be extended in a number of directions. First, we have showed that it can be problematic to infer clear conclusions on the effect of influential factors, such as online marketing campaigns, on the number of applications based on historic recruitment data. Since the data is not obtained in an experimental set-up, the usage of such influential factors can be rather a response to too few applications, hence suffer from reverse causality. A question for further research would therefore be how this reverse causality can be efficiently accounted for, either by incorporating it into the model, or by collecting data in an experimental set-up. Besides only considering online marketing, also the effect of other recruitment endeavors could be examined, such as the effect of using job-boards on the application rate.

Second, this research can be extended to also incorporate the quality of applicants. Although multiple studies have considered the quality of applicants [15], literature is scarce on the relationship between applicant quality and quantity. Further research could therefore consider not only this relationship, but also how recruitment departments can use this information to optimize their recruitment process.

Third, this study considered that the number of applications on the entire vacancy portfolio was independent of time. It is however likely that other corporate career websites will show a drift or seasonality in the number of applications. Estimation of this seasonality can be problematic, as recruitment data might not have sufficient history for proper estimation. Further research could therefore consider how the methods proposed in this paper should be adjusted to incorporate this time dependency.

REFERENCES

[1] C. de Ruijt, S. Bhulai, H. Rusman, and L. Willemsens, "Predicting candidate uptake for online vacancies," *DATA ANALYTICS 2016*, pp. 63–68, 2016.

[2] R. Greenspan, *Job seekers have choices*, 2003, URL: https://www.clickz.com/job-seekers-have-choices/76679/ [accessed 2017-05-09].

[3] F. Suvankulov, "Job search on the internet, e-recruitment, and labor market outcomes," DTIC Document, Tech. Rep., 2010.

[4] E. Galanaki, "The decision to recruit online: A descriptive study," *Career development international*, vol. 7, no. 4, pp. 243–251, 2002.

[5] S. Lang, S. Laumer, C. Maier, and A. Eckhardt, "Drivers, challenges and consequences of e-recruiting: a literature review," in *Proceedings of the 49th SIGMIS annual conference on Computer personnel research*. ACM, 2011, pp. 26–35.

[6] W. Cascio and J. Boudreau, *Investing in people: Financial impact of human resource initiatives*. Ft Press, 2010.

[7] B. Stevenson, "The impact of the internet on worker flows," *The Wharton School, University of Pennsylvania*, pp. 1–24, 2006.

[8] E. Parry and S. Tyson, "An analysis of the use and success of online recruitment methods in the UK," *Human Resource Management Journal*, vol. 18, no. 3, pp. 257–274, 2008.

[9] S. D. Maurer and Y. Liu, "Developing effective e-recruiting websites: Insights for managers from marketers," *Business horizons*, vol. 50, no. 4, pp. 305–314, 2007.

[10] R. E. Petty and J. T. Cacioppo, *The elaboration likelihood model of persuasion*. Springer, 1986.

[11] P. W. Braddy, A. W. Meade, and C. M. Kroustalis, "Organizational recruitment website effects on viewers perceptions of organizational culture," *Journal of Business and Psychology*, vol. 20, no. 4, pp. 525–543, 2006.

[12] J. P. Tong, V. G. Duffy, G. W. Cross, F. Tsung, and B. P. Yen, "Evaluating the industrial ergonomics of service quality for online recruitment websites," *International Journal of Industrial Ergonomics*, vol. 35, no. 8, pp. 697–711, 2005.

[13] H. Sylva and S. T. Mol, "E-recruitment: A study into applicant perceptions of an online application system," *International Journal of Selection and Assessment*, vol. 17, no. 3, pp. 311–323, 2009.

[14] B. J. Jansen, K. J. Jansen, and A. Spink, "Using the web to look for work: Implications for online job seeking and recruiting," *Internet Research*, vol. 15, no. 1, pp. 49–66, 2005.

[15] S. Strohmeier and F. Piazza, "Domain driven data mining in human resource management: A review of current research," *Expert Systems with Applications*, vol. 40, no. 7, pp. 2410–2420, 2013.

[16] S. Mehta, R. Pimplikar, A. Singh, L. R. Varshney, and K. Visweswariah, "Efficient multifaceted screening of job applicants," in *Proceedings of the 16th International Conference on Extending Database Technology*. ACM, 2013, pp. 661–671.

[17] M. Tosik, C. L. Hansen, G. Goossen, and M. Rotaru, "Word embeddings vs word types for sequence labeling: the curious case of cv parsing," in *Proceedings of NAACL-HLT*, 2015, pp. 123–128.

[18] M. Burgard and F. Piazza, "Data warehouse and business intelligence systems in the context of e-hrm," *Encyclopedia of Human Resources Information Systems: Challenges in e-HRM: Challenges in e-HRM*, 2008.

[19] J. A. Hartigan and M. A. Wong, "Algorithm as 136: A k-means clustering algorithm," *Journal of the Royal Statistical Society. Series C (Applied Statistics)*, vol. 28, no. 1, pp. 100–108, 1979.

[20] M. Kuhn, "Building predictive models in R using the caret package," *Journal of Statistical Software*, vol. 28, no. 5, pp. 1–26, 2008.

[21] D. A. Belsley, "A guide to using the collinearity diagnostics," *Computer Science in Economics and Management*, vol. 4, no. 1, pp. 33–50, 1991.

[22] J. Friedman, T. Hastie, and R. Tibshirani, "Regularization paths for generalized linear models via coordinate descent," *Journal of statistical software*, vol. 33, no. 1, pp. 1–24, 2010.

[23] T. Hastie and J. Qian, *Glmnet Vignette*, 2014, URL: http://web.stanford.edu/~hastie/Papers/Glmnet_Vignette.pdf [accessed 2017-05-09].

[24] W. Qian, Y. Yang, and H. Zou, "Tweedies compound poisson model with grouped elastic net," *Journal of Computational and Graphical Statistics*, vol. 25, no. 2, pp. 606–625, 2016.

[25] E. J. Atkinson and T. M. Therneau, "An introduction to recursive partitioning using the rpart routines," *Rochester: Mayo Foundation*, 2000.

[26] A. Liaw and M. Wiener, "Classification and regression by randomForest," *R news*, vol. 2, no. 3, pp. 18–22, 2002.

[27] A. J. Smola and B. Schölkopf, "A tutorial on support vector regression," *Statistics and computing*, vol. 14, no. 3, pp. 199–222, 2004.

[28] A. Karatzoglou, A. Smola, and K. Hornik, *The kernlab package*, 2007, URL: https://cran.r-project.org/web/packages/kernlab/kernlab.pdf [accessed 2017-05-09].

[29] D. C. Liu and J. Nocedal, "On the limited memory BFGS method for large scale optimization," *Mathematical programming*, vol. 45, no. 1-3, pp. 503–528, 1989.

[30] B. Ripley and W. Venables, *Package 'nnet'*, 2016, URL: https://cran.r-project.org/web/packages/nnet/nnet.pdf [accessed 2017-05-09].

Template Based Automatic Generation of DRC and LVS Runsets

Elena V. Ravve
Software Engineering Department
Ort Braude College
Karmiel, Israel
Email: cselena@braude.ac.il

***Abstract*—In this paper, we make the first step toward automatic design, implementation and verification of software products. The problem strongly depends upon the specification of the product. Our special case under consideration is writing of Design Rule Checker and Layout Versus Schematic runsets for verification of layouts of electronic devices. Design Rule Checker is a program that guarantees that the chip may be manufactured as a set of polygons of different chemical materials. Layout Versus Schematic comparison determines one-to-one equivalency between a circuit schematic and its layout. We propose a method to compose design rule manuscript (specification of the runsets) in the way that totally automatizes design, implementation and verification steps of the runsets development as well as significantly improves their maintenance. We plan to extend our methodology to other special cases of software products.**

Keywords*–*Design Rule Manuscript; Design Rule Checker Runset; Layout versus Schematic Runset; Test Cases; Templates; Automatic Generation.

I. INTRODUCTION

This paper presents an extended and improved version of [1], where we introduced the general framework for automatic generation of DRC and LVS runsets.

The main steps of software development are: specification, design, implementation, verification and maintenance. As a rule, specification is written as a free-style document allowing different interpretations. As the same story about Sherlock Holmes is differently interpreted in different movies according to the fantasy of the producer, the same specification may be differently implemented by different programmers, see Fig. 1. The dream of fully automated software design and implementation is hardly feasible. In theory, due the Kleene's Theorem, cf. [2]: if the specification is formulated as a regular expression then its implementation is *automatically* given by the corresponding finite automaton. More results about characterization of complexity classes by the type of logic, needed in order to express the languages in them, may be found in [3]. However, the automated code generation is hardly doable. In this paper, we try to make a step in the direction.

In this contribution, we propose a systematic approach to automated code generation of DRC and LVS runsets. Design Rule Checking (DRC) and Layout Versus Schematic (LVS) runsets are programs, written manually like any program in the corresponding (as a rule special purpose) language. The runsets are aimed to check that the given chip may be successfully manufactured in a foundry. In our research, we closely cooperated with R&D team of TowerJazz foundry [1].

Figure 1. Multiple interpretations of texts

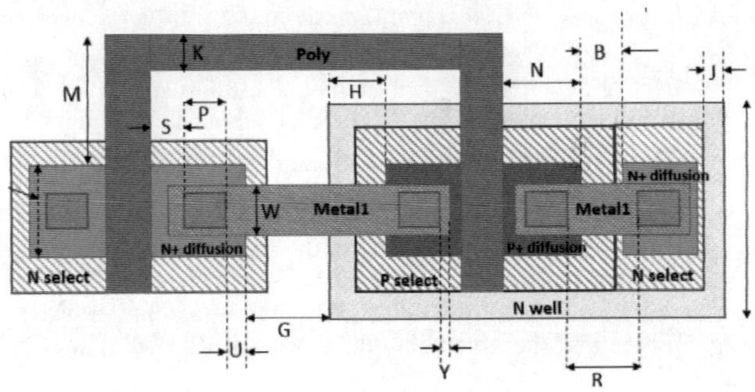

Figure 2. Layout of an inverter

The design of modern electronic devices is presented inter alia by its layout. Typical layout consists of billions of polygons for different chemical layers. For each such a layer, there exist dozens of design rules (DRs), which define how the polygons must be drowning. An example of layout of an inverter and the corresponding DRs is shown in Fig. 2 [2]. Any semiconductor manufacturing process/technology contains a

[1]TowerJazz, the global specialty foundry leader, specializes in manufacturing analog integrated circuits for more than 300 customers worldwide in growing markets such as automotive, medical, industrial, consumer and aerospace and defense, among others; see http://www.towerjazz.com/overview.html, last visited 26.02.2017

[2]The picture is taken from http://www.vlsi-expert.com/2014/12/design-rule-check.html; last visited 25.02.2017

Figure 3. May my design be manufactured?

Figure 4. Verification tools, sent from the manufacturer

set of physical DRs for geometrical configuration of available layers, wiring, placement and so on.

DRs are series of quantitative limitations, provided by semiconductor manufacturers, which enable the designer of an electronic device to verify the possibility of its production. DRs have become increasingly more complex with each subsequent generation of semiconductor process. Every chip, which is expected to be manufactured in the given technology, must satisfy the limitations of the DRs, see Fig. 3. Design rule checking runsets are provided by the manufacturer in order to guarantee that the given chip does not give the DR violations, see Fig. 4.

The document that contains all these rules: Design Rule Manuscript (DRM) is the specification of the runsets. DRM includes dozens of tables for each layer with free style description of the limitations. The fact leads to various problems, starting from inconsistency in the understanding of the meaning of the rules and going on to lots of bugs in coding of the rules in DRC as well as poority of test cases in verification of the DRC runsets. DRM is changing and enriching all the time. Moreover, as a rule, one DRM has different derivatives for special conditions of the manufacturing. The derivatives may be changed independently upon the main DRM that makes the maintenance of the runsets very intricate, see Fig. 5.

On the other hand, in fact, usually almost all the DRs may be divided into a relatively small set of categories and subcategories, such as width, space/distance, enclosure, extension, coverage, etc; see Fig. 6 [3]. Unfortunately, DRM is still not a regular expression, which would guarantee its automatic

[3]The picture is taken from http://www.vlsi-expert.com/2014/12/design-rule-check.html; last visited 25.02.2017

Figure 5. Derivatives of DRMs and runsets

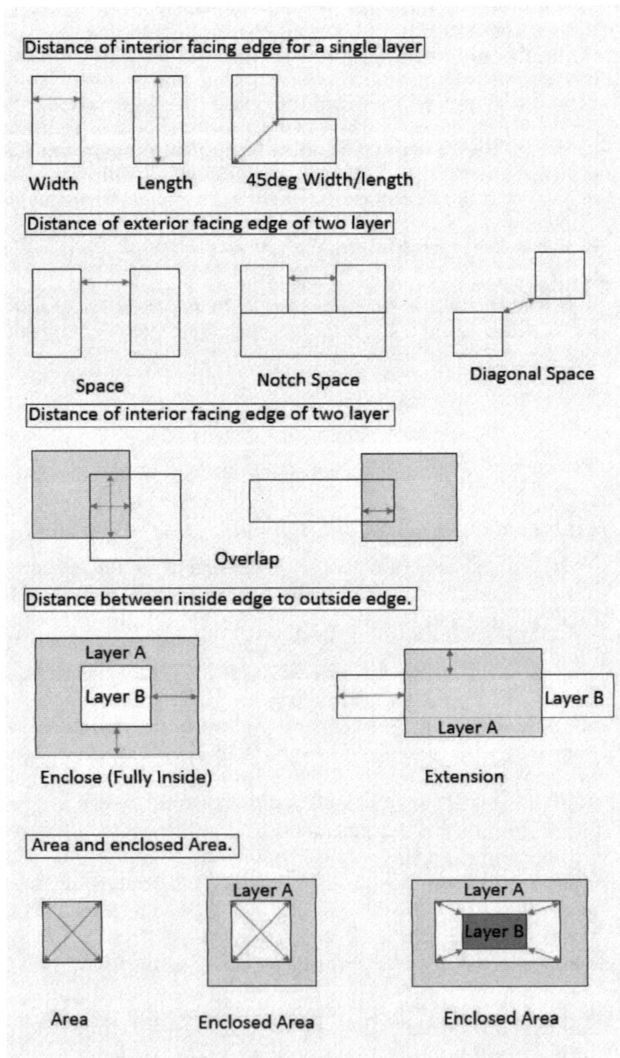

Figure 6. The main categories of geometrical restrictions

implementation according to Kleene's Theorem, but it is more formally formulated than a typical specification of a software product.

In this paper, we use these categories in order to derive a set of patterns. These patterns are the basis of an environment that allows the integrator, who writes the DRM, to use the pre-defined patterns in order to compose the DRM rather than to write it. DRC runset is then *fully automatically* generated, based on the instantiations of the patterns in the DRM.

DRC runsets are provided in order to guarantee that the given chip does not give the design rule violations. The correctness and completeness of the DRC runsets are verified using test cases, which contain shapes of different chemical layers, representing various failing and passing conditions for each rule of the technology. We aware that we would need formal verification tools in order to prove that a runset is correct and complete for all possible configurations. In this paper, we are dealing rather with testing of runsets.

Creation, modification and maintenance of the complete set of test cases is complicated and time consuming process that should be automatized. Now, we enrich the derived set of patterns, used for DRC runset generation, by the option to create a set of test cases, which corresponds to the pass condition or to failures of the DRs. When the option of failures or passing is chosen, the particular type of the failure or of the passing is defined as well as the form of the report. In addition, particular subsets of the test cases, generated by the given pattern, may be chosen by the user, etc.

The set of the varied parameters for the test cases generator may be extended upon request. When all parameters are defined, the set of test cases would be again created *automatically*.

The complete set of the parametrized patterns may be (but not necessary) organized as a library. For any design rule for a given technology, one chooses the relevant parametrized pattern or set of patterns, provides the specific values of the required parameters, and puts the obtained instances into the set of test cases, which corresponds to the technology. The instantiation and (or) modification process may be automated as well. Using this method, the complete set of test cases for the full set of DRs for the given technology may be created and easily maintained and (or) modified.

Any semiconductor manufacturing process allows a finite set of legal devices, supported and recognizable in the process. Layout versus schematic (LVS) comparison runsets determine one-to-one equivalency between an integrated circuit schematic and an integrated circuit layout. The correctness and completeness of the LVS runsets are verified using test cases, which contain shapes (with connectivity) representing failing and passing conditions for each legal device of the technology.

In this paper, we briefly explain how our general approach may be extended to the case of automatic generation of LVS runsets and sets of test cases in order to verify them. The proposed innovation is based on the fact that again the set of legal devices for any process or technology may be divided into final set of technology independent categories and subcategories such that transistors, capacitors, resistors, diodes and so on.

The environment that partially implements the approach is provided. We restricted ourselves to the case of automatic generation of a DRM and a DRC runset, which define and verify limitations, related to width of different layers, as well as the automatic generation of the corresponding set of test cases. The complete tool would produce automatically the DRM, the DRC/LVS runsets and the testcases to test them in a uniform way for all layers and legal devices.

It means that for DRC/LVS runsets, we propose a method to compose DRM (specification of the runsets) in the way that fully eliminates design, implementation and verification steps of the runsets development as well as significantly improves their maintenance. The benefits of the presented invention are:

- Total elimination of the design, implementation and verification steps of the runsets development;
- Common methodological basis for different processes, technologies and verification tools;
- Formal approach to DRM composition that allows precise and consistent formulation of physical design rules and description of legal devices for different processes, technologies and verification tools;
- Human independent accumulation of knowledge and its application;
- Significant reduction of human factor and manual writing;
- Total elimination of manual coding and re-use of patterns;
- Better quality and confidence level of the delivered DRM, DRC/LVS runsets and test cases;
- Significant reduction of time and effort to implement DRM, DRC/LVS runsets and test cases;
- Full coverage of all physical design rules and legal devices and the corresponding test cases;
- Effective, consistent and safe way to change, update and maintain DRM and the corresponding DRC/LVS runsets as well as test cases for all verification tools;
- Detection and correction of mistakes and bug at earliest stages of the flow;
- Effective, consistent and safe way of bug fixes;
- Comfortable GUI.

The paper is structured in the following way. In Section II, we consider the previous results in the field under investigation. Section III is central in our paper and describes our general approach to solve the problem. In Section IV, we describe in great detail a particular implementation of our general approach for creation of a DRC runset for verification of width related DRs. In Section V, we provide the implementation details. Method of automatic generation of test cases for verifying DRC/LVS runsets, using process independent predefined generic set of parametrized patterns is described in Section VI. Section VII summarizes the paper.

II. Review of Previous Works

Various attempts to improve the process of creation of DRC and LVS runsets have long history. They start at least from 90th, cf. [4], where a process flow representation was proposed in order to create a single, unified wafer processing representation, and to facilitate the integration of design and manufacturing. Even before, in early 80th, hardware assisted

DRC was considered in [5], [6], [7], but quickly returned back to software based solutions, cf. [8]. There exist a lot of patents, which attack the same problem. We provide here the description of the most relevant patents taking almost verbatim.

In [9], a method for generating test patterns for testing digital electronic circuits, is defined. It fully specifies some primary inputs, while other primary inputs are specified in accordance with selected series of codes. The test pattern template is then repeatedly converted into a stimulus pattern, using different integers in the selected series of codes, and fault simulation is performed on a circuit under test using each stimulus pattern. A stimulus pattern is then saved for subsequent testing of the circuit under test whenever fault simulation using that stimulus pattern shows that fault coverage has increased.

Another close approach was proposed in [10], which considers automatic generation of DRC runsets, using templates per verification tools. The main idea of the invention is that instead of a user creating runsets in a language of a specific verification tool (also called "native language"), the user expresses the DRC rules in a high level programming language (also called "meta language") that is independent of the native language. The meta language includes, in addition to normal constructs of the high level programming language, a set of keywords that identify DRC rules from an abstract viewpoint, unrelated to any native language.

In [11], an approach to deal with programming language, such as C, C++, Perl or Tcl was proposed. In addition, DRC templates of the type described herein capture the expertise of the template author for use by numerous novice users who do not need to learn the native language of a verification tool.

In our approach, we eliminate the need to use any (either experienced or novice) user/programmer in order to write the DRC/LVS runsets. In order to reach the target, we propose to force the DRM composer (who is assumed to remain in the game in any case) to instantiate the relevant pre-defined generic patterns rather than to write the DRM as a free-style document. When these patterns are instantiated and the relevant information is extracted and stored in the suitable way, we use the patterns for DRC runsets generation and similar (new proposed) patterns for LVS runsets generation for any particular verification tool.

In [12], use of patterns for improving design checking was proposed but in another context. Moreover, one aspect of the present invention includes a method for generating functional testcases for multiple boolean algorithms from a single generic testcase template. The method includes the preliminary step of creating a generic testcase template containing user-entered mask levels shapes and grouping the shapes within each mask level of the template. Next, testcase generation code comprising mask build language is developed to copy and rename the mask levels from the template into the desired input levels necessary to test a mask build operation. Finally, testcase generation code is executed to generate a testcase. The testcase generation code can be easily modified as necessary to change the mask levels. Additionally, shape interactions for new mask level builds can be added into the generic testcase template, allowing the patterns to be reused to generate additional testcases, see also [13].

A more general approach to use patterns was proposed in [14]. During the design of semiconductor products which incorporates a user specification and an application set, the application set being a partially manufactured semiconductor platform and its resources, a template engine is disclosed which uses a simplified computer language having a character whereby data used in commands identified by the character need only be input once, either by a user or by files, and that data, after it has been verified to be correct, is automatically allocated to one or more templates used to generate shells for the specification of a final semiconductor product. Data must be correct and compatible with other data before it can be used within the template engine and the generated shells; indeed the template engine cooperates with a plurality of rules and directives to verify the correctness of the data. The template engine may generate one or more of the following shells: an RTL shell, a documentation shell, a timing analysis shell, a synthesis shell, a manufacturing test shell, and/or a floorplan shell.

In [15], an automatic LVS rule file generation apparatus, which includes a definition file generating unit and a rule file generating unit, was proposed. The definition file generating unit generates definition files used for a layout verification based on first data and templates that are used for the layout verification in a layout design of a semiconductor apparatus. The rule file generating unit automatically generates a LVS rule file based on the definition rule files. The templates includes first parameters indicating three-dimensional structures of the semiconductor apparatus. The definition files includes second data with respect to the first parameters. However, unlike our approach, a template for an automatic LVS rule file generation is used for generating a LVS rule file that indicates a rule for a layout verification of a layout design.

In [16], a method for comprehensively verifying design rule checking runsets was proposed. It seems to be the most relevant patent to our test cases generation approach. The patent describes a system and method for automatically creating testcases for design rule checking, which comprises first creating a table with a design rule number, a description, and the values from a design rule manual. Next, any design specific options are derived that affect the flow of the design rule checking, including back end of the line stack options. Then, the design rule values and any design specific options are extracted into testcases. Next, the testcases are organized such that there is one library with a plurality of root cells, further comprising one root cell for checking all rules pertaining to the front end of the line, and another root cell for checking design specific options including back end of the line stack options. Finally, the DRC runset is run against the testcases to determine if the DRC runset provides for design rule checking. However, while the patent deals with the general flow of testcase creation for a particular technology, we propose a general method for instantiations of technology independent generic patterns.

In [17], a system and method for automatically creating testcases for design rule checking was proposed. The method first creates a table with a design rule number, a description, and the values from a design rule manual. The design rule values and any design specific options are extracted into testcases. Finally, the DRC runset is run against the testcases to determine if the DRC runset provides for design rule checking. Other methods for verifying design rule checking were proposed in particular in [18] and [19].

One more techniques for verifying error detection of a design rule checking runset was introduced in [19]. Another method for verifying design rule checking software was proposed in [18]. One more technique for verifying error detection of a design rule checking runset was introduced in [19]. However, all the mentioned methods and approaches do not reach our level of generality. Moreover, they do not use sets of pre-defined patterns in the consistent way.

III. A Systematic Approach to Automatic Generation of DRC and LVS Runsets and the Corresponding Test Cases

A set of Design Rules (DRs) specifies certain geometric and connectivity restrictions to ensure sufficient margins to account for variability in semiconductor manufacturing processes. DRC is a major step during physical verification signoff on the design. Each process allows a finite list of legal devices, which may be used and recognizable in the process. LVS comparison runsets determine one-to-one equivalence between an integrated circuit schematic and an integrated circuit layout. DRM may contain hundreds of physical design rules and definitions of dozens of legal devices.

Like each physical DR must be implemented in DRC runsets, each legal device must be recognized by LVS runsets. Wafer foundry must provide customers with DRC and LVS runsets, implemented in all required verification tools and languages. Creation, modification and maintenance of the complete set of DRC and LVS runsets is a complicated and time consuming process that should be automatized.

The proposed approach is based on the fact that the set of physical design rules for any process or technology usually may be divided into a final set of technology independent categories such that width, space, enclosure and so on. Moreover, the set of legal devices for any process or technology may be divided into a final set of technology independent categories such that transistors, capacitors, resistors, diodes and so on.

In our methodology, we propose to create one set of parametrized patterns for DRC purposes, such that one pattern (or rather sub-set of patterns) corresponds to a DRC category. In addition, we propose to create another set of parametrized patterns for LVS purposes, such that one pattern (or rather sub-set of patterns) corresponds to a LVS category. The parameters of the patterns may contain in particular (but not limited to): the involved layout layers, specific design values, connectivity, additional constrains, etc. The set of parameters may be enriched upon request. While the earlier proposed methods involve the patterns in pretty late stages of the runsets generation, we propose to force the DRM composer (integrator) to fulfill the templates, defined by the patterns, (in any relevant way, for example, using GUI) instead of free-style writing of the document. It means that the templates are involved in the first steps of the design rules' definition but not their implementation.

Our scenario of the composition of DRM is as follows: For any design rule or legal device for a given technology,

- Integrator chooses the relevant parametrized pattern or set of patterns;
- Integrator provides the specific values of the required parameters or (preferably) chooses them from a choice list.
- The obtained information is transformed and stored as a data structure. The information will be used then by different automatic tools for different purposes, such that automatic generation of DRM itself as well as automatic generation of DRC and LVS runsets in particular verification tools and so on.
- All devices of the process are put in the list of legal devices with their description in DRM.

In addition, any verification tool uses different commands, key words and options for features. When free style is used for DRM writing, different interpretations and further implementations of sentences are allowed that may lead to unexpected results in runs of DRC/LVS runsets. Moreover, when different formulations are used for definitions of derived layers as well as special options, hardly detectable effects in DRC/LVS runsets may be produced.

In order to overcome the obstacle, the following flow is proposed.

- **Specification:** First, we start from precise definitions of all derived layers or options, which are expected to be used in physical design rules or descriptions of legal devices. The step is made once. The definitions lead to a final fixed set of key words and/or notations, which are allowed in physical DRs or descriptions of legal devices. The set might slightly vary for different processes but it is expected to be pretty stable. In extreme cases, the set may be extended after profound analysis and justification.
    - The set may contain, for example, entries for definition of such notions as $GATE$, $HOT\ NWELL$, $NTAP$, $BUTTED\ DIFFUSION$ and so on.
    - In addition, the set may contain more information, extracted from the technology file, such that the names and purposes of layout layers, value of grid and so on.
    - The set may be divided into sub-sets, such that only values from a particular sub-set are allowed in certain fields of certain templates.
    - Moreover, the set may contain key words to choose between minimal, maximal, exact options for the values and so on.
- **Exploitation:** When the specification is fixed and stored as the relevant data structure, the DRM composer may pass to the stage of filling the fields in the pre-defined set of templates for physical design rules or descriptions of legal devices.
    - Any field that is aimed to contain a value from the (sub-)set of key words, either is checked on-the-fly for its correctness or is presented as a choice list.
    - Only fields for the numerical values (for example, the particular value of the width) will not be so.
    - Moreover, many other checking procedures may be involved at this step. For example,

check precision on the given numeric values against grid, etc.

- The precise information, obtained as the result of the filling of the templates is stored as a relevant data structure and will be automatically exploit for particular patterns for further generation of DRM as well as DRC and LVS runsets, implemented in particular languages or tools.
- Moreover, the information will be used also for the automatic generation of the corresponding test cases for the DRC and LVS runsets.

In our particular application case, we have managed to enumerate and name for all possible specification all allowed / possible circumstances.

IV. From Rule Definitions to DRM and DRC: Proof of Concept

A. Cooperation with TowerJazz foundry

In order to demonstrate how our general approach may work, we cooperated with the corresponding specialists of TowerJazz foundry. We had a lot of meetings with the target audience of our tool: the integrators. We wanted to understand what are the main difficulties of the task.

After analyzing and summing these meetings, we realized that the Achilles heel of the traditionally used practice is exactly the entangled manner of the design rule writing.

Example 1 (Device and voltage specific rules): Assume that we consider nMOS transistors and the gate layer with 3.3V voltage. In this case, we approve one particular value of its minimum width. Unlikely, if we use pMOS transistors for the same gate layer with 5V voltage then we approve an absolutely different value of the minimum width.

Example 2 (Area depending rules): TowerJazz uses two layers in order to define thick gate oxide 5V for mask generation and device recognition. **AREA2** defines area with thick oxide either 3.3V. **AREA6** marks thick oxide as 5V for DRC, LVS and MDP purposes.

Now, we consider a more complicated example.

Example 3 (Wide metal rules): We consider only a **M2**-wide rule; the corresponding rules for other wide metals **MI.W.2** for I=3,.,6 are formulated similarly. **M2.W.2** -wide rule is formulated as follows:

> Minimal width of M2 line, connected to a *wide* M2 is approved to be of a certain value.

In order to better understand the above formulation, we look at the rule's layout in Fig. 7 and especially at the red dotted area. Now, we descry that layer M2 is connected to a so-called *wide* M2. On the other hand, the so-called *narrow* metal, according to other DRs, is approved to be minimum of another value!!! Otherwise, if it is smaller, our runset must report the violation.

The metal is *wide* if it dimensions are equal or bigger then 35um. Unfortunately, the definition does not appear at all in the original formulation in the rule and it is expected to be *known* from the *common knowledge* of the integrators' team.

In this case, these determinative details are hidden in the original formulation of the rule and must be extracted from other sources of knowledge if any.

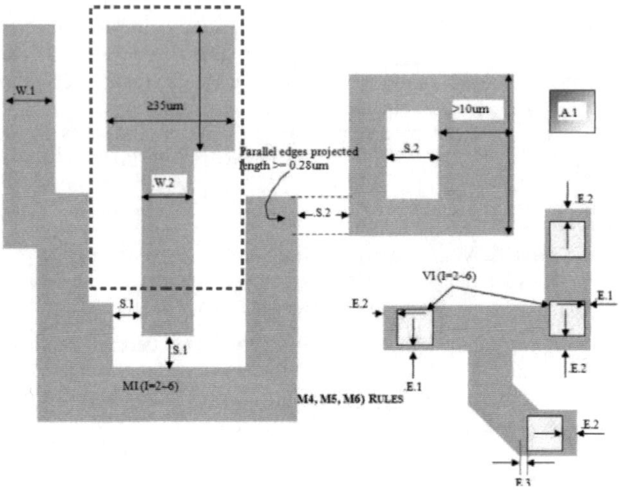

Figure 7. **M2.W.2** design rule

More generally, adding or even changing a rule without considering the previously written rules or even the way, how they were exactly formulated, may cause inconsistency in the DRM as well as the derived runsets. Moreover, the traditionally used approach is patching of a new sentence into the old design rule wording. The patch describes the new feature, without changing all the rule from scratch. In the long run, we get hardly understandable and interpretable patched up statements.

In order to illustrate how the obstacle may be overcome using our approach, we decided to start with DRC runsets. More precisely, teamwise with the TowerJazz's experts, we decided to concentrate our limited research resource on evaluation of all width rules of a particular existing DRM of the foundry.

First, we collected all the width rules for all the corresponding layers. Typically, every design rule consists of:

- the rule number;
- the rule parameter such as width, space, overlap, etc.;
- the layer name, followed by the description of the rule;
- the last thing is the minimal (fixed, recommended, etc) allowed size.

In addition, a rule may be exclusive for specific voltages, devices, combinations of layers or purposes and so on, see Examples 1, 2 and 3.

Then, we transformed every rule to a set of short expressions. We proved that an integrator, who writes DRM, may compose any width rule as detailed as she/he wants by shuffling these expressions without having to add anything manually.

The main problem in the maintenance of DRMs and the corresponding runsets is that, as a rule, the well defined, consistent and well supported source of the knowledge does not exist at all and it is rather replaced by some common local folklore, transferred verbally in the integrators' community. Our approach starts from precise definitions of all such shortcuts, which are reviewed by the corresponding experts and supported in a uniform way.

B. Evaluation of width related rules

With the help of the TowerJazz's experts, we analyzed every width rule and divided it into its components in one long table. In this table, we took in account what is the purpose of each one of the rules as well as what are the corresponding constraints. Altogether, we concluded that we may map all the additions to the width DRs into six main categories:

1) Rules for special layers like marking layers;
2) Rules for layer under other layers;
3) Device dependent rules;
4) Voltage dependent rules;
5) Area despondent rules, see Example 2;
6) Purpose dependent rules.

In order to translate all these short sentences into one rule, we got help from Mentor Graphics experts with profound knowledge how *Calibre* works.

For example, the simplest width related rule will be coded as follows:

```
XP.W.1 {
    @XP.W.1: XP width, min. 0.XX (XP.W.1)
    internal XP< 0.8 region singular abut> 0 < 90
}
```

Now, let us code the rule of Example 3 for M2:

> Minimal width of M2 line, connected to a *wide* M2 is approved to be of a certain value.

in *Calibre*. In our particular case, first of all, we must distinguish between *wide* and *narrow* pieces of metal. To do so, we define the following **M2NRW** shortcut for *narrow* pieces of metal, which actually is coded in *Calibre* as:

```
M2NRW = ((M2MS or (M2slits interact M2MS))
interact M2WIDE) not M2WIDE.
```

Now, we continue to code the rule according to the *Calibre* syntax:

- The first thing, to be written in the runset file, is the rule name, followed by {. In our specific example, it should be:
  M2.W.2 {
  In this way, we know where this rule begins.
- Next, usually, we want to write comments for this rule to make it easier maintained. We start the comment with sign @. That leads us to the next line in the runset:
  @M2.W.2: Width of Narrow Metal, Connecting to Wide Metal min. **0.YY** (M2.W.2)
- Now we put the body of the rule for constraints, which are interpreted as violations for this specific layer:
  ```
  X2=not outside edge M2NRW M2WIDE
  EX2=expand edge X2 by 0.01
  area EX2 < 0.02
  ```
- Sign } finishes the composition of the rule, so that we determine where it ends.

As the result of our coding, we receive the following automatically generated portion of the runset:

```
M2.W.2 {
    @M2.W.2: Width of Narrow Metal, Connecting to
    Wide Metal min. 1 ( M2.W.2 ).
    X2=not outside edge M2NRW M2WIDE
    EX2=expand edge X2 by 0.01
    area EX2 < 0.02
}
```

The considered example represents a single rule of dozens of rules, while each such a rule has dozens of layers. Eventually, each rule must be translated into DRC statements. In this section, we have shown how the coding may be automatized, for two particular rules.

V. Implementation Details

In this section, we show in great detail, how our general approach is implemented in a particular toy-tool. We start from a complete snapshot of the GUI, see Fig. 8; then, we explain each step.

A. Let us start

As usual, the user (integrator) is expected to provide her/his password, when activating the tool, see Fig. 8 step 1 and Fig. 9.

B. What about the process?

Using the tool, the user may add a new process, remove an existing process or use a stored process, see Fig. 8 step 2 and Fig. 9.

C. Which layer?

When the process is chosen, see Fig. 8 step 3 and Fig. 9, the user gets the list of all available layers, see Fig. 10. The techfile of the chosen process is used in order to access the list of the available layers.

D. Composing a rule

When the layer is chosen, see Fig. 10, the user gets the list of all available categories of the rule. By double-clicking on the desired category, the user gets all the pre-defined subcategories, available in order to compose the new rule, see Fig. 8 step 4 and Fig. 11. The sub-categories include in our particular case (but not limited in the general case to):

- the list of all layers from the techfile as well as special layers, like marking layers; see Fig. 12;
- the list of purposes and recommended options; see Fig. 13;
- the list of not relevant cases and available devices; see Fig. 14;
- the list of voltages. see Fig. 15.

The user may choose any allowed combination of the sub-categories for the new rule, see Fig. 8 step 5. If some combination of the sub-categories is not allowed then the fact is checked automatically by the tool and the user is updated accordingly.

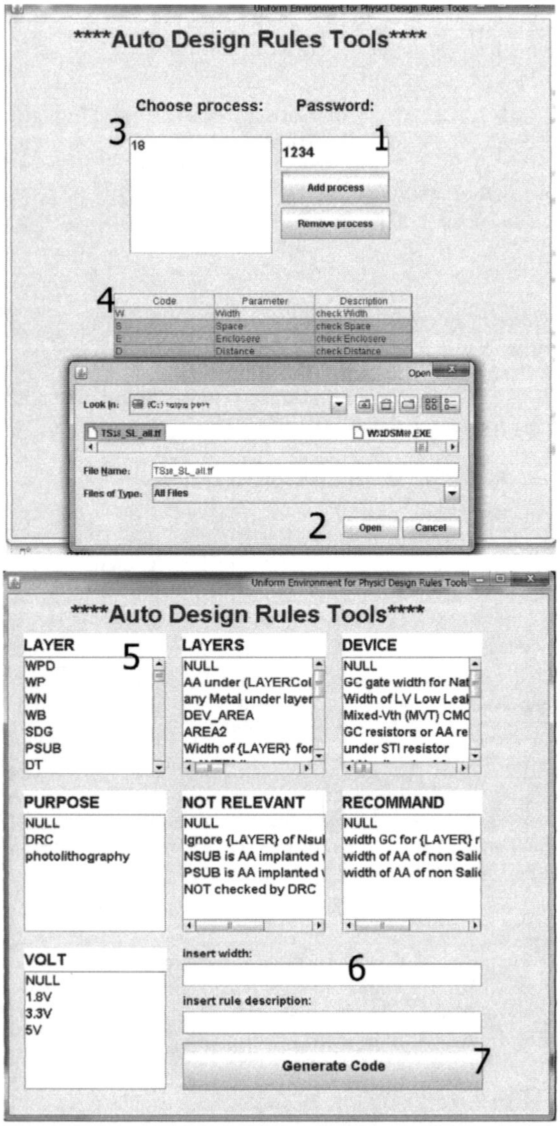

Figure 8. Complete snapshot of the GUI

Now, the user should insert the value of the rule: width in our particular case, as well as a free style comment, see Fig. 8 step 6 and Fig. 15. These are the only values, which are inserted and not chosen from pre-defined options. Then, the corresponding DR is put to its place in the DRM.

E. Generating the code of the rule

It remains to choose the corresponding tool: Calibre in our example [4], see Fig. 8 step 7 and Fig. 16. The corresponding code is generated automatically by the tool; see Fig. 16.

[4]Other languages or other tests may be used in the same way.

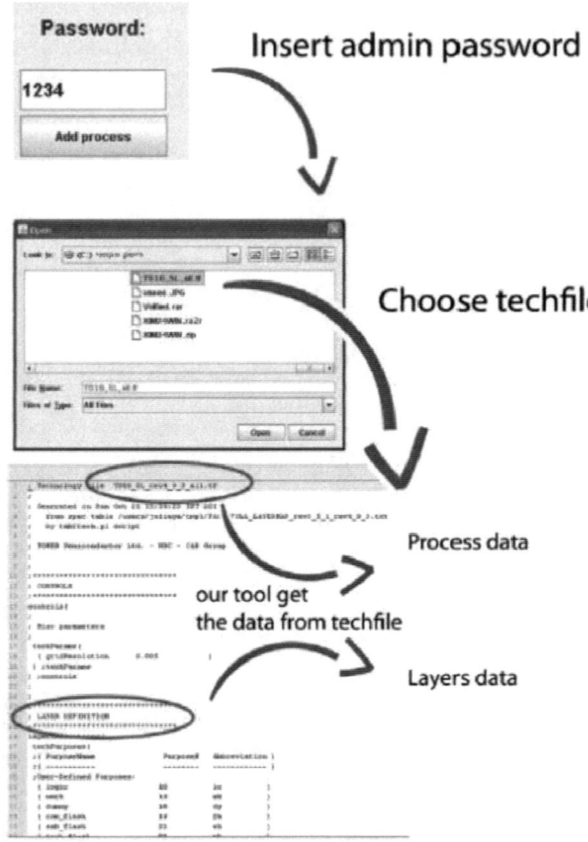

Figure 9. Initiation of the tool

F. Testing the generated code of the rule

In order to test the generated code, we composed a simplest layout with the corresponding DRC violation, see Fig. 17. The violation was found and reported by the automatically generated runset (see Fig. 18).

VI. METHOD OF AUTOMATIC GENERATION OF TEST CASES FOR VERIFYING DRC/LVS RUNSETS, USING PROCESS INDEPENDENT PRE-DEFINED GENERIC SET OF PARAMETRIZED TEMPLATES

In general, dozens of test cases per a design rule should be provided in order to guarantee correctness and completeness of all DRC runsets implemented in all tools and all languages. Moreover, different test cases should be created for failing and passing conditions per each design rule. In addition, all the test cases must be maintained and modified according to any relevant change in DR. As for now, both code of DRC runsets and the corresponding test cases are manually created and maintained. All the above justifies that automated methodology and system should be proposed for these tasks.

We propose a new approach to the automated test cases generation for DRC runsets again based on the fact that there exists a finite fixed set of categories, which may be defined

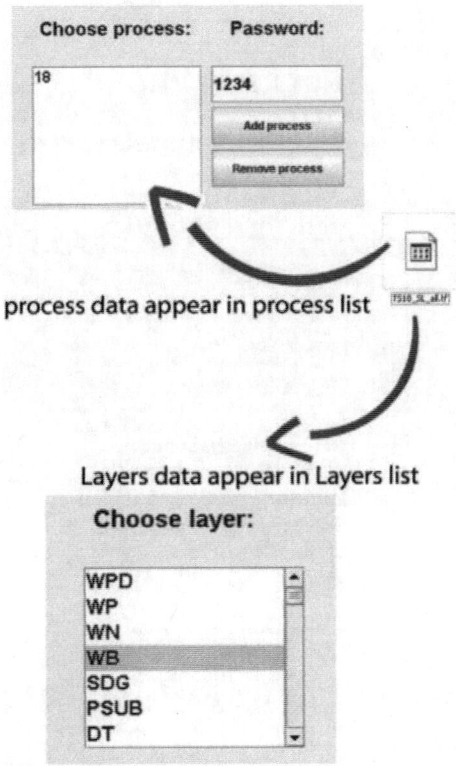

Figure 10. Choosing a layer of the process

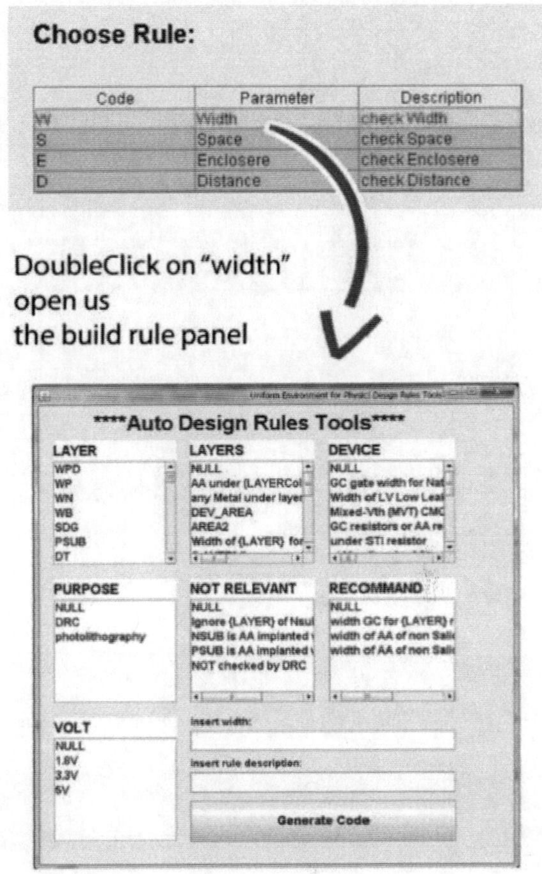

Figure 11. Menus of the DRC generator: choosing (sub)category

at once. The categories cover all (or most) design rules for any given process or technology. The set again contains such categories as width rules, spacing rules, enclosure rules etc. Then, we propose to re-use the parametrized patterns, defined for DRM generator, for each category such that, the pattern may be tuned to the particular testing purposes by assignment of the corresponding parameters.

Figure 19 illustrates the concept. The example shows some part of the technology parameters such as the layout layers and purposes as they are defined in the technology file, different values taken from DRM, as well as parameters, related to the testing purpose such that the failing or passing case and its particular version.

In addition, the corresponding report format may be defined using, for example, error layers and so on. All the parameters (or any part of them) may be assigned either manually or in some automated way. The assignment procedure leads to creation of a particular instance of the template that corresponds to the chosen pattern, testing purpose, etc.

Figure 20 illustrates one of the possible implementation of such instantiation. The particular test case generator was written in SKILL and it is included as an integrated part in the proposed tool.

This approach may be extended to the case of automatically created testcases for LVS checking as well. In fact, the list of legal devices of the process as well as their detailed description is available in DRM. DRM may contain dozens of legal devices such that their final list for the process may be combined from different sub-sets, according to additional options or limitations. LVS runsets are implemented, using different tools and program languages, each one with its own algorithms and particular implementations of checking procedures for different features.

Hundreds of test cases per a legal device should be provided in order to guarantee correctness and completeness of all LVS runsets, implemented in all tools and languages. Moreover, different test cases should be created for failing and passing conditions per each legal device and/or their combination. In addition, all the test cases must be maintained and modified according to any relevant change in DRM.

Our method comprises first of all creating of a data structure (say, a table) with a device identifier, its description (including involved layers and connectivity), and the corresponding values from DRM. The data structure contains all legal devices for the process. Any design specific options or limitations, which affect the recognition process, may be added.

Then, the device descriptions and design specific options are implemented into a set of test cases. The implementation

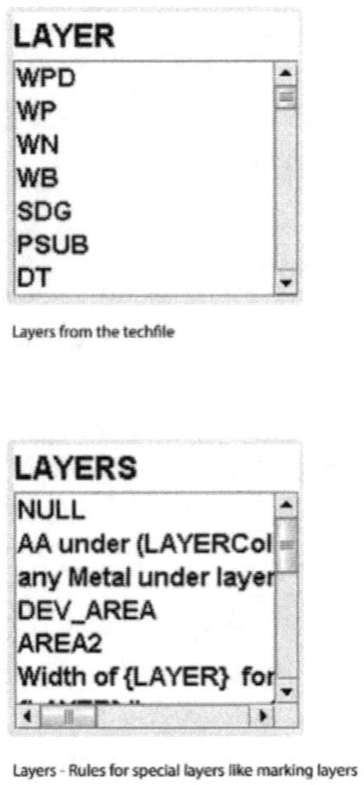

Figure 12. Menus of the DRC generator: choosing additional layers

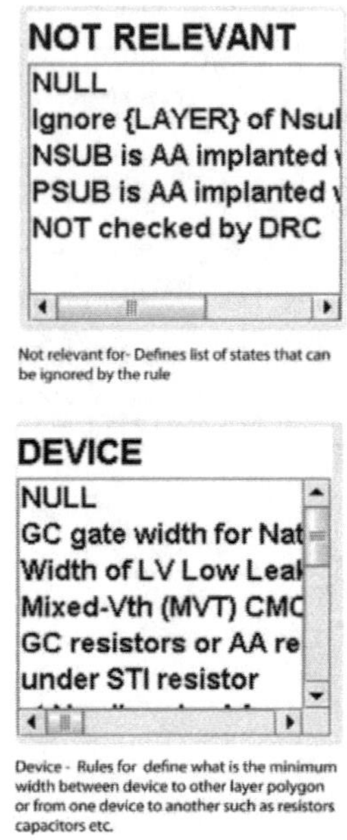

Figure 14. Menus of the DRC generator: choosing device and exception

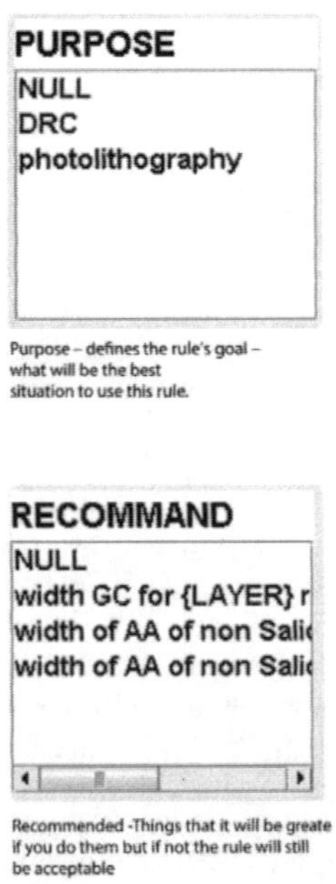

Figure 13. Menus of the DRC generator: choosing purpose and severity

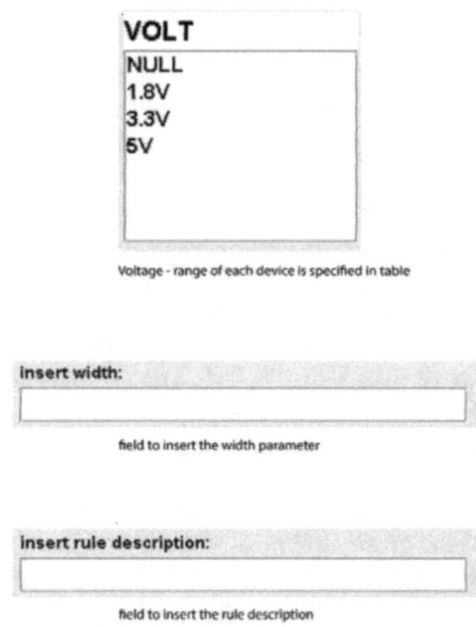

Figure 15. Menus of the DRC generator: choosing voltage and the value of the rule

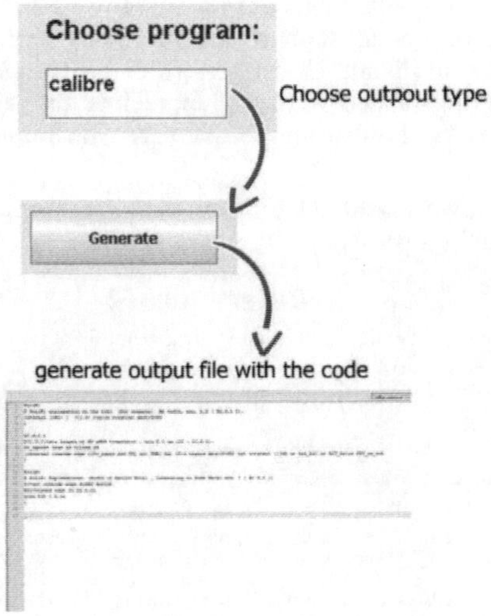

Figure 16. Menu of the DRC generator: generating the code of the rule

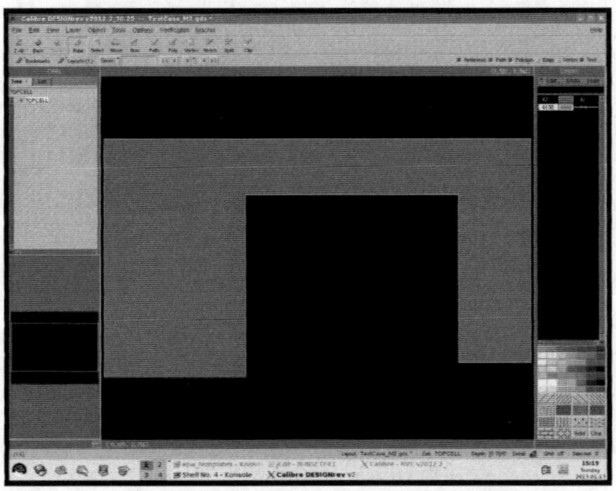

Figure 17. Layout with a DRC violation

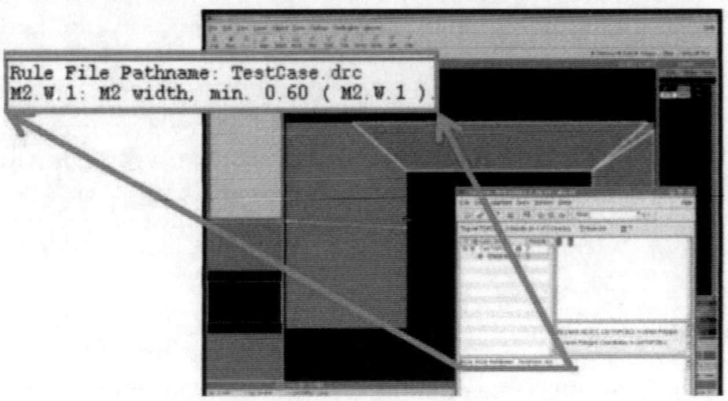

Figure 18. Layout with the reported DRC violation

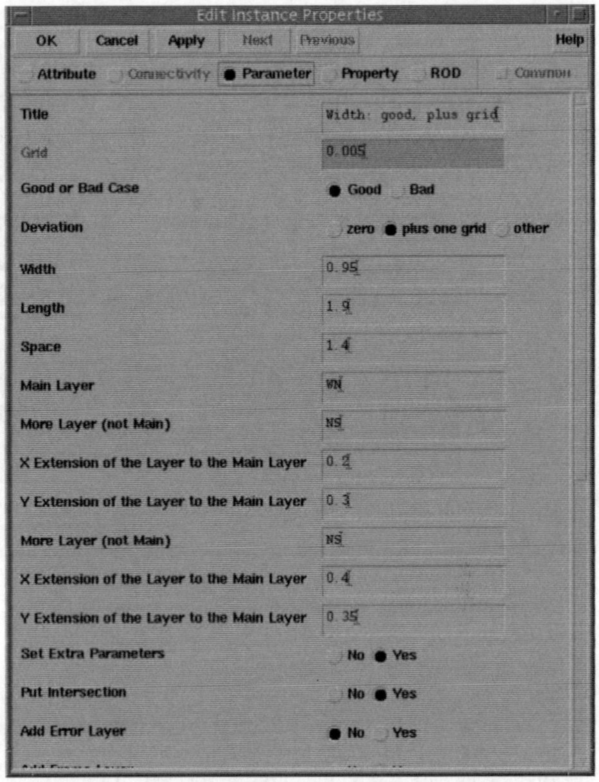

Figure 19. Menu to generate test cases

is expected to be automatic for both failing and passing conditions. Next, the testcases are organized in a data structure (say, a library) that is suitable for the further run of LVS checkers. Finally, the LVS runset is run against the testcases to determine if the LVS runset is correct and complete. The corresponding information about either faced violations or successive result is stored for the further use and reported in the pre-defined way. In addition, the completeness of the LVS runset is verified (either automatically or manually) against the full list of legal devices, in order to guarantee that no device is lost. The LVS test case generator is still not included in the implemented tool.

VII. Conclusion and Outlooks

In this paper, we made the first step toward automatic design, implementation and verification of software. The problem strongly depends upon the specification language. For specification languages, restricted to regular expressions, the problem is solvable due to Kleene's Theorem.

Our approach is based on categorizing properties of the domain and the specifications to a general level and using those as a basis to design a tool and its features to support the domain workflow, and build a basis for automated analysis of the specifications.

Our special case under consideration is writing of DRC and LVS runsets for verification of layouts of electronic devices.

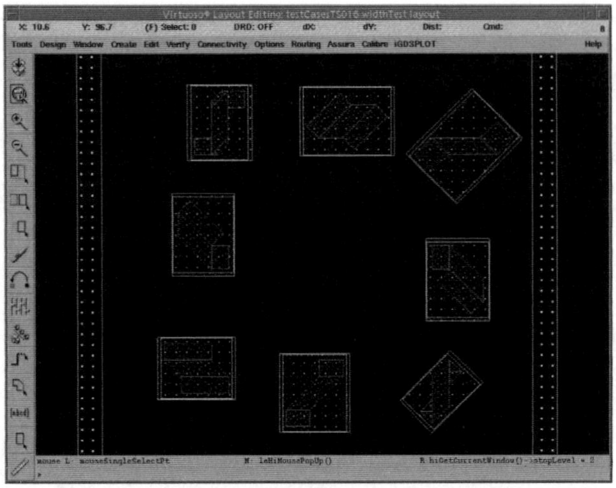

Figure 20. Automatically generated test cases

The verification rules are provided in DRM (specification of the runsets).

We propose a method to compose DRM, which is still not a regular expression, in the way that totally automatizes design, implementation and verification steps of the runsets development as well as significantly improves their maintenance. The proposed general approach is based on a final set of predefined patterns. The particular instantiations of the patterns in the DRM generator are then used for automatic generation of DRC and LVS runsets as well as the corresponding test cases.

The approach is based on the fact that usually almost all design rules may be divided into relatively small set of categories: width, space/distance, enclosure, extension, coverage, etc. Moreover, the set of legal devices for any process or technology may be divided into final set of independent categories: transistors, capacitors, resistors, diodes and so on.

The environment that partially implements the approach is provided.

We restricted ourselves to the case of automatic generation of a DRM and a DRC runset, which define and verifies limitations, related to width of different layers, as well as the automatic generation of the corresponding set of test cases. The complete tool would produce automatically the DRM, the DRC/LVS runsets and the testcases to test them in a uniform way for all layers and all legal devices.

The approach may be extended to automatic generation of other runsets, say, antenna runsets and the corresponding test cases. In general, the approach may be applied in a uniform way to all steps of the of masks' generation and verification.

We plan to extend our methodology to other special cases of software products such as, for example, automatic verification and (partial) implementation of specifications of smartphone applications, cf. [20]. We aware that there were proposes many techniques in that area. We plan to compare our approach and their own.

Acknowledgments

We would like to thank T. Estrugo (TowerJazz) for valuable discussions, general support and his many suggestions. We would like to thank U. Krispil (Mentor Graphics) for his technical assistance. We also appreciate the effort of our students M. Ankonina and N. Mazuz, who implemented the tool.

Finally, we would like to thank the referees for their careful reading and constructive suggestions.

REFERENCES

[1] E. Ravve, "Template based automatic generation of runsets," in Proceedings of ICCGI-2016, The Eleventh International Multi - Conference on Computing in the Global Information Technology, November 13-17, 2016, pp. 52–57.

[2] S. Kleene, "Representation of events in nerve nets and finite automata," in Automata Studies, C. Shannon and J. McCarthy, Eds. Princeton: Princeton University Press, 1956, pp. 3–42.

[3] N. Immerman, Descriptive complexity, ser. Graduate texts in computer science. Springer, 1999.

[4] E. Ünver, Implementation of a Design Rule Checker for Silicon Wafer Fabrication, ser. MTL memo. Massachusetts Institute of Technology, Department of Electrical Engineering and Computer Science, 1994.

[5] L. Seiler, A Hardware Assisted Methodology for VLSI Design Rule Checking, ser. MIT/LCS/TR-. Mass. Inst. of Technology, Laboratory for Computer Science, 1985.

[6] T. Blank, M. Stefik, and W. vanCleemput, "A parallel bit map processor architecture for DA algorithms," in Proceedings of the 18th Design Automation Conference, ser. DAC '81. Piscataway, NJ, USA: IEEE Press, 1981, pp. 837–845.

[7] R. M. Lougheed and D. L. McCubbrey, "The Cytocomputer: A practical pipelined image processor," in ISCA, J. Lenfant, B. R. Borgerson, D. E. Atkins, K. B. Irani, D. Kinniment, and H. Aiso, Eds. ACM, 1980, pp. 271–277.

[8] D. Wittenmyer, Offline Design Rule Checking for VLSI Circuits. University of Toledo., 1992.

[9] K. Bowden, "Method for generating test patterns," Apr. 18 2000, uS Patent 6,052,809.

[10] G. Richardson and D. Rigg, "Method and system for automatic generation of DRC rules with just in time definition of derived layers," Aug. 26 2003, US Patent 6,611,946.

[11] D. Shei and J. Cheng, "Configuration management and automated test system ASIC design software," Dec. 30 1997, US Patent 5,703,788.

[12] S. O'Brien, "Methods and systems for performing design checking using a template," Aug. 4 2009, US Patent 7,571,419.

[13] P. Selvam, "Method for generating integrated functional testcases for multiple boolean algorithms from a single generic testcase template," Feb. 24 2009, US Patent 7,496,876.

[14] T. Youngman and J. Nordman, "Language and templates for use in the design of semiconductor products," Oct. 11 2011, US Patent 8,037,448.

[15] K. Okuaki, "Automatic LVS rule file generation apparatus, template for automatic LVS rule file generation, and method for automatic lvs rule file generation," Oct. 6 2005, US Patent App. 11/093,100.

[16] D. Shei and J. Cheng, "Configuration management and automated test system ASIC design software," Dec. 30 1997, US Patent 5,703,788.

[17] J. Crouse, T. Lowe, L. Miao, J. Montstream, N. Vogl, and C. Wyckoff, "Method for comprehensively verifying design rule checking runsets," May 4 2004, US Patent 6,732,338.

[18] W. DeCamp, L. Earl, J. Minahan, J. Montstream, D. Nickel, J. Oler, and R. Williams, "Method for verifying design rule checking software," May 16 2000, US Patent 6,063,132.

[19] J. Lawrence, "Techniques for verifying error detection of a design rule checking runset," Jul. 23 2009, US Patent App. 12/017,524.

[20] K. Korenblat and E. Ravve, "Automatic verification and (partial) implementation of specifications of smartphone applications," in preparation.

A Motivation and Evaluation of Hierarchical Data Structures for Application in Automotive Demand and Capacity Management

Konrad Pawlikowski
Faculty of Business Economics
Bochum University of Applied Sciences
Bochum, Germany
email: konrad.pawlikowski@hs-bochum.de

Daniel Fruhner
Institute IDiAL
Dortmund University of Applied Sciences and Arts
Dortmund, Germany
email: daniel.fruhner@fh-dortmund.de

Katja Klingebiel
Faculty of Business Studies
Dortmund University of Applied Sciences and Arts
Dortmund, Germany
email: katja.klingebiel@fh-dortmund.de

Michael Toth
Faculty of Business Economics
Bochum University of Applied Sciences
Bochum, Germany
email: michael.toth@hs-bochum.de

Axel Wagenitz
Faculty of Business & Social Sciences
Hamburg University of Applied Sciences
Hamburg, Germany
email: axel.wagenitz@haw-hamburg.de

Abstract— **The demand and capacity management (DCM) is an essential component of the automotive supply chain management. Resource requirements in the automotive supply chain result from future or already realized market demands. DCM synchronizes these requirements with capacities and restrictions of the supply chain and production system. Demand uncertainty and volatility are especially challenging for DCM. Product variety and supply chain complexity intensify this problem. Here, an efficient product data management may increase transparency and support the DCM processes effectively. This contribution analyses and evaluates the benefits of an integration of distributed product data into a hierarchical tree structure and its applications in DCM against the background of complexity reduction. Moreover, the underlying optimization algorithms are described. The results of this study prove that a hierarchical integrated information model provides a significantly improved basis for a scenario-based DCM planning process. Data from a German automotive manufacturer (OEM) has served as basis for this evaluation.**

Keywords- product structure; automotive production; demand and capacity management; optimization; complexity; BOM rules.

I. INTRODUCTION

This contribution is an extended version of work published in [1]. The previous work has been extended, e.g., by evaluation of a full product spectrum of an OEM to provide greater insights into the effects of the integration of the distributed product data into a hierarchical tree structure. In addition, an elaborated overview of different types of product structures has been integrated.

To compete in international markets automotive manufacturers, i.e., original equipment manufacturers (OEMs), tend to offer their customers a huge variety of models which can be individualized by several hundred options. These options comprise design elements (i.e., colors), functional components (i.e., climate control system) and nowadays assistance systems (i.e., navigation and driver assistance systems). Furthermore, OEMs constantly update their product range with increasing frequency [2].Though customers have to deal with the rapidly changing variety of models, they tend to expect that their vehicle orders can be re-customized anytime, i.e., changed even shortly before actual production, and that the produced car is rapidly delivered on the formerly planned date [3][4].

In this context, logistics plays an important role. The core competence of a car manufacturer has shifted to product marketing, the coordination of suppliers, assembly of supplied parts, and the distribution of the end product [5]. Nowadays, suppliers do not only produce simple components, but also develop complex modules [6]. They also have to manage product complexity and variety and need to know in time if the OEM revised the production program for a specified model and market. Hence, the effective integrated management of the automotive production and supply chain is critical. The anticipation of the future market demand, the timely derivation of resource and component requirements as well as the integrated and coordinated capacity planning are indispensable prerequisites [7]. Most critical, resource requirements resulting from anticipated or realized market demands need to be synchronized with resource capacities and restrictions of the production and supply chain by an effective demand and capacity management (DCM). DCM processes identify demand- and capacity-asynchronies and implement appropriate countermeasures in a timely manner. DCM acts as an essential interface between market, production and supply chain processes [8][9].

Caused by the increasing number of variants and options the complexity of this process has continually increased over the past decades. A typical car consists of about 3000 to 6000 material items. If different variants and their parts are considered, it results in about 15000 to 20000 items per car (as of 2010) [10]. The planning systems have been extended continuously to manage the resulting complexity. Nevertheless, the relevant DCM data is typically kept in a highly fragmented system landscape. Data fragments are handled by different systems and thus overall transparency is limited.

For example, within DCM processes part demand is typically gradually derived from sales figures in a number of sequential processes taking into account a variety of systems [11][12][13]. These systems consider historical sales data (e.g., car rentals), retailers' annual model requests, companies knowledge about the local customer preferences and on marketing capabilities to influence customer demand [12]. Since automated processes only allow the identification and reporting of formal inconsistencies, additionally a human planner has to review the process. But, due to the increasing variety, it is more and more difficult to review the product information manually. The success of the overall process is highly dependent on the planner's experience.

Even more so, variants are often quite similar and a significant amount of information is redundant. For example, typically several car series of one OEM are based on the same vehicle platform. Additionally, the common-part-strategy supports the installation of identical modules, e.g., navigation systems, in numerous car models of different series [14][15]. If a common part is changed or even not deliverable, this effects several series. These possibly wide-spread bottlenecks are difficult to identify and control in a fragmented system landscape.

As it is easily understood, an integrated information base could reduce the complexity and increase transparency of the DCM processes immensely. The advantage of this integration is the faster and easier access to relevant data and its innermost dependencies, as well as the reduction of redundancies. Therefore, an innovative system's concept ought to integrate all related data from sales to supply chain data into a consistent and integrated information structure. Only this information model may provide the essential basis for a continuous and effective DCM process.

In general, several types of data structure types are offered by literature and practice, which may form the basis to realize such an information model. Especially, graph structures and here tree structures are an intuitively attractive approach because of their proximity to car design principles. In this context, this paper analyses and evaluates the benefits of a hierarchical tree-based data structure for the integration of DCM relevant distributed product data. The evaluation is performed against the background of complexity reduction and transparency increase. In comparison to [1] not only two car series, but a full product spectrum of a German OEM has been analyzed.

In the next section, the state of the art of automotive DCM processes is given. Afterwards promising information structures are presented in section III and the tree structure is chosen for further analysis. In section IV, an introduction to tree based data optimization methods is given, whereas section V analyses the complexity reductions gained by the application of an integrated and optimized information model for the DCM process. A conclusion including a summary and a perspective on future research and development is given in section VI.

II. State of the Art in Automotive DCM Processes

Before product data and information models may be discussed, an illustration of the state of the art in automotive planning processes and the embedded DCM process is necessary.

Today, the typical DCM planning cascade is initiated by the sales department with forecasting and planning of medium-term future market demand [16]. In this step, model volumes (e.g., number of VW Golf Trendline 2.0 TDI.) and option quotas (e.g., ratio of models with LED light or a certain navigation system) for worldwide sales regions are being planned for a horizon of 12 to 24 months. A model is typically defined by a specific series, body type, engine and gear type. The underlying forecast is based on current information about the automotive market (market shares, economic forecasting), but also on current and historical orders [17][18][19]. Furthermore, sales quotas for options are influenced for example by the sales region, technical restrictions, strategic decisions or customer preferences.

In a second step, the production planning integrates these figures with existing order volumes which may already be available for closer time periods. Next, the sales plan is translated into a production program for all sites [17].

The planning complexity of both steps is tremendous due to the variety of products. For example, a typical mid-class series (e.g., VW Golf, BMW 1 Series, Audi A3) offers about 30 to 50 different car models with up to 200 options. This results in several thousand volumes to be planned for one car models in all sales regions over a specific granular time period (e.g., month, week or day depending on planning granularity) and some 10 million related option quotas. To illustrate this complexity an easy example shall be given: Assuming three options are valid for a sound system in 40 different car models (e.g., standard radio system, comfort radio system and full navigation system). In result, for this small planning fragment 216,000 option quotas for assumed 12 months and 150 worldwide sales regions need to be planned.

The compatibility of options for a respective model is described by a highly complex set of technical rules, while the relationship between the fully-configured car order and the corresponding parts is described by the bill of material (BOM) (see Fig. 1). Technical rules define the technical feasibility of customer selectable options and further OEM-internal technical options. These rules equal restrictions and may prohibit or force options for specific models (e.g., no sunroof for convertibles), force specific combinations of options (e.g., LED head light only in combination with LED back lights) or prohibit combinations (e.g., a navigation system rules out all other radios). In addition, sales constraints (e.g. not all options are available for all models or regions) and customer preferences need to be included. So, even the planning of consistent volumes and option quotas is complex in itself and requires the integration of human experience and intuition (cf. [20]).

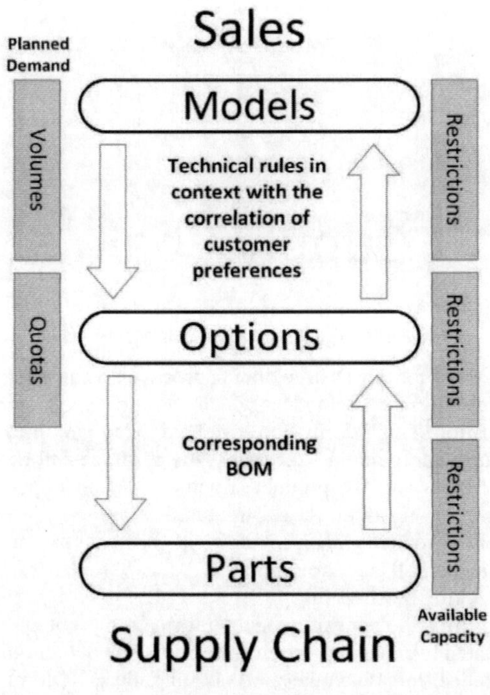

Figure 1. Bridging the gap between demand information and capacity information

The resulting sales plan needs to be balanced with production and supply chain restrictions. Capacity constraints (e.g., the maximum number of leather seat coverings per month) are present on sales level, production level and supply chain level. To balance volumes and resource requirements with constraints and restrictions in order to identify possible bottlenecks, it is necessary to bridge the gap between demand information and capacity information [13][16][11].

If fully specified orders are available, the gap is easily bridged. Fully specified orders allow to derive part demands by BOM explosion; possible bottlenecks can be determined by comparison of capacity restrictions with capacity demands. Nevertheless, because of short order-to-delivery lead times in contrast to partly long supply chain lead times, DCM process have to work on forecasts and plans rather than orders to a great extent. And it is obviously impossible to predict the exact future vehicle orders, as customers can choose from billions of possible configurations for each car type [21][10]. Forecast uncertainty, demand volatility, rapid product changes, as well as changes in the supply chain complicate this task significantly.

Even more so, a huge number of the resulting resource requirements for production or logistics depend not only on single model volumes and quotas for options, but on a particular combination of model, options and sales region (e.g. the BMW 3 series with 143hp, option = "sun roof" is anticipated to be sold 1000 times in the sales region Germany in February 2005). Therefore, some part volumes are harder to predict than others until the exact configuration of the vehicle, i.e., the order, is known. Nevertheless, as replenishment lead times in global supply networks can be long, a certain number of vehicle parts has to be ordered long before customer orders are known (cf. [16]).

In summary, the DCM process is challenging. Because of market dynamics, complexity in car configurations and correlations among models, options, and parts, the planning itself is complex [12]. But even more so, it is also characterized by conflicting goals. Sales departments are forced to react to volatile markets, increased global competitions and changing customer requirements: flexibility and reactivity is requested. Production is interested in a stable production program, which guarantees both high capacity utilization and optimal operating results. Material planning wants to fix part requirements as early as possible to avoid bottlenecks proactively as well as to negotiate the flexibility of suppliers appropriately.

This conflict can be named the dilemma of automotive DCM (cf. [22]). Typically, it is solved by planning cycles of four to six weeks, which are based on numerous workshops and committee meetings between sales, program- and material planning [17] [12] . The consequence of this long planning cycle is insufficient flexibility in reaction to market changes. To counteract this, the program is adjusted manually between program approvals and even after program freeze, i.e., within the so-called frozen period [17]. However, these adjustments cause a lack of program stability and poor transparency on future demand for parts on the supply side. The probability of bottlenecks increases and induces additional internal costs, as well as deterioration of the delivery service to the customer.

To overcome these problems, there are two theoretical approaches for the integration of these sequential planning processes in an effective holistic DCM process.

The first approach focusses on the early inclusion of resource restrictions into the sales and program planning. This requires to trace back restrictions on all levels to the decision variables, i.e., to planned volumes and quotes. As discussed, model volumes and option quotas typically include several million variables. Furthermore, technical rules and BOM rules relate these planning variables amongst each other and to part demands and thus capacity restrictions.

For example, a capacity restriction may limit the installable volume of a specific powerful battery. As a matter of fact, the installation of this battery may depend on several combinations of options, e.g., the battery is only selected if specific but several electronical options are chosen in combination. To derive the resulting limitations on model volumes and option quotas all BOM rules and technical rules that relate directly or indirectly to that battery have to be analyzed. In case of a mid-class model this may amount to a significant proportion of the overall number of rules which amount to about 15,000 technical and 600,000 BOM rules. Even more so, between option quotas and model volumes partially unmanageable correlations exist. These result not only from technical restrictions, but also from product strategy, customer preference, and marketing strategies. A customer preference for the combination of navigation systems and seat heating modules shall be given as an example for such correlations: these two options may be independent from the viewpoint of the customer, but historical data has shown that most customers who chose the navigation system also selected the seat heating; customers who do not select the navigation system rarely choose the seat heating. Consequently, when planning option quotas for navigation systems and seat heating, the high correlation of these two options and the resulting relation to the powerful battery as a part restriction needs to be integrated (based on [23]).

In result, not all restrictions may be deterministically traced back to the decision variables. This is aggravated by ramp-up and run-out processes (continuous change in options, models, etc.), dynamic changes in capacity information, multiple use of parts, commonality strategies and other restrictions that may change daily. The complete derivation of restrictions on planning variables harbors an immense complexity and is not deterministically feasible. Even if such a complete deterministic derivation process would be possible, no planner would be able to comprehend or verify the results. Hence, the early inclusion of resource restrictions into the sales and program planning only allows to focus on selected, historically critical restrictions. But of course any limitation is problematic against the background of an effective and holistic DCM process.

Consequently, the most promising perspective of an effective holistic DCM is seen in the second approach, the iterative scenario-based planning process, which is outlined in Fig. 2. Starting with a planning scenario, resources and part demands are derived by propagation of volumes and quotas by application of the full product structure. Typically, planned orders are applied here to transform planning scenarios into explodable orders. In a third step, capacity bottlenecks are identified and disclosed by backtracking to the point of origin in the planning scenario and revision of the plan.

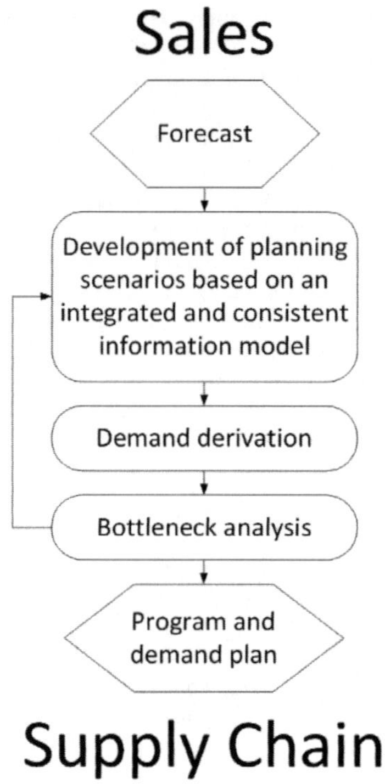

Figure 2. Integrated, scenario-based DCM process

The basis for this DCM planning process is a consistent and holistic information model, which comprises all relevant information. This information may be divided into three data partitions: the planning scenarios, the resource information (restrictions) and the product structures. Whereas planning scenario and restrictions are structured in a simply way, an efficient product representation is critical to provide transparent holistic information and allow for an efficient backtracking mechanism.

Typically, the relevant product information is complex and distributed over several systems, i.e., different data fragments as technical rules, volumes and option quotas, BOM are not integrated in a common information base.

But to efficiently support a scenario-based DCM planning process, all relevant information needs to be integrated in one common data structure. Though enhanced technologies and database infrastructures have been introduced in the last decades, an extensive data preprocessing and reduction is necessary to provide a compact yet comprehensive information basis for the later analytical data processing.

After the DCM process has been described, a general overview of different suitable product structures will be described in the next section.

III. Product Structures in the Field of Automotive Industry

According to Schuh [24], a product structure is generally a structured composition of the product and its components. Typically, structure levels are introduced to represent assemblies, which bundle components in the product structure. Product structures support the multiple use of assemblies and parts. Another important objective is seen in the reduction of production data and the support of the information flow [24].

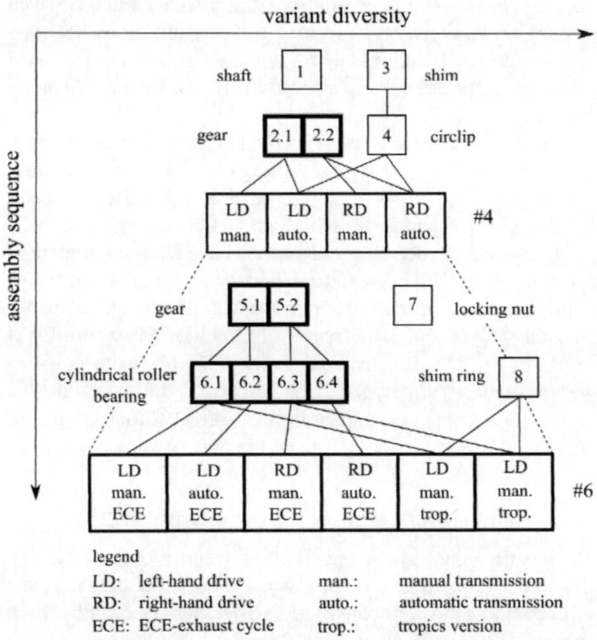

Figure 3: Variant tree [based on [30][32]]

From a technical perspective, product representations are product knowledge composed into its elementary components [25]. A component can be either a physical or a non-physical artifact (service and software components) [26]. The next larger unit are called modules. Klug [10] defines a module as an assembly of several components or assembly units. The module may comprise a variety of functions. The modules can generally be replaced (e.g., door, seat, cockpit, power pack, roof). They are used within a so-called modularization to subdivide a system. Aspects of the product life phase such as development, procurement, production, distribution, utilization and disposal may lead to modularization [27][28][29].

Especially, tree structures as product representation have proven to be promising for various applications. Kesper [30] differs between feature trees and variant trees, whereby the widely propagated feature tree is often incorrectly also referred to as a variant tree. The trees differ in their representation and the integrated information. While feature trees illustrate the variety resulting from the combinatorial of characteristics and their properties, the variant tree represents the variety of semi-finished products arising during the assembly process [30][31]. Thus, the variant tree forms the basis for the reduction of variants by means of product structure optimization or assembly sequence optimization.

The variant tree is often used to graphically represent component and product diversity, that arises in assembly processes [30][32]. Schuh [32] identifies variant trees as important means to design and evaluate product variants. The different components are symbolized by different boxes (see Fig. 3) [30]. According to Schuh and Schwenk [31], variant trees are constructed in defined steps. First, the product characteristics and their properties are captured. Then, the prohibitions of combination and other constraints on combinations of properties are defined. Thereupon, variants are generated. After integration of part information and allocation of part usage, the assembly sequence is determined. As the last step, the variant tree may be depicted graphically [30].

The feature tree is an instrument for visualizing variants or spectra with a focus on their characteristics and properties. Usually, the feature tree is started with a "root". The tree is then branched from left to right (see Fig. 4).

Each vertical level represents precisely one feature. One branch of the tree corresponds exactly to one variant. The extent and shape of the feature tree depends on the order of features. A different order alters the total number of the feature expressions to be displayed [30]. This kind of tree is not only used to depict features, it also allows the visualization of the diversity resulting from the combinations of characteristics and properties.

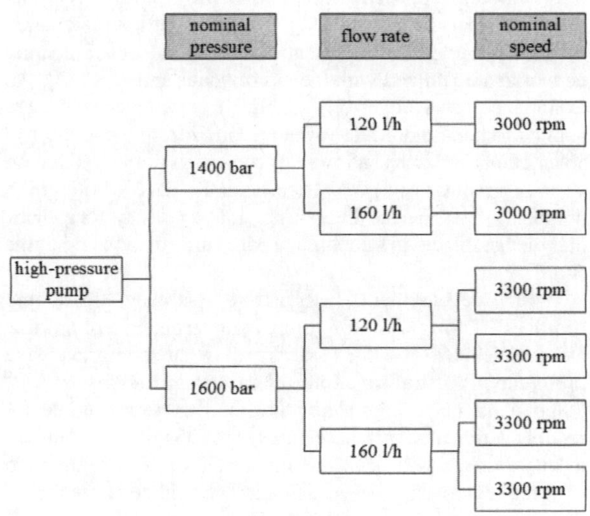

Figure 4: Feature tree [based on [30]]

Not just the product structure itself, also relationships between a product, its components and the relevant assembly tasks have to be considered within a product representation. These can be described in an extended product tree structure originally proposed by Zeng and Gu [33]. In an extended product tree, two types of nodes are distinguished. A component node represents a product or component while an assembly task node represents simplified assembly information included in the product structure. The connection between two component nodes is a parent-child relationship. A parent component (or assembly) consists of all its child components. A connection between components and an assembly task signals that the respective component is assembled by the appropriate assembly task. All nodes together form a recursive product structure tree [25]. Different end products can share the same modules as long as functional requirements and cost-effectiveness persist [34].

Also, a bill of material (BOM) is typically part of the product structure. Parts and components that constitute the product in the context of an assembly, subassembly, or model are listed within a BOM [35]. In the automotive industry, BOMs are considered an integral part of the product representation. Information on components (e.g., compressor, cable, etc.) that are necessarily installed in a product to implement a function (e.g. climate control system) can be looked up in BOMs [20]. A similar, but more detailed specification of BOMs can be found in [36]: Brière-Côté describes a BOM as a list of subassemblies, components, parts, and raw materials which is applied to construct higher-level assemblies. This list illustrates the type and quantities of each to build a finished product.

Newer approaches to depict product structures are based on ontologies and semantic networks. An ontology defines a uniform vocabulary for researchers who need to exchange information in a particular field; an ontology allows inter alia reuse and analysis of knowledge [37]. In contrast, a semantic network is a graphical representation of knowledge. Semantic networks are realized with the aid of nodes and arcs [38]. An example presents Vegetti et al. [39]. Here, two hierarchies are applied to handle product variants from different angles. The abstraction hierarchy allows to represent product data on various granularity levels to efficiently deal with a high number of variants. The structural hierarchy organizes knowledge related to structural product information and to the BOM.

From development perspective, "Design Structure Matrices" (DSMs) denote a compact representation of product element contexts [25]. DSMs allow a comprehensive presentation of information (elements of any type, i.e., components or process steps) and are therefore suitable for models with many variant features. The DSM is illustrated as a square matrix with the same number of rows as columns to map the relationships of parameters between components. In general, only one type of relationship (e.g., "...is linked to...") per DSM can be defined. Furthermore, for larger systems with several hundred elements, it is difficult to keep an overview and ensure the manageability of the matrix representations [26].

To conclude, a variety of types of product representations is available today. As mentioned before, especially graph structures and here tree structures are an intuitively attractive approach because of their proximity to car design principles. Nevertheless, ontologies and semantic networks offer a perspective for integration of additional information. To allow for a real-time analysis of the feasibility of a planning scenario, an integrated DCM requires the application of smart quantitative methods on a holistic information model to derive future resource requirements from market requirements. Innovative processes and methods for DCM (e.g., approaches of [13][40][41][20] have been evaluated in [42]. None of those approaches unites the criteria of part demand calculation from market predictions, realistic lead time assumptions between market demand and resource demand and process based description for at least a part of DCP (Demand and Capacity Planning).

Based on these findings, a product representation has been developed which merges the concepts of variant trees and ontologies into a holistic information model concept. Furthermore, algorithms, which base on the generation of planned orders to derive part demands have been implemented for this product representation and have been validated in combination at several German OEMs. The respective tool suite is known under the name of OTD-DCM, where OTD refers to the basic instrument OTD-NET (order-to-delivery and network simulator, cf. [20]). The next section presents the underlying concepts and optimization methods that are applied in this approach to reduce the data complexity.

IV. Hierarchichal Product Structure and Optimization Methods used in the DCM

It is necessary to assure consistency and avoid redundancy in and between all data entities when integrating data into one information model. Inconsistencies occur for example when subsets of technical rules or BOM rules contradict each other so that orders cannot be specified fully. In the development cycle of a car, rules are added and revised within different IT systems, thus rules are partially redundant and sometimes even contradictory. Hence, it is necessary to process planning-relevant information regarding structural requirements (syntax and semantics) and to verify their consistency.

As a result, the implemented data processing in OTD-DCM has been based on the principle of generating a hierarchically-linked structure of variant clusters (cf. [43]). Here, a variant cluster contains by definition a subset of allowed vehicle variants (typically car models), that have common properties (example: sales region = Germany, fuel type = diesel, gear type = automatic). Each variant cluster is characterized by its temporal validity, the technical rules and the lists of allowed and forced options which apply for all in the cluster included vehicle variants.

Within the hierarchy-linked structure of clusters, each variant cluster inherits all characteristics of his parent cluster.

The first pre-optimization of the product structure comprises the generation of a hierarchical tree where tree levels are based on subsequently detailed variant cluster specifications. The initial tree structure can be derived from automotive engineering principles: Tree levels, which de facto group models, may be based on model characteristics like car series, fuel type, sales region and many more (see Fig. 5). It should be mentioned that the level sequence influences directly the later optimization results and the optimal structure may differ for different applications or different OEM or car series. The sequence applied in this paper has been developed in close communication with all involved departments of the OEM providing the example presented. It is subject to confidentiality and shall not be detailed in this contribution.

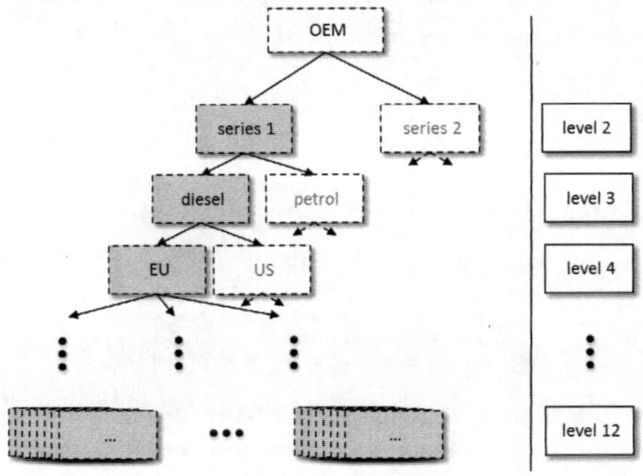

Figure 5. Extract of the generated tree structure

Nevertheless, each tree level can have one or many nodes, depending on the level and type of models clustered (e.g., 90 kW or 150 kW for the engine nodes). Options, technical and BOM rules but also volumes, quotas and restrictions are related to the tree nodes in a last step to obtain a holistic DCM information model.

Among all integrated information, rules are identified as the most complex data fragment. Technical rules represent the technical feasibility by Boolean expressions, e.g., "if engine = 90 kW then transmission = 6-speed manual gearbox". BOM rules follow the same Boolean schema but link options to part demands, e.g., "if engine = 90 kW and radio = "Radio Basic" then parts 5678973 and 5678974". Further, a free definable period is typically specifying the validity of a specific technical or BOM rule. It should be noted that the temporal validity of all data fragments has to be handled within this tree structure [42]. Also, all algorithms working on the product tree have to process the temporal validity.

In the following, the algorithm integrated in this approach will be presented. After initial tree generation all rules are listed on the lowest level; the nodes on this level relate to models one to one. As described in section II, the possible number of BOM rules for a fully specified car amounts to over 600,000 and the number of technical rules to 15,000 per series. The optimization of rules has been subdivided into three subsequent optimization steps. The call sequence of these steps is stated in the following algorithmic code: The procedure starts to identify all points in time within the planning interval where the validity of any rule may change (see Pseudocode 1). Next, the function for the reduction of the number of properties as well as the function for the reduction of the number and length of rules are proceed.

```
// optimize allowed properties and rules
FUNCTION optimizationSteps(variantcluster, originalData)
    LIST timePoints = get points in time of any changes
                      in originalData
    FOR EACH timePoint IN timePoints
        ARRAY of allowedProperties FROM originalData
        LIST originalRules =  get original rules from
                              originalData
        // function to reduce the amount of properties
        reduceProperties(allowedProperties)
        // function for reduction of number and length
        newRules = reduceNumberAndLength(originalRules)
    END FOR
    RETURN allowedProperties, newRules
END FUNCTION
// recursively move rules upwards
CALL function pullRulesUP WITH masterVariantCluster
            as argument
```

Pseudocode 1: Overview call sequence

The objective of the first optimization step is to identify all forced options, i.e., the options that have necessarily to be chosen for a specific variant cluster (e.g., every car for the German market has necessarily a specific exhaust system). Therefore, principally allowed options for one variant cluster are reduced by excluding non-feasible options.

```
FUNCTION reduceProperties (allowedProperties)
    BOOLEAN reduceAllowedProperties = TRUE
    WHILE (reduceAllowedProperties)
        LIST forcedProperties = calculate forced
                                properties of
                                possible allowed
                                properties
        FOR EACH property IN allowedProperties
            SET property IN forcedProperties
            BOOLEAN valid =  check temporary
                             Configuration against
                             all technical rules
            IF (NOT valid)
                REMOVE property FROM allowedProperties
            ELSE
                reduceAllowedProperties = FALSE
            END IF
        END FOR
    END WHILE
END FUNCTION
```

Pseudocode 2: Reduce properties

This is done by checking intelligently selected, partly specified theoretical configurations against all applicable technical rules (see Pseudocode 2). In a sub-step, fixed options are set, i.e., the ones that define the variant cluster. Afterwards all currently available options are temporarily added. If a contradiction occurs, the option will be deleted from the set of allowed options. When this process leads to only one possible option from a set of alternative options, this option is set as forced.

An inner inconsistency is identified if an identified forced property violates a technical rule. An outer inconsistency is identified if a positive demand quota for an option has been planned, but the option itself is technically not allowed. Another outer inconsistency is identified, if the sum of all planned quotas for all allowed options within a subset of alternative options in a specified time period does not equal 100%.

The second optimization step reduces the number and the length of rules by, e.g., application of the Identity Law of the Boolean algebra (cf. [44]). In a first sub-step, the so-called negative normal form is constructed, where negation operators are only occurring directly at variables and not at brackets. Factorization is achieved by counting the occurrences of each sub-term in a current term. Afterwards, the sub-term will be factored out (see Pseudocode 3).

```
FUNCTION reduceNumberAndLength(originalRules)
    LIST newRules
    FOR EACH rule IN originalRules
        BUILD negation normal form of rule
        REMOVE tautologies
        DO WHILE (successful optimizations)
            REMOVE redundant structures and expressions
                   from the tree
            FACTOR identical subterms out
            REMOVE redundant expressions in child nodes
            REMOVE constants
        END DO
        ADD newRule TO newRules
    END FOR
    RETURN newRules
END FUNCTION
```

Pseudocode 3: Reduce number and length

It should be noted that these steps are valid only for one variant cluster and a specified, fixed time period. Consequently, these steps need to be executed for each variant cluster and all relevant time periods. In a next sub-step, the OTD-DCM implementation shortens rules by merging similar rules that belong to more than one resource, i.e., workstations, assembly lines and more [42][23]. Next, the algorithms aim to further reduce the actual length of all rules by Boolean simplification of terms. If the optimized length of the rule is shorter than the original one, it is replaced by the new representation. Example: The Boolean expression "$\neg$ ($\neg$A $\wedge$ B $\wedge$ $\neg$C)" will be reduced to "$\neg$B $\vee$ A $\vee$ C". This simplification does not only reduce the amount of data, but allows the following step to identify identical rules.

The third and last optimization step tries to identify commonalities for nodes in the hierarchical product structure. For example, the rules that are valid for each child node of one variant cluster are moved upwards to the parent node, i.e. variant cluster, and deleted from all children. The preliminary condition for this step is that all derived variant clusters share this rule over the same time period. Example: The forced option "Owner's manual in German language" may be valid for all variant clusters within the sales region = Germany. Hence, it can be transferred upwards to the variant cluster "variants - German" [42]. The last pseudocode (Pseudocode 4) represents this step including a method to limit intervals of the rules: If the interval of a rule contains the whole validity interval of the variant cluster, the interval of the rule will be adapted.

```
FUNCTION recursivelyMoveRulesUpwards(variantcluster)
    FOR EACH child OF variantcluster
        recursivelyMoveRulesUpwards(child)
    END FOR
    //move identic rules upwards
    GET valid interval for variantcluster
    LIMIT interval of rules
    LIST rulesToMoveUpwards
    GET rulesOFChildren FROM all rules
    FOR EACH rule IN rulesOfChildren
    ADD rule TO rulesToMoveUpwards
        FOR EACH child OF variantcluster
            GET allRules for child
            IF allRules CONTAINS rule
                // rule can be pulled up
            ELSE
                REMOVE rule FROM rulesToMoveUpwards
            END IF
        END FOR
    END FOR
    FOR EACH child OF variantcluster
        REMOVE rulesToMoveUpwards from rules
        of the child
        REMOVE rules with invalid interval
    END FOR
    GET valid interval of variantcluster
    REMOVE rules with invalid interval
    from rulesToMoveUpwards
    ADD rulesToMoveUpwards TO rules of variantcluster
END FUNCTION
```

Pseudocode 4: Recursively move rules upwards

Concluding, the described optimization process eliminates redundancies and identifies inconsistencies within the integrated information model. In the next section will be shown that this leads to a significant reduction of data complexity in relation to the data entities and thus dependencies.

V. ANALYSIS OF COMPLEXITY REDUCTIONS

The evaluation of the previously described optimization steps has been analyzed in a first step for real data of one middle class series [1] of a German OEM. In addition, to provide greater insights into the effects of the optimization steps, the full product spectrum of this OEM, which consists of currently 54 series has been analyzed in a second step. As BOM rules follow the same principles as technical rules, the illustration in this contribution is limited on BOM rules only.

In the following, a tree node represents a variant cluster as described in the previous section. The parameter $n(l)$ is defined as the number of tree nodes on a level (as mentioned before, e.g., fuel type). The respective sum of BOM rules before optimization is defined as $r^{pre}(l)$ and after optimization as $r^{post}(l)$. The number of average rules per tree node within a level is defined as

$$a^{pre}(l)= r^{pre}(l) / n(l) \qquad (1)$$

and

$$a^{post}(l) = r^{post}(l) / n(l). \quad (2)$$

A null-entry rule characterizes a rule without condition, i.e., this rule is valid for the whole variant cluster. The total number of null-entry rules on a specific level l before optimization is defined as $v^{pre}(l)$ and on a specific level l after optimization as $v^{post}(l)$.

As described before, the first evaluation is based on one middle class series, which is mirrored in $n(2)=1$, i.e., the number of nodes on level 2 relate to this series. The built hierarchy structure consists of 12 levels and 819 nodes on all levels.

Table I illustrates in the third column that the lowest level of the hierarchical tree structure contains all existing BOM rules $r^{pre}(l)$ before all optimization steps. Levels 1 to 11 do not contain any rules because these levels have been generated artificially in the first pre-optimization step in order to construct the primary tree structure. After optimization, a significant proportion of BOM rules has been hoisted to higher levels resulting in $r^{post}(l)$.

Furthermore, the overall number of rules is reduced from 3,688,514 to 284,219, which amounts to a reduction of 92.3% in relation to the original number.

The reduction as well as the average ratio of rules per node are comparable by columns $a^{pre}(l)$ and $a^{post}(l)$. The weighted average considers the number of nodes of the whole tree per level, where the reduction in this case also results in 92.3%.

TABLE I. INDICATORS WITHOUT OPTIMIZATION (PRE) AND WITH OPTIMIZATION (POST)

level l	$n(l)$	$r^{pre}(l)$	$r^{post}(l)$	$a^{pre}(l)$	$a^{post}(l)$	$v^{pre}(l)$	$v^{post}(l)$
1	1	0	1,568	0	1,568	0	1,208
2	1	0	0	0	0	0	0
3	2	0	918	0	459	0	126
4	2	0	0	0	0	0	0
5	9	0	8,525	0	948	0	1,867
6	9	0	0	0	0	0	0
7	14	0	2,918	0	208	0	572
8	26	0	13,767	0	530	0	2,399
9	31	0	4,745	0	153	0	1,691
10	35	0	4,418	0	126	0	555
11	54	0	6,154	0	114	0	1,856
12	635	3,688,514	241,206	5,809	380	965,379	18,537
	sum	**sum**	**sum**	**weighted average**	**weighted average**	**sum**	**sum**
	819	3,688,514	284,219	4,504	347	965,379	28,811

This analysis of one middle class series illustrates the immense complexity reduction by application of the OTD-DCM hierarchical tree structure.

When a specific variant cluster at lowest level is regarded (for example, for generation of fully specified planned orders) it is necessary to take into account all valid rules for this specific node, because rules at parent nodes are valid for all child nodes. Thus, the rules on the upper levels need to be propagated downwards to all child nodes when evaluating the total number (sum) of valid rules for one variant cluster.

TABLE II. PROPAGATED RULES PER VARIANT CLUSTER AT LOWEST LEVEL (LEVEL 12)

propagated rules - level 12	pre-optimization	post-optimization
sum	3,688,514	2,672,905
average ratio	5,806	4,215
median	6,671	4,424
minimum	0	2,408
maximum	7,620	5,943

Table II shows the number of propagated rules on the lowest level. As a positive side effect, the reduction of the overall number of rules for the car series in focus of this analysis amounts to 27.5%.

Since only a small information model of one car series has been considered here, an analysis of a full product spectrum is of interest to provide greater insights into the effects of the optimization steps. The full product spectrum of the analyzed OEM consists of 54 car series. The results of the full spectrum analysis are presented in Table III and generally confirm the scale of the reduction. The overall number of rules could be reduced from 67,668,544 to 6,575,089. Concluding, this results in a reduction of 90.3%.

Compared to the first results, it is interesting to note that there are no rules, which could be moved upwards to the first level. Nevertheless, it is of course not surprising that no rules exist, which are valid for every car in the spectrum of the OEM. This again reflects the significance of chosen hierarchy levels and their respective order.

TABLE III. INDICATORS WITHOUT OPTIMIZATION (PRE) AND WITH OPTIMIZATION (POST) FOR FULL SPECTRUM

level l	$n(l)$	$r^{pre}(l)$	$r^{post}(l)$	$a^{pre}(l)$	$a^{post}(l)$	$v^{pre}(l)$	$v^{post}(l)$
1	1	0	0	0	0	0	0
2	54	0	92,017	0	1704	0	59,811
3	98	0	63,145	0	644	0	26,328
4	150	0	97,377	0	649	0	30,102
5	360	0	309,627	0	860	0	105,810
6	360	0	0	0	0	0	0
7	510	0	145,359	0	285	0	37,739
8	823	0	434,216	0	528	0	69,239
9	1083	0	196,330	0	181	0	68,823
10	1246	0	175,603	0	141	0	32,884
11	1307	0	17,953	0	14	0	5,226
12	11,810	67,668,544	5,043,462	5,730	427	15,022,405	677,528
	sum	**sum**	**sum**	**weighted average**	**weighted average**	**sum**	**sum**
	17,802	67,668,544	6,575,089	3,801	369	15,022,405	1,113,490

To gain more insights into this effect a door hinge as a part (named here P24139) has been traced through the optimization steps. Upon start, the rules that refer to this part are linked to nodes on the lowest level (level 12) of the product tree. There are 2711 variant clusters referencing this part. After execution of all optimization steps, the number of rules is reduced to 40. An extract of the results is mapped in Fig. 6, which displays those nodes (named N306, N74313,...) that contain the corresponding part for the first five levels of the tree. On levels seven to nine four more door hinge rules exist which are not illustrated here. Referring to the rules that are hoisted upwards, the situation that both – parent and child – nodes refer to the same rule (cf. node 306 on level 2 and node 212 on level 3 in Fig. 6) is valid, because time period for parent and child may differ. The specific rule on child level is so only valid for this specific variant cluster. This example demonstrates the effectiveness of the complexity reduction.

Also, for the full product spectrum, a reduction in propagated rules on the lowest level may be noted as a positive side effect. Whereas the overall reduction amounts to 7.7%, this effect varies widely among the car series: for a high-class car series a reduction of 49% is realized, but for other car series the number of propagated rules have increased slightly caused by the interval split. This indicates a starting point for further optimizations on OEM side as well as algorithmically.

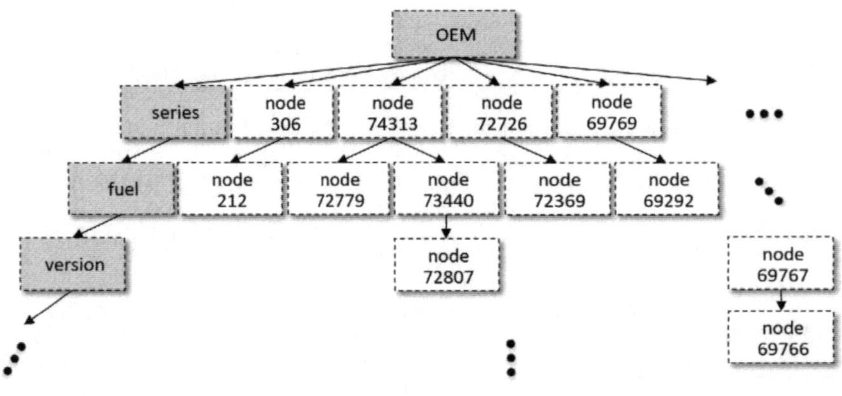

level	No. of nodes referring to door hinge (P24139) rules
1	0
2	13
3	5
4	5
5	13
⋮	⋮

Figure 6. Trace of door hinge as a part after execution of optimization steps

VI. Conclusion and Future Work

An integral component of the automotive supply chain management is DCM, where resource requirements resulting from future or already realized market demands are synchronized with capacities and restrictions of the supply chain and production system. Because it is impossible to predict the exact future vehicle orders, part demand is typically gradually derived from sales forecasts in a number of sequential processes involving a variety of systems as well as experienced human planners. A transparent, lean but holistic product representation plays a key role for the effective facilitation of this DCM process.

This paper has given an overview of different types of product structures. Especially, the tree structure is an intuitively attractive approach because of its proximity to car design principles. Newer approaches based on ontologies and semantic networks complementary benefits. Thus, the integration of distributed DCM data into an extended hierarchical tree structure has been analyzed against the background of complexity reduction.

This study did not only perform the analysis for one middle class series, but moreover for the full product spectrum of an OEM. For a better understanding of the results, the applied algorithms have been described in form of pseudo code. It has been demonstrated that by choosing a hierarchical tree structure the total number of BOM rules could be reduced by a factor of 10 (reduction of nearly 90%) whereas the number of BOM rules related to a specific variant cluster (i.e., propagated rules) decreases as well. In contrary, this number can often be decreased massively in parallel by elimination of surplus information. As a door hinge has been traced to visualize the result of the optimization steps and to demonstrate how rules are reduced, merged and hoisted upwards within the tree structure.

In summary, the hierarchical integrated information model provides more transparency as redundant and surplus information is dramatically reduced. Thus, it proves to be an enhanced basis for a scenario-based DCM planning process for the automotive industry, which relies on transparent and consistent data. A sound DCM process will increase program stability and transparency on future part demand. Bottlenecks and the resulting deterioration of delivery service levels will be decreased. Furthermore, if the mentioned applications use the information model, it will save computation time and memory space [42].

Nevertheless, the complexity of the car as a product increases more and more. Trends like embedded systems and e-mobility are not yet considered in full within the product structures. New dependencies of technical and electronical components and the compatibility between hardware and software will change the car architecture and therefore influence logistics and thus the DCM process. Thus, this information needs to be integrated into the product representation in the near future.

Even more so, when targeting an integrated product structure, further product characteristics from other departments like sales or productions may need to be taken into account. In consequence, it is believed that a more generalized graph structure instead of the applied tree structure may hold further benefits in terms of complexity reduction. Against this background, generic graph structures shall be analyzed by the authors in the near future.

Acknowledgment

Special thanks to the German "Bundesministerium für Forschung und Bildung" (BMBF) for making this study possible by providing funding to the ILogTec project. The funding of BMBF was granted with Funding-ID 03FH008IA5 and 03FH008IB5.

References

[1] K. Pawlikowski, D. Fruhner, K. Klingebiel et al., "Benefits of an Integrated Hierarchical Data Structure for Automotive Demand and Capacity Management," in ICCGI 2016: The Eleventh International Multi-Conference on Computing in the Global Information Technology, C. Merkle Westphall, K. Nygard, and E. Ravve, Eds., pp. 20–25, ThinkMind, Barcelona, Spain, 2016.

[2] J. Schuberthan and S. Potrafke, "Die Anforderungen des Kunden…," in Logistik in der Automobilindustrie: Innovatives Supply Chain Management für wettbewerbsfähige Zulieferstrukturen, F. Gehr and B. Hellingrath, Eds., pp. 8–18, Springer Berlin Heidelberg, 2007.

[3] D. Alford, P. Sackett, and G. Nelder, "Mass customisation — an automotive perspective," International Journal of Production Economics, vol. 65, no. 1, pp. 99–110, 2000.

[4] E.-H. Krog and K. Statkevich, "Kundenorientierung und Integrationsfunktion der Logistik in der Supply Chain der Automobilindustrie," in Das Beste der Logistik, H. Baumgarten, Ed., pp. 185–195, Springer Berlin Heidelberg, Berlin, Heidelberg, 2008.

[5] S. Meissner, Logistische Stabilität in der automobilen Variantenfließfertigung, Technische Universität München, Garching b. München, 2009.

[6] A. Trojan, "…und die Auswirkungen auf den 1st-Tier-Lieferanten," in Logistik in der Automobilindustrie: Innovatives Supply Chain Management für wettbewerbsfähige Zulieferstrukturen, F. Gehr and B. Hellingrath, Eds., Springer Berlin Heidelberg, 2007.

[7] R. T. Yu-Lee, Essentials of capacity management, Wiley, New York, 2002.

[8] E. H. Krog, G. Richartz, R. Kanschat et al., "Kooperatives Bedarfs- und Kapazitätsmanagement der Automobilhersteller und Systemlieferanten," Logistik-Management : internationale Konzepte, Instrumente, Anwendungen ; Zeitschrift der Kommission Logistik im Verband der Hochschullehrer für Betriebswirtschaft e.V., 2002.

[9] D. Arnold, H. Isermann, A. Kuhn, et al., eds., Handbuch Logistik, Springer, Berlin, 2008.

[10] F. Klug, Logistikmanagement in der Automobilindustrie, Springer Berlin Heidelberg, Berlin, Heidelberg, 2010.

[11] J. Gebhardt, H. Detmer, and A. L. Madsen, "Predicting Parts Demand in the Automotive Industry: An Application of Probabilistic Graphical Models," Proc. Int. Joint Conf. on

Uncertainty in Artificial Intelligence (UAI'03, Acapulco, Mexico), Bayesian Modelling Applications Workshop, 2003.
[12] H. Meyr, "Supply chain planning in the German automotive industry," OR Spectrum, vol. 26, no. 4, 2004.
[13] T. Stäblein, Integrierte Planung des Materialbedarfs bei kundenauftragsorientierter Fertigung von komplexen und variantenreichen Serienprodukten, Shaker, Aachen, 2008.
[14] J. Dörmer, ed., Produktionsprogrammplanung bei variantenreicher Fließproduktion, Springer Fachmedien Wiesbaden, Wiesbaden, 2013.
[15] M. Heitmann, IT-Sicherheit in vertikalen F&E-Kooperationen der Automobilindustrie, Deutscher Universitäts-Verlag, Wiesbaden, 2007.
[16] T. Zernechel, "Gestaltung und Optimierung von Unternehmensnetzwerken — Supply Chain Management in der Automobilindustrie," in Die Automobilindustrie auf dem Weg zur globalen Netzwerkkompetenz, F. J. Garcia Sanz, K. Semmler, and J. Walther, Eds., pp. 367–378, Springer Berlin Heidelberg, Berlin, Heidelberg, 2007.
[17] L. Herold, Kundenorientierte Prozesssteuerung in der Automobilindustrie: Die Rolle von Logistik und Logistikcontrolling im Prozess „vom Kunden bis zum Kunden", Dt. Univ.-Verl., Wiesbaden, 2005.
[18] A.-W. Scheer, Wirtschaftsinformatik: Referenzmodelle für industrielle Geschäftsprozesse, Springer, Berlin, 1997.
[19] H. Barthel, Modell zur Analyse und Gestaltung des Bestellverhaltens für die variantenreiche Serienproduktion, Jost-Jetter, Heimsheim, 2006.
[20] A. Wagenitz, Modellierungsmethode zur Auftragsabwicklung in der Automobilindustrie, Technische Universität Dortmund, 2007.
[21] M. Holweg and F. K. Pil, The second century: Reconnecting customer and value chain through build-to-order ; moving beyond mass and lean production in the auto industry, MIT Press, Cambridge, Mass, 2004.
[22] M. Toth, A. Wagenitz, and K. Klingebiel, "Dynamic Supply Chain Planning with Logistic Assistance Systems," in ASOR Bulletin: The Australian Society for Operations Research, E. Kozan, Ed., 2010.
[23] K. M. Liebler, Eine prozess- und IT-gestützte Methode für die Produktionsplanung in der Automobilindustrie, Verl. Praxiswissen, Dortmund, 2013.
[24] G. Schuh, Produktkomplexität managen: Strategien; Methoden; Tools, Carl Hanser Fachbuchverlag, s.l., 2014.
[25] X. Deng, G. Huet, S. Tan et al., "Product decomposition using design structure matrix for intellectual property protection in supply chain outsourcing," Computers in Industry, vol. 63, no. 6, pp. 632–641, 2012.
[26] M. Kissel, Mustererkennung in komplexen Produktportfolios, Dissertation, Technische Universität München, 2014.
[27] C. Blees, D. Krause, and H. Meerkamm, Eine Methode zur Entwicklung modularer Produktfamilien, TuTech Verl., Hamburg, 2011.
[28] P. Gu and S. Sosale, "Product modularization for life cycle engineering," Robotics and Computer-Integrated Manufacturing, vol. 15, no. 5, pp. 387–401, 1999.
[29] D. Krause, G. Beckmann, S. Eilmus et al., "Integrated Development of Modular Product Families: A Methods Toolkit," in Advances in Product Family and Product Platform Design: Methods & Applications, T. W. Simpson, J. Jiao, Z. Siddique et al., Eds., pp. 245–269, Springer New York, New York, NY, s.l., 2014.
[30] H. Kesper, Gestaltung von Produktvariantenspektren mittels matrixbasierter Methoden, Verl. Dr. Hut, München, 2012.
[31] G. Schuh and U. Schwenk, Produktkomplexität managen: Strategien - Methoden - Tools, Hanser, München, Wien, 2001.
[32] G. Schuh, Gestaltung und Bewertung von Produktvarianten: Ein Beitrag zur systematischen Planung von Serienprodukten, 1988.
[33] Y. Zeng and P. Gu, "A science-based approach to product design theory Part II: Formulation of design requirements and products," Robotics and Computer-Integrated Manufacturing, vol. 15, no. 4, pp. 341–352, 1999.
[34] K. Fujita, "Product variety optimization under modular architecture," Computer-Aided Design, vol. 34, no. 12, pp. 953–965, 2002.
[35] J. H. Lee, S. H. Kim, and K. Lee, "Integration of evolutional BOMs for design of ship outfitting equipment," Computer-Aided Design, vol. 44, no. 3, pp. 253–273, 2012.
[36] A. Brière-Côté, L. Rivest, and A. Desrochers, "Adaptive generic product structure modelling for design reuse in engineer-to-order products," Computers in Industry, vol. 61, no. 1, pp. 53–65, 2010.
[37] N. Noy and D. L. McGuinness, "Ontology development 101," Knowledge Systems Laboratory, Stanford University, 2001.
[38] V. López-Morales and O. López-Ortega, "A distributed semantic network model for a collaborative intelligent system," Journal of Intelligent Manufacturing, vol. 16, 4-5, pp. 515–525, 2005.
[39] M. Vegetti, H. Leone, and G. Henning, "PRONTO: An ontology for comprehensive and consistent representation of product information," Engineering Applications of Artificial Intelligence, vol. 24, no. 8, pp. 1305–1327, 2011.
[40] S. Ohl, Prognose und Planung variantenreicher Produkte am Beispiel der Automobilindustrie, VDI-Verl., Düsseldorf, 2000.
[41] H. Wagner, Kollaboratives Bedarfs- und Kapazitätsmanagement am Beispiel der Automobilindustrie: Lösungsansatz zur Sicherstellung der Wandlungsfähigkeit, Huss, München, 2006.
[42] A. Wagenitz, K. M. Liebler, and S. Schürrer, "A Holistic Approach to Demand and Capacity Management in the Automotive Industry," in Innovation in product and production: July 31 - August 4, 2011 in Stuttgart, Germany ; conference proceedings ; 21th International Conference on Production Research, ICPR 21, D. Spath and R. Ilg, Eds., Fraunhofer Verlag, Stuttgart, 2011.
[43] K.-U. Meininger, Abstraktionsbasierte Bereitstellung bereichsübergreifender Planungsdaten für die Produktionsplanung bei Serienfertigung variantenreicher Erzeugnisse, Idstein, 1994.
[44] R. L. Goodstein, Boolean Algebra, Dover Publications, Newburyport, 2012.

iaria journals

www.iariajournals.org

International Journal On Advances in Intelligent Systems
issn: 1942-2679

International Journal On Advances in Internet Technology
issn: 1942-2652

International Journal On Advances in Life Sciences
issn: 1942-2660

International Journal On Advances in Networks and Services
issn: 1942-2644

International Journal On Advances in Security
issn: 1942-2636

International Journal On Advances in Software
issn: 1942-2628

International Journal On Advances in Systems and Measurements
issn: 1942-261x

International Journal On Advances in Telecommunications
issn: 1942-2601

International Academy, Research,
and Industry Association (IARIA)
412 Derby Way
Wilmington, DE 19810

ISBN 978-1-5108-5642-4

CURRAN ASSOCIATES INC.
proceedings.com